The Scientific & the Divine

The Scientific
& the Divine

Conflict and Reconciliation
from Ancient Greece
to the Present

James A. Arieti
and
Patrick A. Wilson

ROWMAN & LITTLEFIELD PUBLISHERS, INC.
Lanham • Boulder • New York • Oxford

ROWMAN & LITTLEFIELD PUBLISHERS, INC.

Published in the United States of America
by Rowman & Littlefield Publishers, Inc.
A Member of the Rowman & Littlefield Publishing Group
4501 Forbes Boulevard, Suite 200, Lanham, Maryland 20706
www.rowmanlittlefield.com

PO Box 317
Oxford
OX2 9RU, UK

British Library Cataloguing in Publication Information Available

Library of Congress Cataloging-in-Publication Data

Arieti, James A.
  The scientific & the divine : conflict and reconciliation from ancient
Greece to the present / James A. Arieti and Patrick A. Wilson.
    p. cm.
Includes bibiliographical references and index.
  ISBN 0-7425-1396-3 (alk. paper) — ISBN 0-7425-1397-1 (pbk. : alk. paper)
  1. Religion and science. I. Title: Scientific and the divine. II.
Wilson, Patrick A., 1962– III. Title.
  BL240.3 .A75 2003
  291.1'75—dc21

                                                              2002014230

Printed in the United States of America

For my friends Linda and Gideon Lidor

Amici magis necessarii quam ignis et aqua.

—JAA

For my parents, Robert L. and Margaret E. Wilson

—PAW

Contents

Preface

> If only God would give me some clear sign! Like making a large deposit in my name at a Swiss bank.
>
> —Woody Allen

The goal of ancient science was absolute, immutable, universal truth based on a thorough understanding of an object's material, shape, generation, and purpose. For the most part, this truth was to be obtained through the power of human thought alone, without the help of sensory data or experimentation. One of the features of modern science, by contrast, is its revisability. Instead of aiming at absolute truth, it produces experimentally testable—ideally, falsifiable—theories. Among the modern criteria of judging a theory, in other words, is the theory's fit with empirical evidence. A theory always runs the risk of having to be revised or eliminated in the light of new evidence. Hence, instead of immutable truths, modern scientists prefer to speak of "current models," as in such expressions as "our current model of the atom." Modern science by its very nature depends heavily on experimentation and on the ability of experiments to be replicated by persons other than the original investigators. Modern scientific theories, always sensitive to empirical data, have achieved remarkable success in describing the natural world with elegance, mathematical precision, and technological fruitfulness.

One goal of religion, both ancient and modern, is an awareness, and, where possible, an understanding, of the divine in the affairs of the human and natural worlds. Religious philosophers and scientists alike have sought compatibility between their scientific conclusions and their religious beliefs ever since the beginnings of science in ancient Miletus in the sixth century B.C.E. The search for reconciliation between these apparently disparate views of the world continues in the academic world today. Despite the profound differences between ancient and

modern science, despite the diversity of religious belief in the West, despite even
the move from paganism to religions affirming the Bible and the variations of belief within religions affirming the Bible, there has been throughout Western history a remarkably continuous effort to reconcile science with the divine.

As we shall see, the first scientists, a group of natural philosophers known as
pre-Socratics, formulated questions about the divine and about science that have
scarcely ever been improved upon. Next, the Greek philosophers Aristotle and
Plato and the Roman Cicero exercised their genius on the question of accommodating science and religion. This book will devote a good deal of attention to
these early questions and to early attempts at integration such as these. There are
several important reasons for doing so.

First, we anticipate that few, if any, readers of this book are pagans. Yet paganism treats many of the same phenomena as revealed religion: miracles,
epiphanies, moral qualities, creative powers, and the like. Because pagans were
not bound by the requirements of a *revealed* faith, however, they remained free
to reflect on the nature of the divine, unencumbered, as it were, by the required
dogmas of faith, for faith was not a pagan virtue. Perhaps more significantly, the
Greek pagans possessed the tool of logic as a discipline, a formal, systematic
methodology not practiced elsewhere. Thus they could reflect on theological difficulties with a rigor that arrived in Islam, Judaism, and Christianity only in the
Middle Ages, when Greek philosophy with its system of logic was rediscovered.
Hence, it is possible for modern readers to recognize and appreciate in pagan
texts complex theological issues with a clarity and objectivity not easily available
to those whose own religions are being examined. The case here is much the same
as with ancient history. Moderns can read about the Peloponnesian Wars and observe the follies of both the Spartans and the Athenians with a detachment still
not possible to Americans when they read about the American Civil War, their
hearts palpitating over the despised or beloved Generals Lee and Sherman.

Second, Western philosophy is a continuing conversation, where thinkers, finding problems in a previous speaker's claims, set out to solve those problems by
rejecting, modifying, or adding to earlier claims. The theologians of the revealed
religions developed many of their views from the conclusions of the early
philosophers. Looming large over Augustine was Plato; over Averroës, Maimonides; and over Aquinas, Aristotle. A good deal of modern science, especially
from Galileo to Darwin, has been aimed at rejecting Aristotle's claims. Both Aristotle and Plato found themselves compelled to respond to Parmenides, one of the
most powerful thinkers who has ever lived, one whose views framed the conversation in the West for over two millennia.

Third, the attempts, successful and unsuccessful, at reconciling religion and
science show both the limitations and the grandeur of the human mind. Here we
can see that human minds—and human nature—have not changed: the broad patterns of accommodation are identical; only the details have changed.

There have been five ways of accommodating science and religion that are at
least logically consistent. The first is outright and complete denial of the divine,

that is, declaring that all causes are natural or in accord with physical laws. The second is outright and complete denial of science, declaring that all causes are supernatural, that is, from the divine. The third is defining the divine in such a way as to be consistent with the conclusions of natural science—for example, defining God *as* the laws of physics or interpreting religious texts in some manner other than the literal. The fourth is separating science and religion into distinct and non-overlapping spheres of authority, assigning to religion "how to go to heaven" and to science "how the heavens go." The fifth is declaring that God and his operations are unknowable. These five ways appear to us to have the advantage at least of logical consistency. Whether they satisfy religious cravings or can be made consistent with religious dogmas is a topic that we shall address. Most problematic, as we see it, is the reconciliation of specific religious claims with science. The doctrine that Mohammed is the last prophet, for example, or that Jesus ascended into heaven, or that the various commandments were delivered by God at Sinai represent the greatest challenge to accommodation with natural science.

The first chapter of this book will identify various approaches to understanding the world, approaches that exemplify religious, scientific, and religio-scientific modes of explanation. The second will examine the nature of human reason and explain why reconciling science and religion is a craving of human nature itself. The nature of ancient and of modern science will be the subject of the third chapter. In the fourth chapter, we shall discuss the origin of science and the views of the first natural philosophers. The fifth chapter will treat the early pagan philosophers' first attempts to reconcile science and religion through adjustments made in understanding the nature of God. These attempts show how logic might be applied to understanding God, represent the founding theology of the West, and anticipate even contemporary theological debates. These five chapters on scientific and religious approaches to understanding the world constitute the first of the book's two major parts.

The second major part deals with attempts to reconcile God and science. Chapters 6 through 13 will trace such attempts from antiquity to the early twentieth century, with special attention paid to the fiery disputes in the Muslim, Jewish, and Christian Middle Ages. Chapter 14 will investigate the state of the debate at the turn of the twenty-first century, when theories in quantum mechanics, chaos, and mathematical probability seem to offer hope that a breakthrough in reconciling God and science is imminent. In the concluding chapter, we shall reflect on where the debate has gone and where it has now arrived.

I

SCIENCE AND RELIGION

1

The Problem

Ah, Love! could you and I with Him conspire
To grasp this sorry Scheme of Things entire,
Would not we shatter it to bits—and then
Re-mould it nearer to the Heart's Desire!

—*Rubaiyat of Omar Khayyám*

All human beings, Aristotle writes at the beginning of the *Metaphysics,* have a desire to know. Unfortunately, many things cannot be known in the way we humans wish to know them. We wish to know in black and white with absolute, total, inviolable certainty. We wish to know in a way that seizes, conquers, and obliterates doubt. Science promises to offer us knowledge; religion boasts that it offers truth. Both claim to satisfy this most exclusively human craving for intellectual satisfaction. Can scientific knowledge and religious truth differ? Do they use different languages to say the same thing? "The human brain wants to know; the human heart wants to believe." Is there a war between our internal organs? To what extent will a mind that wants to know be satisfied by heartfelt poetry, by metaphors, by analogies, by fables? Do the conflicts—or seeming conflicts— between science and religion resolve into differences in storytelling?

The easiest way out of the apparent conflict of the claims of science and religion is the exclusion of one or the other. The success of science implies that there is no need for religion to explain nature; indeed, the expulsion of religion from human life has been a goal of some prominent thinkers from antiquity's earliest natural philosophers to the scientists of today. Religion says that answers may come directly from a divine voice and that, were we to grant validity to any other claims to knowledge, the authority of the divine voice would be diminished. In most parts of the world, including our own country, this claim, echoing the stentorian tirade of Tertullian that Athens had nothing to do with Jerusalem,

3

continues to resound. Others wish to accommodate both in order that, so to speak, the waters of the Athenian Illissus River might mingle with the sacred waters of the Jordan—and a cottage industry has grown up to satisfy this need.[1] This attempt to find room for both science and religion is nothing new: it is already found two thousand years ago, in Philo's work to reconcile the Judaism of his day with the best contemporary science, that of the schools of Pythagoras and of Plato. It is found in the parallel endeavors of Maimonides, Avicenna, and Aquinas to pour Aristotelian light over Judaism, Islam, and Christianity.

The aim of this book is to show the continuity of the issues involved in the attempt to reconcile science and religion, from the origin of the issues in antiquity to the present. By focusing on ancient formulations of the various problems in the relationship of science and religion, we can consider the issues with objective clarity. Just as ancient history enables us to examine the follies and greatness of human actions with a dispassion we cannot easily bring to recent events, so we can gain understanding of the relation between science and religion by looking at the questions posed by the ancient thinkers and seeing their reflection in contemporary issues. Thucydides will be relevant in international politics so long as human nature remains the same; in the same way, the Greek philosophers will be relevant so long as humans aim at understanding the universe and their place in it. This book, then, will begin by looking at ancient and medieval science, philosophy, and theology so that the issues may be seen in the starkest relief possible. We shall then turn to modern versions of the same ideas. Our goal is understanding, of science, of religion, and, most significantly, of human nature.

One extremely curious fact is that from Thales in the sixth century B.C.E. to Albert Einstein and Stephen Hawking, many scientists themselves bring God into their discussions. Equally curious is the fact that although men like Tertullian might completely reject Athens—a metaphor for science—others eagerly look to it for religious support. Thus in the modern era, Pope Pius XII saw in the modern theories of cosmology proof of divine creation. Are both sides trying, like Pascal, to hedge their bets? Or do they sincerely believe that one can learn from the other? What is going on?

When scientists, speaking in their role as scientists, talk of God, what do they mean? What do the religious thinkers mean? What conceptions of God, if any, are compatible with reason? Are the various proofs of the existence of God offered in the Western tradition consistent with science? What of the idea of "double truth," a truth for science and a separate truth for religion? Was this idea really found in the Middle Ages? In any case, is it valid? Or is it a surrender to the inherent incompatibility of science and religion?

The principal value of the classics is their discovery and exploration of issues most fundamental to our lives. The search for meaning in human life, the simultaneous denigration of and yearning for glory and ambition, the unending awe at the contrast between the incomprehensible magnitude of the universe and the smallness of humankind, the agonizing realization that the divine in humankind is mingled with the bestial—these are insights the ancient Greeks bequeathed to us. The question of whether human reason alone can explain the world was first advanced by the fathers of philosophy, Thales, Anaximenes, Parmenides, Heraclitus, and the others known as pre-Socratics. The question of whether God is immanent in the natural world or transcendent in a more mysterious spiritual abode we find in Plato and Aristotle. The attempt to reconcile the truths of philosophy with the truths of Scripture—a process we call theology, the application of *logos* to God—we find first in the work of Philo, whose solutions are surprising similar to those of the moderns who try to include God in the science of our day. These are some of the concerns that we shall visit in this and the following chapters.

SOME PRELIMINARY EXAMPLES

Here follow four passages: from Sophocles' *Oedipus Rex,* a passage concerning the cause of a devastating plague in Thebes; from the *Problems,* an ancient book of intriguing questions that is attributed to Aristotle, a passage explaining why it is cold at dawn; from Augustine's *City of God* (16.7), a passage dealing with the question of whether very remote islands received their animals from those preserved on Noah's ark; from the *Mishnat ha-Middot* of Rabbi Nehemiah, a Jewish mathematician of the second century C.E., a passage that tries to reconcile the value of pi with a biblical description of a circular bowl in the Temple. A careful reading of these passages will reveal a contrast among religious, scientific, and religiously scientific ways of thinking. Our reason for including the Sophocles passage is to show a clear religious causality (the anger of Apollo); the passage from the *Problems,* a purely natural causality; the passage from Augustine, a religious approach to a scientific question; and the passage from Nehemiah, a formidable (and successful) attempt to reconcile an apparent biblical value of pi as three with a mathematical value slightly greater than three.

Sophocles

In the first passage, Creon has returned from a mission to the Delphic Oracle on behalf of King Oedipus to learn why Thebes is suffering from a grievous plague and what may be done about it. This is the dialogue between Creon and Oedipus:

> *Creon.* With thy leave, I will tell you what I have heard from the god. Phoebus our lord bids us plainly to drive out a defiling thing, which (he saith) hath been harbored in this land, and not to harbor it, so that it cannot be healed.
>
> *Oedipus.* By what rite shall we cleanse us? What is the manner of the misfortune?
>
> *Creon.* By banishing a man, or by bloodshed in quittance of bloodshed, since it is that blood which brings the tempest on our city.

Oedipus. And who is the man whose fate he thus reveals?
Creon.   Laius, king, was lord of our land before thou wast pilot of this State.
Oedipus. I know it well—by hearsay, for I saw him never.
Creon.   He was slain; and the god now bids us plainly to wreak vengeance
            on his murderers—whosoever they be.[2]

From the passage we learn that one of the gods, Phoebus Apollo, is angry at the
city of Thebes because many years earlier its King Laius was murdered without
the capture or punishment of the perpetrator. Because this murderer, this "defile-
ment," remains unpunished, the entire city, its fields, and its livestock are all dying. We have here a clear example of religious causality. Because a human's conduct has violated a deity's sense of right and wrong, the deity intervenes in the
human world by sending a natural affliction to elicit the desired response. Perhaps
there is some justice in the suffering of the entire city, for the whole civic community failed to seek the murderer of its ruler. Though many years have passed,
no commission was ever established, no investigators engaged. Nothing was done
to solve the mystery of Laius's murder.

Oedipus's response reflects a total acceptance of Creon's claims. Indeed, it
seems almost natural for people everywhere to accept that they or their city could
be punished by a god for some wrong they have committed against that god.
Homer's *Iliad* also begins with a plague, it too caused by Apollo's anger over a
perceived wrong. In Exodus, the plagues Egypt suffers because of God's anger
seem perfectly expected. We might note that in all of these instances the deity operates through some natural means. He does not appear in his own godhead, bran-
dishing a sword and slaying all comers, but works through disease and famine
and other hardships that appear to have natural causes. That the causes are in fact
supernatural is known only because the deity wishes that fact to be known, for
unless it is, no corrective action can be taken.[3]

That supernatural causes can be known, at least sometimes, is essential for reli-
gion, which requires some form of communication between humans and the deity.
In the present instance, the actions of Apollo appear to be reasonable, for he is up-
holding the authority and sanctity of kings, whom one cannot kill with impunity.
Nevertheless, a great deal of arbitrariness goes unexplained. For example, why has
Apollo allowed so many years to elapse before taking any action? How can justice
be served by allowing so many innocent children and animals to perish? Why does
Apollo not punish only the humans responsible for pursuing the murderer? Why,
indeed, does Apollo not simply name the villain or strike only him? Of course,
these and similar questions are not even addressed, let alone explained, in the text.
It is part of the religious milieu and dramatic context that the situation be accepted.

Now if any work of pagan literature celebrates the powers of a human mind to
solve profound intellectual problems, it is *Oedipus Rex.* At the beginning of the
play the crime seems so deeply hidden in the mists of the past that it will be impossible to track down the relevant clues, which have grown cold. Moreover, the
only report of the crime by an eyewitness contains erroneous details. The report

says that King Laius was killed by a *band* of thieves, but we learn in the play's discovery scene that in fact Laius was killed by one man acting alone. Through a brilliant, persistent use of his intellectual powers, Oedipus is able to solve the mystery. He continues to pursue the truth even when doing so becomes personally torturous. Nevertheless, at the core of the tragedy's universe lie arbitrarily cruel destinies and capricious gods. The play, however, is profoundly religious: the gods and their will are earnestly accepted as reality.

Aristotle

Aristotle's *Problems* contains inquiries about various matters along with replies. The following is typical:

> Why is it that it is colder at dawn, although the sun is nearer to us? Is it because the period of the sun's absence is then at its longest, so that the earth has become more cooled? Or is it because towards daybreak the dew falls, as does the hoar-frost, and both of these are cold? Or do they too fall because the heat which rises from the earth is overpowered, the reason that it is overpowered being the absence of the sun? So that they do not fall when the sun is farther away, but when it is nearer they fall and become congealed, because the longer the sun is absent the cooler the ground becomes. Or is it because the nocturnal breezes tend to cause cold toward daybreak? Or do we only imagine that it is colder because then the food within us is concocted [i.e., digested] and, the stomach being emptier, we are more liable to feel the cold? This can be illustrated by the fact that we feel very cold after vomiting.[4]

Regardless of the truth or falsity of any of the explanations offered, the passage seems wholly scientific in spirit. The question itself involves physical reality and the apparently true observation that it is colder at dawn than at other times of the day. This phenomenon seems counterintuitive, for one would expect the day to be warmest when the sun is closest, as Aristotle thinks it is at dawn. By evenhandedly assessing various theories, Aristotle reveals a resourceful, undogmatic mind. Each of his various hypotheses is recognizably scientific in approach. No gods are brought in, no myths told. At the conclusion of the paragraph, there is a startling admission, that it may not really be colder at dawn but that the coldness may be imagined by people. Even if it is imagined, however, Aristotle assumes that the imagining itself has a physical cause, one having to do perhaps with digestion and the fact that people with empty stomachs are sensitive to the cold. The modern-sounding notion that psychological events, even hallucinations, arise from physical conditions, has a clear precedent in Aristotle.

Augustine

The above two passages exemplify religious and scientific ways of looking at various phenomena. The next two passages illustrate the method of reconciling religion and science by suitably interpreting the claims of religion. The first passage is Augustine's discussion of how animals on remote islands are related to those rescued on Noah's ark. The second, presumably by Nehemiah, attempts to deal with a biblical description of some temple ornaments that would give an incorrect measure of pi.

In *The City of God*, Augustine writes,

> There is a question raised about all those kinds of beasts which are not domesticated, nor are produced like frogs from the earth, but are propagated by male and female parents, such as wolves and animals of that kind; and it is asked how they could be found in the islands after the deluge, in which all the animals not found in the ark perished, unless the breed was restored from those who were preserved in pairs in the ark. It might, indeed, be said that they crossed to the islands by swimming, but this could only be true of those very near the mainland; whereas there are some so distant that we fancy no animal could swim to them. But if men caught them and took them across with themselves, and thus propagated these breeds in their new abodes, this would not imply an incredible fondness for the chase. At the same time, it cannot be denied that by the intervention of angels they might be transferred by God's order or permission. If, however, they were produced out of the earth as at their first creation, when God said, "Let the earth bring forth the living creatures," this makes it more evident that all kinds of animals were preserved in the ark, not so much for the sake of renewing the stock, as of prefiguring the various nations that were to be saved in the Church; this, I say, is more evident, if the earth brought forth many animals in islands to which they could not cross over.[5]

The problem Augustine is addressing arises from the apparent conflict between what is written in the Bible and what is observed in nature—that islands far out to sea contain animals incapable of swimming there from where Noah landed and unloaded the ark after the flood. Although Augustine takes as historically true the story of the flood and Noah's rescue of all the animals, he does not accept the apparent inconsistency unquestioningly but tries to resolve it. He is aware of the physical limitations of animals and does not believe that they can violate their nature. In this respect he accepts a measure of scientific thinking. On the other hand, he allows the possibility that humans might have carried the animals to the islands, though he thinks it highly unlikely. He accepts completely the existence of angels and entertains the possibility that angels performed this labor. But, he adds, God did not need the ark to renew the animals after the flood; after all, he created them in the first place by speech and could do so again. Augustine concludes that God created the animals on the islands a second time. This solution is consistent with the animals' presence on the islands and with Augustine's religious faith.

Augustine realizes that his solution raises the further question of why Noah would have had to make the ark and put the animals in it in the first place. Was not the purpose to preserve them? Augustine concludes that it would be inconsistent with God's power to require Noah to save them when it was so easy for God himself to renew the animal populations. Then, in a theologically innovative inspiration, he suggests that the reason for Noah's ark was "to prefigure the various nations that were to be saved in the Church." In other words, the actual historic event occurred for the sake of symbolism for people who were to be born thousands of years later, when the Catholic Church was saving souls. The inconsistencies between physical nature and the biblical text are eliminated by denying neither the presence of the animals on the islands nor the biblical account of Noah, but by proposing for the biblical event a new, symbolic purpose.

Nehemiah

To understand the final passage, one must keep in mind that the biblical verses to which it refers describe a very large bowl used by the priests for washing.

> And he made the molten sea [this is the bowl: *hayam mutzek*—literally, a "cast or molten sea"] of ten cubits from brim to brim, round in compass, and the height thereof was five cubits; and a line of thirty cubits did compass it round about. And under the brim of it round about there were knops [i.e., gourds] which did compass it, for ten cubits, compassing the sea round about; the knops were in two rows, cast when it was cast. It stood upon twelve oxen, three looking toward the north, and three looking toward the west, and three looking toward the south, and three looking toward the east; and the sea [i.e., the bowl] was set upon them above, and all their hinder parts were inward. And it was a handbreadth thick; and the brim thereof was wrought like the brim of a cup, like the flower of a lily; it held two thousand baths [a "bath" is a measure of liquid, roughly six gallons].[6]

For our purposes, the important part of the description is the length given for the diameter of the bowl (ten cubits) and that given for the circumference (thirty cubits). Given that the number pi equals by definition the circumference of a circle divided by its diameter, we obtain from the above passage a value for pi of 30 divided by 10 equals 3. At the time of 1 Kings, however, the value of pi was known to be larger than 3, probably lying somewhere between $3\frac{1}{8}$ and $3\frac{1}{7}$.[7] As in the case of Augustine's discussion of the animals on remote islands, the question is how to reconcile the inviolable, absolute word of Scriptures with a mathematical fact. Here science and religion seem to be saying different things, and not in a fanciful and indistinct metaphor, but in an actual measurement.

Rabbi Nehemiah, a mathematician and religious Jew, confronted the inconsistency. In the *Mishnat ha-Middot,* a geometry text, he writes:

> (1.4:) The circle has three aspects: the circumference, the thread [i.e., diameter], and the roof [i.e., area]. Which is the circumference? That is the rope surrounding the circle; for it is written: *And a rope of thirty cubits did encompass it round about.* And the thread? That is a straight line from brim to brim; for it is written: *From brim to brim.* And the roof itself is the area. . . .
>
> (5.3:) And if you want to know the circumference all around, multiply the thread into three and one seventh . . . (5.4:) Now it is written: *And he made the molten sea of ten cubits from brim to brim, round in compass,* and yet its circumference is thirty cubits, for it is written: *And a line of thirty cubits did compass it round about.* What is the

meaning of the verse *And a line of thirty cubits* and so forth? Nehemiah says: Since the people of the world say that the circumference of a circle contains three times one seventh of the thread, take off that one seventh for the thickness of the walls of the sea on the two brims, then there remain *thirty cubits did compass it round about.*[8]

Nehemiah resolves the inconsistency by arguing that we must measure the inner circumference and the outer diameter of the bowl, that is, the circumference of the inside rim but the diameter from the outer edge of the brim to the outer edge of the brim on the opposite side. The width of the bowl's walls makes up for the difference and resolves the discrepancy between an apparent value of three for pi and the real value of somewhat greater than three.

Nehemiah's accomplishment saves both the mathematical value of pi and the literal word of the biblical text. Examining his procedure, we see that he has taken two apparently inconsistent statements and shown that they are in fact consistent. Obviously, one of the claims had to bend a little, and Nehemiah resourcefully found room for flexibility in the description of the temple ornament. No doubt his very success in finding the solution confirmed his view that there was no contradiction between God's word and mathematics. To the objection that he was splitting hairs, he might reasonably have asked what difference it made that he was hair-splitting? Law often draws fine distinctions; what matters is that for a learned geometrician and religious Jew there is no irresolvable inconsistency.

Where Nehemiah differs from Augustine is that, although both read their texts in a nonliteral manner, the mathematician did not have to engage in metaphor or symbolism in order to make sense of the difficulty. His was a satisfactorily practical solution. We might, of course, say that other solutions were possible for Nehemiah. He might have claimed that the Bible was giving only an approximation—an approximation aimed at most readers, who would not have noticed the mathematical discrepancy. Or he might, like some German commentators, have claimed that the bowl must have been hexagonal or some other shape.[9] Instead, he looked for the mathematically consistent reading closest to the literal sense of the text.

We may consider the preceding approaches as representative. Religions, at least those of the West, tend to look for explanations in terms of divine will. Science looks for explanations in terms of physical causes. Where there seem to be irreconcilable differences between the divine will literally construed and a commonsense understanding of physical causes, an appeal to symbolic meaning or an appropriate adjustment in the religious or the scientific claim (or both) sometimes aids in the reconciliation. Augustine kept the biblical text as the constant and made adjustments in natural causes. He took the story of Noah, as well as the obvious presence of animals on remote islands, as a given. The presence of those animals, however, he attributed to a supernatural cause—creation ex nihilo by God. In short, he was willing to sacrifice natural causality to resolve the apparent inconsistency. Nehemiah took the mathematical understanding of pi as his given and sacrificed a strictly literal reading of the Bible in order to resolve an apparent inconsistency.

DISCUSSION QUESTIONS

1. Although human reason has been immensely successful in a wide range of human activities, from probing the ocean depths to landing human beings on the moon, it is nevertheless held in suspicion by some people as incapable of probing the inner depths of human hearts or landing persons into meaningful and fulfilling lives. Why do you suppose that there is this double attitude towards what seems to be humanity's single greatest attribute?

2. How pervasive today is the attitude exemplified in the passage from Sophocles' *Oedipus Rex?* Do people really believe that when they watch a sporting event on TV, even thousands of miles from the game, something they do—for example, go to the refrigerator for a soft drink—will magically affect the outcome of the game? Have you ever held such a notion? How seriously have you held it? How successful have you been at banishing it?

3. What compromises have Augustine and Nehemiah made in their reconciliations of the Bible with science? Who seems to have compromised more?

NOTES

1. See, for example, the journals *Zygon: Journal of Religion and Science* and *Science and Spirit,* as well as numerous newsletters and Internet resources.

2. Sophocles, *Oedipus Rex,* trans. R. C. Jebb (Cambridge: Cambridge University Press, 1914), 95–107.

3. There seems in early thought a merging of the idea of the deity's will and what is right. It is right to do what the god wants in order to avoid his anger. We shall take up later the question of whether something is right because the deity wishes it or whether the deity wishes it because it is right. (See "Plato's God," pp. 96f.)

4. Aristotle, *Problems,* trans. E. S. Forster, in *The Complete Works of Aristotle: The Revised Oxford Translation,* ed. J. Barnes (Princeton, N.J.: Princeton University Press, 1984), 888b26–39.

5. Augustine, *The City of God,* trans. M. Dods (Chicago: Encyclopaedia Britannica, 1952), 16.7.

6. 1 Kings 7:23–26, Masoretic text.

7. Petr Beckmann, *A History of π* (New York: St. Martin's, 1971), 15–16.

8. Nehemiah, *The Mishnat ha Middot: The First Hebrew Geometry of about 150 C.E.; and The Geometry of Muhammad ibn Musa al-Khowarizmi: The First Arabic Geometry (c. 820) Representing the Arabic Version of the Mishnat ha Middot,* trans. S. Gandz (Würzburg: jal-reprint, 1973), 5.4.

9. J. Tropfke, *Geschichte der Elementarmathematik. Vierter Band: Ebene Geometrie* (Berlin-Leipzig: Vereinigung wissenschaftlicher Verleger, 1923), 210, cited in Beckmann, *History,* 191n35.

2

Is Human Reason Able to Explain the World?

On Saturday, July 30, Dr. Johnson and I took a sculler at the Temple-stairs, and set out for Greenwich. I asked him if he really thought a knowledge of the Greek and Latin languages an essential requisite to a good education. *Johnson.* "Most certainly, Sir; for those who know them have a very great advantage over those who do not. Nay, Sir, it is wonderful what a difference learning makes upon people even in the common intercourse of life, which does not appear to be much connected with it." "And yet, (said I) people go through the world very well, and carry on the business of life to good advantage, without learning." *Johnson.* "Why, Sir, that may be true in cases where learning cannot possibly be of any use; for instance, this boy rows as well without learning, as if he could sing the song of Orpheus to the Argonauts, who were the first sailors." He then called to the boy, "What would you give, my lad, to know about the Argonauts?" "Sir, (said the boy,) I would give what I have." Johnson was much pleased with his answer, and we gave him a double fare. Dr. Johnson then turning to me, "Sir, (said he,) a desire of knowledge is the natural feeling of mankind; and every human being, whose mind is not debauched, will be willing to give all that he has to get knowledge."

—James Boswell, *Life of Johnson*

REASON AND HUMAN NATURE

Many qualities of human nature are relevant to the kinds of questions asked about the divine. Whether God made human beings in his image or whether human beings created God and gods in *their* image, there would be an affinity between the human and divine. Since much of what is thought about the divine realm is extrapolated from what we know about the human, it will be useful for

12

understanding later discussions in this book to make some preliminary comments about human nature. It will, we trust, become clear how conceptions about the divine developed from contemplation of the various features of human nature and human reason. As we shall see, language and logic themselves have been highly productive of theology.

The Nature of Reason

Except at the fringes of serious thought, no one denies that what distinguishes human beings from other animals is the ability to reason. Even most of those who are committed to the notion that many animals have some smaller capacity to reason will agree that the difference in degree between the human ability to reason and the ability of other animals is so great as almost to constitute a difference in kind. A children's sandbox and the Sahara Desert are both made of sand, but the difference is so great as to refute any identification of the two.[1]

Those who conceive of a rational deity claim that the deity also shares in the capacity to reason. Of these, pagans, for the most part, believed that the gods' capacity to reason was no greater than that of humans, though some, like Xenophanes, as we shall see, believed that the capacity to reason in humans was far beneath the divine capacity. Some Christians distinguished between the reasoning of humans and angels. But before these various distinctions can be appreciated, it would be well to define our terms, starting with "reason" itself, a term often used but seldom defined.

In a nutshell, to reason is to make generalizations. The basic unit of reason is the word, and every word is a generalization, a fact that is evident in the meaning of what grammarians call "common nouns." For example, we use the word *car* to describe something like a four-wheeled vehicle driven by an internal combustion motor for the purpose of transporting people, pets, and groceries from one place to another. Not every car, perhaps, will fit this definition perfectly, but when one person uses the word *car,* another will know what he means because cars share the same *generalized* meaning of the term. Now no two cars are absolutely identical, not even when they are of the same model, for small variations—variations in their matter, to use an ancient locution—will always exist. Even if they were in every respect materially identical (an impossibility at the microscopic level), they will occupy different space and in this respect, at least, will be different. But because they are *generally* the same, we call them both cars. All words are such generalizations, that is, they take a diverse array of things and call them by the same name.

Although the name *Aristotle* seems to refer to only one person on the planet and therefore seems not to be a generalization, even proper nouns are generalizations, for generalizations may arise from time as well as from material. Just as no two cars are identical in material, so too, in a strict sense, no individual is identical to himself at any two moments. Heraclitus's statement that "you cannot step in the same river twice," a statement out-epigrammed by his student Cratylus to "you cannot step in the same river *once*," applies to all things. (This changing nature of physical things, their *temporal* nature, will also be relevant later, when we explore the attempts to find something that exists outside of change, of which the deity is a prime candidate.[2]) So Aristotle is a generalization of the same qualities that remain stable over a period of time. While Aristotle or any individual is a little changed every day, he remains, *in general,* the same.

Verbs are words that generalize the way in which a thing exists in time. For example, in the sentence, "Barbara will swim this afternoon," the words "will swim" show how the thing, in this case "Barbara," will exist in time. The sentence makes sense to someone else because the one hearing the sentence understands the generalization represented by the words "Barbara" and "swim." Whatever peculiarities there might be in Barbara's stroke—or in Barbara herself—the sentence gives a general sense of how she will pass her time. The other parts of speech similarly have a generalized meaning.[3] Language is the best expression of reason. It is, so to speak, reason itself, as even its constituent elements, words, are units of reason. In classical Greek, the word *logos* (which we shall see later as one of the Christian terms for God) means both "language" and "reason."[4]

It would appear that only human beings have a sophisticated ability to use language. If apes or dolphins use some prototypical form of language, the difference in the complex, grammatical languages of humans and the primitive languages of other creatures is so great as to constitute a distinct difference. We shall therefore be careful to avoid metaphorical uses of the word *language.* When dogs bark to frighten off a stranger, to be sure, they are communicating, as are birds attracting others with mating calls, or skunks warding off with an odiferous spray a potential enemy, or human automobile drivers making obnoxious gestures. But none of these forms of communication is language in the strict sense. Language must be made of words that conjure up images in the minds of the people hearing or reading them. Thus, despite the conventional metaphor, music is not a language, for the sounds convey no generalized mental images.

What we call logic, another derivative from the Greek *logos,* consists partly in the rules governing the making of generalizations. While the study of logic may help one to refine the kinds of subtle generalizations one makes, it is not necessary to study logic as an academic subject to fulfill one's nature as a human being. At least with respect to simple generalizations, people think logically most of the time, and where they make mistakes, it is typically from laziness rather than from lack of ability. Those whose powers of logic are seriously impaired suffer from a mental illness.

The thesis of the preceding paragraph can be illustrated with a couple of examples. If the first two pipe-smokers that someone has ever seen turn out to be professors, the person may conclude that men who smoke pipes are professors. His generalization would be based on two samples. Although the process of generalizing is logical, the generalization in this case would have been reached on the basis of insufficient data: a bit of diligent investigation might reveal that some men who smoke pipes are not professors. Most people would understand the rashness of making a hasty generalization on the basis of too small a sample once the risks of doing so were brought to their attention. In fact a good deal of humor is based on the intentional use of obvious fallacies—rash generalization, equivocation, and the like.

Mental disorders in human beings also exhibit a defective capacity to reason. The woman who says, "My name is Mary and I am a virgin; therefore I am the Virgin Mary," and believes that she is actually the mother of Jesus, exhibits what in psychiatry is called "palaeo-logic" and is said to have schizophrenia. Despite the relative rarity of such mental disorders, it is clear that the problem uniquely affects human beings and is a disorder of the human faculty of reason.[5]

The question arises whether a human being may, either through a voluntary suspension of reason or through some acquired second nature of a barbaric kind, cease to be wholly under the sway of his rational faculty. Though we very frequently make reference to people as "beasts" or "animals" in our common speech, we shall argue that it is not possible for someone to violate his nature in this fundamental way. A person can no more choose to cease being a human than a dog can choose to cease being a dog or a cockroach a cockroach. In *The Oration on the Dignity of Man,* Pico della Mirandola argues that man's special quality is that he has control over an inherently indeterminate nature: man can make himself into an angel or a beast. Pico was speaking metaphorically: a man of extraordinary goodness might behave like an angel; one of extraordinary badness, like a creature devoid of reason. But metaphors are metaphors, and human beings cannot literally become irrational beasts. Too often in human culture have the metaphors gotten away from their metaphorical limits and been taken literally. This book will try to avoid that fate.

Even when under the influence of alcohol or other mind-altering drugs, a human being still reasons. The obvious proof is that he can still speak in sentences. The content may be deficient, but he retains his humanity by using language in a way no other animal can. Let us say the drug-user begins to shout and behave violently towards people he chances upon. No matter how obnoxious he becomes, he still maintains the faculty of speech and can still engage in complicated operations, such as driving. He still understands cause and effect. At no time does even the most intoxicated lout ever wholly abandon his humanity. We may call him a beast, but the name is a rhetorical expression of our condemnation of his behavior.

Nor do we human beings do anything at all without reason playing a part at some level in our actions. Thus, we perform in peculiarly human ways even those actions that originate from our animal nature. Like the other animals, we are born, eat, sleep, mate, excrete, bury our dead. But the human versions of these actions are governed by conventions, habits, rituals, and rules that have arisen from thought and dictate the times, places, amounts, and other details that are appropriate. Even when we choose to exert independence by flouting the rules, the very flouting is the result of rational thought. In short, try as we might, we cannot consciously escape rationality: it is the substrate that underlies everything we do, from the moment we awaken to the moment we go to sleep. Insofar as our dreams contain conversations, even in our sleep we do not abandon rationality.

Of all the activities that humans share with other animals, sexual reproduction is special for human beings because, unlike other animals, humans know that sexual intercourse is what brings new life. No other creature seems to understand the cause and effect of reproduction. How could it? Hence because the creation of new life has always been regarded as an almost magical event—we cannot help but speak poetically here—the "magic" has transferred to the sexual intercourse itself, which is subject to rules in every culture. Even when those rules are violated, sex retains the magical status because of the cultural knowledge of its effects. The rituals that surround sexual intercourse develop from a rational awareness of its nature.[6]

Similarly, as living animals, we must eat. But consider all the rituals we associate with food! Every moment of the process of acquiring, preparing, and serving food is associated with rituals that have resulted from thought. The rational concerns of nutrition, sanitation, and taste pervade our eating. Prayer may precede eating; foods may be eaten in a certain ritual order. For humans, eating is accompanied by worries about the future, about the availability and costs of food, about the climate for growing food, about food's effect on health, even about the morality of eating various kinds of living things.

Finally, as we have mentioned earlier, the exclusively human diseases are mental diseases that involve a distorted form of reasoning. No doubt there are diseases that also affect the mental apparatus of other animals. A canine mental disorder would affect a dog's mental abilities that are manifested when it acts like a dog, just as human mental disease affects human mental functions. What is important to see is that a mentally ill person still retains, albeit in a misshapen form, his essential humanity, his sophisticated faculty of reason. And this is true even of those who commit the most heinous crimes.

All Men Desire to Know

At the beginning of the *Metaphysics,* Aristotle writes that all human beings by nature (i.e., by their *human* nature) desire to know.[7] The claim is a very strong one. First, it is universal, excluding no one. Second, it uses the powerful word *know,* a word we shall investigate carefully later (pp. 17–18). Third, it uses the term *desire,*[8] which, since it means "to acquire a perceived good," might be thought to imply that knowledge is for human beings a good, a view that will itself be debated by later classical and medieval writers, especially among some pious thinkers who will place limits on what knowledge *should* be sought. Fourth, Aristotle claims that the desire to know is an innate and therefore unavoidable part of human nature.

Knowledge as Universal

Perhaps all animals wish to know where danger threatens or where an ample food supply is lying, and so perhaps it seems as if there is nothing special in the human desire to know. Aristotle's claim, however, refers to the kind of knowing that is not for the sake of usefulness but is desired exclusively for its own sake, as an end in itself, and that brings pleasure to the knower in its acquisition. The pleasure may come from knowing trivial things or profound things, the knowledge of which is sought for its own sake; or it may come from gossip and snooping or from an almanac and encyclopedia, independently of any utility such knowledge may also have.

Now it is not always easy to disentangle our motives for asking why. If an earthquake destroys a city and little children die, we may ask from a desire for useful knowledge. For instance, we may wish to be told, as was Oedipus by Creon's report from Delphi, whether the city is being punished by a deity for someone's sin. Such information would be immediately useful, presumably because making amends for the sin would prevent further suffering. If a scientist gives an explanation in terms of tectonic plates, however, we would not—at least, at present—have an explanation that is of any utility; yet the desire to know for its own sake and apart from any utility is partially satisfied. (It will not be entirely satisfied until all aspects of the why-question are addressed.) Similarly, when people ask questions about an unsolved crime that occurred a hundred years earlier and either speculate about it or investigate it, they are attempting to satisfy the human desire to know even when there is no possible use for the resulting knowledge.

We may ask different questions, those that begin with the famous journalistic interrogatives who, where, when, what, and why. Human beings desire to know answers to all of these questions, says Aristotle, but especially answers to why-questions. Such inquiries into questions of causes figure essentially in our exploration of science and religion. When questions go unanswered, especially why-questions, one feels an aching pain of unsatisfied desire, even when the knowledge concerns something trivial. That is why one child may mock another by claiming to know a cause or a bit of information that he refuses to tell. When the claim to knowledge is about a serious matter and the refusal to tell is boldly made, the reaction will be righteous anger. In *Oedipus Rex*, when Tiresias claims knowledge about the murderer of Laius but refuses to reveal that knowledge, Oedipus rightly responds with intense anger.

The ubiquitous gossip magazines and tabloid periodicals cater to this most human of desires. We may deplore the desire to know about the private lives of others, a knowledge that can have no possible utility for ourselves, but it would be impossible to deny that everyone shares to one degree or another in the desire for this kind of knowledge. It forms the content of a good deal of social intercourse. Except in cartoons or fables, where the animals are really people, it is impossible to imagine a squirrel or a wolf having the slightest interest in the private affairs of another member of the species. The essential point is that the desire of knowledge for its own sake, whether that knowledge be sublime or base, is pervasive in and unique to human life.

Degrees of Certainty

The word *know* is notoriously difficult to define; in fact, a whole branch of philosophy, epistemology, concerns itself with the nature of knowledge. A spectrum of words covers cognitive awareness of reality, words like *belief, opinion, faith,* and so forth. In different contexts, different standards of proof are required to satisfy claims of knowledge. Thus, as is now common knowledge (whatever this means), the standard of proof of culpability in civil cases is less than that in criminal cases. When Aristotle says that all humans desire to know, however, he has in mind the strongest possible certainty, a standard beyond reasonable doubt, nay, beyond any doubt whatsoever. Of course, not every desire for knowledge can be satisfied. Yet when we desire to know something, what we are desiring is certainty. We do not want to settle for "pretty sure"; we want to know without qualification. When we want to know about a celebrity's private life, for example, we are not looking for probabilities and approximations. We want to know *exactly* how much a movie star paid for a yacht; and we want to be *certain* that the illicit affair occurred. Although we very often must content ourselves with opinions and beliefs—lower and less intrinsically desirable levels of cognitive awareness— this contentment is an accommodation we make to necessity.

In addition to the question of certainty, another matter that will arise frequently in our discussions of scientific and religious ways of knowing is the difference between knowing through causes and knowing through effects. If a person awakes one morning, looks out his window, and sees that the streets and sidewalks are wet, he will conclude, most reasonably, that it has rained during the night. By looking at the effect—wet streets and sidewalks—he draws a conclusion about the cause of the wetness. Although it probably did rain in such circumstances, how certain is that conclusion? Someone may have washed the streets with a hose; a pipe might have burst; snow might have melted. A conclusion reached from effects is called a conclusion a posteriori, that is, from what is posterior to, or after, the cause. Knowledge of effects is in such cases more certain than knowledge of the cause, given that there are several possible causes. If, on the other hand, the person had awakened in the night, looked out the window at the rain falling, and then stayed awake until dawn to ascertain that nothing else had happened, then he would, to Aristotle's satisfaction, have seen the cause of the wetness, and his knowledge of how the streets had gotten wet would be a priori in the sense of being knowledge of a cause. (Let us emphasize that we are using *Aristotle's* sense of a priori here, not the sense used by modern philosophers of being independent of experience.)

Unfortunately, we fail to witness the causes of most things in our lives and hence have much less a priori knowledge than we might desire. No one is a witness to his own conception, yet he has highly certain knowledge of his existence. Of his actual identity, however, he has only a posteriori knowledge. He looks at the documents and listens to what his parents tell him, but the certainty that he has of these matters is not by any means absolute, as Oedipus found out. In a great many cases what knowledge we have can be only a posteriori, for the nature of the world precludes any other way of knowing. (Here we are using the term *knowledge* in a sense less strict than Aristotle's absolute knowledge.) For example, when we look at dinosaur bones we may draw all sorts of conclusions about what the dinosaurs were like, all of which conclusions are a posteriori, from effects. As an example of how frail a posteriori conclusions can be, note how frequently reconstructions of dinosaurs in the nineteenth and early twentieth centuries have been subject to revision as more information has become available. Because it is impossible to go back into time and have firsthand information about dinosaurs, we are limited by the nature of the subject matter to a posteriori conclusions.

Scientific theories, from Big Bang cosmology to biological evolution, suffer from the same intrinsic weakness that attends all a posteriori conclusions. Scientists must reason from observed effects back to an often unobserved cause that is almost always one of several possible causes. The a posteriori and revisable nature of such conclusions in no way means that they are false or automatically suspect. Nevertheless, the degree of certitude we have about them is less than that for perfectly deduced a priori conclusions, such as those in mathematics and logic. When people object to Darwin's theory of natural selection as "only a theory," they are degrading the theory perhaps because it is a posteriori and hence cannot be absolutely known in the strongest sense. Those who refer to the theory of evolution as "only a theory" are expressing, especially in the word *only,* their hearts' desire to have the strict knowledge that attends matters known through their causes. (They are of course also conflating the colloquial use of the term *theory* as "unsubstantiated hypothesis" with the scientific use of the term for a hypothesis that is *well* substantiated—by observation, experiment, logical elegance, consilience with other well-substantiated theories, etc.)

In criminal trials as well, the highest degree of certainty we can achieve is that of well-substantiated but a posteriori knowledge, but this limitation is no reason to call all criminal verdicts into question. Let us say that a man is on trial for a murder that no one else has actually witnessed. There may be a great deal of circumstantial evidence against him. He may have had motive and opportunity; traces of his hair and blood may have been found at the scene; etc. Is he guilty? Is it possible to know in the strict Aristotelian sense that he is guilty? To the degree that knowledge of his guilt can be only a posteriori, i.e., derived from the experiential evidence rather than from logically deduced causes, his guilt will always be in an important sense provisional. To what degree can doubts about his guilt be "reasonable"? To those willing to apply the term *knowledge* only to what they know absolutely and through firsthand experience of causes, no a posteriori knowledge will satisfy, and there will, to them, always be room for reasonable doubt. But such a lofty standard of certainty applies no more in legal contexts than it does in scientific ones. If legal verdicts are ever to be reached, or even the most universally accepted scientific claims to be adopted, we must very often be content with a posteriori knowledge. Indeed, all our knowledge of George Washington and of the Spanish–American War and of most things is a posteriori.

There are, of course, many, many other questions that deal with knowledge, some of which will arise later, as we explore the kind of knowledge that we can have of God, the kind of knowledge that God himself could have, the influence of problems concerning knowledge on theology, and so forth. Let it suffice for now for us to claim that all men desire to know and that what they really desire, or desire most, is knowledge in the strict sense of cognitive awareness of what is absolutely true. Given a choice, one would always choose the most unqualified kind of knowledge.

Knowledge as a Good

"Desire" is always aimed at what the one desiring perceives to be a good, so it may safely be said that desire is the wish to obtain a good. In this respect, literally everything that we do, we do seeking what we perceive to be a good. We eat for the good of nutrition or simply for the pleasure that eating provides; we exercise for the good of health; we may go to work for the good of obtaining a living. Even when we do things that are bad for us, we do them for the sake of some perceived good. One smokes for the sake of taste, or for the sake of eliminating the painful craving for nicotine, or for the sake of "looking cool," or for a mild "high." A person commits a crime for money, a thrill, or revenge—all goals that he perceives as goods. It may be, of course, that an action is in fact more harmful than beneficial, more bad than good, but the one performing the action is aiming only at the perceived good, not at the bad, unless the bad effect is part of the perceived good, as in the case of someone with suicidal tendencies. It may be, to return to the example of smoking, that smoking will lead to lung cancer or heart disease—but the one who lights up a cigarette is not aiming at these evils when he lights up; he is aiming at one of the perceived goods. The immediate good, because it is immediate, often appears larger or makes a stronger impression than the remote evil of disease.

When it comes to desires, one is obviously far better off desiring things that are in fact good rather than merely perceived to be so. Moreover, the better the objects of one's desire actually are, the happier one will be. The person who loves justice and charity and holds them as excellent objects of desire will be much less inclined to criminal activity than a person who puts the possession of money or pleasure as the highest good. Much of the job of parents is to train children in what to desire and what to shun, i.e., to train their perceived goods to correspond to actual good. Parents train children in this way by instilling values about what is good—the proper object of desire—and what is bad. Here, as in so much, actions speak much more forcefully than words, especially since children are often incapable of distinguishing perceived goods from actual goods. The child who sees his parent smoking will infer not only that smoking is perceived as good by his parent but that smoking is actually, all things considered, a good habit to acquire. If the child comes to the conclusion on his own that smoking is actually bad, he will have less faith in his parent's judgment. If his smoking parent tells him not to smoke, the inconsistency between words and deeds will undermine respect for the parent. The same might be said of the parent who spends all his time seeking wealth, as though wealth were the highest good, or sexual encounters, or television-watching, or anything else. One's objects of desire indicate what one thinks of as good, and what one thinks of as good constitute one's values. Telling one's children other-

wise will be to no avail. But where parents seek healthy foods or seek to participate in healthy activities, the children will likely conclude that these habits are
both perceived by their parents as good and actually good in themselves.

Since all men desire to know, knowledge must be understood to be at least a perceived good. The question arises of whether it is a qualified good, such as the merely
perceived goods above, or an unqualified good, which we have been referring to as
actual goods or proper objects of desire. A good is qualified when it is good only under some circumstances or only in certain ways. An unqualified good is one that is
always good without any restrictions. For example, chocolate cake is a qualified
good: it is good only if fresh, if consumed by a non-diabetic or non-allergic person
in the right amount and at the right time, and so on. Wisdom, the ability to make intelligent choices in significant ethical matters, is an unqualified good, for there are
no circumstances in which being wise would not be desirable.

For finite creatures such as human beings, we must conclude that knowledge,
though one of the greatest goods, is a qualified good. To explain this limitation,
it is necessary first to recognize that knowledge in the abstract, apart from any
subject matter, does not exist. There is no such thing as knowledge in general;
knowledge must be *of* something, i.e., it must have a subject matter. Just as a parent does not exist without being the parent of an offspring, so knowledge must be
the knowledge of a particular truth. We know that Napoleon lost the Battle of Wa-
terloo, or we know that in a right triangle the square of the hypotenuse equals the
sum of the squares of the other two sides. The question of whether knowledge is
a qualified or unqualified good therefore depends on the subject matter. For example, it is not a good thing for a robber to know the combination to the bank
vault, nor for a person to know every thought that passes through the mind of
every acquaintance of his. The finitude of the human mind is also relevant to
whether certain types and amounts of knowledge are unqualified goods. Knowing every detail of world history, if such a feat were possible, would deprive a
person of much other, more valuable knowledge. The question of whether knowledge or complete knowledge is a qualified or unqualified good for God, or under
what conceptions of God, is one we shall return to later in this book (p. 169).

The Rationality of Desiring Knowledge

Most interesting of the claims in the opening of the *Metaphysics* is that all humans desire to know *by nature*. Since, as we have observed, the distinguishing characteristic of human nature is the capacity to reason, the question is whether the desire for knowledge or understanding—that is, knowledge of what and how the
world works—is a necessary consequence of reason.[9] Is it possible to be rational
and not to desire understanding?

It seems reasonable to conclude that for the most part it would be irrational not
to desire understanding. In certain special cases, of course, a person might declare
that he does not wish to understand something or that it is better not to know. But
these declarations would almost certainly be the result of believing the knowledge

to be painful or wicked rather than believing that knowledge itself is undesirable. For example, a man might not wish to know that his wife is committing adultery, and he might deliberately turn away from the information that would confirm the deed. Another person might choose not to learn that he has a dreaded disease, again because of a fear of the pain such knowledge would cause. These cases are exceptions to the general rule, but only because of the fear of pain or some other woe that is involved. In general, people wish to know, for they have an innate sense that it is better to know than not to know, even when the knowledge may be painful, even when it may do no good to know. It is part of the nobility of human nature—perhaps the noblest part—that we crave knowledge so profoundly.

Why maintain that the desire to know is a *necessary* consequence of the faculty of reason? To reason, as we have defined the term earlier (p. 13), is to make generalizations. As in any natural activity, the tendency is to attempt the activity in as excellent, efficient, and effective a manner as possible. When we breathe, for example, our lungs try to take in air properly and in a manner conducive to health. When our eyes operate, they try the best they can to see clearly, and so too with ears and every other organ of the body. By analogy, then, we may say that the faculty of reason, in its effort to make generalizations, tries to make them as accurately as possible. Hence, when it comes to making generalizations about the world, our reason tries to make them consistent with true information, with things known. If someone uses a word, unless he has some special and unusual purpose, he wants to use the word accurately. If one says "tree" he wishes the object to which he has referred to be a tree. For his conversation to be meaningful he must know what a tree is. Thus it will be plain that in virtually all cases the desire to know is so inborn, so automatic, that we no more think of it than we think of our desire for food or water. Because we naturally tend to use our faculties effectively, the proper use of reason leads almost inevitably to a desire for knowledge.

Knowledge may be desired because it contributes to an activity, because it helps us to make or acquire some other thing, or as an end in itself. One may wish to learn how to swim for the sake of the activity of swimming. Or one may wish to learn the science of medicine in order to bring about health in other people or in oneself, and so the knowledge of medicine is acquired for the sake of a product, health. Another person may wish to learn a skill for the sake of making something, say a crystal radio, and here the goal is a product. Very often, however, human beings seek knowledge that is wholly useless, simply because of the pleasure in knowing. We may enjoy learning the details of a deceased baseball player's life. The knowledge has no utility whatsoever, but there is a joy in learning about a famous life. Most of what we read in the newspapers has no bearing on our lives at all, and indeed, most "human interest" stories are printed because of *human* interest, the natural tendency of people to want to know about their world and the things, including people, in it. Occasionally we meet people who claim to eschew all useless knowledge, and they don't read the newspapers except for the movie listings or the "do-it-yourself news," but such people, if they really exist, are rare. Most of us have known many who made such claims but who also listened to useless gossip with greedy delight.

The ancients, especially those belonging to the Platonic and Aristotelian schools, claimed that the philosopher was the best human being, for, unlike the artisan or athlete, he sought knowledge for its own sake. Pythagoras is said to have divided humankind according to the three types found at the Olympic games. The worst type, he said, is the hawker of refreshments and other items, who is not interested in the games at all, only in the monetary profits he can acquire. Next worst are the players, who limit their vision to their part of the field and, though they are playing for the sake of victory, see only what is in their immediate vicinity. Best of those at the games are the spectators, who, above the fray, watch the entire playing field and understand how all the parts contribute to the whole. Taking pleasure in this contemplation of the whole, their position is most like that of the gods, their motive neither gain nor glory. Philosophers, like the spectators at the games, who seek knowledge for its own sake alone, are the most exalted.

The philosophers who made these claims, even though they were *Greek* philosophers, were mistaken here. While they were looking quite rightly at the purpose or goal of the knowledge, they were overlooking a fact we observed in the previous section (p. 21), that knowledge does not exist apart from its subject matter. The subject matter of a particular instance of knowledge in part determines the value of that piece of knowledge and in some cases outweighs the motives for which the knowledge is sought. If one wishes to memorize the heights and weights of various baseball players, for example, that knowledge is neither productive nor practical and, though trivial, is sought for its own sake. But its being sought for its own sake hardly makes it superior to, say, knowledge of the Heimlich Maneuver, which could save a life but is of little theoretical value as knowledge for its own sake. Although the ancients did not conceive of this weighing of subject matter versus motives and did not adequately appreciate the value of practical motives as applied to practical subjects, it seems clear that trivial knowledge, despite the fact that it may be sought without ulterior motive, should not be deemed better than highly practical knowledge, even if the latter is sought for precisely its practical benefits.

The question of whether—and exactly how—knowledge can be valued in proportion to its purposes or subject matter is a question that has been associated with both science and religion from antiquity to our own day. Debates still take place in the United States, for example, over the relative values of so-called pure and applied scientific research. One of the major justifications of the space program in the popular imagination is that it will continue to produce useful technological devices and applications collateral to the subjects under investigation, i.e., that its subject matter and purposes are at least in part practical. Such claims were made in the belief that Congress would never fund pure research. The argument over whether the United States should spend its money trying to learn about distant galaxies or about how to solve the many pressing problems on earth exemplifies disagreements about the relative value of knowledge for its own sake versus useful knowledge.

As for religion, theology has been often hailed as the "queen of the sciences," an epithet that has sometimes referred to its sovereignty over all other subjects, sometimes to the superior quality of its subject matter, God. Is knowledge of God something to be sought at all? How can such knowledge be obtained? Is the only knowledge of God a posteriori, and, if so, how reliable is it? Is a knowledge of God purely theoretical or can it have some practical advantages? Does such knowledge bring pleasure or pain? These are questions that shall follow us as we survey the attempts to reconcile God and science through the millennia.

Human Nature and Human Questions

Wolfgang Amadeus Mozart is said to have been a difficult child to rouse from his slumbers in the morning. Because he wished to loll in bed instead of heed his parents' wish that he get up, his father devised an ingenious scheme to stir the musical genius. He would go to the piano and play the first seven notes of an octave— do, re, mi, fa, so la, ti. . . . Such was the young Mozart's discomfort at not hearing the eighth note that he would jump out of bed, rush to the piano, and hit the last note. This anecdote nicely illustrates a human psychic need for closure, completeness, and order. The desire for order is a necessary concomitant of our rationality, which, as we have seen (p. 13), leads us naturally to classify and generalize about the things we encounter in the world.

Reason involves making generalizations, and generalizations require that things that fall into categories or exhibit general patterns. We classify something as a bird, for example, if it shares with other birds the qualities or pattern of what me might call "birdness." Notice how uncomfortable we are with an animal we cannot identify. Is it a cat? Is it a dog? Is it dangerous?

Categorization can give us a sense of comfort or closure even in cases in which we do not understand the category in question. If a birder identifies a bird as "an ivory horn-billed scarlet kinglet," the nonexpert is usually satisfied, even if he has never heard of the bird and has no idea whether the identification is accurate. Nevertheless, he has a sense of order and closure about the matter, because he now believes that the bird fits into a category or pattern, even one that is known only by experts.

For the most part, people are just like Mozart in wanting closure. The violated octave ruined the pattern, destroyed the harmonious order of the scale, and upset the young Mozart's peace of mind. Until he played the eighth note he could not enjoy repose. The person who wants to know the name of the mysterious bird, even though that knowledge serves absolutely no practical purpose, feels a similar, though probably less severe, discomfort.

Part of Aristotle's genius lay in first enunciating the various patterns that constitute the knowledge that human beings long for and in showing how, if any of these are incomplete, knowledge will be incomplete and the discomfort we have been discussing will ensue. When we talk about a thing, Aristotle said we want to know (a) what it is made of (the material cause), (b) who or what made it (the efficient cause), (c) what it looks like and how it is put together (the formal cause), and (d) what its purpose is (the final cause). These are known as "Aristotle's four causes." If we are speaking of a house, for example, we want to know that it is made of bricks and wires and glass and so on, that it was constructed by Joe and Alice and Maureen and Scott, the carpenters, electricians, and plumbers, that it is a colonial house, and that it was made for the purpose of housing the Gibson family. We want to know, in other words, how to categorize the house: as "brick house," "colonial house," etc. Aristotle's four causes provide four fundamentally different ways of categorizing things, four fundamentally different aspects of knowing things. If we knew only that the house was made of bricks, our knowledge would be incomplete, as it would be if we knew everything about the house *except* what it was made of.

Aristotle's formulation works best for things made by human beings for express purposes and less well for things in the natural world. For example, we might ask about a certain mosquito that bit a guest in our garden last night. We might be able to say what the mosquito was made of; we might be able to explain "who made it"—its mosquito parents; we might even understand its anatomy and shape. But what is its purpose? Those who cheerily grant purposes to nature might say that the mosquito's purpose is to supply food to birds and so to participate in the chain of being. Others might say that the mosquito is fulfilling a purpose assigned it by God. Those, like the vast majority of evolutionary biologists, who say that the mosquito has no ultimate purpose, must acknowledge that the denial of purpose to things in the world creates a tension in rational human desires, which cannot find closure unless all four causes are understood. Cosmic objects, such as asteroids orbiting the sun, pose similar difficulties for understanding purposes. *Why* does a particular chunk of rock continue in its orbit for billions of years? There seems to be no obvious purpose, goal, or ultimate end in such cases. If there is a purpose or design in the motion of an asteroid—or in the universe as a whole—the purpose is far less obvious than the purpose of houses for accommodating people.[10]

The search for purposes is called teleology. Ancient thought is dominated by teleological thinking, because the ancients, with some notable exceptions, could not easily conceive of a universe or of anything in the universe that lacked a purpose. Aristotle dismisses the notion of purposeless things and events as absurd.[11] In modern times, the idea of a purposeless universe is, in intellectual circles, quite prevalent; indeed, part of the challenge to modernity is facing the possibility of purposelessness, especially in the evolution of life and in the development of the universe. The challenge is greatest for religious people, since it is not easy under most conceptions of the deity to admit both a superintending God and a purposeless universe. These are questions that we shall take up in the final chapters of the book.

Bad Answers and Socratic Ignorance

To return to the ivory horn-billed scarlet kinglet, we confess that there is no such bird. We made it up! Nevertheless, it is safe to suppose that readers who do not know enough about birds to know that this one is an imaginary creation identified with the sense of contentment in the identification of the bird by species. The upshot is that the classification of a bird or a flower or anything else brings the satisfaction of having an understanding of one of Aristotle's four causes and that even a false understanding—provided one does not know it is false—gives the satisfaction of understanding. If one knows that he does *not* know, on the other hand, he can feel no sense of calm satisfaction. A bad answer he can live with (again, provided he does not know that it is bad or so wholly bad as to be false). A believable answer gratifies the human desire to know, whereas the admission "I don't know" leaves one hungry and ill at ease. We see this phenomenon all the time in the news. A plane crashes for mysterious reasons, or a bomb goes off without any hint of the perpetrator, and people want to know why it happened, its causes, who was responsible, and what the purpose was. In the absence of a motive and in the absence of the order and harmony produced by the prosecution, conviction, and punishment of a criminal—or at least convincing evidence that the event resulted from natural causes—there is no sense of calming closure.

Socrates is reported by Plato to have claimed that his superiority over others lay in knowing that he did not know what others falsely claimed to know.[12] When Socrates talked with someone who claimed to know what courage or justice is, for example, Socrates always discovered that the person's claim to knowledge was misplaced. Because Socrates knew one thing—that he lacked knowledge—he deemed himself wiser than the person who falsely claimed he knew something. It is certainly possible that Socrates was joking when he proclaimed this wisdom, for in the Platonic corpus he is frequently portrayed as knowing his own knowledge. (In the *Symposium,* for example, he claims that he knows one thing alone—what love is. In the *Crito* he seems to claim the knowledge that one wrong does not justify another.) There is, at any rate, a certain amusing arrogant humility in his claim that his wisdom consists in lacking knowledge.

If we look at Socrates' life as a metaphor, we see that he went around seeking to learn what he knew he did not know. Not content with not knowing, he wanted others not to be content with not knowing either. Socrates undoubtedly realized that in order to seek truth, one must first know that one does not have it. Consider a trivial example of even the practical advantages of knowing what one does not know. No one would take the trouble to locate his theater tickets if he thinks he already knows where they are. But by the time he discovers that he really does not know where they are, it may be too late to find them and he would have been better off knowing that he did not know where they were.

While there are obvious advantages to Socratic ignorance—knowing what you don't know—nevertheless we humans prefer to know. Now when it comes to understanding human actions and human motives, explanations are reasonably easy to come by. If a person does not state his motive (in Aristotle's language, the final cause), for the most part we could assume that his motive is one of the motives generally experienced by our fellow human beings. When considering the motives for crime, for example, the number of possibilities is limited: revenge, greed, jealousy, envy, thrill-seeking, power, and perhaps a few others. When examining the motives for noble actions, the number is similarly small. In short, we humans are not terribly difficult to comprehend. If in our ignorance of the true motive we attribute a false motive believing it to be right, we will have a satisfying sense of closure. And, because the repertoire of human motives is quite limited, we shall probably not be very far wide of the mark.

But what about the natural world? Why does the sun rise? Why does the wind blow? Why are particles of sand small? Why are beetles shiny? Why are there earthquakes? Why is there disease? Why are there rainbows? Why does sexual intercourse result in birth, but only sometimes? Here are questions whose answers do not automatically come by extrapolation from human motives. Here are phenomena whose causes are not so neatly comprehensible. Yet, as we have observed, the human mind cannot live easily with unanswered questions. The human mind, rational to its core, needs to fit data into patterns; it needs to formulate answers consistent with its rational nature. And the answers must consist of generalized patterns of explanation, such as those related to Aristotle's four causes. Thus far in our history, there have been two fundamentally different routes to achieving explanatory satisfaction, the religious and the scientific. What qualifies as a satisfactory explanation will depend on the confidence we put in the premises, the consistency of the evidence, the internal coherence of the arguments, the authority of the agent issuing the explanation, and the like. History shows that explanations now rejected, like Empedocles' theory of the four elements or pagan polytheism, gave just such satisfying closure for a very long time.

RELIGION'S ANSWERS

God as Explanatory Principle: The Positive

Some might fret that using God as an explanatory principle is too easy: when in doubt, attribute the cause to God. God makes the sun shine, the wind blow, sand small, beetles shiny; God makes earthquakes and diseases; God makes rainbows; and God determines when sexual intercourse will result in a baby. If we do not like the outcome, and we cannot find any human actions to blame, we can say that God works in mysterious ways or that if God had wanted us to know, he would have told us. When we do like the outcome, we can thank God for his blessings. Perhaps, however, before glibly rejecting God as an explanatory mechanism, we ought to consider the attractiveness of such a mechanism. There are important respects in which attributing causality to God or to the divine makes sense, is satisfying both emotionally and intellectually, and is complete. These advantages account for the ubiquity of the practice in human history. Indeed, it may be part of the nature of human reason to develop a belief in God.

It may perhaps seem premature to discuss God without having first defined his nature—if it can be defined—or at least before having explored the various conceptions of God. The nature of God will be addressed in detail in later chapters.[13]

For now, let it suffice that the underlying conception of God be of a power above or outside of nature, having a capacity to reason and a power to communicate akin to mankind's, an agent who can intercede in nature at will. This definition will, of course, be subject to intense criticism by philosophers, who will attempt to deduce a less anthropomorphic or humanlike deity, but we shall postpone more rigorous definitions of God for later.

Despite the contentious and perennial philosophical debates over the real existence of a free will, we humans certainly know what it feels like to experience freedom of the will. All of our conscious actions, whether good or ill, seem to result from our will. Other humans, as well as many nonhuman animals, though perhaps to a lesser extent, seem also to perform their conscious actions as a result of their will. Unlike inanimate objects, animals seem to choose their direction of movement, their method of pursuing food, and their way of avoiding danger. Inanimate things, on the other hand, cannot move independently of something that moves them. A rock does not decide to move to the other side of a tree in the way that a squirrel might. The rock moves there only if someone or something moves it. If the thing moved is of such a kind as not to be moved by an animal or human being, then the mover must be of a special sort. Thus when what are moved are clouds, winds, waves, or celestial objects, it seems to make great sense, on the surface at least, to assume that the mover is some supernatural entity, which one might refer to as God.

For a species that sees itself as intellectually superior to other animals in virtue of our faculties of language and reason, it is tempting for us to think that what happens happens with us in mind or as a result of what we do. Thus if we are good or make sacrifices to the deity, it follows that the deity, responding as a human being would, ought to be gracious to us, protect us from danger, or grant us special benefits. If we should be somehow obnoxious, on the other hand, it makes sense that the deity, again responding as a human being would in similar circumstances, might be vexed with us and bestow upon us various miseries. Conversely, if we should experience an earthquake or a plague, it makes sense to assume that somehow we have distressed the deity; if we are successful in our enterprises and our crops grow lush and healthy because of good weather, it makes sense that our actions have pleased the deity, who causes the weather.

This way of looking at nature and attempting to explain good fortune, bad fortune, and everything in between is prevalent in the ancient myths that form the intellectual substrate of our culture. For example, in the Bible, the flood that results from forty days of rain is a punishment for sin; the misfortune of linguistic differences, a punishment for arrogance; the storm that tosses the ship bound for Tarshish, a punishment for Jonah's escape from a divinely mandated mission to Ninevah. When the Assyrians destroy Israel, there is no analysis in the Bible of the world's geo-political situation: the destruction has come about because Israel has sinned. In pagan mythology, the plague at the beginning of the *Iliad* comes because Apollo is furious with the Greeks for not ransoming the daughter of one of his priests. The action of the *Oedipus Rex,* as we saw above

(p. 6), comes about because the city of Thebes has allowed a regicide to go undiscovered and unpunished. In the Christian tradition, the defects of nature are blamed on human action. As a direct result of Adam's disobedience, all nature is believed to have changed: whereas the antelapsarian lion dandled with the kid and the rose was without thorns and the weather was always a happy blend of spring and fall, in the postlapsarian world nature became violent and hostile, always wrought with danger.

In modern times many of the same thoughts occur. A child dies, and a parent concludes that the death is punishment for a parental sin; a house catches fire and it is retribution for some offense. Some have attributed AIDS to God's justice in punishing homosexuals.[14] Of course, the attribution of supernatural causality is not limited to undesired conditions or to the direct action of a deity. Very often we find sports fans believing that something they do will affect the outcome of a game. A baseball fan, watching a game in the comfort of his own easy chair thousands of miles from an actual baseball stadium, may think that, if he steps into the kitchen for a soda, or wears a certain cap, or leans in a peculiar way in his Lazy Boy recliner, the outcome of a play or of an entire game will be affected. The beliefs by some that an alignment of the stars and planets will affect what happens on earth by some supernatural mechanism, or that Tarot cards or tea leaves or palm lines or flights of birds can reveal the divine knowledge of the future, attest to the ubiquity of belief in supernatural causation and in the ability of humans to discern its operation.

The literature of the West has validated these views. From Homer and the Bible to Toni Morrison, we find deities and spirits responding to human actions. The presence of the supernatural is a staple of television and cinema. Our children from their cradles have become accustomed to the mythology attending ghosts and genies and angels, and can respond to dramatic situations on the basis of their familiarity with the commonplaces of the various genres. The English language contains many expressions the use of which so accustoms us to supernatural concepts that these ideas become a part of our cultural infrastructure. Who doesn't immediately understand such notions as "star-crossed," "jinxed," "unblest," "lady luck," "Midas touch," "godsend"? How many take for granted the efficacy of amulets, rabbits' feet, and other lucky objects?

Our point is that the tendency to view the world in these terms is built in to human nature and that people derive a good deal of comfort from worldviews that accommodate supernatural causality. In literature, the correspondence between human actions and divine responses assures us that the gods are on their watch. It is comforting to think that crime will not pay, at least not in the end, and that justice will always eventually be achieved. A murderer will be always be discovered, for if the clues prove impossible for human intelligence to find, divine help will bring the villain in. Aristotle describes a beautiful example of the kind of justice we find in poetry. A man is killed when the bust of a person he murdered falls on his head. When we see such an incident in a drama or read of it in a novel, we feel that the knots have been untied, the loose ends brought together. We believe that whatever chaos has taken place in the course of the story is only temporary, that in the end, order prevails. Because our rational minds crave order, we have traditionally found art tasteful when it is orderly and reflects our underlying view that the world, with deities superintending, with celestial bodies moving in regular paths, is a place of stability and order.

Although the view that God's motives can be known is not without its detractors,[15] the presence of a deity who oversees human affairs is deeply satisfying to our rational natures. To the most difficult questions for which we are unable to find any answers, we can attribute divine causes and a divine plan. Like Boethius in *The Consolation of Philosophy*, we can say that adversity tests and builds our character. If the adversity ends in the premature death of a young child, we can say, "God knew that if he had lived, he would have had a miserable life, so God in his mercy spared him," or "God knew that he would commit crimes if he had lived." Or we can say that only God sees the big picture, the interplay of all the various parts of the universe, and has a plan by which the apparently unhappy event will have good consequences. Most of us, having at some time experienced cases in which one disappointment led to a greater opportunity that would not have occurred without the initial disappointment, can find a parallel hope in God.

When a loved one is sick, real comfort is found in believing that a deity will hear our prayers for the recovery of the individual. When we are suffering, it is calming to ask God for strength or deliverance. Prayer has always been a source of great comfort to human beings. As Freud observed, God is like a parent who will come to our aid in times of stress to help us.[16] If the causes of our pain are God's doing, perhaps God can remove them if we make vows or promise a sacrifice.

Belief in divine causes is satisfying for various reasons. It is intellectually satisfying because it provides commonsense explanations akin to explanations of human actions. When we say that "God created the heavens and the earth," we are explaining what happened in a way that can be, at some level, easily understood. Even if the exact causal mechanisms are inscrutable, the answer is in some respects quite satisfying. Invoking divine causality is like attributing the construction of an airplane to intelligent human beings: one does not need to know exactly how it was built in order to accept the fact that engineers designed it and aeronautical workers built it. The claim that the airplane came about "because of an engineer" is more satisfying than the reply "I don't know how it came into being," especially given our direct experience of the capabilities of human engineers. Since for the most part we tend to describe God in human terms, our minds can readily accept much of what he does and says. If he often works in mysterious ways in which we do not, the mystery is a quality we can also accept because we have become accustomed to it through constant familiarity. The attribution of causality to God and the explanatory closure that that attribution brings are a source of comfort and hope. Many human minds find the answer of God as cause very compelling, so compelling that relatively few ever seriously question God's existence.

God as Explanatory Principle: The Negative

There is a negative side as well to using God as an explanatory principle. The problems include the unreliability of the evidence for God, the general uncertainty and vagueness that surrounds God, the difficulties that arise from the reliance on and fear of willful powers outside of our control, and, perhaps most strikingly, the plurality of opinions about God.

It is obvious that whereas a belief in the divine is almost universal in humankind, there is no agreement about the exact nature of the deity. The deity's — or deities' — names, attributes, number, morality, appearance, and accessibility to humans are only a few of the matters about which people differ, often considerably. The rituals associated with worship, the requirements of faith, the standards of behavior, the dictates of law all differ greatly among religions and among individuals. The openness to others, the justice, even the courtesy, with which others must be treated is another matter that varies from religion to religion. In short, there is probably almost as much difference in concepts of the divine as there are individual human beings. If the near universality of belief in the divine supports a divine reality, the diversity and, what is worse, the *incompatible* diversity, of those beliefs undermines that reality. A religion that asserts the truth of many gods cannot exist alongside a religion that asserts the truth of one and only one deity — not if they mean the same thing by "deity." Adherents of a religion or a particular sect often believe that they alone have the truth and that everyone else is misguided.

The diversity of religions comes as no surprise given the fact that many religions establish as their first principles claims of magic and supernatural activity and nonrationality. For example, in Christianity there is the claim that Jesus is man *and* God and that one and the same God exists in three persons. These claims, which Christians make no attempt to explain in rational terms, must be accepted as matters of faith. The lack of constraints on the motives and methods a deity might have is a particularly effective generator of a plurality of religious beliefs.[17] A deity might choose to test people's faith, for example, by making dinosaur bones appear to be tens of millions of years old when they are really only a few hundred years old. Each different deity, with its different motives and methods, is a candidate for worship by a different religious sect. If faith supersedes rational criteria in the acceptance of religious first principles, and if virtually any scenario can be fitted into the mold of a religious explanation, then it is impossible to judge whether one religion is more or less plausible than another. The religions of the ancient Greek and of the aborigine living in the Brazilian Amazon Basin have an equal claim to credibility. Which religion to accept out of the numerous available choices becomes a matter of taste. Yet it seems somehow abhorrent to conclude that the profoundest matters that we can conceive, matters over which so much thought and blood have been spent, should devolve into a question of taste.

To a disinterested observer, it may appear as if many claims of particular religions have been rather fanciful and hence invented by a creative imagination.[18] No doubt many people have believed sincerely in what they have only imagined, and no doubt the religious voices that some have heard have been as real to them as the sightings of alien spaceships have been to others.[19] Humans seem able to convince themselves of all manner of beliefs and superstitions. The earlier in childhood one hears a view and the longer the view goes unchallenged, perhaps the more entrenched it becomes in the mind. (Perhaps even a plausible evolutionary story can be told about the general human tendency to credulity and obsequiousness in the suspected presence of the ultimate alpha-male.) Part of the difficulty with religion is that a person can never be sure that he is not accepting his religious first principles simply because he learned them at an early age. Because the principles are imbibed with mother's milk, so to speak, they are never questioned but simply taken for granted as the way things are.

Although first principles are the hardest to question, let alone to shed, we admire those capable of staging such a cognitive revolution in their own minds. We admire Abraham, for example, when he destroyed the idols in his father's shop because he came to realize that there cannot be many different gods made of wood and stone. His intuition that there is only one incorporeal God caused him to shed the principle of idol-worship and polytheism that he had inherited from his ancestors. To take an example from science, the geocentric and heliocentric views of the Solar System are like firmly held religious first principles: learned from an early age by their respective advocates, difficult to shed, and seemingly obvious. Those raised on the heliocentric view think it self-evident that the earth moves and are unable to appreciate the fact that pre-Copernicans thought it self-evident that the earth stands still. In retrospect, we admire Copernicus, Kepler, and Galileo for being able to overthrow what their teachers and their own senses told them and for defending a revolutionary new Solar System. It requires some extraordinary insight to overthrow long-held first principles; when they are successfully overthrown, as in the cases of Abraham or the early Copernicans, we admire the courageous thinkers as virtual demigods.

We see in our own time many first principles that have only now been challenged. For example, it had been a rarely challenged principle from the beginning of recorded history until the nineteenth century that women are morally and intellectually inferior to men. The notion was based on mistaken scientific views and customs passed down in various prominent religions. Because the idea was taken for granted, because it simply seemed *the way things are,* it was never questioned. Those few brave pioneers who did question it were treated as we would treat a person who woke up one morning and claimed that the number seven was and always had been even. People rarely challenge first principles; instead they modify and adjust their lives so as to act consistently with them. First principles are the "brute facts" that we simply accept. We are going to die, parents are older than their children, when water freezes into ice it floats—we accept these facts without question because they seem indisputable and are regularly confirmed by the world around us. The earth is flat, the sun moves around the earth, women are not capable of hunting or governing—people accepted these claims for the very same reason. God's creation of the heavens and the earth, the inheritability of sin, the ability to affect the condition of our souls in an afterlife, the division of the afterworld into heaven, hell, and purgatory—these are views so often repeated, so often portrayed in art, so much a part of daily consciousness that as first principles they were invulnerable to doubt.

The longer a first principle is around, the more authority it gains and the more its very longevity seems to confirm its truth. A religion's age is often taken as evidence of its truth. Moreover, religious people hold their faiths very deeply and tend not to tolerate challenges with equanimity. A cliché of cinematic westerns is the gratuitous insult to a gunslinger's mother: "Say anything about *me;* but don't say anything about my mother." When the villainous and provocative gunman continues to insult his interlocutor's mother, the mandatory saloon brawl commences. In real life, the mildest of questions about something held sacred is likely to engender the bitterest of feelings, which can last for a very long time. We need only look around the world at the centuries-old animosities that exist because of religious differences.

Of course, not all first principles are equal. Some certainly seem to conform to a reality that can be objectively verified. The axioms of geometry or those of Aristotelian logic, for example, are of this kind. The first principles of most religions, on the other hand, are said to have been *revealed* to prophets and are thus not amenable to objective verification. Revealed first principles depend on faith, which is often considered a virtue, and indeed the more so the more incompatible it is with evidence and reason. Thus Tertullian said, "I believe *because* it is absurd," as though if the view made rational sense, there would be less virtue, less merit in faith.

It is clearly possible for the first principles of Aristotelian logic and those of various religions to clash. When the first principles of one religion are diametrically opposed to those of another, and both make a claim of universality and absolute truth, the difficulty of inconsistency arises. The logical principle of non-contradiction declares that no statement and its denial can both be true. In short, the fact that there are so many contradictions between the claims of different religions draws us to the conclusion in Cicero's *Nature of the Gods:* since it is impossible for all religions to be true, either one alone is true and all the others are false, or all of them are false. History resoundingly confirms that people prefer the former alternative. People have declared almost universally that their own religion is true and that all the others are false.

Lucretius, the Roman author of *On the Nature of Things,* a poetic account of the philosophy of the atomic theorist Epicurus (whose work will be discussed in more detail on p. 86), suggested that the chief problem of religion is that far from giving us the calm and intellectual satisfaction discussed in the previous section, it instills fear and dread. Some deities demand cruel sacrifices, for example. Lucretius gives as typical the case of the sacrifice of Iphigeneia. On the way to Troy to recover Helen, the Greek fleet was stalled at Aulis by unfavorable winds. In order to obtain favorable winds, Agamemnon, the supreme commander of the Greek allies, was required by Poseidon to sacrifice his own daughter Iphigeneia. After being deceived into thinking she was going to be married, she came to the altar and was slaughtered by her father. Lucretius says that human sacrifice is the extreme horror to which religion leads us but that our lives are permeated by superstitions and foolish rituals.

Lucretius's discussion offers several insights into some of the problems that religions present. Secure in one's own rituals, one will look at the customs and rituals of the next person's religion as superstitious and nonsensical. The Hindu practices of suttee or of putting a murdered person's corpse into the foundation of a building to assure it safety and strength; the Jewish separation of foods into meat and dairy or refusal to work on the Sabbath; the Christian belief that bread and wine are actually turned into the flesh and blood of their savior or that baptism removes inherited sin; the Muslim belief of a heaven filled with sensual delights or that a hair from Mohammed's beard possesses magical powers; the Calvinist belief that God chooses who will be saved or damned for eternity before they are even born; the Native American belief that talismans can bring good fortune—but there is no need to go on: books on comparative religion and anthropology are filled with religious practices that are sincerely believed.[20] Very often a reader will shake his head in wonder at the bizarre beliefs and practices of other religions while adhering most firmly to those of his own. He believes his own religion is true, sacred, in touch with God, whereas other religions are bunk and nothing but superstitions.

What standard of choice can we apply to religion? Shall we be content, with Pascal, to place a wager on the truth of our own religion so that if it is true we will have won paradise, but if it is false we will have lost nothing? *Will* we have lost nothing? If the particular religion we have picked turns out to be false, and if it is true that only the one true religion opens the door of paradise, we shall in fact have lost everything! And if all religions turn out to be false, we shall have lost the opportunity to make the most of a rational life in our one moment of existence in the universe. For our one moment we shall have lived a lie. So the questions are critical: are there any ways of knowing which religion is true or whether any of them are? And how can we know that we know? The answers to these questions will involve a discussion, in the next chapter, of knowledge in general. Suffice it to say for now that the solution is far from easy, and the persistent fact that there are many different religions keeps alive the suspicion that they may all be false. Moreover, the very sincerity with which believers hold to their religions is a monumental obstacle to rational investigation, for it prevents questioning the first principles of religion and it makes many people hostile to those who do. The claim that we must respect all religious views is also an obstacle to rational investigation, for what it really means is that we must not offend anyone by pointing out the foolishness of those views, or, if not the foolishness—for we do not wish to offend anyone—then the kind of nonrational assumptions upon which a religion is based.

SCIENCE'S ANSWERS

Scientific Explanations: The Positive

In many respects, science appears to be free from the defects of religion. Whereas religion appears to originate in the untestable imagination, science proceeds from investigations of nature, carries out experiments and observations that are, at least ideally, repeatable and testable, and constructs its explanations without reference to the supernatural. Any scientist from any country and at any time can in principle repeat an observation or experiment and validate results. Prophecies and magic, on the other hand, are exclusive to the subjective experience of particular individuals. Every tribe has its own religious views, as does practically every individual; but science claims universality and objectivity. Chemistry, for example, describes the periodic table of the elements and atomic theory for everywhere, not only for Europe or America or the planet earth, but everywhere in the universe. Where religion offers up a host of inscrutable, even capricious, deities, science serves up nature, a nature that may be utterly impersonal but is never willfully malevolent. As Lucretius says, understand the laws of nature, and you conquer fear.

The science of the last several centuries has been like no prior science in the history of the world: it has probed the vastness of space, the smallness of subatomic particles, the mysteries of life, and a multitude of other hitherto mysterious phenomena. It has earned our trust in its ability to work out solutions to vexing problems of disease and hunger. Science has lengthened and improved the lives of us in the developed world and promises to do the same for all humanity. If the inventions and discoveries have sometimes been abused or used for foul ends, the cause is human evil, not science itself.

The technology of our modern world relies on the discoveries of science. We can do what our forebears thought impossible: we can travel in the sky vast distances in machines that weigh hundreds or thousands of pounds. (This notion of heavier than air flight was so fanciful in just our grandfathers' and great-grandfathers' generations that the U.S. patent office refused to grant a patent for airplanes until seven years after the Wright Brothers flew at Kitty Hawk!) We have been able to send humans to the moon and spacecraft to the outer reaches of the solar system. We have been able to broadcast our voice with nearly instantaneous speed to continents on the other side of the globe and engage in conversations so clear that the respondent seems only a few yards away. We have succeeded in performing complex calculations in a moment that could not have been performed in centuries if the entire human population had been working continuously on them. These examples merely hint at the modern technological marvels that are based on an underlying, thoroughly naturalistic, science.

The satisfaction that scientific explanations afford is distinct from that provided by religious explanations. The answers that science gives are satisfying to the mind, though perhaps not satisfying in the same respects as the answers of religion. Not only does science tell us a great deal about the how and the what, that is, about the efficient, material, and formal causes of things, but its explanations are typically characterized by a quantitative or definitional precision that religious explanations lack entirely. If, for example, one wants to know about the variations in the tides, a physicist can give a convincing, and of course readily testable, answer in terms of the gravitational pull of the sun and moon at precise times of the day or month. Such an explanation largely satisfies the human need to understand. In fact, the more one presses the physicist for details about gravitational theory, the more impressed one becomes about the elegance, mathematical precision, accuracy, predictive power, and technological applicability of the theory—not to mention its impressive historical track record and its extreme generality, i.e., its ability to explain not only the tides, but everything from the fall of an apple to the rotation of a distant galaxy. The explanatory success of natural science has been so great that one need not understand the details of a scientific theory to accept it. For some, in fact, it is sufficient to believe that there are physical answers available, even if one does not wish to take the trouble to understand them. For example, an engineer might assure us that there is an explanation for how a television works—that it is not a magical instrument—and we might very well be satisfied that there is such an explanation, even if we do not wish to hear the details of cathode ray tubes and transistors. Because one has found science successful and persuasive in so many other areas, one is tempted to believe that scientists will be persuasive in an unknown area.

Scientific explanations thus satisfy the deep human desire to know in ways that no religion claims to be able to. Not limited to the interests of a given sect or country, science takes us away from earthly affairs, inward to the unimaginably small particles that all matter comprises and outward to the hundred billion galaxies that populate the observable universe. No religion professes expertise in this range of physical phenomena, yet the human mind desires knowledge of them too. Scientific explanations of these phenomena are not based on subjective feelings or unconstrained imagination but on independently testable observations, experiments, laws, and theories. Anyone from any country is free to observe the motions of Mercury to see if they conform to current physical theory; anyone can reproduce Galileo's experiments with the pendulum; anyone can work with Boyle's laws of gases; and anyone can investigate the evidence confirming the theory of evolution. But not just anyone can experience what Paul did on the road to Damascus or share the visions of the medieval mystics. No experiment can repeat or verify such experiences or visions. That is partly why the universality of science and the independent constraints on its explanations are satisfying to persons eager for knowledge but wary of being gullible.

When scientific experiments repeatedly fail to confirm a theory, an adjustment in or overthrow of the theory becomes necessary, whereas any experience, no matter how seemingly contradictory to one's religious beliefs, can always be attributed to the inscrutability of the divine will without necessitating a modification of one's religious beliefs. To use statistical language, the motives of a deity present a variable that cannot in principle be controlled for. As Aquinas shows (see p. 213), one cannot limit the deity to goodness itself. The caprice of the deity or deities makes the beliefs of the religious person unfalsifiable. Scientists, by contrast, actively try to falsify one another's theories and, if they are particularly ambitious, to revolutionize their field. They know that their experimental and theoretical results, since they are objectively repeatable and testable, are open to the scrutiny of the entire scientific community and to anyone else. They are also fully aware of the intense pressure on any group of scientists to disconfirm the work of rival groups (in an objectively repeatable manner, of course). The falsifiability of scientific theories, as well as the active attempts by rival scientists to falsify each other's results, makes theories that have withstood numerous tests all the more satisfying, especially to persons who suspect that unfalsifiable claims come dangerously close to the explanatory equivalent of snake-oil remedies.

Scientific explanations satisfy not only for their objectivity and testability, but for their elegance and precision, their predictive ability, and their technological fruitfulness. Although no one ever claimed that every scientific theory possesses all of these qualities—or should be expected to—striking examples of each feature are easy to cite. The mathematical elegance of Einstein's equations and a precision to ten significant digits in confirmed predictions of quantum mechanics are a rich source of cognitive satisfaction, for they are a sign that the theorists have hit upon some universal truth. Religions may make predictions of the type that "sinners will be punished," but the accuracy of such predictions cannot be tested and, further, cannot match that of scientific predictions of solar and lunar eclipses, the accuracy of which has been confirmed down to the second in hundreds of cases. Predictions of eclipses are neither vague nor difficult to falsify; surely, their success is evidence that the theories on which they are based provide sound explanations. Although predictions in the quantum realm are more esoteric than in planetary astronomy, their higher level of precision makes them even more satisfying. Scientific explanations thus possess a number of distinctive features that set them apart from religious explanations and provide satisfaction of the innate human desire to understand the world.

Scientific Explanations: The Negative

Because science has been so successful, it is tempting to afford it more respect than it deserves. Just as parents would be wrong in going to their child's pediatrician for advice on the moral upbringing of their child—for the pediatrician, insofar as he is a pediatrician, is expert only in matters that pertain to a child's physical health—so one would be mistaken in going to a physicist or chemist in their capacities as physicist and chemist for military or matrimonial advice or on a question of home decor. Yet scientists, because they are proficient in a particular area of science, very often feel qualified to make pronouncements in a different area. They are like the specialists Socrates mentions in Plato's *Apology,* who, because they really are excellent in their own area, believe that they are excellent in other things as well.[21] (One might have expected that any particular excellence would have taught them what is required in achieving excellence and that therefore they would be more modest in their claims about other areas, recognizing that they were not achieving the same degree of success as in their areas of expertise. This expectation—alas—continues to be vain.)

A witty example of this tendency to assume expertise in unrelated matters is illustrated in the story of the German mathematician Leonhard Euler (1707–1783). One day he decided to refute the famous atheist Diderot, the French encyclopedist. Euler filled a page with abstruse mathematical equations, from which he concluded that God exists. "Show me where the error lies," he challenged Diderot. "Disprove the calculations!" Diderot, who knew hardly any mathematics, was at a loss. There is a general danger that scientists will extend their authority into areas in which it does not belong. Yet, even when they speak ex cathedra on matters about which they have no special claim, because of their success elsewhere they are often credited as sages.[22]

More serious than unjustified authority, however, is science's inability to address the questions most meaningful to our lives. Despite its broad explanatory power in physical matters, science cannot answer questions of a nonphysical nature, e.g., questions about how beauty, love, hate, and kindness give meaning to our lives or about the purpose of our existence in general.

When we recall Aristotle's four causes (see p. 24), we recognize that science can tell us about three of them, the material, efficient, and formal, and—in a limited way for the biological sciences—about the fourth, the final. Science can tell us, perhaps, what the dinosaurs were made of (their material cause), how they were generated (their efficient cause), what they looked like (their formal cause), and, to a certain extent, even the purposes of their various bodily organs (for example, that their hearts had the purpose of pumping blood). But science cannot tell us the purpose of the existence of dinosaurs in the first place. A purpose in this sense, a purpose in the complete context of things, is just what science does not address and indeed declares is not scientifically addressable. Humans nevertheless want to know *why* we are here, *why* the dinosaurs once existed, *why* there are stars in the sky, *why* there is suffering and apparently gratuitous pain spread throughout the living world. Our minds cry out for the answers to these questions. Science responds, self-consciously, with total silence, neither affirming nor denying ultimate purposes.

The ancient Greeks rejected the idea of a purposeless universe, and as we mentioned earlier (p. 25), refused to discuss it. Modern science, by refusing to discuss a *purposeful* universe and, more importantly, by offering strikingly successful explanations that make no appeal whatsoever to ultimate purposes, drives towards the conclusion that there is no purpose in the universe—a proposition that stirs horror in human souls. Jesus asks in Matthew, "What is a man profited, if he shall gain the whole world, and lose his own soul?"[23] We might ask a similar question of science: what good does it do us to understand the workings of the universe if it costs us the tranquility of being able to find meaning and ultimate purpose in our lives? One of the chief concerns of part 2 of this book is to analyze attempts throughout history to reconcile a universe that is scientifically explainable without appeal to purposes with the existence of a benevolent and purposeful God.

DISCUSSION QUESTIONS

1. We have written that human beings retain their basic humanity, i.e., their faculty of reason, even when they are engaging in the most heinous and despicable behaviors. Why is there a tendency to refer to these behaviors as "bestial," and why do we metaphorically refer to such people as "animals"? Is the metaphor of calling despicable humans "beasts" fair to animals? In other words, does one need to possess the faculty of reason in order to engage in truly wicked behavior?

2. There is a long tradition in the West—perhaps best symbolized in Dante's *Inferno* (canto 26) by Ulysses, whom we find in hell in the circle of the evil counselors—of apprehension towards those who would seek to know too much. Dante hears Ulysses repeating this "sin" in the impassioned address he delivers to his crew, urging them to seek knowledge of the unknown, knowledge of what lies beyond the Pillars of Hercules. The very act of seeking this knowledge brings the crew destruction. Is knowledge an unqualified good? Is it necessary to qualify what we mean by knowledge before we determine whether it is an unqualified good? For example, is knowledge about trivial things, say, how much a particular person paid for a particular dress, real knowledge? Is knowledge ever an evil, even if it is not necessarily a good?

3. We have said that human beings wish to know the answers to all the journalistic questions that begin with *who, where, what, when,* and *why,* but especially to the questions that begin with *why.* Questions about causation and motive concern the most invisible of the subjects. With our eyes we can see the who, where, and what, and we all have an experiential sense of time, but the why is known only intellectually. Is there a connection between the invisibility of why (and its intellectuality) and our desire to understand?

4. How would our lives be changed if instead of a posteriori knowledge we possessed only a priori knowledge? Are there circumstances that would be drastically altered? What would a legal system be like if the standards of proof were the standards of a priori knowledge? Would it even be possible to have a legal system under such circumstances?

5. Everyone, we think, acknowledges that humans have only finite knowledge. Unlimited and perfect knowledge is attributed, in some conceptions, to God. What kinds of assumptions do we make about what unlimited knowledge would be like? What are some of the problems that need to be solved given the assumption of perfect, unlimited knowledge?

6. While it is often said that a pragmatic people like Americans could not be excited by pure research, we nevertheless find that many are willing to pay for research into the ancient pyramids of Egypt, dinosaur bones, prehistoric spiders, black holes, and galaxies so distant that it would take billions of years to reach them. Are there secret feelings that this research might yield practical results, even as by-products of the main research, that explain the willingness to fund this research? Or are people perhaps willing to pay to satisfy their curiosity about these matters? Is there in fact a feeling that money ought to be spent only for practical results? Does this pragmatic feeling extend towards theology? Should there be funding for metaphysical inquiries into the nature of God? Should there be funding to discover practical ways to keep people from sinning?

7. Is the assigning of purposes to things in nature an example of a sort of anthropomorphism—that is, a casting onto nature of an invisible quality of human beings, in this instance, the motive or final cause?

8. While we praise Socrates for "knowing that he did not know," and while we acknowledge that his condition of knowing that he did not know was superior to that of others who thought that they knew when they did not, nevertheless would you be satisfied with this purely negative sort of knowledge? Given what we've concluded earlier about the human desire to know, is the Socratic position in any way unnatural? Is it possible to reconcile this Socratic position with human nature?

9. How can we explain the certitude that people feel in their own religions while at the same time they laugh at the credulity of others who have different religions? The linguist Max Weinreich defined language as a dialect with an army and a navy (cited in Steven Pinker, *The Language Instinct* [New York: HarperPerennial, 1995], 28). Can we define religion similarly, as a superstition with an army and a navy? Does religion stir up jingoism in the same way that national interests do?

10. Science prides itself on the testability and repeatability of its claims. Yet there are many matters that science studies that are not testable or repeatable, such as the extinction of dinosaurs, the origin of life, and the Big Bang. Can single events be "known"? What exactly is the difference between knowledge of single events and that of generalized matters (such as the claim that in all triangles the sum of the interior angles equals the sum of two right angles)?

11. If a religion makes a claim to exclusive truth by revelation, is there any way to assess the validity of that claim from within the religion itself?

Does the ability or inability to assess such a claim have any bearing on the truth or testability of the religion?

NOTES

1. Perhaps an analogy may be drawn with wings, which evolved from limbs that became at some point able to lift their possessors off the ground. Thus even a continuum marked by differences in degree will be punctuated by what in normal discourse we take to be differences in kind. We thus speak of limbs and wings as different in kind, even though in a strict evolutionary sense they differ only in degree. A color spectrum serves as another example. Though the various colors differ in degree of wavelength, for the purposes of discourse we distinguish them into separate colors. We treat red and blue as different colors despite their representing simply different wavelengths along the same spectrum.

2. See p. 81.

3. For a discussion of prepositions and articles, which Aristotle calls "connectives" and "joints," see *Poetics,* 1456b20–1457a10.

4. For *logos* as a Christian term for God and as both language and reason, see p. 148.

5. This example comes from Silvano Arieti, *Interpretation of Schizophrenia,* 2d ed. (New York: Basic Books, 1974), 230–31.

6. Augustine (*City of God,* 14.19) has pointed out a difficulty for human beings in the matter of sex. Humans want rational control over all parts of life, including sex. But sexual urges sometimes seem to exercise a will of their own. Hence comes the struggle to put the urges under the control of reason. One of us (James A. Arieti) has argued ("Nudity in Greek Athletics," *The Classical World* 68 [1975]: 431–36) that the Greeks saw their own sexual control as a sign of their moral superiority over the barbarians, who, according to the Greeks, lacked it. Perhaps even the use of pornographic materials is an attempt to control when sexual urges will occur and when they won't—in other words, an attempt to put the urges under the control of a presumably reasoned will.

7. Aristotle, *Metaphysics,* 980a1. We have translated the Greek word *eidenai* as "know," although H. G. Apostle, whose translation and commentary we are using, translates it as "understand." In his commentary, however, Apostle explains that "understanding" means "knowing through the causes"—a concept we shall discuss in chapter three and a view most eloquently repeated by Cicero in *De Finibus,* 5.48–50.

8. The Greek word is *orgesthai.*

9. For a discussion of the words *knowledge* and *understanding,* see note 7 above.

10. We discuss at length this notion of design and its possible application to natural objects and the universe as a whole on pp. 251ff.

11. Aristotle discusses the impossibility that something may arise in nature by chance and without purpose in *Physics,* 198b10–199b33. In *On the Heavens,* 271a34, he explicitly says that God and nature create nothing that is pointless. He expresses the same view repeatedly (e.g., *On the Soul,* 415b16, 432b21, 434a30, and many other places).

12. Plato, *Apology,* 21–22.

13. In chapter 5, we shall discuss the kind of God that philosophers have defined. In chapters 6 to 14, we shall consider the God of religion in the context of attempts throughout history to reconcile science and God.

14. Rev. Jerry Falwell has called AIDS a "gay plague." See Peter David, "Moral Majority Intervenes," *Nature* 304 (1983): 201, and, for commentary on his remarks, M. McGrory's column, "The Spread of Fear," *Washington Post,* 17 September 1985, A2.

15. The view that God's plan can be understood by reason is sharply criticized, for example, by al Ghazali in "Vivification of Theology." He writes:

> Let us imagine a child and a grown-up in Heaven who both died in the True Faith, but the grown-up has a higher place than the child. And the child will ask God, "Why did you give that man a higher place?" And God will answer, "He has done many good works." Then the child will say, "Why did you let me die so soon that I was prevented from doing good?" God will answer, "I knew you would grow up to be a sinner; therefore it was better that you should die as a child." Then a cry goes up from the damned in the depths of hell, "Why O Lord, did you not let us die before we became sinners?"

The challenge implicit in the story is that it is impossible to explain rationally everything attributed to God. See al Ghazali in "Vivification of Theology," in *Averroës' Tahafut Al-Tahafut,* trans. S. Van Den Bergh (London: Gibb Memorial Trust, 1978), x.

16. S. Freud, "A Philosophy of Life, Lecture XXXV," in *New Introductory Lectures on Psycho-Analysis,* trans. W. J. H. Sprott (New York: Norton, 1933), 223–24; S. Freud, "A Neurosis of Demoniacal Possession in the Seventeenth Century," in *Collected Papers,* trans. J. Riviere (New York: Basic Books, 1959), 4:449–50; and S. Freud, "The Question of Weltanschauung?" in *The Complete Introductory Lectures on Psychoanalysis,* trans. J. Strachley (New York: Norton, 1966), 626–28. For a discussion of Freud's view of religion as illusion and neurosis, see M. Palmer, *Freud and Jung on Religion* (New York: Routledge, 1997).

17. We shall see later (chapter 6, p. 96 and chapter 8, p. 166) that even the claim that God can do only good raised objections, for it was seen as an attack against God because it limited God's freedom.

18. E. O. Wilson suggests that religions result from the mental illnesses of their founders: "From the delusions and visions of madmen have come some of the world's despotisms, religious cults, and great works of art." See his *Consilience: The Unity of Knowledge* (New York: Knopf, 1998), 145. For another take on the imaginative source of religion, see Hobbes, *Leviathan,* 1.12.

19. For an account of the striking similarities between religious experiences and alien abductions, see Carl Sagan, *The Demon-Haunted World: Science As a Candle in the Dark* (New York: Random House, 1995).

20. For suttee and foundation sacrifice, see N. Davies, *Human Sacrifice in History and Today* (New York: Morrow, 1981), 76, 107–26.

21. Plato, *Apology,* 22D.

22. The story of Euler and Diderot is told in Aristotle, *Aristotle's Posterior Analytics,* trans. H. G. Apostle (Grinnell, Iowa: Peripatetic Press, 1981), 135. Perhaps scientists should not be blamed more than others, and at least they do not seem to make claims outside their expertise for money. When William Shockley, the inventor of the transistor, made claims about race, or Linus Pauling about vitamin C, they were sincere. Sports stars, however, who advocate coffee pots or cars or brands of beer are paid to make pronouncements about the excellence of the products they are hawking. Then again, perhaps—since the truth value is equally nil—the known insincerity of those who are paid proves less dangerous to the public welfare than the trusted *gratis* sincerity of the scientists.

23. Matt. 16:26.

3

What Is Science?

If all men were students of philosophy, the social order would be destroyed and the human race quickly exterminated.

—Maimonides

THE ANCIENT VIEW

Our word *science* comes from the Latin verb meaning "know" (*scio*). When ancients said "science," for them it was like saying "knowledge." Hence to understand the ancient concept of science it is necessary to know what they meant by knowledge. The definition of *knowledge,* from Aristotle through the Stoics and down to the first century C.E., as well as thereafter, is remarkably consistent: an apprehension that cannot be tripped up, that is strong and sure, and that cannot be faulted by argument.[1] The model science is geometry. Geometry begins with very few axioms and definitions, on which all people agree, not arbitrarily but because the axioms and definitions seem self-evidently true; building upon these, geometry draws its conclusions deductively. The truths that geometry reaches are not dependent on any actually existing elements. For example, truths about triangles do not depend on there being any actually perfect triangles in the world that embody those truths. In fact, any drawn or physical triangle will be defective, at least if inspected closely enough (where the jagged edges of a drawn line will be visible). Hence, geometry describes truths distinct from those applicable to the material world; in fact, its claims do not pertain to material objects at all, which, as we have said, only approximate perfect points and lines. The question, then, is whether we can have an absolute science like geometry about things in the material world.

This question is particularly pressing because nowadays we tend to think of science as concerning *only* the physical world. If a topic does not deal with the physical universe or the laws governing it, then, we feel, we should not use the word *science* in discussing that topic.

The first step in knowing something and in being able to talk about it is to know its name.[2] It might be possible, but it would surely be difficult, to talk about squirrels if we do not use the word *squirrel* or an equivalent. But in order for there to be a word for a thing—and a word has meaning only if it is able to communicate something—the thing indicated by the word has to have an identity that remains the same for a measurable amount of time. In fact, one of the problems in knowing whether a subatomic particle actually is something is the brevity of its existence. In order to be recognized as something, a particle must have an existence that abides for a measurable moment. Luckily for us, most things *seem* to have a sustained existence for a measurable amount of time.

Please note the word *seem.* Whether physical things actually do sustain an identity through time is one of the fundamental problems of ancient (and perhaps modern) science. The question may appear at first naïve, but, as we shall see, it goes to the heart of what science is and can be. In what follows, we shall first lay out the problem, then examine the ancient attempts to deal with it, attempts that at first made the problem only knottier until Plato and Aristotle offered solutions. We shall then try to define the ancients' concept of science. It will become apparent how the nature of science, that is, the nature of knowledge, bears on the various problems associated with understanding the deity.

THE PROBLEM

As we discussed briefly in chapter 2 (p. 24), we feel that we have some sense of what a thing is when we know its name. Simply by calling a certain tree an *oak,* we are accepting the fact that it has a recognizable, nameable nature that distinguishes it from other trees. When we think about the oak more deeply, we realize that it is always changing. The oak tree is never in an absolutely fixed state, because its chemistry is dynamic, its sap flows up and down, its leaves grow and then fall off or get nibbled by bugs or rustled by the wind. In short, the tree is never in a stable condition. Can we then say that we know the oak? Even if we actually know all the properties and conditions of the oak at one moment, once that moment has passed, can we say that we know the oak the following moment?

What is true for the oak tree is true for everything else. Everything physical, animate or inanimate, is subject to aging, radioactive decay, bombardment by various kinds of waves, constant repositioning of its atoms and electrons, and so forth. In a word, everything is in a constant state of flux. This view, that all is in a state of flux, that *everything flows,* is the view of the ancient philosopher Heraclitus, who, as we mentioned in chapter 2 (p. 13), is famously remembered for the statement that you cannot step into the same river twice, a beautiful metaphor for the whole concept of the world's constant change. Because a river is constantly changing, its waters constantly moving downstream, a moment after you have stepped into it, it is in a sense a different river. Surely, if everything is constantly in flux, even *once,* as Cratylus observed (p. 13), it is of such short duration as to be meaningless.

Yet the river has an identity, just as we do, despite its condition of constant change. When a person wakes up in the morning and looks at himself in the mirror, in a strict Heraclitean sense he is not the same person he was yesterday: he is older and more decrepit, has longer hair—or, if he has gotten a haircut, shorter hair—and has forgotten yet another piece of information that he once knew. Still, he *does* recognize himself: there's his familiar mole, the same squint in his eyes, the usual, ever more despairing disheveled look, and so forth. Clearly there has been a constancy that has remained the same from the preceding day, and so, like the river, the person has an identity. He can be classified a *thing,* that is, something whose identity has remained the same, at least in some way, for a measurable amount of time. It is obvious that though there might be truth in Heraclitus's claims, those claims are not true without qualification. On the other hand, perhaps the impression of abiding identity is merely an illusion.

At the other end of the spectrum of thought lies Parmenides, one of the most strikingly brilliant and provocative philosophers who ever lived.[3] According to Parmenides, there is no change; all apparent change is illusory. Parmenides' famous dictum captures this insight: "Whatever is, is; whatever is not, is not." This simple expression of his philosophy belies its complexity.

What Parmenides means is that there is something called *being* and that whatever has being, is. All being is the same insofar as it is being. For example, a flea and a house can both be said to be; with respect to their being they are identical. The same is true for subatomic quarks, solar systems, galaxies, and everything else. All being, as being, is the same. This part of Parmenides' meaning seems fairly simple to grasp. But his meaning becomes much harder to grasp when we consider the negative. When we say, for example, "I have no money," what is denoted by the concept "money" has no being; we cannot in the strict sense even talk about nonexistent money or anything else that does not exist. Other sorts of negatives indicate similar cases of nonbeing. If we say "the house is not green," "not-green" has no being, and hence no meaning, for the mind cannot conceive of "not-green" any more than it can conceive of the nonbeing of anything. If you imagine the house as blue, you are imagining blue rather than "not-green." "Not-green" in itself cannot be imagined. Hence, according to Parmenides, minds can conceive only of things that have being.

Parmenides' most famous application of this principle is to motion. To move means to go from a place where you are to a place where you are not. But "are not" cannot be; hence motion is impossible. In the end, we are left with a very powerful logical argument that says that one thing cannot differ from another, that there can be no motion, and indeed that there can be no change of any kind whatsoever. Although the argument seems manifestly absurd, for we can disprove it by moving—or seeming to move?—it is not so easy to point to any logical flaw in it. Parmenides leaves us with a universe that is an undifferentiated, unchanging, eternal sphere. This strange idea seems to be the conclusion of his book *Way of Truth.*

This problem of change was one of the fundamental problems of ancient philosophy, one that has serious theological implications. What are we to say of the divine? Is it, too, in a state of constant flux? Is it now one thing, now another? Or, if Heraclitus is right for the physical world, is the divine somehow exempt from constant change? If so, how and why is the divine exempt? And how can a changeless divinity operate on a universe that constantly changes? On the other hand, if the world is nothing except an unchanging, undifferentiated sphere, and if this sphere includes everything, does *everything* include God? And if God is unchanging, as he must be, does this condition preclude God's acting or even thinking? After all, to think or to act is to undergo change. How is absolute constancy compatible with divinity? Later we shall examine in closer detail this question of change and the nature of God.[4] One of the central problems of western theology is to explain how God's nature allows him to be absolutely unchanging while still able to act in the world—and therefore to change.

PLATO'S SOLUTION

Perhaps it will be useful to consider how mathematics, a field to which Plato was devoted (he merged his school with that of the mathematician Eudoxus), may have contributed to his understanding of the problem of change and its solution.

In geometry, when we speak of points, lines, circles, triangles, and the rest, we are able to distinguish the geometric figures that we draw from the perfect ones that exist only as concepts in our minds. This distinction is critical, for it enables us at once to recognize that the mental points and other figures are indestructible, unchanging, eternal, and universal. They are apprehended only by the mind. The approximate physical embodiments of geometric shapes, on the other hand, whether portrayed by chalk or paint or shapes in wax, are destructible, changing, temporary, and particular. In other words, the mental figures are akin to things spiritual; the drawn shapes, to things physical. It follows also that our senses are unable to perceive what is nonphysical. The tongue cannot taste a mental image of a triangle; the ears cannot hear it; the eyes cannot see it; the nose cannot smell it; and the hands cannot touch it. It can be apprehended only by the mind, which itself is not perceived by the senses.

The intelligibility of perfect, unchanging things—like geometric shapes— suggests that alongside the physical realm there exists an abstract realm that is perfect and unchanging. In this insight that reality consists of two different realms, Plato found his solution for problem of change. For the physical world, which Plato called the "World of Becoming," everything is changing. In the

"World of Becoming," just as Heraclitus proclaimed, all things flow. For the world of mental images, which Plato called the "World of Being," however, all is constant, unchanging, and universal.[5]

This solution is known as Platonic dualism, perhaps one of the most powerful and abiding conceptions in the intellectual history of the West. Its advantages are considerable. It accepts the apparently true fluid condition of the materiality with which we are familiar. At the same time, it accepts as true the apparent constancy that enables us to recognize things and to communicate with one another by referring with fixed names to things that are in some sense fixed. Plato succeeds in reconciling the opposite views of Parmenides and Heraclitus by means of the insight that each view is partly right but refers to a different part of reality, one to the World of Being, the other to the World of Becoming.

What is fixed seems to be an immaterial part of reality. A house may change, but the *idea* of a house remains the same. Indeed, one's idea of a house may remain the same in one's memory even while the house grows old and things in it fall apart.[6] Living things, or things that appear to be alive, seem to change more than inanimate materials. Animals change more than rocks. Nevertheless, we also say that living things have an identity that remains the same even in the midst of a changing corporeal part. Now if we say that an unchanging fixed identity is akin to the immaterial ideas, perhaps we can call this part the living thing's soul. Hence we can define *soul* as the part of a living entity that remains the same, or has the greatest claim to remaining the same. It is not too difficult a stretch of the imagination, then, to see why for Plato, the abode of souls is the World of Being, and the aim of each person is to prepare his soul for habitation there. His body will decay and remain in the World of Becoming. And so a person should worry about his soul, not his body.

Platonic dualism involves a dualism of body and soul, of that which changes and that which remains the same. The two are not equivalent, for the one is entirely subject to corruption, while the other may be improved to the point that it can dwell in everlasting peace and stability. The job of someone during this life is to cultivate the soul, the non-corporeal part, so that it will enjoy its happy permanence. In the Platonic scheme, rewards and punishments are meted out to souls in accordance with their owners' behavior in the World of Becoming. In some dialogues, perhaps humorously, Plato discusses the reincarnation of souls into bodies suited to their earlier behavior. Apish souls are reincarnated as apes, flighty souls as birds, and so forth.

The problem in all dualistic systems comes at the point of contact. How can immateriality and materiality meet and impinge upon one another? The idea of a triangle, as something without weight or other physical qualities, is clearly nonphysical. It exists only as a concept since there are no perfect triangles in the physical world. Yet the abstract idea governs our behavior with regard to the approximate triangles we encounter in the physical world. On the other side, corporeal human creatures seem to discover or invent new ideas. One aspect of this general problem with dualistic schemes is the "mind-body problem," how apparently incorporeal thoughts can affect our bodies. For example, the beauty of a word or an image may cause a physical sensation. But the beauty itself, even if it is *of* a physical thing, is not itself physical. The question of course is how the physical affects the nonphysical and vice versa.

The simplest solutions to the problem of dualism are those that eliminate the problem altogether by reducing everything either to bodies or to spirits. The former alternative is often called materialism or physicalism; the latter, idealism. Scientific solutions tend to be materialistic, i.e., to account for everything in terms of physical particles and combinations of them at various levels of complexity. What we think of as incorporeal ideas and concepts are manifestations of physical processes. They emerge from mental operations that are generated by neurons and their purely physical connections. Ideas are perhaps analogous to the music heard from CDs and tapes: a heavenly excrescence from a physical substrate and a physical mechanism of propagation. Materialists think of concepts that no one has yet discovered or that have been forgotten in exactly the same way they think of physical objects that have not yet come into being or that have ceased to be. For example, there would be no CD of music that has not yet been composed, and there would be no music where a CD has perished with the only recording of a score. And just as the data encoded on a CD emerges as actual music only when the CD is played on a CD player, so a concept that lies buried in the words of a dusty book hidden in a library alcove emerges as an actual concept only when it is read and understood in a thinking human brain. (Of course, the issue of the existence of past and future objects is metaphysically distinct from the issue of whether material objects, immaterial things, or both, exist.)

The alternative of reducing everything to spirit has not been nearly as accepted as the option of finding a place for both matter and spirit. Religious solutions, at least in the West, do not reduce everything to spirit, except perhaps for Leibniz and his theory of monads (to which we shall return in chapter 12, pp. 228ff.). Nevertheless, spiritual substances most definitely occupy a central position in most religions. For some, the corruptible physical world is but a trial the spirit must endure until it can move into a world of pure spirit. In religious terms, a version of Plato's "World of Being" is called "heaven" or "the afterlife." In parts of Christianity, Islam, and Judaism, at some point there will be a re-merging of body and soul in what is called a "resurrection." Belief in such a resurrection must be held as an article of faith because its details elude scientific investigation and precision.[7]

In the Hebraic tradition, in the Book of Genesis, God is described as creating the heavens and the earth by commanding the various parts to come into being. The problem of whether God is physical or spiritual is not addressed in the text, no doubt either because it was not considered a question of interest to its original audience or because the whole story was to be interpreted as a metaphor or, as Philo puts it, as a preface to the Laws, to give them dignity and authority. Obviously, it is incomprehensible how a purely spiritual entity could create physical things. A nonphysical spirit is something like the *idea* of a triangle—how can an idea, all by itself, create anything? On the other hand, it is difficult to see how a physical entity could create the universe in the manner described either, where God creates by voice alone. If God is himself physical, where would he be before the creation of the world? These are questions to which there are no easy or uncontroversial answers, and we can laugh at Augustine's joke that before creation God was creating a hell for people who asked such questions.

Plato never explicitly tells us what he means in any of his extant works. He is said to have written or to have communicated his most deeply held views in some works, but these, known as his "esoteric" writings, if they ever really existed, have all been lost. All that remains are his public writings, the dialogues. While some of them make for fairly tedious reading and are read only by patient scholars or forced students, others are delightfully entertaining. The greatest of the dialogues are immensely stimulating at many different levels. They provoke readers to argue with the various participants in an intellectual drama of high tension. Many of the dialogues are best understood as works of drama whose lessons are the kind that can best be communicated through drama. While the various interlocutors—as the people who talk together in the dialogues are called—discuss profound questions, Plato's playful spirit, the personalities of the characters he has created, and the various barbs at his rivals, all render Plato's meaning unclear. (The very lack of clarity has given rise to radically divergent interpretations of the dialogues.[8]) On the most perplexing topics, such as the immortality of the soul and the nature of the World of Being, Plato offers no conclusive answers, and the dialogues cannot be relied on to provide significant insights. Some of them—the *Euthyphro* and the *Timaeus* in particular—have nevertheless been of immense influence in the struggle to reconcile science and religion. We shall have more to say about them later.

For the ancients, the notion of science as knowledge leads to vexing metaphysical issues that include the nature of the material world, change and permanence, material objects and immaterial ideas, and the mode of interaction between impermanent matter and changeless ideas. Plato's metaphysical view, to the extent that we can ascertain it, has change characterizing the World of Becoming and permanence the World of Being. This view raises but does not solve the problem with all forms of dualism: how do matter and spirit interact? Materialists, whether scientific or not, avoid the problem by denying the existence of immaterial entities. Religious thinkers, who typically posit an immaterial deity, face the problem directly but with solutions couched in mystery and with appeals, ultimately, to faith.

ARISTOTLE'S CONCEPTION OF SCIENCE

Although most people are unfamiliar with Aristotle's understanding of science, they intuitively hold to a view just like it and shape their thinking about science and religion as a result of that view. For most of history, Aristotle's views held a powerful position in the philosophical thought of the West and have, wholly without Aristotle's intentions, lent fuel to the fire of the debate on science and religion. We need to remember here that when we speak of Aristotle's demand for *scientific knowledge,* we are speaking redundantly. For Aristotle, *science* and *knowledge* are the same word, the Greek word *episteme.* The philosopher puts such strong requirements on knowledge (i.e., science) that very little can actually meet the requirements of being known in the strict sense. Eight hundred years after Aristotle, Augustine used this Aristotelian conception of science to applaud the humility of Catholicism in its call for *belief* in matters that cannot be demonstrated, i.e., matters that cannot be known in Aristotle's strong sense. Other religions, such as Manichaeism, claimed to have knowledge on various subjects even without the requisite demonstrations.[9] For Augustine, the Catholic Church was more intellectually respectable than the Manichaean sect, for the Church was honest in its more modest intellectual claims.

Briefly stated, for Aristotle scientific knowledge is universal knowledge of necessary truths through their causes. Because the goal of attaining this sort of knowledge is difficult, if not impossible, to reach, Aristotle distinguishes between the exact and the inexact sciences. For example, in chemistry one might learn that if chemical X is mixed with chemical Y the resulting compound is chemical Z. While the facts may be true and it may indeed be true that every time chemical X and chemical Y are mixed they produce chemical Z, the science is inexact, for there is no knowledge of the cause: it is not known *why* these two chemicals result in the third. Our lives, of course, are full of this sort of inexact knowledge. All cooks know that if they apply heat to a raw egg in a frying pan, the egg hardens, but few can explain why. In such cases, there is knowledge of *what* happens, but no *scientific* knowledge. In the same way, we might turn on our televisions and change the channels by pushing a button. If we do not understand the full causality of *why* the channels change, we do not have scientific knowledge. And, of course, a full knowledge of the causes would involve an explanation of all four causes (as discussed above, p. 24).

Moreover, scientific knowledge explains causes and effects in such a way as to be universally applicable. To know scientifically would be to know the *why* for *all* eggs, or to know the *why* about changing the channels on *all* televisions. Scientific knowledge discards accidental, contingent, and irrelevant factors such as the color and size of an egg or the brand of a television.

Although we have accurately represented Aristotle's philosophy of science as he lays it out in his *Posterior Analytics,* we note at the outset that the conclusions presented in most of his philosophical, biological and other writings are not as strictly scientific as he himself deems desirable. Indeed, few, if any, scientific results have ever met Aristotle's full requirements. Yet the views in the *Posterior Analytics* are very enlightening because they underscore the problems of reconciling science and religion. A few words about Aristotle's philosophy of science here will help us to see the full dimensions of our culture's preoccupation with this reconciliation of science and religion.

Aristotle says that all teaching and learning that comes through discourse, either spoken or written, proceeds from previous knowledge. The first level of knowledge in discourse is, of course, knowing the meanings of the words we use in order to learn from others. But knowledge of the meanings of most words falls short of knowledge in the strong Aristotelian sense, for it is not universal knowledge of necessary truths through causes. For example, when we hear the statement, "The monkey is sitting in a cage," we understand the meaning of the remark because we understand the meaning of the separate words, but we do not know the word *monkey* in a scientific sense because we do not know the causes that have resulted in the universal concept of "monkey."

Understanding a word means knowing the general category into which the word fits and also the various qualities that make the thing denoted by the word different from everything else. A monkey will fit into the general category of animals and also has certain simian characteristics that distinguish it from all other animals. But scientific knowledge, which includes a knowledge of definitions, requires more: it requires knowing the cause through which something exists and knowing that the thing cannot be other than what it is.[10] When it comes to monkeys and most everything else, neither we nor anyone else has this full knowledge, for such knowledge would include more than what can be comprehended by human minds: why did a particular sperm fertilize the particular egg that led to the monkey; why do monkeys have just these and not other characteristics, and so forth.

One of the biggest problems in knowing in the strict sense we have been discussing comes from the apparent truth that all learning and teaching comes from previous knowledge, which has several requirements of its own. First, the starting principles of the original knowledge must be true; that is, they must accord with the universe as it actually is. Second, the principles must be primary; that is, they cannot themselves be demonstrable. If they were, they would proceed from other principles that had to be demonstrated as well, and so on in an infinite regress. Clearly, if there were to be such an infinite regress, we could never know anything, for our lives would be spent in an endless search for more and more basic principles. Third, the principles from which new knowledge is acquired must be more known to us than the new knowledge. For example, if one is studying cell division, one must first understand cells. Or if one is studying triangles, one must first understand lines and angles. The starting principles, Aristotle holds, are the causes of the conclusions because we reason from them to the conclusions.[11]

Perhaps, given Aristotle's admonition that certain terms be thoroughly understood, it would be useful to list some critical Aristotelian terms, along with brief comments that will hint at some of the topics that we shall take up later.

Contradiction: a pair of statements one of which is the explicit denial of the other. The pair of statements "The elephant is pink" and "The elephant is not pink" constitute a contradiction. It is important to note that, necessarily, one of these statements is true and one false. Here the denial ("The elephant is not pink") is true. The pair of statements "God exists" and "God does not exist" is also a contradiction. Here too one of the statements must necessarily be true and one false. Which is true and which is false may be debated, but so long as "God" is taken as a definite thing with a meaning, one of the components of the contradiction will be true, the other false. It is important to note that the pair of statements "The elephant is pink" and "The elephant is gray" does not constitute a contradiction, because neither statement is an explicit denial of the other.

Affirmation: the part of a contradiction that affirms. In the above example, "The elephant is pink" is the affirmation.

Denial: the part of a contradiction that denies. In the example, "The elephant is not pink" is the denial.

Thesis: an indemonstrable statement that is used as a premise in a syllogism or investigation. Aristotle suggests that the thesis may be either a definition or a hypothesis when these are to be applied to the question at hand. For example, the definition of a monkey need not be investigated if we are endeavoring to learn about the endocrine system of monkeys. We take as a thesis (sometimes also called a "posit") what a monkey is. It is not necessary for an investigator to work out a definition of "monkey" in order to investigate the hormonal system of a monkey.

Axiom: the kind of thesis that is necessary for someone to learn something in a given science. For example, if in geometry we are studying the equality of vertical angles, we must take as an axiom that "equals from equals yield equals." Axioms, also called "common doctrines," though they *may* be used as premises, are different from premises, in that they can be used in a demonstration. For example, in demonstrating that vertical angles are equal, the axiom that "equals from equals yield equals" is not used as a premise, but is drawn on in the process of the demonstration.

Hypothesis: the thesis that takes the form of a statement in a particular demonstration, a statement that either denies or affirms and is immediately taken as true and used as a premise. A synonym for *hypothesis* is *assumption.*

We know premises to a higher degree than we know the conclusions based on those premises. For example, a premise might be that a certain club allows only teenage members. We know that Fred is a member of the club and thus conclude that Fred is a teenager. But we have far more certitude about the premise than the conclusion. (It is possible that a precocious twelve-year-old Fred passed himself off as an older boy.) Or, to take another example, we might say that a gold watch is more expensive than a silver watch. We know the premise, that gold objects are more expensive than silver objects, better than we know the price of any pair of gold and silver watches.

In addition, we are more *convinced* of the premises than we are of the conclusions. For example, a person might be quite convinced that he likes chocolate. But if someone offers him a piece of chocolate pie, he will not be quite as convinced that he will like it. The example is of course necessarily imprecise, for chocolate is not something fixed in the way that numerical quantities are. The recipes for it differ; the quality of the beans varies; and so forth. If by a process of reasoning one is to obtain demonstrated knowledge through causes, one must be absolutely convinced not only of the premises but of the secondary facts—here the expertise and quality of the rest of the process of making the pie—but, as we have discussed above, one cannot be as certain of secondary facts as of premises.

Aristotle points out that there are two opposite types of mistakes about knowledge. One involves believing that there is no knowledge whatsoever because it is impossible to come up with premises that do not depend on demonstration. Those who hold this view argue that one cannot know unless one knows what is prior, that is, what a claim is based on. But since one is led into an infinite regress in constantly seeking prior premises and since an infinite regress, by its very nature, is impossible to traverse, one can never have knowledge in the strict sense. Because they accept Aristotle's requirement of demonstration through causes, they are unwilling to accept any principles whatsoever. Hence they claim that knowledge in the strong sense is logically impossible. Even children, who never tire of asking *why* no matter how far the series of explanations goes, seem to share this view.

The second sort of error involves thinking that there can be a demonstration of *everything*. Persons who hold this view are mistaken, according to Aristotle, because they think that premises *can* be demonstrated. When a conclusion is reached, they say, we have a demonstration of the premises. If, for example, a certain club that allows only teenagers to be members actually has only teenagers in it at a certain time, this fact would purportedly be a demonstration of the premise that only teenagers are allowed to be members. But it should be clear that this demonstration would not constitute scientific knowledge of the premise.

Aristotle rejects both positions. In the first instance, he accepts the idea that there can be indemonstrable truths, truths that are understood by intuition or intellect. The axiom that a thing cannot both be and not be is such an indemonstrable truth. Although knowledge of such truths, for Aristotle, is not *scientific* (i.e., demonstrated) knowledge, it is knowledge nonetheless. There are very few truths of this sort, however. Concerning the second sort of mistake, Aristotle rejects the kind of circular demonstration illustrated in the argument about the club that admits only teenagers. The problem with these faulty demonstrations is that each of the terms is taken as a prior truth in one context but a posterior one in another. If we allowed such demonstrations, then any statement X could be proved by a circular argument of the form "Given that X is true, it follows that X is true." In the argument about the teenage club, for example, after accepting the premise that only teenagers are allowed to be members—a "prior" claim—we conclude that only teenagers are present—a "posterior" one. When we claim that the conclusion proves the premise, however, the fact that only teenagers are present becomes the prior claim, and the fact that only teenagers are members becomes the posterior claim. Taking one and the same statement to be both prior and posterior obviously prevents the proof from being a satisfactory one. The proof that Bush is president would be that Bush is president.

Now for Aristotle, unqualified knowledge is known in an absolute way and cannot be other than it is. Not only does scientific knowledge, i.e., demonstrated knowledge, proceed from necessary premises for Aristotle, but demonstrations are of things that are themselves necessary. Aristotelian demonstrations require necessary, not merely true, premises. As an example of a demonstration that fails to meet Aristotle's criteria because it has a true, but not *necessarily* true, premise, consider the following. From the fact that Einstein knew that Rio de Janeiro was the capital of Brazil it follows necessarily that Rio is the capital of Brazil. But the premise is not necessary, i.e., although it is true that Einstein knew about the capital, he merely happened to know about it, and thus the premise stating his knowledge is not *necessarily* true. Hence, the conclusion, although it follows from the premise, has not been demonstrated in the Aristotelian sense of following from a necessary premise. To take an example in which a premise involves a contingent property rather than a contingent truth, and in which the conclusion similarly fails to measure up to Aristotelian rigor, consider trying to derive a conclusion from the fact that a carpenter is tall. Tallness may indeed be a property of the carpenter, but it is only a contingent, not a necessary, property of being a carpenter. Therefore, any conclusion derived from the tallness of the carpenter will fall short of being demonstrative, regardless of whether the conclusion—say, that the carpenter is not short—really does follow from the premise. The reason for the non-demonstrativeness of all such arguments is that their premises do not embody necessary truths or do not involve essential attributes.

We have seen that Aristotelian knowledge involves demonstration that is universal, through causes, and from premises that are prior, more convincing, and necessary. Perhaps it will be beneficial at this point to consider one more significant feature of Aristotle's conception of science. If in an investigation the premises are universal, then the conclusion of a demonstration correctly made from these premises will be unchanging. In other words, premises about changeable, destructible things cannot figure into unqualified demonstrations, and hence there can be no unqualified knowledge about destructible things. To be sure, we can make claims about destructible things, but these claims will never be universal. Here again we see the close attention by ancient philosophers to the constant flux of physical things.

The import of the foregoing discussion is that Aristotle effectively limits the kinds of things we can know in the full sense of the term to sciences such as geometry and logic—deductive sciences that have indestructible, immaterial things as their subject matter. All the other branches of learning that we call science—geology, biology, physics, chemistry, botany, physiology, astronomy, and so on—are lesser forms of science for Aristotle, because they cannot achieve knowledge in the full sense. In physics, for example, we may know about various constants or about the rate of decay of certain isotopes, and we may draw all sorts of conclusions from this knowledge. But we do not have knowledge in the Aristotelian sense because, perhaps among other shortcomings, our premises are never necessarily true. We know what occurs, but we don't know the causes. A geometric or mathematical proof, on the other hand, is conclusive to those who understand it because the axioms possess an intuitive necessity and the conclusions follow necessarily from what is prior. But a posteriori arguments, as we observed in chapter 2 (p. 19), are never known fully known, in the Aristotelian sense, since they are developed from effects and not from causes.

Our consideration of Aristotle's epistemology has raised the crucial questions of the standards of rigor and the methods of demonstrating conclusions in various fields. Although it is fairly clear that some sort of hierarchy of rigor distinguishes, say, geometry from physics, what is less clear is the level at which rigor becomes high enough to constitute knowledge. Should the line be drawn just below mathematics and logic, as Aristotle did? Or should it be drawn low enough to take in physics, chemistry, and the other modern natural sciences as well? Does the indemonstrability of one's ultimate premises—whether in science or in religion—make all claims to knowledge in this respect on a par? Or does the intuitive plausibility of the premises favor science? Or religion?[12]

PROBLEMS CONCERNING RELIGION AND SCIENCE IN THE LIGHT OF ARISTOTLE

A number of interesting problems present themselves when we reflect on Aristotle's strict requirements for scientific knowledge. A survey of these problems will prove useful at this stage in our discussion and will anticipate many of the issues that will arise later, when we discuss attempts at reconciling science and religion.

As we have noted, very few subjects lend themselves to the kind of demonstrable proofs that yield Aristotle's strict scientific knowledge. Indeed, beyond various logical principles and mathematical theorems, it is difficult to see where one can apply the requirement of knowing necessary facts through their causes. From antiquity through Hobbes and perhaps even further, philosophers have therefore looked to geometry as the model demonstrative science. It begins with very few axioms, to which virtually all people readily assent, and its proofs proceed with logical rigor. Aristotle might have been thinking of some forerunner of Euclid's *Elements* when he wrote the *Posterior Analytics*.[13]

Religion, however, is not Euclid's *Elements*. It does not start with the self-evident claims of geometry. If it did, it is likely that its claims would have been as persuasive to rational souls all over the planet as the claims of geometry have been. The problems of life, as well as political and ethical questions, do not lend themselves to the rigorous demonstrable proofs of scientific knowledge in the Aristotelian sense. Aristotle in fact observes in the *Ethics* that each area of inquiry should be investigated with the precision appropriate to its subject matter.[14] Hence we should not expect geometric proofs from a politician or political rhetoric from a geometrician.

There have been attempts—and we shall examine some of these in chapter 5—to work out truths about the nature of God by means of logic. The attempt to do so, without the aid revelation, is often called "natural theology." As we shall see, the kinds of claims that natural theology makes are far from the religious experience of most people. For example, let us say that the proofs we find in question two of Aquinas's *Summa Theologica* for the existence of God as the unmoved mover or first cause give a logically persuasive argument. Does an unmoved mover satisfy the soul's craving for a recipient of our prayers? Does an unmoved mover offer any guidance about how we should behave towards one another? At the very least, the religiously inclined person would like to see the conclusions of natural theology supplemented in a way that makes them more spiritually satisfying.

Even if "revealed truth" is added to the mix, and a step is taken in the direction of combining logical rigor with spiritual satisfaction, once the revelation falls into human interpretation, it fails to meet Aristotle's rigorous requirements for scientific knowledge. The debates that we find in the Talmud provide an excellent example of how, even if we start with what is accepted as biblical revelation, we cannot work out with logical precision what the text signifies, and hence often very different interpretations oppose one another. The Talmudists were themselves aware of the difficulty of obtaining the meaning even when God himself speaks. Consider the following classic story:

> Rabbi Eliezer ben Hyrcanus used every argument in the world to support his opinion that a certain oven was ritually clean, but the other rabbis opposed him.
>
> He said, "if the *halakhah* [i.e., the religious law] is with me, let this carob tree be uprooted from the earth!"
>
> And the carob tree rose into the air and flew five hundred feet before it crashed to the ground.
>
> But the rabbis said, "You cannot prove anything with a carob tree."
>
> Then he said, "If I am right, let this stream of water flow backwards!"
>
> And instantly the stream reversed its course and flowed the other way.
>
> But the rabbis said, "A stream can't prove anything."
>
> Then Eliezer ben Hyrcanus shouted, "If the law is with me, let the walls of this study house prove it!"
>
> And the walls immediately began to teeter, but Rabbi Yehoshua reproached them and said, "Is it any of your business, walls, if scholars disagree about the Law?"
>
> And out of respect for Rabbi Yehoshua, the walls stopped falling. But out of respect for Rabbi Eliezer, they did not right themselves either. Thus they remain tilted at an angle to this day.
>
> Then Eliezer raised his voice and called out, "If the *halakhah* is with me, let heaven itself prove it!"

And a heavenly voice rang out, "Why are you opposing Rabbi Eliezer? Don't you know that the Law is always as he says?"

Rabbi Yehoshua now jumped to his feet and cried, "The Torah is not in heaven!" What did he mean by that?

Rabbi Jeremiah explained, "The Torah was given to Israel on Mount Sinai. Therefore, we need not listen to heavenly voices, for the Torah itself teaches us that the majority rules in matters of Law."

Later, when Rabbi Nathan met the prophet Elijah, he asked him, "What was God's reaction to Rabbi Yehoshua's outburst?"

Elijah replied, "God smiled and said, 'My children have gotten the better of Me! My children have bested Me!'"[15]

The Talmud is itself considered to be a work of revelation, even with its opposing positions. But what *is* the meaning of the present story? Whatever it means, it does suggest that the rabbis are not after scientific knowledge à la Aristotle. An historian—though not a Churchman—might look in the same way at the debates at the Council of Nicea and at all the politicking that preceded votes on such matters as the nature of the Trinity, each side convinced that it alone understood God's will.[16]

How, then, if illustrious rabbis disagree, can *we* evaluate the various claims to religious truth? Indeed, what kinds of evidence attest to the truth of religious claims? Traditionally, people have pointed to the reality of miracles, the healing of the infirm, the restoration to life of the dead, and the various appearances of a supernatural entity on earth. Accounts of miracles, however, admit of a host of different interpretations and typically persuade only those who are already convinced, while the skeptics remain skeptical.[17] As Gibbon reports,

At such a period [during the early growth of Christianity], when faith could boast of so many wonderful victories over death, it seems difficult to account for the skepticism of those philosophers who still rejected and derided the doctrine of resurrection. A noble Grecian had rested on this important ground the whole controversy, and promised Theophilus, a bishop of Antioch, that if he could be gratified with the sight of a single person who had been actually raised from the dead, he would immediately embrace the Christian religion. It is somewhat remarkable that the prelate of the first eastern church, however anxious for the conversion of his friend, thought proper to decline this fair and reasonable challenge.[18]

Others point to the test of time and claim that the longevity of a religion is sufficient substantiation of its truth: "A religion that has lasted X thousands of years *must* be true." The history of the world has brought forth a thousand thousand charlatans, and yet so strong is the human desire for absolute inviolate truths even in matters not subject to demonstrable proofs that standards of belief are lenient and believers are everywhere found.

Is there any kind of cause that *can* be known by human beings? As we discussed in chapter 2, we understand best the things that we ourselves do. Hence we best understand effects that are willed by conscious beings who operate for reasons, as we do. Indeed, we tend to read conscious activity into all sorts of events we observe. Even if we cannot always perceive, or conceive of, a suitable motive, we assume that every action has a motive and has been willed. There is also a strong human tendency to assume that events in nature have purposes and are also products of someone's will. When we posit God and attribute human-like will to him, we have a cause that is understandable and satisfying.

Most people care far more for what happens in their lives than for truths about the angles of a triangle or other geometrical phenomena. The desire to *know* what to do to meet life's crises is very strong. In view of Aristotle's strict requirements for scientific knowledge (again, recalling that "scientific knowledge" is a redundancy), however, it is not possible by means of reason to reach knowledge about the events of our lives. The subject matter does not lend itself to demonstrable proofs, that is, proofs depending on necessary truths (see p. 50). For revealed religions—and these include those in which a soothsayer or shaman reveals the divine will—one must admit a different standard of truth altogether.

But if we wish to satisfy Aristotle's requirement for knowledge through understanding the causes, we have our best opportunity in willed actions. If we see someone eating ice cream, it is not difficult for us to guess that he likes ice cream and so has chosen to eat it. We may, of course, be mistaken. It is possible, even if barely so, that someone is forcing him to eat the ice cream against his will. But, in general, willed actions are intelligible and reliably comprehended. They are satisfying, even if they do not fit the requirements for demonstrable proofs.

We observed earlier (p. 51) that science begins with axioms that are themselves indemonstrable. Religion also begins with axiomatic claims. Since both science and religion begin with indemonstrable claims, is it simply a question of "paying your money and taking your pick"?

If the claims of a religion are wholly implausible but nevertheless proclaimed as truth, there will be no way within the religion itself to question the claims. For the most part, however, religions of the West have sought to press the case for the plausibility of their doctrines by means of logical arguments. The Talmudists and the Christian and Muslim philosophers have employed the tools of Aristotelian logic in defense of their positions. Even Martin Luther, the instigator of the Protestant Reformation, while maintaining the supremacy of unproved assertions and totally rejecting arguments, himself used logic to make his case.[19] Debates within particular denominations over doctrine or ritual also consist of logical arguments whose validity is based on their conformity and consistency with the premises of a given religion.[20] In short, at least in the western world, and despite the central role in many religions of inscrutable mysteries, religions have not chosen to abandon the goal of scientific knowledge.

But how do we assess the validity of intuitively implausible first principles? How likely is it for a proposition to be both implausible and true? Are plausibility and implausibility merely in the eye of the beholder? In Plato's *Symposium,* various individuals give a description of the nature and behavior of a certain deity, Eros. The accounts are wholly different. Among them are the accounts of Agathon and Socrates. According to Agathon, Eros is wealthy, a lover of luxury, and walks in expensive shoes on soft, dainty feet. According to Socrates, Eros is poor, a lover of simplicity, and walks on tough, bare-footed feet.[21] Plato, the author, sees to it that Socrates' account is the loveliest—and most persuasive—of all that are given. But why should Eros be as Socrates describes him? Does the eloquence of an account correspond with its truth? The point of the dialogue in fact seems to be that theological pronouncements take their character from the nature of the speaker and that their validity does not necessarily correspond with eloquence.

In Christianity, among the premises are that Jesus was both man and God, that he died and was resurrected, and that through him the way to heaven is available to all who believe in him. On what logical or intuitive bases are these claims more valid than those of paganism or any other religion? In Islam, Mohammed claims to be the last and truest of the prophets, after whom there will be no true prophets to contradict what he said. On what logical argument should we accept these claims? At the beginning of the Ten Commandments, God claims moral authority for commanding them: he says that he took his people out of Egypt, out of the house of slavery. But what evidence is there that Jews were ever in Egypt, that an Exodus took place, or that God himself gave the commandments rather than that some lawmaker—Moses or someone else—made them up?

If we adopt Aristotle's concept that knowledge is reached only through demonstration, we shall have to conclude that there can be no knowledge about any of the premises of religion or about the conclusions drawn from those premises and therefore no principled way of preferring one to another. Gibbon, referring to Roman religion, writes, "The various modes of worship, which prevailed in the Roman world, were all considered by the people, as equally true; by the philosopher, as equally false; and by the magistrate, as equally useful."[22] The impossibility of logically differentiating among religions is reinforced by the capriciousness of some deities. Indeed, the more capricious the divinity that is assumed, the more impossible it will be within the religion to assess the plausibility of that religion on the basis of logic.

The Aristotelian concept of science presents both shortcuts and roadblocks to thinking about God. One of Aristotle's favorite arguments—one of the shortcuts to thinking about God—concerns the impossibility of an actual infinity. According to Aristotle, there cannot be an actual infinite regress, including an infinite regress of prior knowledge: there must be a stopping point, as we have seen, in the search for premises. There must be first principles that are not themselves demonstrable. Likewise, there must be a cause that is itself uncaused, a mover that is itself unmoved. Philosophers, including Aristotle, sometimes find it convenient to call this starting point God, although such a God bears little resemblance to the loving father figure in which many people take comfort. Philosophers also sometimes concur that God, defined as first mover or first cause, is unique.

God's uniqueness, however, leads to a serious philosophical roadblock. To understand the problem, let us recall that the starting place of wisdom is knowing what to call something and that words are generalizations. Let us recall as well that when we define a word, we put it into a general category, a genus, and we list the ways in which it differs from other things—its differentia. Thus we say that a human being is an animal with a rational soul, where "animal" is the genus and "with a rational soul" is what distinguishes humans from other animals. But how can we define something that is unique? What is the genus to which God belongs? If there is no genus, there can be no definition, and if we cannot define something, how can we know it? God is therefore unknowable in a very important respect: because God belongs to no genus, we cannot fulfill the basic requirements of a definition of God. This idea of God's unknowability has been very important in the West. Surprisingly, it has contributed one answer to the problem of evil. One sometimes hears, "God works in mysterious ways" or "We cannot know God's plan." These claims, based on God's unknowability, give the hope that the evil we may be suffering actually serves some secret good purpose, one known only to God. But unknowability also generates confusion for those who wish to have faith. In the opening of the *Confessions,* Augustine wonders how he can pray to a God he cannot know, for if he does not know God, perhaps he will pray to something else by mistake.

The strongest measure of falsity in Aristotelian science, and philosophy generally, is the presence of contradiction. If a contradiction is present, one knows absolutely that a claim is wrong. One does not merely "believe" or "have no doubts" or "trust" that the conclusion is wrong; one *knows* it. In philosophy, one contradiction in a theory is sufficient to require that the theory be modified until the contradiction is resolved. In modern science, where apparent contradictions are sometimes called anomalies, a similar, though somewhat weaker, principle applies. If an observation appears to contradict a theory, then the theory must be either modified to accommodate the apparent contradiction or rejected—unless, of course, the theory is so well supported by *other* observations (and considerations such as elegance) that the anomalous observation is what should be rejected, or at least temporarily set aside.

Greek logic abhors contradiction, and western religions, insofar as they are influenced by Greek logic, have, like philosophy and modern science, sought to avoid contradictions or face the charge of irrationality. Christianity, which early in its history adopted the tools of Greek philosophy, had to face the problem of explaining its many apparently contradictory principles. A God who is both man and God? A God who is one and "not-one" (and is "three")? A God who is merciful and just at the same time, even when mercy is not just?

Perhaps a brief glance at this contradiction between God's mercy and God's justice will be useful. When the writers of the New Testament wished to express the idea of mercy, they could not actually find a word in Greek to express it, so they chose the nearest word they could find, the Greek word *"eleos"*—pity. Now Aristotle defines pity very carefully in the *Rhetoric* (1385b13ff). It is the sense of pain that arises whenever we see some destructive or painful evil coming to someone who does *not* deserve it. That the person does not deserve it is significant, for when we pity someone we wish to help the person out of his distress, on the grounds that he does not deserve to suffer. Mercy, however, is quite different; it is directed at someone who is about to suffer *deservedly.* Furthermore, whereas we can pity someone who is about to suffer at the hands of someone else, we can have mercy only towards those who have wronged us. Hence we can hope for pity from a stranger, but we can ask for mercy only from one whom we have offended.

To the degree that we are asking someone to be merciful, we are asking him to be unjust in the strict sense, for we are asking him to give us other than what we deserve. Our conception of God is therefore caught in a dilemma. On the one hand, the thought of an unjust God is almost unthinkable; whether we believe in God or not, we wish him to be, if he does exist, a just God. On the other hand, we regard mercy as a virtue, and we want God to have all the virtues. But if mercy contradicts justice, then we want God to be a living contradiction. We can save God from the contradiction by foregoing either justice or mercy; but if we do, we appear to lessen the perfection of God. Of course, to the degree that we lessen his perfection, we make God less worthy of being God, less worthy of our admiration and love. In fact, to the degree that he lacks virtues and perfection, we are, and believe ourselves to be, justified in not believing in him.

What can we do to escape the contradiction? In many cases a contradiction can be avoided by discovering some other sense in words, by making a new distinction, by finding a loophole. In the *Pirates of Penzance* of Gilbert and Sullivan, for example, there appears a humorous example of what one can often do to avoid contradiction. A young man, Frederick, is apprenticed to a group of pirates until his twenty-first birthday. In the comedy it happens that though he is about to finish his twenty-first year of life, he is about to celebrate only his fifth birthday. The confusion arises because Frederick was born in a leap year, on the twenty-ninth of February, so that while he has lived twenty-one years, if his age is calculated by birthdays, he is a little boy of only five. So what seems to be a contradiction is really a *paradox,* that is, a statement that at first appears to be a contradiction but which upon closer examination contains an equivocation. A theological example would be the Christian doctrine that the last shall be first and the first last. If taken literally, the statement is contradictory, for it says that the last shall be first and not last. But if we see that two standards of priority are being used—that of heaven and that of earth—the contradiction disappears. Those who are first in status and power and authority on earth will be last in heaven; those who are lowly and meek and humble on earth, low in power and authority and status, will be first in heaven. Later (p. 114), we shall investigate some other apparent contradictions, such as human free will and God's foreknowledge, as well as the simultaneous existence of a God who has created everything good and the presence of evil in the world.

Of course, what appears to one person as a brilliant resolution of a contradiction into an innocuous paradox may appear to another as casuistry, chicanery, trickery, the kind of maneuvering expected more of slick lawyers than of philosophers. Yet so powerful is the abhorrence of contradiction that casuistry is much preferable to it. We can live with distinctions so fine as to be almost invisible. We cannot live with contradiction.

Not all contradictions, however, have been able to be converted into paradoxes. Mercy and justice have not been shown to be resolvable by the detection of some hidden equivocation. Nor has the oneness and threeness of God. Here, at least, Christianity has declared that something called a "mystery" applies.[23] A mystery is a kind of knowledge that by its very nature is inexpressible and incapable of being grasped rationally. The doctrine of mystery involves declaring that an apparent contradiction is merely apparent, even though human reason is incapable of explaining why it is merely apparent—by means of a hidden distinction or by any other means. When Christians wish to avoid some theological contradictions, they decide that mysteries exist that are beyond the power of human reason to understand. In short, they declare mysteries to be not contradictions but paradoxes. If one says that a paradox is ultimately resolvable by reason, a Christian will agree that the mysteries will be resolvable when we are intelligent or perceptive enough to learn God's language and detect the equivocation. With mere human intelligence, though, mysteries will remain mysterious, and apparent contradictions must be taken on faith to be only paradoxes.

Although the concept of religious mystery would probably not have arisen if not for the influence of Greek philosophy, with its emphasis on avoiding contradiction at all costs, nevertheless, to proclaim the truth of a doctrine by calling it a mystery is distant indeed from the Aristotelian concept of scientific knowledge. The difference between the thinking of Aristotle and that of Augustine is particularly striking. The doctrine of mystery seemed perfectly respectable to Augustine, indeed preferable to exaggerated claims of knowledge. The Manichaeans, with whom he had become disenchanted, had claimed knowledge but were shown not to know what they claimed to know. The Catholic Church did not make claims of knowledge about many subjects; instead it asked for faith, a humble admission that it did not have knowledge.[24] In fact, it made faith—not knowledge—one of its three cardinal virtues.

Another way of resolving contradictions may be observed in the controversy between Galileo and the Catholic Church over whether the sun or the earth is the center of the planetary system. Galileo agreed with the Church that there can be no contradiction between the revealed word of God and astronomers' correct observations of nature. He argued that the sense data of the observations constituted a "better known" (not in an Aristotelian sense) and more reliable set of premises than the word of Scripture, for the observations could be confirmed by anyone who took the trouble to look at the sky, whereas Scripture is often understood in a variety of nonliteral senses. Therefore, argued Galileo in his "Letter to the Grand Duchess Christina," the data from observations of astronomers should be taken as the premises, provided that those data have been sufficiently well confirmed, whereas the interpretation of Bible, whose words are often metaphorical, should be adjusted to accord with the observations, rather than vice versa. In this way, any contradiction will be shown to have been merely apparent, and neither scientific nor religious claims will need to be substantially modified.

The division that Aristotle draws between those who think that nothing can be known and that everything can be known also has its counterpart in religion (see p. 53). There are those who believe that the cause of everything is known: everything that happens is attributable to God's will. On the other side, there are those who believe that nothing can be known because no one can understand the mind of God. The first group, who think that the cause of everything is attributable to God's will, do not, of course, have scientific knowledge, for they do not have knowledge of logically necessary facts through causes (see p. 50). A second group thinks that nothing can be known because everything is attributable to the will of God and that will cannot be known.[25] There is a third group that believes it would be wrong to investigate causes, for man ought to be "lowly wise" and not aspire to know what is outside human prerogatives. This last group is not interested in reconciling science and religion, unless we consider the suppression of science a form of reconciliation.[26]

Arguments that appear circular have been profoundly important in theological investigations since Plato. In the *Euthyphro,* Plato has Socrates ask whether something is pious because the gods love it or whether the gods love it because it is pious. The choice of answer makes a great deal of theological difference. In the first formulation, that something is pious because the gods love it, the will of the gods is primary. The gods are the standard. What they say goes. This concept would appear to be the underlying one for revealed religions in which the deity or deities give commands that must be followed without question. The commands are right because the gods say so. The commands are like those that come from parents who tell their children, "Do what I say *because* I say it." The circularity in this first answer results from the absence of a higher standard of piety or rightness, as the case may be. *Why* do the gods love piety? Because their loving it *makes* it pious.

In the second formulation, that the gods love something *because* it is pious, some external standard beyond the gods is primary; even the deities or deity yields to the objective standard, and there is an escape from the circularity. A divine command, on this interpretation, is like that from a parent who says, "Do what I say because it is *right.*" The problem here is that the deity appears subordinate to a standard that is separate from himself, or the deity appears limited by the standard to which he must conform. Is a subordinate, limited deity still a deity? One solution to the problem is to say that God is indistinguishable from the standard, or that God is the standard. But this solution is also problematic, for it suggests a nonpersonal God, since it is hard to conceive of how a standard can listen to our prayers. One does not address prayers to a yardstick or to an abstract standard of perfection or to beauty itself.

Finally, a word or two must be said about Aristotle's idea that we can have knowledge only about indestructible things and not about things that are constantly changing. The Platonic distinction between the Worlds of Being and Becoming leads to a devaluation of things in the corporeal realm, the realm of opinion, shadow, appearance, and change, with no fixed reality. During the Hellenistic period, the three centuries between the death of Alexander the Great and the reign of Augustus—roughly between 323 B.C.E. and 31 B.C.E.—the philosophical and religious milieu was enormously complex, with philosophy and religion mixing freely and confusedly. Paralleling various philosophical developments, in the Mediterranean world there occurred a breakdown of the *polis,* the form of society in which people lived in relatively small city-states. In these small communities every person was a substantial part of the whole and every person mattered. When Alexander and his successors replaced the *polis* with the *cosmopolis,* or world-state, one's individuality mattered far less, and people generally saw less meaning in communal and civic life. For these people a more meaningful world of the spirit beckoned.[27] The vast bureaucracy of Rome and the Hellenistic empires afforded little satisfaction to souls craving some sort of significance. To fill their need for meaning, religions arose that were known as the "mysteries" and that offered communion with the spiritual world. Entrance into this spiritual world had been made attractive by the philosophical ideas circulating, ideas that denigrated the physical, corrupt world and elevated the world of the unchanging incorporeal spirit. It was, of course, in this context that Christianity arose, a religion that, like the mystery religions, offered unchanging stable salvation from this turbulent, corruptible world.

Aristotle's ideas have been stimulating to religious thinkers for over two millennia. The concept that knowledge must be of the unchanging and the idea that only something whose nature is totally constant could be perfect led to the notion that one could have true knowledge only of the divine, for only the divine is perfect. The irony is that the uniqueness of the deity precludes any knowledge of him, for knowledge requires definitions, and definitions by their very nature impose limits. In the following chapters we shall investigate how various thinkers deal with these and other problems generated from the various notions embedded in Aristotle's thought. In a certain respect Aristotle's thought was like that of Albert Einstein: it stirred developments that the thinker himself could not have foreseen.

MODERN VIEWS OF SCIENCE

An observer of modern science, like the Supreme Court justice talking about pornography, might say, "I don't know what it is, but I can recognize it when I see it." When we see chemists or biologists working in their laboratories, we are reasonably sure that they are "scientists," and when we see dentists or butchers or construction workers, we are reasonably sure that they are not scientists. But philosophers of science have always disagreed on the question of what exactly science is. The fundamental difference between Aristotle's philosophy of science and modern philosophy of science, however, concerns the level of rigor required for the acceptance of scientific claims. For Aristotle, the goal of science is the discovery of truth—inviolable, unchanging, eternal, absolute, and universal truth. Because "to know" means to know the truth conceived in this way, scientific knowledge in the Aristotelian sense is limited, as we have seen, to axiomatic and deductive fields like geometry. Modern philosophers of science, on the other hand, tend to have a more inclusive conception of what counts as science and tend to be less preoccupied with absolute truth. Both the criteria scientists use in assessing theories and the willingness of scientists not to consider their theories unalterably "true" have changed dramatically between the time of Aristotle and the dawn of modern science in the seventeenth century.

Having already surveyed the modern criteria for theory-choice in our discussion of the positive aspects of scientific explanation at the end of the preceding chapter (p. 35), it will suffice to emphasize here the fact that theories falling short of Aristotelian ideals—i.e., all theories that we would today classify as science rather than as mathematics—can nevertheless be justifiably held with confidence. Indeed, the reason that science provides such satisfying explanations of the world is that its theories pass rigorous, even *reasonably* rigorous, tests of empirical adequacy, mathematical elegance, and technological fruitfulness. Because there are already numerous accessible books on the modern philosophy of science, including ones that underscore the ability of science to discover truths,[28] and because one of our goals in this book is to emphasize both the richness and the shortcomings of ancient views, with which most readers are likely to be less familiar, we shall content ourselves in what follows with a brief survey of the opinions of a few nineteenth- and twentieth-century philosophers of science. We hope thereby to convey the flavor of what distinguishes the interests, methods, and agendas of modern philosophers of science from those of their ancient predecessors.

Perhaps a suitable place to begin is the philosophy of John Stuart Mill (1806–1873), the most influential English philosopher of the nineteenth century. Mill took as axiomatic the principle that nature displays a certain uniformity and, what amounts to the same thing, that every event has a cause. Although the uniformity and causal structure of nature is confirmed by experience, one of the basic problems of science is that the generalizations we draw from experience are sometimes erroneous. Hence, one of Mill's chief concerns was the character of scientific induction, i.e., how theories are generated from observational evidence. Among the philosopher's many legacies are "Mill's methods"—of agreement, difference, residues, and concomitant variation—for uncovering causal relationships and general explanatory principles. The method of agreement states that if two or more instances of a phenomenon have only one circumstance in common, then that circumstance is the cause or effect of the phenomenon. If a number of healthy people die from ingesting arsenic, but in all other respects live different lives—with different bedtimes, diets, and racial backgrounds—and the only circumstance they have in common is that they have ingested arsenic, then we can conclude that arsenic is the cause of their deaths. The method of difference states that if a phenomenon occurs in one instance but does not occur in another instance that is identical except for one difference, then that one difference is the cause (or effect) of the phenomenon. If, for example, we have two people who are identical in every possible respect except that one ingests arsenic and dies while the other does not ingest arsenic and lives, we may conclude that arsenic was the cause of the death. This is, of course, the familiar method we see when control groups are employed in experimentation. The methods of residues and concomitant variation also search for correlations as clues to causation. For Mill, the goal of science, even if it is achieved only rarely, is to induce laws of nature, i.e., to derive them from empirical evidence and to continue to test them through their empirical consequences. Like Aristotle, Mill was an empiricist through and through, and like Aristotle he sought general explanations of the empirical facts. But Mill emphasized the specific methods for generating those generalizations and was far more concerned than Aristotle with empirical tests than with deductive rigor and eternal, a priori truth.

Mill's methods produce a far lower degree of certitude than that produced by Aristotelian syllogisms. If the complaint can be made that Aristotle's conclusions are already implicit in his premises and thus teach us nothing new, the complaint against Mill is that causal relations are notoriously difficult to pin down. Indeed, it is often impossible to isolate the elements of agreement and difference that Mill's methods require. For example, it used to be believed that the one element that people suffering from ulcers have in common is anxiety. But later it was discovered that a bacterium is also a common element. In the case of controlled experiments, it is impossible to find subjects that are in every way alike, given the variability at the molecular level. Even so-called identical twins are far from identical.

An empiricist like Mill, Ernst Mach (1838–1916) sought to make rigorous the logical foundations of science by reducing theorizing to the organization of sensations. By claiming that the world is reducible to sensations, he took empiricism to its limit and denied that science achieves any sort of Aristotelian rigor, a priori knowledge, or truth. To claim otherwise would be to contaminate science with metaphysics, towards which Mach was particularly hostile. Rather than dabbling in metaphysics, science, for Mach, merely describes the world and does so in terms of the sensations of those who observe it. Because scientific theories are therefore just a shorthand for the original sensations on which they are based, theories must always be testable by reference to those original sensations. Theories are thus always provisional; they are useful predictive tools rather than statements about reality. Whereas Mach, like Aristotle, desired scientific rigor and valued empiricism, Mach departed sharply from Aristotelian thinking in his disdain for metaphysical truth, his view of theories as descriptive and provisional, and his reduction of much of science to what amounts to a collection of subjective sensations.

The question of whether a theory precedes one's understanding of what one has observed and hence helps to shape that understanding, or whether a theory is developed from one's observations, has a parallel in historiography. There are Marxist historians, for example, who begin with the Marxist theory that every human action springs from economic motivations. When these historians write, in every historical situation they find class warfare and economic struggle. Other historians, like Thucydides and Herodotus, describe events and then draw from the events conclusions about human nature. The methodological question is whether theory or observation is the starting place for understanding. Both approaches were seen in the incident with cold fusion: there were scientists who began with theories and then tried to explain what was happening as conforming to those theories; and there were scientists who began with the observations and then tried to adjust their theories to fit the observations.

For Mill and Mach, theory does not suggest ways of looking for new facts; theory is what is suggested by the facts themselves. One studies the data, and theories simply arise. These views clearly deny any power to theories themselves to help find new data; it is the highly ordered and precise descriptions of data that are powerful, for they generate the theories.

Like Mach, the French philosopher Henri Poincaré (1854–1912) was concerned with the logical character of science and emphasized the provisional nature and predictive utility of all scientific theories. Like Mill, he accepted as a given the facts that the universe exhibits intelligible order and that an inductive method provides our most effective means of uncovering that order. One of Poincaré's chief contributions to the philosophy of science is his claim that theories, including mathematical ones, are linguistic conventions. Even Euclid's axioms, he said, are accepted on the grounds of convenience and, ultimately, convention. Because geometry is a convention, it is possible for one to choose his preferred form of geometry, be it Euclidean or non-Euclidean. One criterion of theory-choice, for Poincaré, is simplicity, but it too proves to be conventional: we start, provisionally, with the simplest hypotheses and laws not because they are likely to be true but because they are the easiest to work with. The danger in Poincaré's conventionalism, of course, is that when the laws of nature are believed to be nothing but linguistic conventions, like so many rules of etiquette, they are easily reduced to arbitrary matters of taste or preference. (It is not difficult to see why this view would destroy the idea that nature is the product of God's art, of an art that obeys fixed laws: did God pick one of a number of physics—perhaps because he liked the sound of one of the constants? Is the Law of Gravity valid because God chose it for the universe?) It does not seem to matter which convention one chooses (although the philosopher claimed, rather inconsistently, that some conventions *were* better than others insofar as what he defined as "facts" produce the same sensations in different people). The extreme contrast between Poincaré, whose conventionalist view of theories verges on relativism about their truth, and Aristotle, who sought objectively true explanations of the most rigorous sort, should be obvious.

The logical positivists of the Vienna circle in the early twentieth century, of whom Mach and Poincaré were intellectual ancestors, also thought of science in linguistic terms. The sharp distinction they drew between observational and theoretical terms was central to their project of distinguishing rigorous science from pseudosciences like astrology. Meaningless theoretical terms could be eliminated, they thought, if there were a requirement that every theoretical term, such as *gravity,* be reducible to observational terms, such as the observed positions of bodies in planetary systems. The positivists placed a great emphasis on logic, for example, in the correspondence rules that were thought to govern the reduction of theoretical terms to observational ones. They also stressed the verifiability of scientific claims, as distinct from the claims of pseudoscience, which of course cannot be verified by actual observation.

Aristotle, too, as we well know, was keenly interested in rigorous knowledge and in a tight logical connection between observations and the principles that explain them, but Aristotle explained observations in terms of their real, underlying causes, and would have had no sympathy at all with the positivists' analysis of science in linguistic terms. Although Aristotle would have shared the positivists' distaste for pseudoscience, had he been aware of the concept, the positivists for their part would have decried Aristotle's formal and final causes as themselves pseudoscientific. After all, how can a thing's essence or purpose be reduced to purely observational language?

The positivist model of science, it turns out, fared no better than Aristotle's in accounting for science as it is actually practiced. After a half-century reign, positivism, the most logically and technically oriented view of science ever, fell prey to its own technical problems. The rules of correspondence between theoretical and observational terms proved intractable, as did the very concept of an observational term devoid of any theoretical content at all. (Does one "observe" a blister on his foot, or does a term like *blister* carry medical—and hence theoretical—meaning? Do glasses or contact lenses contaminate the observation?) Perhaps most importantly, the criterion of verification, which was supposed to separate science from pseudoscience, was found to be itself unverifiable. The entire positivist project rested on a circularity.

Strongly influenced by positivism—especially in his desire to weed out pseudoscience—but intent on avoiding the shortcomings of positivism, Karl Popper (1902–1994) emphasized falsifiability rather than verifiability as the defining criterion of science. The claim of an astronomer that a total solar eclipse will be visible in the central Pacific on 22 July 2009 for 6 minutes and 38.9 seconds, for example, is easily falsifiable, and will indeed be falsified if the predicted eclipse does not occur. The astrologer's claim, on the other hand, that a person will have "good luck soon" is compatible with *all* observations and is so vague as to be entirely unfalsifiable. For Popper (in direct contrast to Mill) a new scientific theory is boldly conjectured, without any logic or justification needed to support the conjecture, and is always held most tentatively. Indeed, the whole point of science is to *disprove* theories with falsifying observations and experiments. For this reason, Popper held broad, highly falsifiable theories in higher esteem than he did those that are narrower in scope and hence harder targets for falsification. In direct contrast to the positivists, Popper held that theories are not only never verified but cannot even be confirmed. The most one can hope for is the "corroboration" that attaches to theories that have survived repeated attempts at falsification.

Popper's bold conjectures, tentatively held theories, and active attempts at falsification would, of course, have been anathema to Aristotle and to the Greek mind in general. Yet Popper's view of science has remained one of the most influential up to the present day. It is far from perfect, however. Indeed, its central concepts of corroboration and falsification have been seriously challenged. Most people, while acknowledging that science never reaches Aristotelian rigor or positivistic verification, think it does better than Popperian corroboration. We like to think of the Big Bang theory, relativity theory, and the theory of evolution as having achieved a status higher than that simply of survivors of attempts to falsify them. Although falsification cannot be as simple as we have outlined—and neither Popper nor his successors thought it is—there are grounds for thinking that it cannot apply to science at all. The chief reason is that theories are "underdetermined" by the evidence, i.e., no single theory can be deduced from any body of evidence, and there is no way to isolate theories in the way needed to falsify them by a single piece of contrary evidence. Theories are more like interconnected, protected webs than sitting ducks for falsification. An apparent anomaly, as we have seen, might mean that something went wrong with an experiment, that some artifact of an instrument has been introduced, that some auxiliary theory has problems, or that one of a host of other assumptions is false: declaring a specific target theory false is by no means the only way to resolve an anomaly.

One of the most influential recent philosophers of science and one of the most influential twentieth-century thinkers in any field is Thomas S. Kuhn, who emphasized the historical character of scientific theories rather than focusing on the logical relationships between theory and evidence, as had so many of his predecessors. Kuhn divided the history of particular scientific fields into periods of "normal science," during which a "paradigm" governs research and "revolutionary science," when the old paradigm is in the process of being replaced by a new one. A paradigm, typically based on a single work, such as Copernicus's *De Revolutionibus,* defines a line of research, provides scientists with a way of looking at the world—the heliocentric way, for example—and defines the set of problems appropriate for further research. This research, this explication and fine tuning of the paradigm, constitutes normal science under the paradigm. During a period of normal science, anomalies besetting the paradigm accumulate, and finally a crisis period ensues in which scientists scramble either to shore up the existing paradigm or—especially if they are newcomers to the field—overthrow the old paradigm with a whole new way of looking at the phenomena. During the sixteenth and especially seventeenth centuries, for example, the field of astronomy underwent a crisis that ended in a paradigm shift from the Aristotelian and Ptolemaic earth-centered cosmos to the revolutionary new view of Copernicus, Kepler, and Galileo. Although most of scientists' time is spent spelling out the details of a paradigm, e.g., computing exact planetary orbits according to the prevailing cosmology, every scientific field witnesses multiple revolutions and paradigm shifts during its history. Thus Aristotelian physics shifted to Newtonian and Newtonian to Einsteinian. If such shifts occur, the natural question is whether science provides us any sort of objective, ahistorical truth. According to Kuhn, a given paradigm does not bring us closer to the truth but simply delimits a new "gestalt," a new way of looking at the observed phenomena. Science is as aimless and purposeless as the evolution of living forms, as Kuhn emphasizes in the final chapter of his revolutionary *Structure of Scientific Revolutions.*

> We may . . . have to relinquish the notion, explicit or implicit, that changes of paradigm carry scientists and those who learn from them closer and closer to the truth.
>
> It is now time to notice that until the last very few pages the term "truth" had entered this essay only in the quotation from Francis Bacon. And even in those pages it entered only as a source for the scientist's conviction that incompatible rules for doing science cannot coexist except during revolutions when the profession's main task is to eliminate all sets but one. The developmental process described in this essay has been a process of evolution *from* primitive beginnings—a process whose successive stages are characterized by an increasingly detailed and refined understanding of nature. But nothing that has been or will be said makes it a process of evolution *toward* anything. Inevitably that lacuna will have disturbed many readers. We are all deeply accustomed to seeing science as the one enterprise that draws constantly nearer to some goal set by nature in advance.
>
> But need there be any such goal? Can we not account for both science's existence and its success in terms of evolution from the community's state of knowledge at any given time? Does it really help to imagine that there is some one full, objective, true account of nature and that the proper measure of scientific achievement is the extent to which it brings us closer to that ultimate goal?[29]

In Kuhn's insistence on the inescapably historical character of science, in his somewhat unsettling notion of paradigm shift, and in his disavowal of objective scientific truth, modern philosophy of science reaches perhaps its most extreme departure from the Aristotelian view of scientific knowledge as unchanging, objective, and truth-seeking in the most rigorous sense. It is worth noting that later analyses of Kuhn's work, as well as commentaries by Kuhn himself, reveal him to be less radical than first impressions might indicate. He is quick to point out, for example, that theories and paradigms are not generated willy-nilly: there *are* criteria for theory-choice, and these include the familiar ones of simplicity, elegance, scope, empirical adequacy, and potential to generate fruitful future research. It is worth noting as well that most scientists themselves are unconcerned with the philosophical analysis of their work. At a natural, intuitive level, scientists, like other people, are driven by a passionate desire to *know* and not merely to construct linguistic or logical models that might have little connection to reality. Those who study the mysteries of the distant universe or prehistoric animals and plants or the formation of mountains and rivers or the slow drift of the continents are not driven by dreams of wealth or fame or romantic love. They are driven by that desire to know that Aristotle observed as the core of human nature. To be sure, some of them deny that they are looking for *truth*—for they have been enough influenced by the philosophers to be embarrassed by such a word, but they are all the same likely to admit off the record that they are looking for the way the world really works, not just for a mental construct or a hypothesis that has survived attempts at falsification. The situation is rather like that in G. B. Shaw's *Major Barbara,* where the moral principles of Barbara's father are infinitely better in practice than in his pronouncements. Our scientists and mathematicians would have won the approbation of Aristotle for what they *do,* even if he would have blushed at what they sometimes *say.*

FAITH AND SCIENTIFIC KNOWLEDGE

People of faith find satisfaction in ascribing the cause of many phenomena to the divine, some even taking comfort in the view that God or angels participate directly in their lives. Unfazed by the lack of scientific proof for their beliefs, they rely not on demonstration but on faith, which, after all, is one of the Christian cardinal virtues. In chapter 11 (p. 171), we shall consider arguments for a necessary dichotomy between faith and knowledge, i.e., whether matters of faith can simultaneously be matters of knowledge. Despite the fact that faith, for the believer, ideally represents the pinnacle of conviction and certitude—as epitomized by martyrs, who die for their faith—for the philosopher it nevertheless lacks the objectivity, the demonstrability, the intuitive self-evidence, and the explanation in terms of causes that knowledge in the fullest sense requires. In this sense, religious people are like modern scientists, who, because their subject matter is the natural world rather than the deductive realm of mathematics, cannot in principle achieve eternal, a priori, deductive truth. Both religious believers and modern scientists acquiesce in a level of cognitive certitude that falls short of full knowledge. As a Christian might aim at faith, so a Kuhnian aims at a successful paradigm, a Popperian at a corroborated hypothesis, and a positivist at a theory reducible to observational terms. Although only the Christian among these thinks his beliefs literally true, clearly neither he nor the scientists of the various persuasions has an Aristotelian handle on the truth. All share the natural human desire for absolute, unqualified certitude *and* absolute truth, yet all must be satisfied with something less.

If there is such a thing as the truth about the world that all people desire to know, and if part of that desire consists in an unwillingness to give up Aristotle's fundamental principle of truth—that truth cannot be self-contradictory—then the conclusions of science and those of religion, at least insofar as they approximate the truth, must be consistent with one another. But knowledge of the truth consists at least in part in knowledge of the causes, and it is part of the operational definition of science that God not be invoked as a cause. Hence if science and religion are to coexist, we must establish the consistency of explanations of the world in purely naturalistic terms with accounts of the same world in terms of an overarching divine cause. In the following chapters we shall survey some of the attempts to do so from the very beginning of science in ancient Miletus.

DISCUSSION QUESTIONS

1. In the western world there has been a tendency to think of nature as *natura naturata*—a consistent, complete, finished entity—rather than as *natura naturans*—a changing, dynamic, growing, unfolding entity. The Greek word for "nature," *physis,* which predates the rise of Greek philosophy, comes from the verb *phyo,* meaning "grow." While the idea of *natura naturata* is perhaps shown in physicists' favorite pre-twentieth-century metaphor for nature of billiard balls, whose behavior is subject to deterministic causes and effects, the ancient idea of nature embodies a metaphor of growth, conflict, and death. In what ways is one's conception of nature related to various ways of understanding the divine, as a polytheistic mélange of competing gods, for example, or as a monotheistic unity of the divine qualities of perfection, knowledge, and power? How are varying conceptions reflected in the philosophies of Heraclitus and Parmenides?

2. What are the strengths and weaknesses of Plato's reconciliation of the competing ideas of Parmenides and Heraclitus? Does the Platonic reconciliation avoid the defects of each of the pre-Socratics, or does it repeat the errors in a different though more sophisticated form?

3. One of Aristotle's contributions to understanding science was his ability to make distinctions, many of which have been formative of subsequent discussions in epistemology, the philosophical inquiry into the nature of knowledge. Do you think that Aristotle's work has so controlled the discussion as to have made thinking in non-Aristotelian categories virtually impossible? Have Aristotle's distinctions won acceptance because they are true? Or is this last question itself impossible to answer without escaping somehow from Aristotelian modes of inquiry?

4. Aristotle's strict definition of knowledge as involving a demonstration that is universal, through causes, and from premises that are prior, more convincing, and necessary would severely limit the number of things known. Is it nevertheless useful to have so rigorous a standard? Will such a standard inspire or demoralize those in fields like biology, chemistry, geology, and astronomy, where the material nature of the subject matter prevents these strict criteria of knowledge from ever being met?

5. If Aristotle's strict definition of knowledge allows for perfect understanding of things in the nonmaterial world, should it be able to be directed toward understanding an immaterial deity? Or is immateriality a necessary yet not sufficient cause for perfect knowledge? What difficulties might, in principle, impede the process, or even foreclose on the possibility, of having knowledge in the strict sense about the deity?

6. The Talmudic story about whether a certain oven was ritually clean shows an attempt to determine exactly God's intention by human means. Is it possible that in the story God's actual intention is that the process of debate

about God's meaning *is* the holy act? Does this notion hint at some sort of reconciliation of God and science?

7. Aristotelian logic, with its emphasis on understanding things by examining their generic nature and by categorizing them by genus and species, encounters a serious obstacle when it comes to understanding things—such as God or the universe as a whole—that are unqualifiedly unique: such things cannot be generalized about and cannot be categorized. Is it possible for such things to be understood at all? Does the meaning of *understand* have to be altered significantly in order to accommodate such things?

8. Does the distinction between *contradiction* and *paradox* offer promise of settling the apparent difficulties in reconciling science and religion? Is the hope that apparent contradictions can be resolved into paradoxes itself a religious hope? What successes have offered confirmation of the hope?

9. In what ways do modern philosophers of science attempt to develop a science that aims at a lower degree of certitude than Aristotle would have claimed for his strict definition? How, for example, do Mill and Mach try to develop a science that embraces both the logic of human minds and the materiality of the objects towards which they are applying the logic?

10. Have the various claims about modern science altered your acceptance or rejection of Aristotle's claim that "all human beings by nature desire understanding"? Should we revise the claim to say that "all human beings by nature desire to show that the claims of modern science are falsifiable" or that "all human beings desire to find anomalies in the latest paradigm"? Have the claims of the modern philosophers of science successfully updated what we mean by "understanding"?

NOTES

1. See *Fragments of the Ancient Stoics,* 1.68; and *Philo on the Preliminary Studies,* 41.

2. E. O. Wilson quotes a Chinese saying that makes this point. He writes, "The first step to wisdom, as the Chinese say, is getting things by their right names." See his *Consilience: The Unity of Knowledge* (New York: Knopf, 1998), 4. See also our discussion above in chapter 2, p. 24.

3. Alfred North Whitehead, who said that all of Western philosophy consists of footnotes to Plato, would have been more accurate to have made the claim about Parmenides.

4. For the question of change by the deity, with reference to Aristotle, see p. 101; with reference to Neoplatonism, see p. 112; with reference to Plato, see pp. 136ff.

5. Nicholas of Cusa (1401–1464) went much further than Plato in describing five ways in which mathematics provides a symbolic basis for thinking about God. (1) Mathematics starts with entities we see in the perceivable world. (2) It furnishes us with invisible abstractions drawn from the physical world. (3) It moves us from the uncertainties of the physical (like the uncertainties in Plato's World of Becoming) to the certainties in the invisible theorems. (4) It provides us with the best understanding of the concept of infinity, which enables us to glimpse God by analogy. (5) It provides practical benefits in engineering, just as the

concept of God provides human benefits such as ecumenism or social communities. See S. Dangelmayr, *Gotteserkenntnis und Gottesbegriff in den philosophischen Schriften des Nikolaus von Kues* (Meisenheim am Glan: Anton Hain, 1969).

6. The problem is more vexed, as Plato himself knew (and as he revealed in his dialogue *Parmenides*). If a person redecorates his house, he has produced a new idea of his house. So now he has a fixed idea of his house at time A (before the redecoration) and at time B (after the redecoration). And what about every other moment? Does each moment of each thing reflect a different fixed idea? Does each number? These are very difficult questions for a Platonist.

7. Resurrection has been central to Christianity and Islam from the beginning. The Pharisees added it to Judaism, and Maimonides made it one of the thirteen principles of the Jewish faith. For a modern attempt to reconcile resurrection with science, see chapter 14, p. 285.

8. For a reading of the dialogues as works of drama, see James A. Arieti, *Interpreting Plato: The Dialogues As Drama* (Savage, Md.: Rowman and Littlefield, 1991).

9. See Augustine, *Confessions,* 6.5.

10. On the distinction between definitions through genus and differentia and definitions that involve knowledge of causes, and on Aristotle's occasional use of one or the other, see A. Gomez-Lobo, "Definitions in Aristotle's Posterior Analytics," in *Studies in Aristotle,* ed. D. J. O'Meara (Washington, D.C.: Catholic University Press, 1981), 25–46.

11. Aristotle, *Posterior Analytics,* 71b27–72a5. For Aristotle the causes of a thing are its starting principles, and these may be explained in terms of the four causes. The material principle (or cause) of a house is what it is made of; the efficient principle is who brought it about, and so on.

12. See the next section, especially pp. 58ff.

13. See Gomez-Lobo, "Definitions," 28–30.

14. Aristotle, *Nicomachean Ethics,* 1094b25.

15. E. Frankel, *The Classic Tales: 4,000 Years of Jewish Lore* (Northvale, N.J.: Jason Aronson, 1993), 305–6.

16. E. Gibbon, *The Decline and Fall of the Roman Empire,* Great Books of the Western World Edition (Chicago: Encyclopaedia Britannica, 1952), vol. 1, chapter 15, gives a compelling account of the politicking. The Catholic Church, however, considers the resolutions of councils to be divinely inspired.

17. For David Hume's critique of miracles, see chapter 12, p. 232.

18. Gibbon, *Decline and Fall,* vol. 1, chapter 15.

19. See his debate with Erasmus on free will in Erasmus, *Erasmus-Luther: Discourse on Free Will,* trans. E. F. Winter (New York: Frederick Ungar, 1961), especially 100–101.

20. One might recall the aborted attempt to unite the various Lutheran synods in the 1970s. The process collapsed over arguments about how literally the Bible should be interpreted.

21. For Agathon's account, see Plato, *Symposium,* 195D-E; for Socrates', see 203C-D.

22. Gibbon, *Decline and Fall,* vol. 1, chapter 2.

23. The Roman Catholic Church, by canon law, says, "If anyone say that in Divine Revelation there are contained no mysteries properly so called, but that through reason rightly developed all the dogmas of faith can be understood and demonstrated from natural principles, let him be cursed." See The Vatican Council, Session 3. De fide et ratione, canon 1 (from *The Catholic Encyclopedia*).

24. Augustine, *Confessions,* 6.5.

25. Al Ghazali is perhaps the most prominent of these. See chapter 9, p. 167.

26. The phrase "lowly wise" is from Milton, *Paradise Lost,* 8.173. This third group is perhaps best represented by Tertullian:

What has Athens to do with Jerusalem, the Academy with the Church? . . . We have no need for curiosity since Jesus Christ, nor for inquiry since the Evangel. Tell me, what is the sense of this itch for idle speculation? What does it prove, this useless affectation of a fastidious curiosity, notwithstanding the strong confidence of its assertions? It was highly appropriate that Thales, while his eyes were roaming the heavens in astronomical observation, should have tumbled into a well. This mishap may well serve to illustrate the fate of all who occupy themselves with the stupidities of philosophy.

  This is the substance of secular wisdom that it rashly undertakes to explain the nature and dispensation of God. . . . Heretics and philosophers deal with similar material, and their arguments are largely the same. It is the Platonic ideas which have supplied the Gnostics with their aeons, the Marcionite deity (the ideal of tranquility) comes from the Stoics, the identification of God with matter is a doctrine of Zeno, with fire of Heraclitus, . . . the Epicureans supply the notion of annihilation of the soul; and all alike are agreed in denying any possibility of regeneration for the flesh. . . . Unhappy Aristotle, who supplies them with a logic evasive in its propositions, far-fetched in its conclusions, disputatious in arguments, burdensome even to itself, settling everything in order to settle nothing.

See Tertullian, *De Praescriptione Haereticorum,* 7, quoted in C. N. Cochrane, *Christianity and Classical Culture* (New York: Oxford University Press, 1940), 222–23.

27. See E. R. Dodds, *Pagan and Christian in an Age of Anxiety: Some Aspects of Religious Experience from Marcus Aurelius to Constantine* (New York: Norton, 1965).

28. See, for example, Robert Klee, *Introduction to the Philosophy of Science: Cutting Nature at Its Seams* (New York: Oxford University Press, 1997).

29. Thomas S. Kuhn, *The Structure of Scientific Revolutions* (Chicago: University of Chicago Press, 1970), 170–71.

4

The Origin of Scientific Attempts
to Explain the World

Science moves, but slowly, slowly, creeping on from point to point.

—Tennyson

THE ORIGIN OF SCIENCE IN MILETUS

No one knows how science came into being. Antiquity credited Miletus, a port city on the eastern coast of the Aegean Sea (in present-day Turkey), as the home of the first group of philosophers. Called pre-Socratics, they are famous for their theories about cosmology and physics, in contrast to Socrates, who, according to Cicero, brought philosophy down from the sky (where it had been with the *pre*-Socratics) and placed it in cities and homes. In other words, whereas the pre-Socratics were concerned with natural science, Socrates and his followers were principally concerned with ethics. This division is, however, misleading, for pre-Socratics dealt with ethical matters, and later philosophers dealt with physics, metaphysics, logic, zoology, mathematics, and many subjects other than ethics. Socrates himself, as portrayed in the Platonic dialogues—the principal source for information about Socrates—engaged in conversations on many subjects besides ethics.[1]

Miletus, as a port city, is said to have been a fertile ground for philosophy, for with people coming from and going to different places, there was the opportunity for cross-cultural conversations and new ideas. Of course, ports in antiquity, like modern ports, offered bored sailors more opportunities for vice than coffee houses (or their ancient equivalent) offered intellectuals opportunities for philosophical discourse. Even if we agree that a port like Miletus was a stimulating locale, the claim that it was therefore a fertile place for the birth of science raises the question of why it was *Miletus* and not one of the hundreds or thousands of other ancient port cities.

THALES AND MONISM

The tradition of antiquity attributes to Thales of Miletus the invention of science as a search for natural explanations of the world. Like Abraham, he was an original and independent thinker, one able to observe objectively and then reject the pervasive worldview of his contemporaries. Because we in the West have become habituated to independent thinkers, it is perhaps easy to forget how difficult it is to extract oneself from the cultural and traditional views with which one is surrounded. When Thales looks at the world and asks new questions and proposes new solutions, we ought to celebrate the occasion as one of the truly revolutionary moments in the history of the world. If there were any justice, the nations of the world would choose a day when the original insight came to Thales, and would give children a day off from school, rightly calling the holiday an authentic Founder's Day. Thales also made one of the first *quantitative* predictions of note: he was the first person we know of to predict successfully by mathematical means a total eclipse of the sun. Although Thales' prediction was correct only to the nearest year, the historian Herodotus reports that the occurrence of the eclipse was significant enough to cause the Lydians and the Medes immediately to make peace after six years of war.[2] If the eclipse in question was indeed the one of 28 May 585 B.C.E., the anniversary of that day should be the occasion for parades and speeches at universities and research centers.

Why did Thales have the insight that we should look for explanations of the world in principles of nature rather than in references to deities? This is a question that cannot be answered with certainty. But we can observe that genius often works in the following way. One person has an idea that no one else has ever had. He talks of it to others and it quickly spreads and is refined. In a sense, the idea might be like the very first chemicals that in the primeval cosmic soup were somehow able to replicate. As, according to theorists of evolution, all life has a common origin in that random mix of chemicals, so all science and philosophy can trace its origin to the brilliant mind of Thales. It may be, of course, that others had similar insights, but they are lost to history, and since Thales is the first to have clearly influenced others, we shall do no harm to truth by giving the credit for the insight to Thales. In the same way, it is possible that someone prior to Abraham had the insight that idols were not fully divine, but it is Abraham who communicated his insight to others and hence deserves the credit.[3]

Thales is most recognized for his claim that everything comes from water. As Aristotle records it, Thales held that the material principle of all things is water.[4] Thales may have had in mind the changeable condition of water, i.e., the fact that it can be transformed into either liquid, solid, or gas. Water may thus be a metaphor for the various forms of matter. Alternatively, because life comes from water and because water is a major component of all living things, Thales may have meant the claim as a metaphor for the significance of water for life. Aristotle suggests that Thales came to this conclusion from "observing that all food is moist and that heat itself is generated from the moist and is kept alive by it (and that from which things are generated is the principle of all)."[5] Because the early philosophers tend to be extremely metaphorical in their discourse, employing human ethical terms to describe physical forces—for example, Empedocles speaks of "love" and "strife" as the elemental forces of nature—there is always a danger of interpreting their remarks too literally.

Thales also discusses soul (*psyche*). Aristotle writes that "Thales seems to have understood the soul as something in motion [kinetic]—if indeed he said that the loadstone has a soul because it moves iron."[6] Aristotle adds, "And some say that the soul is mixed in the universe, whence perhaps Thales also thought that all things are full of gods."[7] These passages illustrate how a natural philosopher stretches the limits of his vocabulary in order to make his insights intelligible. Thales seems to be suggesting that soul is the source of movement—a view most people share today, at least in some contexts. We see a motionless corpse and conclude that its soul has departed. We speak of a dead person's body as distinct from the person himself. We'll say, "So and So's body lies in state in the Rotunda," or "the child's body was removed from the river." Perhaps Thales believes that the soul is a god because it causes things to move and that movement is the essence of being alive. Thus rivers, trees, winds, and celestial bodies are gods and are alive (unlike rocks) because they move and seem to have the faculty of self-motion. Independent self-motion is the province of soul; all that seems to generate its own movement is in this sense alive and possessed of soul. As Aetius writes, "Thales said that the mind of the cosmos is the god, and that the whole is ensouled and full of daimons, and that a moving [kinetic] divine power penetrates through the elemental moisture."[8]

Assuming that these attributed comments are accurate, Thales seems to make two different claims about the gods. On the one hand, he seems to say that souls are gods because they are self-moving. On the other hand, he suggests that the mind of the cosmos, its systematic order, somehow penetrates the moisture and is the god. What is revolutionary in this thinking is the depersonalizing of the divine, the making of the divine both the intellectual framework for the world and the actual sustained perpetuation of that framework through the physical world. Thales defines "god" in a non-religious way, as a physical force and as an intellectually comprehended pattern. Though he uses the words *soul* and *god*—the language of religion—his thought is quite distinct from the religion of his contemporaries. There would be no altars, no sacrifices, no hymns to Thales' divinities. They are not appropriate objects of prayer or ritual.

Other early philosophers identified different elements as the principles of all things. Anaximenes and Diogenes say that the primary substance is air. Hippasus and Heraclitus say that it is fire. These philosophers are known as monists because they believe that all matter is reducible to the same one element (the word *monist* comes from the Greek word for *one*). Opposed to the monists is Empedocles, who reduces the world to four physical principles—air, earth, fire, and water. If we reckon influence by the duration of a theory, Empedocles perhaps will carry away the palm, for his theory was the longest lasting of any. It endured into the modern period, not superseded until the founding of modern chemistry in the eighteenth century. Its medical and psychological version is humoral theory, from which words like *melancholy, sanguine, bilious,* and *phlegmatic* survive in our language. Yet another non-monist, Anaxagoras, claims that the basic principles are infinite, that all substances are distinct and unique.

These various theories represent fundamental options that continue to be debated in modern physics. Is there one kind of matter or many? Are all the apparent varieties of things an illusion or the result of various combinations of basic material elements? How many different fundamental particles are there? In modern times physicists have sometimes reduced all matter to one particle—atoms—or to several elementary particles—protons, neutrons, and electrons—or again to one particle—quarks—or again, to three kinds of quarks. But the original question of whether all matter is ultimately reducible to one kind of particle out of which everything is made remains unanswered. Although it appeared that matter and energy were two basic principles, Einstein showed that they are convertible one into the other. Are they, then, like ice and steam, two forms of one underlying unity? Then again, perhaps Anaxagoras's views also remain alive in a way. Even if the contemporary debates reduce the principles to one or several, physicists would accept the uniqueness of every particle in the universe—if we include what is sometimes referred to as the "numerical distinction" between particles, that is, that their ages and their locations in the various fields that act upon them are different. It is, however, a fundamental principle of the physics, or metaphysics, of elementary particles that "different" electrons are in principle indistinguishable, and in a way that does not apply to macroscopic entities. One electron isn't a "different principle" from another in the way Anaxagoras had in mind, and there might not be an infinite number of them. Analogies between ancient physics and modern physics can be pushed only so far, and one must be careful about using the same terms for different concepts. Nevertheless, it is clear that the pre-Socratic philosophers were asking what would come to be enduring questions in western science.

THE PROBLEM OF CHANGE: PARMENIDES AND HERACLITUS

What the world is made of is a question embedded in the context of other questions, the most important of which concerns change. How is change possible?

How are the various kinds of change—movement, growth, generation, destruction, alteration—possible? Is the basic condition of the world one of change or constancy? Can we control change so that we obtain the kind of change we want and avoid the kind we do not want? Is there a connection between change in physics and ethics, and, if so, what is it? Perhaps it would be best here to quote Aristotle, who cautions at the beginning of his discussion of these problems, "Not only is it difficult to arrive at the truth, but it is not even easy to discuss the problems well."[9]

The pre-Socratic philosophers were the first to address the problem of change systematically, although there was far from any consensus on the issue. In Parmenides and Heraclitus we find two philosophers with diametrically opposed views. Parmenides, whom we discussed briefly above, lived in the second half of the sixth and the first half of the fifth centuries B.C.E. He was the thinker who wished to reveal the reality that lay beyond the diversity and flux of things in what he called Being. Being, he reasoned, is the same in all the things that partake of it. It is never different: Being is Being, period. From this seemingly trivial insight, however, came his startling conclusions. If Being is always the same, it cannot cease, nor can it come into being. It is obvious that all things that exist have Being. Hence, because Being and the things that are have only a positive form, he says, there can be no negative claims. For example, to say that there is not a house on the hill is to speak about nonbeing. But to speak about nonbeing is impossible because nonbeing cannot even be thought, let alone intelligibly spoken about. Even implicit negatives are impossible. For example, to say that something has begun is to say that at one time it was not and hence is to speak unintelligibly. The same reasoning applies to motion. To say that a thing is now at location B is to suggest that it was not there before, and not to be there is a form of nonbeing and hence cannot be.[10] Moreover, for Parmenides, Being is indivisible and homogeneous, like a perfect sphere.[11]

Parmenides makes the same claim about plurality, the possibility of which he also denies. For to say that we have a plurality of items is to say that one thing is not or is not like another thing. But "is not" and "is not like" are negatives and hence unintelligible concepts. In the same way, the only permissible qualities are "all" and "full." For to be "tall" would imply "not short," a negative, a form of nonbeing, which cannot exist. So there is only Being, which is expressed in the one-word sentence "Is." Among numbers there is only "one"; in time, there is only the eternal, which must be an unchanging single moment, and in space, only the full or universal. Here is a sample of how Parmenides himself summarizes his thought:

> I shall tell you, and you take good care of what I explain: these are the only ways of inquiry one may conceive. The one way of "Is" and "Not being is not," is the way of conviction (for conviction goes with truth); the other way, the way of "Is not" and of "Not being has to be," that way I tell you to be an unexplorable road, because you could nei-

ther conceive the non-existent (this cannot be consummated) nor state it. For conceiving and being are the same. . . . Being is, and nothing is not.[12]

The consequence of Parmenides' conclusions, of course, is that the world we live in, the world we think is real, cannot be real. One of Parmenides' disciples, in fact, was Zeno, who conceived of the famous paradoxes showing that motion is impossible. Although a flying arrow appears to be in motion, for example, it must really be at rest, for it is stationary at every (infinitesimally short) moment of its flight and is therefore stationary throughout its whole flight.[13]

Despite the seeming lunacy of these conclusions, Parmenides is a philosopher to be reckoned with. He is taken seriously by Plato and Aristotle, and the implications of his thinking are fundamental to our thinking about God. The Christian philosophical position that God resides in an eternity in which a single moment is extended in a timeless, unchanging eternity and alone has true being is reminiscent of Parmenides' insights.[14] The identification of God with Being among the Christian Platonists like Augustine is similarly descended from Parmenidean thought. Zeno's paradoxes describing the impossibility of motion remained baffling until Aristotle showed their flaws and were not really laid to rest until the development of the calculus, with its rigorous treatment of infinitesimal quantities.[15]

One might ask what motivated Parmenides to construct so powerful an argument for the impossibility of motion, plurality, and qualities. While it is, of course, impossible to know his motives, some speculations are possible. First, Parmenides may have had an uncanny ability to suspend disbelief in what would have appeared to him, as to us, to be real distinctions between different things, real motion, and the real possibility of negative claims. In writing his *Way of Truth* he would have *seemed* to be moving his hand, *seemed* to be using different words, and *seemed* to be making negative claims, such as the claim that one cannot conceive of a negative claim. The logic of his claims must have seemed insurmountable both to himself and to those who heard them.

Second, in an era when philosophy and systematic thinking were just beginning to be recognized, perhaps Parmenides wished to show that logic was not the be-all and end-all of human discourse. By making logically irrefutable claims that were absurd, he might have been trying to show the weakness or limited applicability of logic, or proving that logical plausibility and truth are quite different, even opposed. Thus Parmenides may have been a sort of fifth column, subverting and discrediting philosophy from within the philosophical enterprise. In the next century, there were apparently sophists of the sort Plato mocks in his dialogue *Euthydemus,* who make all sorts of contrary claims. Plato himself suggests something of this subversive motive for Parmenides in the dialogue *Parmenides,* in which Plato has the philosopher argue with a young Socrates and manipulate him into agreeing to every manner of contradiction. It is possible—to follow this speculation a little further—that Parmenides' aim is to discredit the new philosophical enterprise; but it is also possible that he was endeavoring to demonstrate his own brilliance as well as the craftiness he could impart to his students. After all, think of the power a lawyer might have if he could so manipulate logic as to persuade juries of things contrary to the most obvious experience of their senses! It is clear that the general public in the century following Parmenides suspected clever speakers of having this latter motive, and so we find among rhetoricians a defense of speaking well along with their frequent claims of being plain, simple speakers.[16]

Completely opposed to Parmenides is his contemporary, Heraclitus (fl. 500 B.C.E.), also of noble birth. According to traditional accounts, Heraclitus dedicated his treatise to the Temple of Artemis, evidence that the treatise was not intended either for posterity or even for a Greek audience. It is just as well, since Heraclitus believed that humans are incapable of understanding his rational explanations.[17] In Heraclitus's view, the world consists of an oscillation between opposites in a continuous flux. He writes, "Living and dead are the same, and awake and asleep, and young and old, for the ones, turned over, become the others, and the others again, turning over, become the one." And again, "The cold is heated, the hot cooled, the wet dried, and the arid drenched." Whereas for Parmenides the world is a unitary, unchanging Being, for Heraclitus nothing exists except change and the constant transformation of one thing into another. He declares, "You enter the same river, but other waters flow unto you." Heraclitus elaborates his doctrine of opposites with the metaphor of a harmony, according to which different tensions on a string will produce a beautiful sound. Consider this pair of fragments:

> United pairs are: whole and non-whole, tending together and tending apart, harmonious and discordant; and out of all things one and out of one all things.
> They do not grasp how the tending apart is in concord with itself, the harmony of tension just as in the bow and the lyre.[18]

The principle of harmony, that things opposed to each other work together in a creative way, is one of Heraclitus's central metaphors for the world. Just as in music high notes and low notes, flats and sharps, long notes and short notes all collaborate to form a concordant whole, so too the various opposite forces and conditions of the world harmonize in forming the whole. This truth is apparent in our lives, where hunger and thirst, pain and pleasure, sleep and waking—all opposites—are necessary components of life and health.

Heraclitus's other metaphor for the operation of the universe is war. Whereas for other people war is the god Mars, destroyer of all that is beautiful and dear, the sacker of cities and ravager of fields, for Heraclitus, war is what generates the creative pairing of opposites: "War is all-father and all-king, and he appoints some gods and others to be men; he made some to be slaves and others to be free." As Werner Jaeger puts it, "War thus becomes, in a way, Heraclitus's primary philosophical experience." The underlying reality is a war, everlasting and all-pervasive, between the opposites of the universe. God is for Heraclitus what keeps the eternal war raging, God, the unity of opposites: "God is day-night, winter-summer, war-peace, fullness-hunger. . . . He changes his appearances, just as oil, when blended with perfumes, is named after the smell of each perfume." For Heraclitus the tension created by the oppositions *is* the world.[19]

In the views of these two early philosophers we see the great divide in conceptions of the universe and in conceptions of God. The motionless, timeless world of Parmenides and the world of an ever-changing harmony of opposites conceived by Heraclitus provide two diametrically opposed starting points for later metaphysics and philosophy of religion. Indeed, we can see in the thought of Parmenides and Heraclitus the origins of the perennial debate over whether God is a unitary, unchanging, simple, single entity or a changing, dynamic force. Both views of God present philosophical difficulties that, as we shall see (pp. 111ff.), have inspired attempts to combine them into some less controversial compromise. Whether any of these conceptions of God is compatible with a scientific view of the world is a matter we shall take up in the second part of this book.

EMPEDOCLES

The influence of Empedocles, a profound and original thinker of the mid-fifth century B.C.E., about a half century after Parmenides, has been far-reaching in Western culture. Perhaps responding to Parmenides' concept of changeless Being, his denial of mobility and plurality, and his view that nothing is entirely created or destroyed, Empedocles proposed a scheme by which the world is made up of four elements—fire, earth, air, and water—under the control of a force of attraction and generation called "love" along with a force of repulsion and destruction called "strife." In addition, Empedocles was a religious mystic, believing in the immortality and transmigration of souls. He seems also to have believed in a "holy mind," an incorporeal intelligence pervading the cosmos.[20]

According to Empedocles, four cyclic periods constitute the life of the universe. The first occurs when all four elements are mixed together by love. During the second period, love passes out of the universe and strife enters. While the universe is in this second period, the elements are partially combined, partially separated. After strife has entered sufficiently, in the third period, love is banished altogether, and the elements are separated completely. In the fourth period, love enters, strife begins to move out, and, with the influx of love, the elements are again combined. At any given time, the world exists in one of the dynamic periods, with its particular degree of mingling of love and strife.[21]

Whereas the ancient poet Hesiod saw love as the principle of creation and Heraclitus saw war, Empedocles saw the combination of the two as the creative principle.[22] In so doing he united the view of Parmenides, with its unchanging, perfectly homogeneous sphere, with that of Heraclitus, with his separated but harmonized opposites. For Empedocles, the world consists of these alternating

periods of mixing and separating. He is, perhaps, the first great synthesizer of philosophy. Thus it is not surprising that Aristotle was especially fond of Empedocles, citing only Plato more frequently in his many references to philosophers.
Empedocles' two principles provide an explanation for rest and motion, the fundamental question of ancient physics. Cosmic love is the cause of rest; strife, the
cause of motion. There is no reduction to all rest or all motion, as in Parmenides
or Heraclitus. Empedocles' theory provides also for an alternative to the choice
of either absolute rest or absolute motion, an alternative in which they are combined and in which the world is permitted to exist in the form we know it. The elements themselves are unchanging and eternal; what seem to be generation and
destruction are really the processes of mixing and separation. The concept is not
entirely unlike the modern scientific view of enduring particles of matter that get
recycled and remixed into everything from stars to living things over vast periods
of time by various attractive and repulsive forces.

One must be careful in thinking about the names that Empedocles gives to his
constituent elements. The material elements—earth, air, fire, and water—he calls
daimones (spirits) and the forces, *love* and *strife*. Whether he intends these appella-
tions to be metaphorical (like our "charmed" and "strange" quarks) is, of course, impossible to know. Ancients do identify what they believed to be natural impulses or
forces of nature with gods. Aphrodite or Venus is sex; Dionysus, drunkenness; Zeus,
the weather.[23] It is often difficult to tell how seriously to take metaphors, especially
religious ones, when scientists use them to describe nature. When, for example, Einstein says that God does not play dice with the universe, is he speaking metaphorically, and if so, what is the meaning of the metaphor?[24] Even if he were referring to
God as a principle of ordered rationality and not as some kind of creator-deity, is not
this a religious view—indeed, not unlike that of Empedocles?

DEMOCRITUS

The idea that there are indivisible atoms of matter is attributed to Leucippus (circa
425 B.C.E.) and Democritus (b. 460–457 B.C.E.). Although the original insight might
well belong to Leucippus, our ancient sources do not clearly distinguish what was
properly Leucippus's and what was Democritus's. Because Democritus is generally recognized to have developed the insight into a complete theory with implications for physics, ethics, biology, epistemology, and politics, we shall use the name
Democritus to refer to the entangled Leucippus-Democritus composite. One of the
consequences of the passage of time, alas, and of the neglect that attends less
prominent thinkers, is that their distinct personalities are lost in the fog of ages.

Democritus offered yet another solution to Parmenides' denial of plurality and
motion. One of the logical consequences of Parmenides' idea that nonbeing cannot exist is that there can be no empty space. Emptiness of course, would be nothing, and, as Parmenides observed, nothing cannot be. (In modern times, the ques-

tion takes the form of whether a vacuum can exist.) If, however, the universe is completely full—if it is what is called a *plenum*—then there can be no motion. The world would be like a telephone booth crowded with playful teenagers, so packed that no one could move in it in any direction. As a solution to this conundrum, Democritus proposed that in addition to matter there exists what he calls "void," also sometimes translated as "vacuity" or "empty space." The void allows for plurality by separating the bits of matter and allows for motion by giving matter space in which to move.

In Democritus's universe the bits of matter separated by void are called *atoms*, tiny, indivisible units, themselves unchanging and eternal—miniature Parmenidean spheres, as it were. The Greek word *atom*, in fact, means "unsplittable." These atoms, constantly in motion through the void, make up different macroscopic objects by their different combinations, just as different structures may be made out of different combinations of identical Lego blocks. Also like Lego blocks, the atoms differ in shape and size. Everything is constructed out of these atoms—mountains, rivers, bodies, souls, even gods. Visual and auditory images are made of atoms too. Finally, according to Democritus, there is an infinite number of atoms.

How, we might wonder, did Democritus come up with the theory of atoms? Because he could not see atoms directly, they were an intellectual model, devised by genius alone, that resulted from various thought experiments and from attempts to make sense of such observed phenomena as plurality and motion. Because matter is divisible into smaller and smaller pieces, one might think that the process of division could in principle go on forever. Perhaps because so far as we can see, every bit of matter is capable of being divided, the indivisible units of matter must be invisibly small. In any case, Democritus assumes that there must be an end to smallness, an absolute smallness that defines the units of matter. Like the existence of a void, this absolute smallness is established as a premise. The existence of all sorts of invisible things, such as wind, smells, and sounds, lends credibility to the idea that there are also invisibly small, indivisible units of matter.

Aristotle will object to the Democritean scheme on two grounds. First he says that any single piece of matter, no matter how small, is able to be divided, at least potentially. Second, he says that there cannot be an infinite number of atoms, for such an actual infinity is impossible. Thus Aristotle's distinction between potential infinity and actual infinity is employed to criticize atomism.

Whereas Democritus introduces atoms to avoid the repugnant notion of infinite divisibility, his notion of the void results from an inversion of Parmenides' argument against motion. Whereas Parmenides argued that, because nonbeing cannot be, motion is impossible, Democritus argued the reverse: because motion is observed all the time and is therefore possible, there must be a sort of nonbeing—void—that makes motion possible. He cut the Gordian knot of Parmenides' problem, not by denying that motion requires nonbeing, but by refusing to deny the existence of motion and therefore accepting the "being" of the void. One might perhaps compare Democritus to Samuel Johnson discussing Bishop Berkeley's proof of the nonexistence of matter. Describing the moment, James Boswell writes, "I observed, that though we are satisfied that his doctrine is not true, it is impossible to refute it. I shall never forget the alacrity with which Johnson answered, striking his foot with mighty force against a large stone, till he rebounded from it, 'I refute it thus.'"[25]

Democritus also has to account for how atoms actually combine into things rather than collect in a pile at the bottom of the universe. His proposal is that the constant motion of atoms enables them to fulfill their function. Both their absolute motion in the universe and their motion relative to one another account for the coming into being and going out of being of everything. Nothing is created or destroyed; atoms are simply rearranged. Furthermore, the rearrangement is, ultimately, random. This universe, with its particular arrangements of atoms, did not have to come to be as it is; all of its atomic configurations originate by chance. For all we know, there may be many other worlds, with many other configurations of atoms.

As to the question of where the motion of atoms originates, Democritus avoids the issue entirely by taking eternal motion as a given. With regard to the question of why atoms collide rather than fall straight down, a later atomist, Epicurus, asserts that occasionally atoms swerve on their own, and so, instead of falling in parallel descents, collide and thereby combine. The swerve also accounts for the appearance of what seems to be free will. This solution, of course, begs the question, for it does not explain how the swerve itself comes to be. Hence, the reflective Cicero rightly rejects the notion of the swerve as an arbitrary contrivance.[26]

Although the physical system of Democritus constitutes a brilliant proposal that embraces a non-teleological explanation of causes, it does not explain the source of motion or of atoms (other than by stipulating that they have no source), does not satisfactorily account for how atoms collide, and does not provide a philosophically satisfying explanation of how nonbeing in the guise of the void can exist. In short, it addresses specific problems in Parmenides in a groundbreaking but explanatorily incomplete manner.

What are the theological and ethical implications of atomism? Most importantly, the Democritean view seems to reduce the universe to purposelessness and meaninglessness, despite the existence of gods. The atomists believe in the existence of gods, albeit atomistic ones. After all, if atoms can combine to create men, then atoms can combine to create gods.[27] The gods of the atomists are bright, beautiful, radiant creatures—like characters in a Noel Coward play—who inhabit the interstellar spaces, lead lives of transcendent happiness, and never give the slightest thought to men. Given the gods' lack of concern for human beings, no atomist ever dreams of praying to the gods. He might, of course, try to imitate them, for they embody the Democritean ethical ideal of cheerfulness. If the universe is meaningless and purposeless, one might as well try to be cheerful.

What is cheerfulness for an atomist? The atomist must first understand how the physical system works. Once he understands the theory of atoms and the void, he can see that the universe is meaningless and that certain ethical consequences follow. For one thing, attempting to do anything that has meaning is meaningless. There is no sense, Epicurus argued, in engaging in what we today call "meaningful activity," in aiming for a career, for fame, for wealth, for power, for success. Stay out of community activities, the atomists say. For an atomist, citizens who fight for their country or who participate in political affairs are foolish. The moment they become involved, the moment they care about an issue—any issue— they have sacrificed their happiness. In the face of these seemingly grim considerations, cheerfulness is achieved in the liberating realization that meaning need not be actively pursued, that death need not be feared because it is simply the re-forming of atoms into other objects with no afterlife full of horrible punishments.

For Democritus, the ultimate standards of happiness are pleasure and pain. His aim is lasting pleasure, pleasure that will not ultimately lead to pain. But sensual pleasures are short-lived and invariably lead to pain: drinking leads to hangovers; sexual liaisons, to physical and emotional suffering. The only true pleasures are those of philosophy, which for the atomists consists fundamentally of friendship, though friendship without the kind of intensity of feeling that can lead to great pain. The friendship of the later atomists known as Epicureans is famous, and justly so. In the face of a meaningless and purposeless universe, what pleasure is there greater and more lasting than that of friendship?

CONCLUSION

Although we have not by any means given a complete account of the pre-Socratic philosophers and their various theories, it is possible, perhaps, to draw some general conclusions about their approach to philosophy. Working with their minds and with the evidence of their unaided senses, the early philosophers from Miletus and elsewhere in the Greek world tried to comprehend the material and dynamic forces of the cosmos. In doing so they anticipated many of the questions that continue to puzzle scientists: are the underlying principles one or few or many? Does change take place by an alteration of accidental qualities such as color and shape, or do the fundamental principles themselves undergo an essential metamorphosis? Is there in physical reality a particle so small and unitary that it cannot be divided? How is motion possible and what are its limits? The pre-Socratics shared with one another, and with modern physicists, the view that because the universe is intelligible and orderly, its wonders yield to human intelligence. For the atomists, all structures are the result of chance collisions, but this very fact about chance is able to be known—and in this sense even chance yields to human reason. One implication of the view of the universe's intelligibility is that the universe exists outside the will or caprice of an independent deity whose mode of operations is his own desire. For these thinkers, either the deity is like the gods of atomism—uninterested and uninvolved in the universe—or, as seems to be the case for Thales and Heraclitus, the deity is itself identical with the order and system of the cosmos.

Despite its genius, pre-Socratic philosophy is fundamentally flawed. The major theories are largely independent guesses at the principles of nature. If a part of one theory turned out to be clearly unsatisfactory, a later thinker would come along with a new theory that would substitute for the unsatisfactory element a new principle designed to resolve the difficulty. But there was no experimentation whatsoever, no steady refinement or progress in the course of knowledge. The theories stand with the names of their authors like works of sculpture in a museum, with no sense of approaching closer and closer to the truth. Perhaps because the thinkers did not have much of a scientific vocabulary at their disposal, they relied too heavily on easily misleading metaphors to stretch their meaning.

In any case, the writings did not survive long as works worth copying. What we possess remains because it was included in summaries by later thinkers, such as Aristotle, who present only a partial précis of what the pre-Socratics said. Moreover, these summaries are often neither accurate nor fair, but are shaped so as to render more acceptable the summarizer's own views. Thus, in most cases, the full original meaning has been lost. Still, to ask questions, to frame inquiries, to wonder about nature as the early philosophers did is one of the great achievements of the human race. When Thales speculated that the fundamental principle of nature is water, he initiated a process of mental activity that would change human life on our planet. His idea that a human mind can explore the secrets of nature because those secrets are at bottom intelligible was a fruitful idea that multiplied, first in Miletus and then in the rest of the Hellenic world, in those minds in which it found a fertile soil.

As we have noted, most pre-Socratic philosophers were concerned somehow to fit the gods into their understanding of nature. In the following chapter, we shall look at early philosophical attempts to understand the nature of God or the gods. We shall end this section of the book with the Neoplatonists, who are the last ancient thinkers to try to avoid conflict with religion by means of a philosophically consistent definition of God. Then we shall proceed to consider attempts to reconcile the existence of God with the conclusions of philosophy and science.

DISCUSSION QUESTIONS

1. It is common for people to explain complicated things in terms that are more familiar. These terms are often metaphors that lend insight into one quality or another of the thing being explained. For example, when Antonio in the *Merchant of Venice* says, "I hold the world . . . as / A stage where every man must play a part, / And mine a sad one" (1.1.81–83), he is suggesting that just as characters in a play do not write their own scripts but must mouth the words and act the role the playwright has assigned—*and hence are not responsible for the qualities that they exhibit*—so Antonio himself has no choice about his sadness. Though Antonio, in using the simile, aims at this single point of his own inability to control his sadness, the

simile nevertheless reflects a worldview, the view that things are predetermined and that people lack the ability to change them. When pre-Socratic philosophers use metaphors to explain nature, are they also inadvertently introducing views that extend beyond the particular point they are making? Can you think of any modern *explanatory* metaphors that have taken on a life of their own, overshadowed the original clarifying similitude, and ultimately done more harm than good to understanding?

2. What difference, if any, does it make to our valuation of our own bodies, and hence to our own self-image, if our bodies are made up of recombined forms of the same single substance or of a wide variety of different primary substances?

3. Of the various theories concerning the number of elements and the functioning of nature, why was the theory of Empedocles the most attractive?

4. From its very start, science has dealt not only with a snapshot description of the current instantaneous state of nature but with the processes of change. The contrasting conclusions of Parmenides and Heraclitus—that change is an illusion and that sameness is an illusion—suggest that each was carving out as extreme a position as possible, as though in a debating contest. Is such competition productive of clarity or does it confuse issues—or does it do some of both?

5. We moderns are perhaps most partial to the thought of Democritus, for it seems most to resemble contemporary theories of physics. But Democritus's theory had less influence on Western civilization than many of the competing theories. What are the features of ancient atomism that rendered it implausible? Was there any way that Democritus could have repaired its deficiencies, or were both its strengths and weaknesses inherent parts of the system?

6. Einstein is said to have engaged in thought experiments that clarified problems and suggested solutions to profoundly difficult questions in physics. The pre-Socratics also engaged in what we might call thought experiments, yet their theories did not prove fertile or inspire further thought. What might account for the success of Einstein's thought experiments? Are there questions in modern science that can be addressed purely by thought, without the need for evidence (*evidence* here being understood consistently with its etymology, as something *seen*)? Does evidence ever impede the search for scientific knowledge? In other words, does what we *can* see sometimes occult, or hide, important facts that we *can not* see? For example, did the "rising" and "setting" of the sun occult the heliocentrism of the planetary system? Did Aristarchus, and later Copernicus, engage in "thought experiments" before offering an alternative to geocentrism?

NOTES

1. For example, the *Republic* deals with metaphysics (the theory of forms), the *Parmenides* with logic, the *Theaetetus* with knowledge, the *Cratylus* with language, and so on.

2. Herodotus, *The History,* 1.74. With regard to reports of successful but isolated predictions, there is always the possibility of a selection effect in the reporting, i.e., there could have been numerous eclipse predictions mathematically on a par with that of Thales but unsuccessful and hence unreported. Thales may just have gotten lucky.

3. Simplicius says that Thales was the first to reveal the correct way of inquiring about nature. Simplicius and Theophrastus say that Thales had many predecessors (though they do not name them) but agree that Thales was so far superior to them as to eclipse them all. The comment is reminiscent of a similar metaphor in one of Sappho's lyric poems, in which she says that her lover's beauty is like that of the moon, which hides all the stars when it comes out.

4. Aristotle, *Metaphysics,* 983b19ff.

5. Aristotle, *Metaphysics,* 983b22.

6. Aristotle, *On the Soul,* 405a19.

7. Aristotle, *On the Soul,* 411a7.

8. Aetius 1.7.11, quoted in G. S. Kirk and J. E. Raven, *The Presocratic Philosophers* (Cambridge: Cambridge University Press, 1966), 95–96.

9. Aristotle, *Metaphysics,* 996a17.

10. Strictly speaking, some negatives are possible if we take them as metaphors. For example, if we say, "The house is not blue," there is an implication that it is another color—green, red, or white—in other words that it is a color *different* from blue. But this difference is an inference in the mind of the person understanding the sentence, a metaphorical transference of the precise meaning of "not blue." "Not blue" by itself in an absolute sense is not a concept that can be pictured in the mind. If one hears "not blue" and has an image of "green" in his mind, then what he is thinking of is "green," not "not blue." That we understand "something different" when we hear a negation is, of course, the main insight in Plato's dialogue *Sophist.*

11. Parmenides, frag. 8.

12. Parmenides, frag. 2.

13. Another paradox states that it will be impossible to move from point A to point B, for before one arrives at B one must go to a point C that is halfway between A and B, and before C to a point D that is halfway between A and C, and so on in smaller and smaller steps—so that one never actually moves from A to B even in an infinity of time. This paradox is reminiscent of a joke about a beautiful woman, an engineer, and a mathematician. The beautiful woman says, "I am yours. Just walk over to me. But each step you take in my direction must be half the one before." The mathematician understands that under these conditions he will never reach her and gives up. The engineer, however, walks over to her and embraces her. The joke was undoubtedly invented by an engineer. It embodies the old conflict between pure and practical science, or, in medieval terms, between superlunary metaphysics and sublunary reality.

14. For a description of the Christian concept of eternity, see E. Stump and N. Kretzmann, "Eternity," *The Journal of Philosophy* 78 (1981): 429–58.

15. For Aristotle's treatment of Zeno's paradoxes, see *Physics,* 239b5–240b7.

16. Socrates, for example, in Plato's *Apology,* begins his speech to the jury by claiming to be—unlike his opponents—a "plain speaker interested only in the truth" (Plato, *Apology,* 17B).

17. See Heraclitus, frags. 1, 17, 34, 56, 57, and 107.

18. Heraclitus, frags. 10 and 51. The three preceding quotations are, respectively, from frags. B88, B126, and B12.

19. The quotations from Heraclitus are from frags. 53 and 67; that from Werner Jaeger is from *The Theology of the Early Greek Philosophers* (New York: Oxford University Press, 1967), 118.

20. Empedocles, frags. 133–34.

21. There is some debate among scholars concerning the number of creative periods. Either there are two such periods, when either Love or Strife is gaining the upper hand, or there is only one. See Jean Bollack, *Empedocle* (Paris: Éditions de Minuit, 1965).

22. For Hesiod's views, see *Theogony,* 120.

23. As we can see from Euripides' *Bacchae,* drunkenness is conceived as a natural force, violated at the great risk of offending the god Dionysus.

24. We discuss Einstein's views on science and religion in chapter 13, pp. 243–43.

25. Boswell, *Life of Johnson,* 1.545.

26. Cicero, *De Finibus,* 6.19, *De Fato,* 22.46–48.

27. Democritus, frag. 166.

The God of Ancient Philosophers

Imagine a bedbug completely flattened out, living on the surface of the globe. This bedbug may be gifted with analysis, he may study physics, he may even write a book. His universe will be two-dimensional.

—Albert Einstein

XENOPHANES' GOD

Xenophanes (570–478 B.C.E.) lived as an exile from about the age of twenty-five, when he left his native city of Colophon in Asia Minor. It is no wonder that he left home: he was an independent thinker and a cheerful critic of his culture's values. Although he speaks of the rewards that will come to someone who wins a victory in the Olympic Games—free board at public expense or a rich treasure— he protests that no athletic skill is as good as his wit. The victorious athlete will "not fatten the storehouses of the city." Xenophanes could have addressed his lament as well today, for some things have not changed: we reward our athletes— at least with earthly gold—far more than we do our scholars.[1]

Xenophanes also offers a biting criticism of his contemporaries' conception of the gods. He writes, "Homer and Hesiod attributed to the gods whatever is shameful and blameworthy in the eyes of men, stealing, adultery, and deceiving one another."[2] The passage is significant for its theological implications. Xenophanes declares that the standard of the gods' character must not be tradition, nor perhaps even faith, but moral purity. The statement goes beyond an attack on mere anthropomorphism. Xenophanes declares that behaving in a way that we would frown upon in human beings is incompatible with the essence of divinity and that therefore the poets are wrong. In other words, he boldly asserts that we can make claims about the divine based on standards discoverable by reason. The gods do not commit adultery, steal, or deceive, because these actions are intrinsically wrong. He suggests, moreover, that the gods live according to a standard beyond their will. Adultery is not wrong because the gods declare it to be wrong; it is wrong, and the gods do not engage in it because it violates an objective standard. The gods too are subject to law. They are, in a sense, less free than the king of Persia, whose will itself is the law.[3]

In a series of three fragments, he exposes the fallacies in anthropomorphic thinking:

Mortals think that gods are born and have human dress and voice and form.
Negroes imagine the gods to be snub-nosed and black; Thracians, blue-eyed and red-haired.
If bulls and horses and lions had hands, and were able to paint with their hands and make sculptures as men do, then they would paint the form of the gods, the horses like horses, the bulls like bulls, and mold their bodies such as they themselves have.[4]

Here Xenophanes shows how human beings cannot help but think of their gods in terms of themselves. To make the point most satirically, he crosses the boundary that separates humans from other animals and says that nonhuman animals would make their gods look like themselves, just as we humans do. Xenophanes' insight is valid enough to be taken beyond species to fashion. One need only look at the various artistic renderings of the goddess Venus throughout history to see how her face and figure follow the current fashions of what is beautiful. The artists Oggiano, Carracci, Canach, and Titian reveal their own ideals of feminine sexuality in their portrayals of the Greek goddess. If one looks at portrayals of the other gods, one will note that in Renaissance painting the pagan gods resemble no one so much as fashionable courtiers of the artists' era and locale. Similarly, in the historical films of the 1930s, historical accuracy is gone with the wind as actors and actresses wear their hair and makeup in the style of, well, the 1930s. Is not the God of the Sistine Chapel a mere few years older and grayer than his Adam? The silliness of anthropomorphizing God seems self-evident as soon as one reads Xenophanes' witty comments.

In a great monotheistic insight, Xenophanes claims that God must be wholly different from both the common conception of divinities and from men: "One god, greatest among gods as among men, not the equal of mortals in form or mind." Xenophanes reasons that it is as foolish to anthropomorphize a god in mental as in physical form. Whatever God is, he must be wholly different from mortals in all his characteristics and capabilities. Xenophanes describes God's intellectual difference: "As a whole he sees, as a whole he perceives, as a whole he hears." Whereas humans can see only parts, never wholes, God has utterly different capabilities. In using words evocative of our most intellectual sensory faculty—sight—Xenophanes stresses his deity's intelligence. In addition, "He remains forever in the same condition, changing not at all; it is not fitting for him to pursue now this and now that; with no effort, by the mind of his thought, he agitates all things."⁵ Here Xenophanes' God seems quite Parmenidean. Xenophanes' God does not move, perhaps because movement implies a lack of completeness or perhaps a better and worse location; for Xenophanes God must always be the same, always perfect. If he did pursue now this and now that, he would perhaps be less than perfect (for one pursues only what one lacks or desires; and if one lacks or desires anything, one is imperfect). The activity of Xenophanes' God is mental; he can even move things with his mind. The notion is perhaps not unlike that in Genesis, where God, in saying "let there be light," creates by simple fiat. We should note that Xenophanes says that God agitates *all* things. The philosopher is not speaking of a local deity, who serves only a part of the earth. He is speaking of one God for the entire cosmos.

Xenophanes extends his mockery of anthropomorphism to anthropocentrism: "If god had not caused yellow honey to be produced, people would pronounce figs so much sweeter."⁶ We humans judge sweetness by what we ourselves experience, making the sweetest food with which we are familiar into the ideal, the standard of sweetness. If it happens that a less sweet food is the sweetest that we have, then that lower degree of sweetness would be the ideal. In short, we set up anthropocentric ideals, ones relative to our acquaintance and not to truth. This concept rejects the ubiquitous human practice of basing judgments on experience. In ridiculing and rejecting anthropocentric standards, Xenophanes does not, however, go so far as to postulate an absolute grounded in a transcendent being.

Xenophanes' view of the arts departs from the tone of dismissal of certain human tendencies. Most of the other ancients believed that gods reveal the arts to humans. Demeter gives the cultivation of grains; Dionysus gives wine-making; and Athena gives weaving. Mythological stories describe how the gods teach these arts. One implication of this view is that the various arts are given to mankind already whole, developed, and perfected. One consequence of this belief is a disinclination to try to improve the arts by inventiveness. After all, if a god has given an art, it must be perfect, and to attempt progress or development would be foolish. Xenophanes rejects this view of the gods: "Not all things in the beginning did the gods reveal to mortal men, but men by searching in time find out what is better."⁷ Here, in the idea of "searching in time" lies the implication of our modern idea of progress. The arts of civilization did not come as the complete, wholly formed gift of the gods, but have been worked out by human beings. If in his other writing Xenophanes diminishes man by taking away his commonness with the gods and his control of standards, here he gives man the power to progress and to develop the arts himself. Of course, attached to this power is an implied imperfection, for progress always aims at improvement, and the capacity for improvement implies a lack of perfection.

One of the views of the Pythagoreans, an ancient group that divided its interests between mathematics and mysticism, is the reincarnation and transmigration of souls, a view with which Xenophanes has little sympathy. As Xenophanes reports, "They say that once Pythagoras passed a puppy that was being maltreated. He took pity and spoke thus: 'Stop beating it, for it is the soul of a dear friend; I recognized the soul by its voice.'"[8] As is his method, Xenophanes exposes the silliness of a view by painting an extreme version of it. In this case, he seems to be mocking his friend also, who has returned as a dog.

Xenophanes expresses unequivocally the limitations of human access to knowledge of the divine.

> No man has seen it clearly, nor will there be any one who has a real (first-hand) knowledge of the gods and of all the things I discuss. For even if one should happen to set them forth ever so perfectly, yet he does it without personal (first-hand) knowledge. However, an opinion is formed for everything. (God, on the other hand, has direct and real knowledge of everything.)[9]

Here we find the great difference between men and God. Man cannot see through to the truth of things. Trapped in humanity, trapped in relativism, he can judge only on the basis of himself. How different is Xenophanes from the Greek poets, for whom the gods are merely more powerful and deathless humans! Heraclitus, to be sure, had said, "Man is considered as infantile by God, just as a boy by a man."[10] But the gulf between man, who sees and understands nothing clearly, and God, who has direct knowledge of everything, is much wider in Xenophanes.

Despite the brilliance of his insights, Xenophanes seems to have had no followers and his deity no worshippers. Xenophanes did find support for his views a century later, in Plato, whose dialogue *Symposium* might be considered a supplement to Xenophanes' attack on anthropomorphizing the gods. In the *Symposium,* Socrates and a diverse collection of his friends engage in a rhetorical contest in which each gives a speech describing and praising *Eros,* the god of sexual desire. What is most conspicuous in the dialogue is the way each draws a picture of the god that resembles the speaker. For example, the physician Eryximachus describes *Eros* as a physician; the tragedian Agathon describes *Eros* as a dainty tragic poet like himself; and finally Socrates, who gives the longest and most spectacular speech, describes *Eros*—sexual desire!—as a bare-footed philosopher like Socrates. It is likely that Plato was trying to expose the silliness of making a deity in the image of humans, and particularly in the image of whoever is speaking (thus making himself the ideal of sexual desire). Perhaps Plato's point is more serious, namely, that if we *do* make a god in the image of a human, we ought to be sure to pick the best human, and that a god who resembles the manly Socrates is superior to one who resembles the dandy Agathon. A strong case can nevertheless be made that Plato is making the Xenophanic point, especially in view of his other comments about the nature of God, to which we shall attend presently.

PLATO'S GOD

One of the best known discussions in Plato's dialogues of the divine attributes takes place in the *Euthyphro*. The dramatic setting is the grounds of the courthouse, where Socrates must answer an indictment on a charge of corrupting youth and of not believing in the city's gods. There he meets young Euthyphro, who is bringing charges against his father for having allowed a slave to die. The two discuss the nature of piety, a subject about which Euthyphro is convinced he is an expert. Socrates says he wishes to avail himself of Euthyphro's theological brilliance and asks the young man to tell him what piety is.

Euthyphro says that "piety" is to prosecute the wrongdoer. As proof he offers the examples of Zeus, who chained his father Cronus for swallowing his other children, and of Cronus, who had his own father Uranus castrated. Euthyphro claims that in prosecuting his father, he is simply following the example of the gods. At this point Socrates says that people believe him to be impious for the very reason that he does not believe such stories. A bit later, when Euthyphro changes his mind and says that piety is what is pleasing to the gods, Socrates points out that in the traditional stories, which Euthyphro believes, the gods are continually quarreling with one another, for what pleases one does not please another. By Euthyphro's definition of piety, the same thing would at once be both pious and impious, for it would please one god and not please another.

It is by such arguments that we can perhaps snatch a glimpse of Plato's theological views. We say "perhaps," because the only writing we have by Plato, aside from a few letters the authenticity of which is hotly contested, is dialogues, in which Plato never speaks in his own person. Moreover, his various characters, including Socrates, are not always consistent or admirable or entirely scrupulous in their logic. Hence we can only guess at Plato's own views. Where Plato returns to the same themes again and again, however, we can be sure that these subjects occupy his thoughts, and where the arguments are solid, we can, perhaps, assume that he tends to agree with them. We can reasonably assume that Plato rejects entirely the view of the gods that we find in Greek literature. These are gods who intervene continuously in human life, who commit adultery among themselves and with human men and women, who steal and commit other crimes. These are gods who become angry and experience the full range of human emotions, no matter how petty or self-destructive those emotions are. They feel pain and sorrow, prefer personal revenge to justice, show favorites, and mock and deceive one another. In Plato's likely view, however, as we see in Socrates' encounter with Euthyphro, the gods must be just and wise and possessed of every virtue. It is not possible for them to disagree, because they all want the same goodness and truth. In short, God for Plato cannot be anthropomorphic, cannot be human.

It does not appear that Plato's views on divine nature are an advance on those of Xenophanes, for they are not in fact different from them. In chapter 6, when we take a look at Plato's *Timaeus,* one of the most influential philosophical works ever written, we shall see Plato's words penetrate into the traditions of revealed religions and contribute fundamentally to the principal Western tradition as we know it. The *Timaeus,* which describes the creation of the universe and of man and includes the operations of God, is not strictly *about* God. For his specific views on God, we can safely say that for Plato God must be logically consistent and morally good. For a complex, rich, and detailed Greek conception of God, we must turn to Aristotle.

ARISTOTLE'S GOD

In working out a conception of God in the *Metaphysics,* Aristotle tries to address a few difficult questions about the kind of knowledge that metaphysics treats. His general technique is to distinguish the subject matter of metaphysics, which for him is the "first philosophy," from other and for him lesser disciplines. After examining Aristotle's conclusions with these questions in mind, we shall assess Aristotle's successes and failures.

At the beginning of the *Metaphysics* Aristotle distinguishes between experience and art. Experience, he says, is knowledge of individual things. We experience individual roses or individual people with the flu, and we know about them in particular. Art, on the other hand, is knowledge of universals. The man who knows about *all* roses—the horticulturist—and the person who knows about *all* people who have the flu—the physician—possess arts. In other words, people who have experience understand the fact *that* something is the way it is, that a particular rose has a fungus or that a particular child has the flu. In addition, Aristotle continues, the people who possess an art understand *why* the rose has the fungus or the child the flu; in short the person of art has knowledge of the causes.[11]

Because a knowledge of plants in general or of horticulture generally, or of all diseases or of medicine generally, is greater than the narrower specialties, the people who have more universal knowledge, says Aristotle, are wise in a higher sense.[12] He says too that the most universal things are on the whole the hardest to understand because they are furthest removed from our experience. What he means is that we start with sensations of individual things and proceed to concepts by a process of abstraction. As the concepts become more and more abstract, since the more abstract concept is developed from the less abstract, the most universal concepts are farthest from sensation. We can trace the course of one child's growth or of one tree at a time, for example, but strictly universal knowledge cannot, unfortunately, be obtained by experience alone, for it is obviously impossible to have experience of all children or of all trees, and so, for Aristotle, universal knowledge must be of concepts.[13] The laws of physics, being as universal as knowledge can be, often represent radical generalizations that depart totally from sense experience, as befits their typically mathematical formulation. A formula like $e = mc^2$, for example, is far more remote from experience than the growth of a single tree.

Continuing to develop his description of metaphysics, Aristotle adds that the most accurate sciences are concerned with first causes, and these are knowable in the highest degree, for it is because of them that other things are known.[14] Given the Aristotelian view that the highest knowledge is of first causes and is most universal, we can see that, according to Aristotle, the field of metaphysics is divine in two ways. Its ultimate subject matter is the first cause of the universe, and that first cause, God, alone possesses the highest knowledge.

Aristotle's views of God are thus in two important respects compatible with those of Western revealed religions. God is the first cause insofar as he does things and produces effects and is not himself caused by something else. At the same time, God has knowledge and perhaps is the only possessor of universal knowledge. The first view, whether in its Aristotelian or modern forms, is of course compatible with even the most materialistic science, depending on how willing one is to define God materialistically, e.g., as the Big Bang or some other initiating cause. The second view is open to the objection that it anthropomorphizes God, giving him a cognitive faculty akin to, even if much superior to, that of mankind.

For Aristotle's other views of God, we must turn to book 12 of the *Metaphysics.* Although Aristotle's views are subtle, they repay careful study, for they reflect the most profound and historically influential philosophical discussion of God in the West. Aristotle's definition of God in shorthand form as the "Prime Mover" is justifiably famous. What exactly this Prime Mover is and how it works is not, however, widely known. To understand the Prime Mover, we must begin with Aristotle's idea of the kind of thing that can move other things, for then we shall understand the kind of thing that defines all movers, including the Prime Mover. Aristotle's theory assumes, of course, that there *is* motion in the universe; everything is based on this assumption, which, despite Parmenides' views, is for Aristotle (as for most of us) observationally evident.

When we inquire about motion, says Aristotle, we are not asking about the efficient cause of motion itself, for motion has no efficient cause: it is uncaused and eternal. Particular motions, of course, are caused by other particular motions. The rustling leaves are caused by the wind, which itself is caused by other winds. But nothing moves motion in general. This means that there never was a time when motion began. In the same way, time must have always existed, and the terms *before* and *after* are meaningless with respect to an (imaginary) period in which there is no time.[15] By this argument, there is no reason for the motion ever to have had a beginning or ever to have an end.

Let us recall, just for a moment, that Parmenides denies all motion and all coming into being. He bases this denial on the idea that if something comes into being, either it has to come from something that is—in which case it would already be—or it has to come from something that is not—an impossibility, since nothing can come from nothing.[16] Aristotle attacks Parmenides' dilemma by distinguishing between actuality and potentiality. Every object has the potentiality to become something else. For example, an acorn has the potentiality to become an oak, and it becomes one by actualizing its potentiality to be one. In a sense, the potentiality to become an oak actually *is* in the acorn, as is the oak's potentiality to be made into a table or chairs or a bookcase. In the sense that the potentiality has being, Parmenides is correct. Aristotle thus says that Parmenides is right insofar as nothing comes into being *absolutely* out of nothing. Things do come into being out of what they are not, but, for Aristotle, the things they are not exist potentially, even if not actually. Thus the oak comes into being out of a thing that is potentially but not actually an oak (but is actually an acorn).[17]

What sort of being is capable of turning potentiality into actuality? It must be something that, in a broad sense, moves the thing and is different from the thing itself. In order to understand this idea, we must first look at Aristotle's conception of matter. For Aristotle, *matter* is what is left when all form is removed. Because matter is experienced only in some form or other, and never by itself, it is impossible to give an example of pure matter.[18] Perhaps it will be helpful, though, to explain the meaning by analogy. A gold statue is made up of a matter or material called gold. But it is not a statue until it receives a form. When it receives a form, it is what Aristotle calls a composite of matter and form. Before the gold is formed into a statue, it has some *other* form (unlike the pure matter), e.g., as a cube, bar, or collection of ingots.

Trying to think of gold itself without any form is like thinking of water or gas apart from the particular shape they take from the receptacle that contains them. Each of the things we make out of gold—statues, cups, dishes, guns, etc.—is distinguishable from other things made out of gold *by its form*. We make a statue out of gold by getting the gold to have a certain form. We do not start with some gold on the one hand and some form on the other, and then put the two together. No form is ever separable from its matter, any more than matter is capable of existing without some form. We cannot take the form out of the gold statue and leave just the gold over here and the form over there: all we can do is destroy the form, as when we melt the gold statue and thereby impart a new form to the gold. Even if the newly formed gold lacks the aesthetic excellence of a statue, it has a form nonetheless.

By considering the relationship between form and matter, we can further clarify the meaning of the term *matter.* Suppose we take a wooden chair as our example. The matter is wood; the form in which the matter appears to us is the form of a chair. Suppose that we chop the chair up into small pieces with an ax. We can see at once that we have destroyed the form of the chair—that is, the remnants of wood no longer look like, or can be used as, a chair. But the remnants of the chair are still wood—that is, the matter has not changed. Now suppose that we take another wooden chair, but instead of chopping it up with an ax, we burn it. Once again, we can see that the form of the chair has been destroyed. In addition, however, the matter of the chair—the wood—has been changed: in destroying the form, we do not end up with wood but with ashes (and some gases, as well, although they dissipate and are not easily detectable). Now ashes are not wood—that is, we cannot take the ashes and, using the techniques of carpentry, make a chair out of them. But the ashes are matter (in the form, perhaps, of a loose pile on the floor), and we can take the matter that is ashes and do something with it.

If we reflect on this imaginary experiment, we can see that both the wood and the ashes are what Aristotle calls "proximate" or "intermediate" matter, not ultimate or final matter. The reason is that wood and ashes have different characteristics — different forms — that enable them to be distinguished, characteristics having to do with their respective smell, color, and solidity, for example. Reduce a chair to wood chips or ashes, and you have reduced it to its proximate matter, not to entirely formless, ultimate matter. Underlying both the ashes and the wood is something that is final and ultimate — what Aristotle calls primary matter or what today we might call matter/energy.

Even though ultimate matter has no form in and of itself, there must be such a thing as ultimate matter lying behind all the matter/form composites in the world. If we do not posit ultimate matter, we end up with what Aristotle absolutely and unequivocally set himself and his powerful intellect against: an infinite regress. If the wood can be changed into ashes — which are matter plus form — and if the ashes can be changed into something else that is matter plus form, and if this process can go on indefinitely, we end with an infinite regress of potential changes, with no starting point.

The connection between Aristotle's doctrine of matter and form and the issue of how potentialities become actualities lies in Aristotle's insight that matter is to potentiality what form is to actuality. Gold in the *form* of a statue is an *actual* statue, although in virtue of its matter it has the potentiality of being formed into any number of things. But gold does not spontaneously form into statues, nor acorns into oak trees. States of potentiality must be actualized by someone or something. And the actualizer must itself be in a state of actuality with respect to the form being actualized. The sculptor does not of course have to *be* a golden statue in order to make one, but the form of the statue must be present in his mind before he can render that form in gold.

Natural processes, such as the maturation of oak trees and even the motions of the stars and planets (although these latter motions do not involve matter taking on new forms), are, for Aristotle, made actual by a being that is actual in the highest sense and that uses a special mode of actualization. The key to understanding the most fully actual sort of being and how it works is to appreciate Aristotle's aversion to infinite regress. If *all* motion and actualization were accomplished by transitions from potentiality to actuality, there would be an infinite regress of such transitions and there could never be any *first* motion or actualization. Hence, there must exist a being of pure actuality, one that actualizes and moves *itself,* without the help of anything else and without a hint of potentiality. This self-moved being, moving eternally, is the ultimate source of all motion and actualization in nature.

How does a self-moved being move other beings? In a dazzling insight, Aristotle defines the unmoved mover — unmoved in the sense of self-moved or not moved by anything else, not unmoved in the sense of "not moving" — as the object of *desire.* Aristotle is capitalizing on the fact that a thing may move other things by being the object of their desire. For example, a river may move a woodchuck or a human being to it by offering to fulfill its desire to drink. An astronomer may be moved to study the distant stars by a desire for understanding. Neither the river nor the knowledge the astronomer seeks is itself affected or moved in any way by those who are doing the desiring. Neither is even aware that it is desired. By being the objects of desire, they move others—hence the term *unmoved movers.*

We can easily see the implications of this concept in the human world. As Aristotle observes in the opening of the *Nicomachean Ethics,* every action and every intention aim at some perceived good. Even our actions that are in an absolute sense bad are aiming at *some* good, e.g., pleasure or wealth or fame. For example, the man who smokes is aiming at the good of pleasure or acceptance by his peers; the man who robs a bank is aiming at the good of wealth. But, of course, Aristotle would say that real goods—health or virtue—are rational, whereas goods that are *perceived* to be good but are not actually good are irrational. In the claim that we always aim at some perceived good, and that this good is the object of our desire, Aristotle is right in saying that the good moves us. If the highest good subsumes all lower goods, and if the highest good is identified with God, we can see that the unmoved mover, God, in an important respect does move every action and every intention.

The problem, as Aristotle's student Theophrastus observed, is how "desire" can move lifeless things. This is a real problem, for how can we speak of stars or trees as having desires? The problem is aggravated because the distinction between living and lifeless is not always clear in Aristotle. In *On the Soul,* Aristotle suggests that "living" things are what have self-nourishment, growth, and decay, but in the *Physics* he suggests, with Plato, that self-motion is what distinguishes the living.[19]

Perhaps Aristotle's insight can be made intelligible by taking his reference to desire as metaphorical. Aristotle talks about the natural impulses and natural motions that inhere in a thing's essence—the tendency of rocks to fall and fire to rise, for example—in much the same way that modern scientists speak of the gravitational "attraction" between bodies or the "attraction" between differently charged particles. Similarly, systems "seek" equilibrium, and various cells "seek out" their counterparts. Aristotle's metaphor of desire should not be unintelligible to those familiar with similar metaphors in modern science.

One of the advantages of this notion of "desire" is that it eliminates the need for physical contact between mover and moved. A necessity for such contact would be a significant obstacle to any plausible concept of the unmoved mover, for in most cases we do not experience any physical contact between the object moved and the mover. In the most obvious physical sense, we do not see any physical contact between, say, a rock let go out a window, and the ground to which it is drawn or any physical contact between a celestial object and its orbiting satellite. Today we say that there is gravity, an invisible "unmoved mover," and we believe that gravity is a physical force, even though the mechanism of it is not understood. For an ancient like Aristotle, a psychological force, like desire or its metaphorical extension in lifeless things to powers like "attraction," was an intelligible way of expressing the notion. In the case of gravity, is it so very different to say that objects "have a de-sire" for one another in proportion to their masses?

For Aristotle, the ultimate source of desire in humans is to fulfill our nature by seeking the good. The desire of everything else is, metaphorically speaking, to fulfill their natures or to move and act in accordance with the laws governing them. If we think of God as goodness itself or as the order and system of the cosmos, then Aristotle's concept of the Prime Mover makes a great deal of sense. But, to be clear, we must not confuse this concept of "God" with Jewish, Christian, or Muslim concepts of "God" as a creator. Aristotle's Prime Mover does not create, because the world, motion, and time are eternal.

Physically, Aristotle's universe consists of a collection of concentric spheres, the outermost of which carries the fixed stars. Beyond lies the Prime Mover. Within the sphere of the stars are the planetary spheres, each in its own proper place. According to this conception, the spheres themselves are self-moved movers and in this sense "alive."[20] On the sphere of the fixed stars, the individual stars are not self-moved but are carried along like ships in a current. The motion of the celestial spheres is circular, because circular motion is the only form of eternal, uniform, perfect motion. The spheres, in desiring what is closest to the Prime Mover's unchanging state, desire the kind of motion most like an unchanging state. There is, of course, an essential gulf between the changelessness of the Prime Mover and the ever-changing movement of the spheres, but the circularity of the spheres is the closest thing to the Prime Mover.

Among the problems with Aristotle's conception of the Prime Mover is that the theory depends very strongly on a metaphorical understanding of the "desire" of lifeless matter. Even in the case of most living things, "desire" must be loosely interpreted. After all, do bacteria feel desire?[21] Do flowers feel a "desire" to bend towards the light? A second problem concerns what the Prime Mover does with itself. Here is Aristotle's description of the Prime Mover's eternal contemplation.

Such, then, is the principle upon which depends the heaven and nature. And its activity is like the best which we can have but for a little while. For it exists in this manner eternally (which is impossible for us), since its actuality is also a pleasure. And it is because of this [activity] that being awake, sensing, and thinking are most pleasant, and hopes and memories are pleasant because of these. Now thinking according to itself is of the best according to itself, and thinking in the highest degree is of that which is best in the highest degree. Thus, in partaking of the intelligible, it is of Himself that the Intellect is thinking; for by apprehending and thinking it is He Himself who becomes intelligible, and so the Intellect and its intelligible object are the same. For that which is capable of receiving the intelligible object and the substance is the intellect, and the latter is in actuality by possessing the intelligible object; so that the possession of the intelligible is more divine than the potency of receiving it, and the contemplation of it is the most pleasant and the best. If, then, the manner of God's existence is as good as ours sometimes is, but eternally, then this is marvelous, and if it is better, this is still more marvelous; and it is the latter. And life belongs to God, for the actuality of the intellect is life, and he is actuality; and his actuality is in virtue of itself a life which is the best and is eternal. We say that God is a living being which is eternal and the best; so life and continuous duration and eternity belong to God, for this is God.[22]

But is this conception of a deity thinking of himself thinking, so that there is no distinction between the thinker and the thought, an attractive concept? Does it satisfy religious cravings? Does it provide us with a deity who is more a congenial recipient of our prayers than the deity of Xenophanes? Aristotle has provided us with the grist for an accommodation of science and religion—but he has not given us a God whom we can love in any kind of emotional way. Perhaps neither science nor philosophy can provide such a deity any more than they can provide us with particularly cuddly laws of physics, mathematics, or logic. Or perhaps the commandment enshrined in the *Shema*—thou shalt love the Lord thy God with all thy *heart* and all thy *soul* and all thy *might*—is not really true, and instead we should desire the goodness, the orderliness, the actuality of God that our *rational* faculties can appreciate.

CICERO'S GOD

Though not possessed of the rare genius of a Parmenides or an Aristotle (but who is?), Cicero, a Roman statesman of the first century B.C.E., possessed an acute mind and an exceptional ability to distill the arguments of complex philosophical systems. He does so beautifully in many of his philosophical works. While he is not to our knowledge generally taught in classes on the history of philosophy, he is owed a tremendous debt. Were it not for his works, much of Greek philosophy—preserved only in his books—would be lost to us. One of these books is *The Nature of the Gods,* a fine assessment of philosophical views concerning the divine.

The work does not address the question of whether gods exist, for their existence is taken for granted. Cicero concentrates on the nature of the gods, an issue on which people differ considerably in their opinions. The opinions that philosophers, including Cicero, have of the gods tend to be based on evidence and arguments rather than on faith and revelation (although appearances of deities in epiphanies, a form of revelation, crop up as a form of argument). A member of the school of philosophy known as the Academy, Cicero believes that truth exists and can be known. But neither the Academy nor Cicero himself accepts *many* things as true, for they hold to a rigorous Aristotelian standard of knowledge. It is in fact one of the central tenets of the Academy to accept no proposition that has not been proved true (in the strong sense).

Even before beginning his examination of the various conceptions of divinity, Cicero warns us that where so many people, and so many wise people, differ, it is best to approach the investigation with some doubts. How different the world's history might have been if his warning had been heeded, for in view of the immensity and complexity of the questions, such doubts might have been a protection against the untroubled confidence that has nourished persecution of those with different views. A sincere sense of uncertainty or skepticism—joined with a willingness to engage in rigorous disputation and, as is always helpful, a charitable heart—is perhaps the proper philosophical disposition.

The investigation begins with the question of why the gods who created the universe suddenly woke up to create the universe.[23] The question is a profound one; indeed, in some religious and mythological traditions our world was created only after other worlds had been created and destroyed.[24] This appeal to a continuing cycle of creation and destruction, however, leads to the obvious question of why the cycle began at one particular time. Perhaps the question of *why* the gods woke up invites the jocular conjecture that they wanted to keep trying until they got creation right.

Should the question of creation be dismissed with such mockery? The issue of how the universe came into being from nonbeing led Aristotle to propose that matter and motion are eternal and hence that the world *never* came into being. In the Middle Ages, the issue of whether the world was created or is eternal was a burning question in the philosophical schools. Although many philosophers wished to be able to prove in the strong Aristotelian sense that it is not eternal— for the idea of creation from nothing is fundamental to Christian interpretations of Genesis—the best of them, Aquinas, finally admitted that none of the arguments for an eternal world is conclusive. It would be better, he said, to admit uncertainty on the matter than to claim certainty for an argument, only to have its deficiencies exposed later, deficiencies that would render the Catholic faith suspect in other matters. Not only is the debate over an eternal versus created world central to the history of philosophy, therefore, but anyone who favors a created world must face Cicero's original question seriously.

The question of *why* the gods suddenly woke up summarizes the problem in obviously anthropomorphic terms. Although human-like gods might sleep, the capacity for sleep, like all human qualities and activities, would be inappropriate in transcendent divinities.[25] If, however, we reject obvious anthropomorphism and ask why the gods at one point decided to create the world, the very question still supposes some human-like decision-making process in the gods' minds.[26] For them to have minds that make decisions is for them to be objectionably anthropomorphic.

After discussing the issue of why the gods created the universe at a particular time, Cicero next asks why they created it at all.[27] This question also attributes a degree of anthropomorphism to the gods, for the question *why* seeks a purpose of the sort that human beings aim at in their own activities. Indeed, when we hear of some "motiveless" human action, we find the claim dubious, and we strain and struggle to find *some* motive. Without a motive we feel that we cannot have understanding. Those actions that really do seem motiveless, even after we have searched for motives, always appear to be *bad* actions, to which no good, regardless of how depraved, can be assigned. (Actions done out of depraved motives—revenge, greed, lust, prejudice—nevertheless have identifiable motives and are to that degree comprehensible.) We never use the term *motiveless* to refer to a good action, for we always assume that the good of a good action is itself a goal of that action. Because human actions require motives to be comprehensible and good, we thus naturally think in anthropomorphic terms when we inquire into the motives of the gods.

It seems difficult to believe that a conscious deity would have created the universe for the sake of lifeless objects like rocks or magnetic waves or microwave radiation instead of creating it for the sake of living, conscious creatures. It is difficult to see what good these lifeless objects would have in themselves, except insofar as they are needed for the development of life in the universe. One might say that the construction of the physical universe would satisfy some aesthetic impulse on the part of the creator and that the satisfaction from admiring and contemplating the order would be motive enough. Yet if we attribute aesthetic pleasure to a deity, we are again anthropomorphizing, and if we anthropomorphize, we need to attribute motives that we *anthropoi,* we humans, find compelling. From our point of view, the most compelling motives would seem to involve the actualization of conscious creatures like ourselves.

Most ancient philosophers, like many religious traditions, do indeed claim that the deity created the world for human beings. Although the view is both anthropomorphic and anthropocentric, perhaps it is the most natural view for humans to have. And yet, let us suppose that some alien creatures from another planet came to earth, observed hummingbirds and roaches, and gave us their unbiased view of creation. Wondering why the earth was made, the aliens could very well conclude from many of the world's features that the world was made for hummingbirds, roaches, or indeed any species. The aliens could point to the fact that there are flowers in most parts of the globe from which hummingbirds can draw nectar, that there are trees in which they can build their nests, that there are people who put up feeders for them—and perhaps the aliens could make their point persuasively. An alien advocate of roaches could point to their ubiquity, their ability to survive on virtually any food, and their invulnerability to radiation. As it is, however, with no unbiased viewpoint as a reference, we humans have a strong tendency to conclude that the universe was made for us and that we occupy the central position in it.

But was the universe made for all humankind or for a special group? Cicero considers the possibilities:

> For the benefit of the wise people? In that case never was so much undertaken for the sake of so few. Then for the benefit of fools? But why should God put himself out for people who do not deserve it? And in any case what would be the point? All foolish people are bound to be unhappy: their own folly will usually see to that. There is nothing like folly to beget misery. But also because there is much unpleasantness in life, which wise men are able to alleviate by the compensation of the good things which they can enjoy. But a fool can neither escape the future nor endure the present.[28]

Why, moreover, if the universe is for the sake of mankind, need it be so big? Is all the complexity of life on earth and is all the vastness of the universe really necessary? Is not some principle of economy violated if so much is created for the sake of so few? These are hard and important questions that Cicero asks about a creator-god.

The next part of Cicero's work consists of an analysis of the theologies of myriad philosophers from Thales on.[29] All the views are rejected on the basis of their inconsistency, their arbitrariness, or their plain silliness. Perhaps no modern reader will find fault with the criticisms. Of course, if we are willing to grant that everyone else's theological views are rightly rejected on the basis of inconsistency or some other deficiency, we shall be obliged to have our own views subjected to the same standard. How many religions will be able to withstand a rigorous philosophical analysis? If they cannot, is there any rational basis for choosing one religion over another? This conundrum is the implicit conclusion of *The Nature of the Gods.*

Cicero then takes up one of the arguments used to prove the existence of a God or gods, the argument of universal assent. Since virtually all people everywhere believe in gods, gods *must* exist.[30] This argument is found also in Judaism, Islam, and Christianity.[31] The argument ignores the fact that sincere, reflective atheists exist (and that assent is therefore *not* universal) and, more importantly, that the gods assume different natures in different cultures. Even if the general assent were universal, it would be assent to many different propositions and hence lose the force of its universality. The Jewish poet Solomon ibn Gabirol says that the wish even of idolaters to worship shows the yearning in the human heart to have an object of worship, and that, in a sense, this desire for an object of worship implies assent to God.[32] The argument is not unlike that of certain Greeks who say that all worship the same deities under different names.[33] Those who wish to reduce all religious beliefs to a single fervor or desire for the transcendent and claim that behind all the variations in religious practice lies a single idea of something greater than man, such as those Christians, Jews, and Muslims who say that these three religions all worship the same God of Abraham, are no doubt motivated by sincere respect for the religiosity of the majority of human beings, as well as by a genuine concern for the moral well-being of the human race.[34] Although they may be right that all the variations are a manifestation of a sense of the divine, nevertheless it is the differences that religious people often care enough about to martyr themselves for their particular cause. The struggles among the faiths, the splitting off of innumerable sects, the frequent fractiousness and division that have so tormented human history have often arisen because of minute differences in the details of belief. Aristotle, in another context, says that people do not really disagree about ends—for they all agree that it is the good that should be sought—but they disagree in their understanding of the good and in the means to be used in pursuing the end.[35] The same is true with the argument of universal assent: is there any meaningful assent if one group thinks God is one, another that God is many, another that God is corporeal, another that God is incorporeal, another that God has a beard, another that God is hairless, another that God is half-man, half-animal? Is it any more meaningful an assent than two groups agreeing that we ought to have a better world, with Group X thinking that the world will be better if it conquers the world and kills all who are not members of Group X, and with Group Y thinking that the world will be better if it conquers the world and kills all who are not members of Group Y? And, of course, universal assent—even when it *is* universal—does not guarantee truth, for it is possible for all people to be mistaken, as they were once about the relationship of the earth and sun or of the impossibility of a heavier than air flying machine or of the ether.

Another popular argument for God's existence discussed by Cicero is known as the argument from design, to which we will devote considerable attention in chapter 14 (pp. 251ff.). It maintains that the world's order, perfection, and purpose must be the work of a divine intelligence. Chance could not have made the universe, the argument goes, just as it could not have created works of literature from a random collection of letters.[36] The argument is old, clear, and appealing to common sense. It seems implicit in Psalm 19.1: "The heavens declare the glory of God, / And the firmament shows God's Handiwork." Nowhere is design more apparent than in biology, in the seemingly perfect marriage of form and function in numerous biological organisms. The ancients cited biology, and especially anatomy, as evidence for the operation of a conscious designer in the world. We shall look closely in chapter 7 at Plato's use of this strategy and return to the issue in chapter 14, where we discuss evolutionary alternatives to design.

The argument that the world is made by a designer seems at first glance powerful and almost self-evident. If we should wander through a museum and find some sort of instrument, we would surely be tempted to conclude that it was made by an intelligent creature for a purpose, even if we have no idea what the purpose was. Indeed, many of us who have visited collections of scientific instruments or laboratories or collections of tools have not had a clue as to an instrument's purpose, but in every case had no doubt that it was designed by humans for a purpose.[37]

The argument from design suggests that every designed object has a purpose intended for it by its designer. Those who defend the design argument often tend to identify purposes even where doing so requires considerable ingenuity. The limit case of the view that the world is designed is the claim that *everything,* the movement of every fish, of every particle of matter down to the tiniest quark, has a purpose. Although there are certainly cases in which the purposes of natural processes seem evident, the ancient principle that nature does *nothing* in vain is quite impossible to demonstrate. Because attempts to do so often refute themselves by their absurdity, Cicero is able to give us a number of examples. Since only man understands the stars, for example, they must have been made for his sake; oxen must have been designed by God for the purpose of toiling under a yoke; pigs were created for no purpose other than to be eaten; and beasts were created so that the humans hunting them could have food and exercise.[38]

If the universe had a designer, does it necessarily follow that the designer is an eternal, universal God with all the other divine attributes? Can the designer not be like the architect of the pyramids, who, having designed his long-lasting work, then died? Perhaps it seems niggardly, having given credit to a designer for the *entire* universe and *all* its complicated laws and fantastic properties, to deny that designer perfect divinity. But no "argument from niggardliness" carries much weight. Although to some it seems self-evident that the universe's designer is necessarily divine, to others the matter is quite controversial.[39]

In addition to the arguments from the consensus of mankind and from design, many believe that gods exist because they feel that they or others whom they trust have experienced the appearance of a deity, an epiphany.[40] Some say that the number and fame of the people who have seen gods, as well as the fine reputation for integrity and virtue that many of these people enjoy, lend credibility to their accounts. The ubiquity of these mystical experiences and their resemblance to one another is additional evidence of their reality.[41] Nevertheless, Cicero's character Cotta replies that the stories of epiphanies are old wives' tales and hearsay. How does one answer such a charge? If someone reports that he has been abducted by a space alien or has seen a ghost, a natural reaction would be skepticism and the assumption that the person is joking or mistaken, or has hallucinated. As we asked in our discussion of the negative aspects of religious explanations in chapter 2 (p. 32), how do visions of deities differ from alien visitations? The real issue is whether a claim of a personal visitation from a deity or anything else can ever constitute convincing evidence for a third party, especially one with a skeptical bent or one insistent on high standards of evidence. If the experience admits of no rigorous verification, then the experience cannot stand as a proof of divine existence. Unless all the alternative explanations of these reports can be conclusively dismissed, the reality of epiphanies can be acknowledged only by faith. Even so, there would be the nagging problem that the deities experienced seem to come in numerous varieties.

Others claim, says Cicero, that the evidence of divination is proof of the existence of gods and of their concern for mankind.[42] The gods are said to know the future and to communicate it to certain humans through the art of divination. Cicero observes that divination is often false. Indeed, he jokes that he cannot imagine how two diviners could meet in the street without breaking out into laughter. Even if the gods *do* know the future, what good is such knowledge if they are unable to use it to change events? Foreknowledge would thus be an argument *against* the power of the gods; and if they lack that power, what reason is there to suppose that they are divine?

Turning to what is known as the ontological argument for God's existence, Cicero gives Zeno's version of the argument and offers a commentary:

Zeno argued thus: "Any being which reasons is superior to any being which does not. But there is nothing superior to the universe as a whole. Therefore the whole universe is a reasoning being." If you accept this argument, then you will have a universe which is proficient in the art of reading books. Because if you follow Zeno's footsteps, you will have to develop his argument as follows: "A being which can read is superior to a being which cannot. But nothing is superior to the universe as a whole. Therefore the universe as a whole can read."[43]

Cicero's criticism of Zeno's argument is compelling: if the superiority of the universe can be used to show its rationality, then the superiority of the universe can be used to show that it has almost any quality that we like. The question, of course, is whether the universe itself is a conscious mind. Cicero argues that having order is not enough to make something divine. And, he adds, those who claim that the universe is itself alive or has conscious thought are mistaken.[44] *The Nature of the Gods* concludes, as is fitting for a work of Academic skepticism, that everything ever brought forward to explain the nature of the gods is dubious.

After Cicero and Hellenistic philosophy, the next major thinkers in the West's philosophical struggle to fathom the secrets of the divine and to untangle the knotty problems that philosophy had uncovered were the Neoplatonists. Their work at first looked quite encouraging to those who hoped that a solution to the various problems could be found.

NEOPLATONISM

The need to reconcile seemingly opposing views of the world has its roots deep in antiquity and continues to the present day. One of the greatest unmet challenges to modern physicists, for example, is the unification of quantum mechanics with the theory of relativity. The remarkable success of both theories in explaining physical phenomena, along with an underlying belief among physicists that nature's order is not contradictory, makes the need for unification all the more pressing. Hence physicists suppose either that both theories are special cases of some underlying or more general theory, or that they are somehow complementary. Showing that they are harmonious and can be reconciled is the holy grail of contemporary theoretical physics.

There was in antiquity a similar desire to reconcile the system of Plato, as it was believed to be a system, with its heavy emphasis on a transcendent World of Being, and the system of Aristotle, with its emphasis on the dynamic and changing world apprehended by the senses.[45] Plato's work, appearing in the mid-fourth century B.C.E., was fresh and ready at hand at the beginning of the Hellenistic period. This was a time when the *polis,* the small, tightly knit community that was the meaningful focus of people's lives, ceased to exist, and large "*cosmo*poleis," such as those of the great Hellenistic kingdoms or that of Rome, became the dominant political order. Many people found themselves lost in the vast insignificance of their political lives and, despising their physical lives, sought meaning in spiritual aspirations.[46] In the Hellenistic period, "mystery" religions proliferated that promised salvation for individual souls and oneness with the divine. Many passages in Plato appeared to describe the spiritual realm

in the legitimizing terms of philosophy. In the *Symposium* there is a description
of a heavenly ladder by which one can ascend from the lowly material world of
the senses to the transcendent world of the spirit. In the *Phaedrus* there is the
brilliant image of a magical chariot by which one can ascend to the divine world
of ideas and obtain true love. Aristotle, who was Plato's student for twenty years,
seemed equally attractive: he presents to his readers the world's most difficult
metaphysical principles in the most persuasively rational manner possible. Indeed, through the greater part of the Middle Ages he appeared—alas—so com-
pellingly persuasive as to seem beyond challenge.

If, then, the theories of Plato and Aristotle could be blended or reconciled, the
transcendent and the immanent—the realms of religion and science, as it were—
could be brought together and all problems solved. A happy marriage of religion
and science would be consecrated! There would be the possibility of a theory of
everything, of the physical and spiritual realms, and mere humans would have a
means to carry their souls aloft to that latter realm. Underlying this grand hope
lay the problematic premise that each of these thinkers was believed to be putting forth the truth in a complete whole, a whole that had to be accepted in its
entirety. The eclecticism of antiquity did not simply take the best pieces of various thoughts and put them together; it was instead a syncretism that sought *synthesis*. Perhaps the analogy with quantum mechanics and relativity is applicable
here too: because the parts of each system seem harmoniously to constitute a
whole, each theory has to be accepted in its entirety, and a blending will need to
show that the two self-contained theories do not contradict one another or at
least that the difficulties in one system are resolved by the other. The second-
century C.E. philosopher Albinus attempted just such a synthesis of Plato and
Aristotle.[47] So did Apuleius, also in the second century, as did Boethius in the
sixth and al Farabi in the tenth.[48] The most successful and well-known attempt
to reconcile Aristotle and Plato, however, was that of Plotinus (204–270), the
person most responsible for devising the system known as Neoplatonism.

The work of Plotinus survives principally in the *Enneads,* a collection of essays published after his death by his student Porphyry (234–305). Plotinus himself studied with a certain Ammonius Saccas, who had been a Christian before de-
voting himself to philosophy. Saccas was the teacher also of Origen, a Church
Father and one of the most capable of the Christian Platonists of Alexandria.[49] Although Plotinus never mentions Christianity itself, there are, as we shall see, so
many points of similarity between it and Neoplatonism that it is easy to understand why intellectualizing Christians like Augustine were so drawn to Neoplatonism and quote from it extensively.[50]

We shall limit our discussion of the rich and complex philosophy of Neoplatonism to the two fundamental features particularly relevant to the attempt to
unify science and religion. The first describes how a philosophically intelligible
God affects the world, i.e., how a deity can retain the qualities of imperturbabil-
ity, constancy, and perfection, and yet be able to create and influence the world.
The second describes how humans can reach the divine, i.e., how a human be-

ing, imprisoned in a body, in the corrupt world of sensation, can find salvation for his individual soul.

How God Affects the World

The ancient mind could not conceive of how the world, if it is exclusively material, could have become an orderly, beautiful place, full of living things hierarchically arranged, with rational, intelligent creatures conscious of their place at the acme of existence.[51] Matter by itself seems incapable of initiating motion or change and of putting itself it order. It appears always to require some external principle to organize it. As we saw earlier (pp. 12–13), it is easiest to comprehend how things are ordered when a mind similar to our own human mind does the work. Of course, the mind that orders the universe would have to be a mind on a scale incomprehensibly grander than ours. This mind, it seems, would itself be immaterial yet somehow able to act upon matter. Although Aristotle and many other philosophers agree that humans are composites of material bodies and immaterial souls, the way in which the immaterial element acts on the material one is the sticking point of all dualistic theories of human nature. Because the divine is absolutely best and therefore can consist only of the best, nearly every philosopher except the atomists holds God or the gods to be purely nonphysical. But the problem remains: how can the nonphysical divine affect the physical world? Although Aristotle's conception of God as Prime Mover equated knower and known by identifying the Prime Mover as thought thinking about itself, this concept explains the effects of God on the world only in terms of desire, a notion hard to defend when referring to things incapable of desiring.

Plotinus proposes a solution to the problem of interaction between immaterial and material entities in his theory of emanation. He posits as a first principle a deity so transcendent, so beyond being, so beyond anything in our experience or imagination as to be wholly ineffable, wholly incapable of articulation. Such a deity cannot be known except by a "way of removing," by which every attribute that can be thought is removed until only God alone is left. Any attribute that can be conceived—and if a word for an attribute exists, the attribute can be conceived—is too limiting. Whereas Aristotle allows a *distinction* between the deity as thinker and the deity as thought—even though this thinker and its thought are as inseparable as the concave and convex surfaces of a lens—Plotinus holds that the unity of the absolute ultimate One is so pure as to be utterly without internal distinctions.

The unity of Plotinus's deity recalls the unity of Parmenides' world and differs chiefly in the theory of emanation. The emanation from the One is the Divine Intelligence, from which emanates the General Soul. From the General Soul emanates everything else, including matter. The first three—the One, the Divine Intelligence, and the General Soul—constitute a "trinity"—an Arian trinity, as it were, of descending hierarchical value.[52] We might compare emanation to the light that shines from a torch: it illuminates what it shines on without itself being diminished. Thus the torch "emanates" light, and the light affects everything within its range, but the torch itself is unaffected by what it illuminates.[53] The emanations occur continuously, without beginning or end and without being willed by the One. As Plotinus puts it, "What is full must overflow, what is mature must beget."[54] Emanation thus provides for continuous creation.

We can illustrate what Plotinus means by creation by elaborating on the analogy with light. Just as an object is continuously illuminated by the torch's light while the torch itself remains undiminished, so Plotinus's One continuously creates but is not diminished by its creative activity. If the torch were suddenly to disappear, so would the illumination of the object. In the same manner, creation continuously depends on the existence of the One. The term *creation* is for Plotinus a metaphor for this relation of dependence of one thing upon another without reference to coming into being. The One is a creator in the sense that, like the torch's light, it is the cause of what depends on it (i.e., the illuminated object). The cause of each successive level of existence—the Divine Intelligence, the General Soul, etc.—is in the previous level, as if the light on the illuminated object should then reflect light on yet another object. Because the subsequent effect mirrors the cause imperfectly, however, each effect is further from excellence than its cause. This process, Plotinus says, is eternal, as is the world. In this way the world is just as eternal as the One—or God—even while the world is caused by the One. Although the world is dependent on God, God is independent of and unaffected by the world. The One is immanent in everything because everything is its emanation; at the same time it is transcendent because nothing at all ever comes even close to resembling it.

As emanations become more distant from the One, Plotinus speaks of a "descent." Thus the Divine Intelligence is a falling away or descent from the transcendent One. Matter, as the level or emanation lowest and furthest away from the One, is in that sense evil, although even it is good and beautiful insofar as it is a reflection of the intelligible world. Plotinus's doctrine of emanation thus undergirds his attempt to reconcile the seemingly contrary notions of immanence and transcendence on the one hand, and good and evil on the other.

Plotinus gives a second, different explanation for the loss of perfection as emanations move further from the source.[55] According to this account, the soul, stirred by a desire to rule, breaks free of the Divine Intelligence. Since the soul can rule over only what is worse, it wishes to separate itself from what is better and becomes involved with bodies. One can hear echoes of the Christian story of the rebellious angels who fell because of their choice to break away from God. Plotinus also speaks of the inferior emanations as a fall.[56] Perhaps Plotinus heard this sort of language from his teacher Ammonius, who had been a Christian before his conversion. Perhaps, then, Plotinus was employing this sort of language poetically, as Plato had done six hundred years earlier.

What has Neoplatonism gained by this theory of emanation? It seems to present a deity that answers many of the requirements of philosophy: it—for such a deity can be referred to only as an "it"—is unchanging and therefore has no will (for a will suggests choice, and choice suggests change). It is not dependent on anything, yet everything is dependent on it. It is knowledge, goodness, and everything else, but not in any definable way, and as both cause and result. If this description makes no sense—and it doesn't—it is because such a deity is beyond comprehension. It is simultaneously immanent and transcendent. It is unmoved and yet is the agent of cause in everything else. The deity was so attractive to a young and philosophically lost Augustine that Augustine suggests that were it not for the absence in Plotinus of the doctrine of the Incarnation, the Neoplatonic view, because of its lofty view of God and its ability to deal with the problem of how God could affect the world without himself being altered, would be entirely acceptable to Catholics.[57]

The defects of the Neoplatonic doctrine of emanation are, unfortunately, only too clear, and additional defects of Neoplatonism will emerge presently as we look at the second salient feature of the philosophical school, the account of how humans commune with the divine. The doctrine of emanation vindicates Cicero's quip that nothing is so absurd as not to have been uttered by some philosopher. Upon reflection, we are forced to conclude that the doctrine of emanation represents nothing more than an attempt to define away such deep metaphysical problems as those involving transcendence and immanence, the interaction between spiritual and physical spheres, and the creative activity of an eternal being. Although it is tempting to lose oneself in the fine-sounding metaphors of Neoplatonism, one relinquishes in the process any standard of logical rigor, including the fundamental human desire for consistency.

Human Access to the Divine

The second problem that Neoplatonism addresses concerns the central promise of religion, namely, the means by which humans might come into contact with the divine. Because many of the writings of Neoplatonism deal with this matter, one might say that Neoplatonism is as much a religious as a philosophical doctrine. The school of thought is, to be sure, religion without ritual and without sacrament; perhaps partly for that reason it appealed to people like Plotinus, rationalists seeking a spiritual comfort more fulfilling than logic alone can offer.

Given the basic Neoplatonic principle that matter is bad and spirit good (to put it plainly), the intellectual challenge to human beings is to achieve for the soul independence from its body—its matter. Various ways of separating the soul from the body and from bodily things had long been discussed. In the *Phaedo,* for example, Plato has his character Socrates define philosophy as a preparation for death. When a mind is engaged in philosophy, Socrates says, it escapes its earthly concerns and dwells, as it were, in the region of ideas. Socrates also suggests a literal escape from the body through bodily death, at which point a philosophic soul takes up residence in the world of the spirit. In the *Republic,* Plato has Socrates divide the soul into three parts, with the appetitive and spirited parts linked quite intimately with the body and the intellectual part the freest from the body.[58]

In Neoplatonism, soul is a wholly spiritual entity independent of the body. By a process known as *theurgy*—a disciplining through ethical and intellectual purification—soul can return to its source. In a process very closely resembling Dante's in the *Commedia,* the soul in a Neoplatonic theurgy travels through the five stages of purifying ascent, (1) purification, (2) illumination, (3) union, (4) mystic union, until it achieves (5) apotheosis and apprehends the absolute One. "Ecstasy" is the soul's escape from the body's prison by these stages. The escape is what is really meaningful, not the time when the body and soul are joined together. When a soul has returned to the source from which it emanated, it is reabsorbed in the cosmic universal soul, and the soul's individual qualities, acquired when it was dressed in a body, are lost. This is its supreme happiness, this its salvation: to be merged into the universal soul.

In its religious doctrine of mystical union, Neoplatonism asserts the fundamental identity of the incorporeal soul with the trinity of the One, the Divine Intelligence, and the General Soul. The matter that one's body comprises is not one's essence; one's essence is one's soul, and that soul is ultimately the same as universal soul.[59] The means by which one achieves this union of individual and universal soul is contemplation. The further one goes in contemplation of the One, the further one is removed from material existence.

This process is reflected in Boethius's *Consolation of Philosophy,* which is not taken to be a Neoplatonic work but is in many respects sympathetic to Neoplatonism. Boethius shared the Neoplatonic project of reconciling Aristotelian and Platonic ideas, for example. At the beginning of his sublime book, the formerly flourishing Boethius laments his sorry state, as he waits in prison for his execution, while experiencing the figurative imprisonment of earthbound values and private pains. The imaginary figure Lady Philosophy argues with him and leads him upwards through a course of Greek philosophy, recalling to him the true nature of fortune, the falsity of the glamorous goods of honor, wealth, and pleasure, the true human happiness of virtue and wisdom, the doctrine that God is not responsible for what appears to be evil, the nature of God as simple unity, the proof that there is no randomness in the universe, and finally, the demonstration that since God resides in a timeless present there is no contradiction at all between human free will and divine foreknowledge. If at the beginning of the work Boethius wallows in self-pity for his private woes, by the end he forgets himself entirely and his spirit soars into the realm where the profoundest divine mysteries are revealed. He and his reader alike achieve consolation for their earthly woes by completely forgetting them. *The Consolation of Philosophy,* one of the glories of ancient literature, provides a practical model of the Neoplatonic program of moving the soul by steps to contemplation of the divine.

We find a similar Christian Neoplatonic text in Dante's *Commedia.* Finding himself lost in a dark forest of private worries and blocked by the three beasts of ambition, pride, and lust, Dante passes through the various levels of wisdom and purification, led first by figures symbolizing reason and love (or perhaps philosophy and revelation) and later by one representing mystic union. At the climax of his journey, he gazes—only for a moment—on divinity itself, his own will merged with God's.

Allegory is especially suitable for Neoplatonism and other philosophies of transcendence. An analogy will illustrate our meaning. In the illusions known as Magic Eye images we first see a pattern of colors. But if we gaze on the pattern for a while, the pattern somehow turns into a three-dimensional picture of something else.[60] Both images are simultaneously present, just as two senses of a pun are simultaneously present, though the mind rapidly perceives one and then the other. Plotinus intends emanation to work in this way, except that there are many images, and each is always present in the others. Allegory works the same way. For example, if we look at a painting of Mars and Venus in amorous embraces, we could see it as just a depiction of ordinary sex. But we might also look upon the painting as a story about the possibility of love to tame war, or as a story about the strife that love or erotic passion involves. In other words, the same image might *simultaneously* radiate several different messages, some nobler, some baser, depending, we suppose, on the soul of the observer. What is particularly useful for Neoplatonism is that in allegory the transcendent is simultaneously present with the immanent. The earthly sex in the painting is simultaneously present with the spiritual doctrine about love and strife. This simultaneity of meanings can be likened in Platonic language to reflection, for the way in which a thing is reflected by a mirror is akin to the way that the ideas are reflected in the physical things. The simultaneity can be likened in Christian language to the simultaneously distinct and indistinct persons of the Trinity. Allegory is an attractive way to confer deep meaning on ordinary things, and it finds a welcoming home in much philosophy and religion.[61] The path for Neoplatonic allegorizing had been cleared earlier, when the Stoics and Pythagoreans had allegorized Homer to render his poetry compatible with their philosophies and Philo had read the Bible to reflect his understanding of Platonic doctrines. Porphyry, editor and interpreter of Plotinus's *Enneads,* interpreted pagan myths to be compatible with Neoplatonic notions. In *Homeric Inquiries,* for example, discussing the Cave of the Nymphs in Homer's *Odyssey* (13.102–112), Porphyry writes that the cave represents the material world; the cave's rock, matter's recalcitrance; the waters in the cave, matter's flux; the cave's darkness, matter's obscurity. Among Jewish Neoplatonists, the ladder in Jacob's dream was taken to be a metaphor for the soul's ascent to the One.[62]

Nevertheless, for all its poetical virtues, and for all its appropriateness to Neoplatonism, a philosophy that attempts to speak of simultaneity, allegory is a sham approach to philosophical truth. The painting of Mars and Venus evokes various ideas in the observer—true; but the ideas are evoked sequentially and depend on prior knowledge of different patterns. While a man might simultaneously be a father, a son, a brother, a husband, and a plumber, he is not all of these things *in the same respect* (i.e., he is not father, son, and brother of the same person), yet being both different and same in the same respect is just what Neoplatonism requires.

Moreover, mystic union is much more easily spoken of than achieved. While some people experience an ecstatic exhilaration from intense contemplative activity, this form of ecstasy is perhaps the rarest and most difficult to obtain. And there is something unsatisfying to most people, at least to those in whom the Greek ideal of individuality is deeply rooted, about salvation into a universal soul, of reabsorption into a cosmic psychic soup, where the soup is not even a vegetable soup where one might be a pea or carrot, but an undifferentiated consommé where perfect unity prevails. This loss of identity seems to compromise whatever rewards attend the arduous five stages of ascent. The greatest difficulty for Neoplatonism, as for dualistic systems generally, is the connection—or the breaking of the connection, as the case may be—between the spiritual and the physical. The Neoplatonic conception of ecstasy thus suffers from the same fatal shortcoming as the Neoplatonic conception of emanation. In this case the breaking, or transcendence, of the connection to the physical is exalted and affirmed by fine-sounding rhetoric but, as before, is unproved by argument. The whole edifice rests on imagined foundations that depend on the willingness of the adherent to suspend disbelief. At the same time, there is an overlay of philosophy, and the system presents itself as a philosophically valid response to all the conundra of the best philosophy.

To those with religious yearnings, Neoplatonism's conception of the deity is unappealing as well. Wholly impersonal, lacking even a will, it cannot answer prayers, let alone hear them. It is not a creator, even as a parent might be a creator. It is more like a radio tower, except that the deity is not even responsible for the programming beamed out, because the beaming occurs in a uniform, unchanging, involuntary fashion. Despite its defects, Neoplatonism was to its believers true science. It claimed knowledge not only of a process by which the divine interacts continuously with the human and material worlds, but of a process by which human souls can move up the ladder of perfection to the Absolute. This sort of transformation or metamorphosis, which could change souls into something better, was seen by later proponents to suggest a means for metamorphosing matter as well and thus encouraged a belief in magic.

One influential Neoplatonist was the Christian Dionysius the Areopagite, who wrote several books combining Christianity and Neoplatonism. The titles of the books suggest why they may have influenced Albertus Magnus and Thomas Aquinas to endorse mysticism and may have, through them, influenced Dante and the mystic traditions of the Middle Ages and Renaissance: *On the Celestial Hierarchy, On the Ecclesiastical Hierarchy, On the Mystical Theology, On the Divine Names.* Dionysius claims that God affects human beings by working sequentially through three groupings of three supernatural beings each: Seraphim, Cherubim, and Thrones; Dominions, Virtues, and Powers; Principalities, Archangels, and Angels. With so many intervening supernatural creatures, it should not be surprising, perhaps, that some of them could be corrupted to do the bidding of manipulative people. Incantation was the easiest form of magic spell, although all sorts of brews, wax images, sacrifices, charms, and so on could also be used to invoke the aid of the spirits. To those who believed in the sign of the cross, the *Ave Maria,* and holy water, the transformative power of words and things into other things, for good or evil, might seem perfectly believable too. To what extent Neoplatonism contributed to the belief in magic or was itself influenced by the general ambiance is of course impossible to determine. Its affinity with certain parts of Christianity and its philosophical authority, however, would certainly have been a contributory element. Perhaps it would be worthwhile to quote Gibbon's assessment of Neoplatonism:

> Several of these masters, Ammonius, Plotinus, Aemilius, and Porphyry, were men of profound thought and intense application; but, by mistaking the true object of philosophy, their labours contributed much less to improve than to corrupt the human understanding. The knowledge that is suited to our situation and powers, the whole compass of moral, natural, and mathematical science, was neglected by the new Platonists, whilst they exhausted their strength in the verbal disputes of metaphysics, attempted to explore the secrets of the invisible world, and studied to reconcile Aristotle and Plato, on subjects of which both these philosophers were as ignorant as the rest of mankind. Consuming their reason in these deep but unsubstantial meditations, their minds were exposed to illusions of fancy. They flattered themselves that they possessed the secret of disengaging the soul from its corporeal prison; claimed a familiar intercourse with daemons and spirits; and, by a very singular revolution, converted the study of philosophy into that of magic.[63]

Let us conclude this brief discussion of Neoplatonism with a word about its revival in the Renaissance, perhaps its last major appearance as an influential system of thought, and with a speculation concerning why it enjoyed this late rebirth. With the fall of Byzantium and the flight of Greek classical texts to Italy, there was, understandably enough, a special fascination with the works of the glamorous, romantic, and lushly eloquent Plato. The intellectual elite, naturally wearied with dry, tediously logical scholastic discourses, were charmed with the inspirational beauty of Plato. Lorenzo (the Magnificent) de' Medici (1449–1492) cheerfully lavished resources in Florence on the Platonic Academy, an association of men devoted to Plato who would meet in Lorenzo's palace for dinner to read aloud a dialogue or two and to discuss philosophy. On Plato's supposed birthday, 7 November, they would crown a bust of Plato with flowers and burn a lamp before it. Pico della Mirandola, Michelangelo, and Marsilio Ficino were among the many famous, if muddle-headed, intellectuals who attended the meetings. Presiding was Ficino, translator into Latin of Plato, Plotinus, and Dionysius the Areopagite and author of *Platonic Theology Concerning the Immortality of the Soul,* who virtually worshipped Plato as a saint and addressed his students as "beloved in Plato." Pico was the great syncretist, a man open to every philosophy and religion—all of which, he tried to show, taught the same truths about man's fluid nature, a nature that could either descend towards the material or ascend towards God. Pico accepted magic and mysticism along with Platonism and Christianity. Given the Christianity of these figures, their love of Plato, and their inability to make studious distinctions among the various successors of Plato (whom they lumped into a homogenized whole), they found among the Neoplatonists both kindred spirits and the philosophical legitimacy that attended the giant of philosophy Plato.[64] That the Church did not frown on Neoplatonism is confirmed by Pope Julius II's 1508 commission of Raphael for the famous painting of the "School of Athens" in the Vatican Stanze just outside the Sistine Chapel.[65] In the painting, in the center of a huge and outwardly radiating basilica, Aristotle and Plato are discussing truth. The painting is evidently influenced by Neoplatonism, according to which the two linked philosophers would represent the one truth that radiates outward to the lesser luminaries. It is important to beware, however, that once one begins to look for Neoplatonism, like a Freudian looking for sexual symbolism, one finds it everywhere.

Neoplatonism represents a final attempt by pagan philosophy to combine science and spirituality. Without an organized structure and without worshippers or adherents, however, without an institutionalization of rituals and observances, without the support of political authorities, it was not destined to endure. Insofar as it was in part absorbed into the elements of Judaism,[66] Islam, and Christianity, it may be said to breathe still, as some of the DNA of the ancient dinosaurs still takes flight in both the eagles and sparrows of our skies.

THE GOD OF PHILOSOPHY

God bothers philosophers. Sometimes their minds drive them to deny, or withhold judgment on, the existence of God because *none* of the arguments concerning God's existence or nature are rigorously compelling. Philosophical speculation about God falls short not only of Aristotle's requirements for knowledge but often of the weaker requirements of probable, experiential arguments. Such speculation rarely converts doubters. Sometimes, however, philosophers' minds drive them to assert the existence of God in order to explain in terms natural to humans how the universe arose and is sustained. The most philosophically plausible deity, one that is totally unanthropomorphized, though, seems to us mere *anthropoi,* to us feeble humans, to be bloodless, colorless, lifeless, and both unworthy of our belief and incapable of satisfying our spiritual needs. The Neoplatonic One is devoid of consciousness and will. Aristotle's Prime Mover would be alone at a party, a most solitary and unengaging bore, who would want to talk only about himself thinking about himself. Reconciling such a "God" with science—as opposed to proving the existence of such a God demonstratively—would be as uninteresting as it would be unchallenging: although deities of this sort play central roles in the unified philosophical systems described in this chapter, we yearn for something more. We desire what religion promises, a God relevant to human needs, even if that God is all too human and all too implausible from a philosophical point of view. Hence, the real challenge of reconciling science and religion will be to reconcile the God of actual religious belief with what science tells us about the world. Attempts to achieve that reconciliation are the subject of part 2.

DISCUSSION QUESTIONS

1. When one contemplates the lamentable history of religious intolerance, one cannot but marvel at the license given Greek thinkers for their philosophical views. How must Xenophanes' revolutionary ideas have been received by his contemporaries? Though he seems to have had no immediate followers and might therefore have been dismissed as a lunatic, is there any sector of Greek society to whom his arguments would have been appealing?

2. Plato and Aristotle seem to have adopted the Xenophanic view of God as a Parmenidean unity of goodness and perfection and immobility, a view that eventually came to dominate Western theological thinking. Does the earlier view—that there is a multiplicity of gods, each god controlling one of the multiplicity of natural forces, each god contending with the others for supremacy but all kept in check by Fates and a dominant king, and that out of this continuous conflict there emerges a dynamic, continuously changing world—have any positive features? Which view seems to fit the evidence of the *senses* better?

3. The distinction that Aristotle draws between actuality and potentiality helps him out of the Parmenidean claim that nothing can come into being, for the distinction enables him to say that the-things-that-are-not exist *potentially*. (For example, the oak that emerges from an acorn exists potentially in the acorn.) But the distinction also requires Aristotle to postulate the existence of a prime matter that has no form at all, a postulate Aristotle is driven to by his wish to escape infinite regress. Which view seems more problematic—the view of an underlying matter that has no form, or the view of an infinite regress? Why does Aristotle think the latter more problematic? How did his choice affect the scientific and theological thinking of the western world?

4. The notion that the unmoved mover works as an object of desire succeeds as an explanation for human beings. When, however, we take the term as metaphorical in its application to things in the natural world, does the concept of the mover as object of desire become problematic? Is the metaphor strained as we transfer it from humans and animals to celestial objects? Does the metaphor clarify or confuse the final description of the unmoved mover's eternal contemplation of itself? Does the description of the unmoved mover become a curious mélange of anthropomorphic and "anti-anthropomorphic" qualities?

5. Cicero dares to ask some very commonsensical questions about the divine: why the creation of the world occurred at a particular moment and not earlier, why the divine bothered to make the world at all, why the world has the size it has. These are questions one seldom hears so simply put. Do these questions have modern formulations? If they do, are the modern formulations more sophisticated versions of the same questions, or just the same questions but in modern dress?

6. Cicero assesses the ancient philosophical conceptions of gods for their consistency and plausibility. Is his approach valid? Is there any other approach? How would such an approach be received today if one were to compile a list of the actual theological views of the myriad churches and denominations and assess them for their consistency and plausibility? How many would survive the test?

7. Cicero reviews the argument that the world was made by a designer in such a way as to ask *for whom* the world was designed, and the answer turns out to be that it was designed for humans, and especially for philosophers. (Stars, for example, were made so that philosophers, from contemplating the heavenly order, might learn number.) This sort of idea, which aims the spotlight on humans, is called *anthropocentrism.* If we say instead that the deity designed the world for his own amusement or his own pleasure or so that he could have an object upon which to bestow his love, we are attributing to the deity human qualities. This sort of idea, which makes the deity to be like humans, is a type of *anthropomorphism.* Is it possible to avoid either anthropomorphism or anthropocentrism or both in formulating the argument from design? Does so formulating the argument affect its validity? If so, how? If not, why not?

8. Cicero's book *The Nature of the Gods* concludes with the skeptical claim that everything that explains the gods is doubtful. What is the range of possible inferences one might draw from an inability to describe the deities and their operation?

9. Plotinus's theory of emanation has the attractive feature of explaining how something might affect other things without being itself affected. Nevertheless, the theory suffers from the fact that the deity is incomprehensible and from the theory's own literalness of metaphor in accounting for the loss of perfection as emanations move further from their source. Was the failure of Neoplatonism to develop into a religion in its own right owing exclusively to its lack of an army and a navy, or is the incomprehensibility of the main character, God, fatal? If the whole system of Neoplatonism could not survive as a religion, have some parts made their way piecemeal into established religions?

10. As we have seen, there were parts of the systems of Aristotle and Plato that have stood the test of time and remain valuable for philosophy. At the same time, there were some speculative parts of those philosophies that in their inception were shakily confused. Neoplatonism aimed at taking on the weak points of each system, at strengthening them by correcting their errors, and, after solving the problems of each system, at reconciling them to create a perfect unity. If Plato and Aristotle had, so to speak, risen from the dead and seen what Plotinus produced, what would their reactions have been?

11. Is allegory ultimately satisfying to the devotees either of religion or of philosophy? To whom is it more appealing? Why is allegory so enduring a feature to the thinking of both?

12. Emotions have an underlying rational element. For example, pity is the painful sense that the object of pity is suffering unjustly; anger is the painful sense that the object of anger has acted unjustly; hence these emotions, like the others, depend on a sense of justice, a sense that derives from the faculty of reason. Yet the deity that the best reasoning of pagan philosophy could describe does not satisfy humans at an emotional level. Does this failure result from a failure of reasoning, or is there at the margins some fundamental conflict between reason and the parts of emotion that are not obedient to reason?

NOTES

1. Xenophanes, frag. 3.

2. Xenophanes, frag. 11.

3. The question of whether God lacks the freedom to do evil because of a necessity to do good vexes philosophers in the Middle Ages. The idea that God is controlled by necessity and hence limited seems to deny God's omnipotence. At the same time, the idea that God can be anything but good contradicts the idea of God as absolute, unqualified good. This matter is taken up in the next several chapters.

4. Xenophanes frags. 14, 16, and 15, respectively. Modern thinkers who defend the anthropic principle seem not to have learned Xenophanes' lesson about the pitfalls of anthropocentric thinking (see below, p. 265).

5. Xenophanes, frags. 23, 26, 25.

6. Xenophanes, frag. 38.

7. Xenophanes, frag. 18.

8. Xenophanes, frag. 7.

9. Xenophanes, frag. 34.

10. Heraclitus, frag. B79.

11. Aristotle, *Metaphysics,* 980a26–981b8.

12. Aristotle, *Metaphysics,* 982a25.

13. Aristotle, *Metaphysics,* 982a20–29; he makes the same point in *Posterior Analytics,* 72a1–5.

14. Aristotle, *Metaphysics,* 982a25.

15. See Aristotle, *Metaphysics,* 1071b5–15.

16. Aristotle summarizes this dilemma in *Physics,* 191a27–31.

17. Aristotle, *Physics,* 191b13.

18. Aristotle's word for matter is *hyle,* a metaphor from the word for wood — perhaps chosen because wood can be easily shaped.

19. Aristotle, *On the Soul,* 412a13; *Physics,* 255a5–7.

20. Aristotle *On the Heavens,* 289b32–33.

21. On whether animals' souls are self-movers, see M. L Gill, "Aristotle on Self-Motion," in *Self-Motion: From Aristotle to Newton,* ed. M. L. Gill and J. G. Lennox (Princeton, N.J.: Princeton University Press, 1994), 15–34, and, in the same volume, D. Furley, "Self-Movers," 3–14.

22. Aristotle, *Metaphysics* (trans. Apostle) 1072b14–31.

23. Cicero, *The Nature of the Gods,* trans. H. C. McGregor (New York: Viking Penguin, 1985), 1.21.

24. The view is found, e.g., in Origen, *de principiis,* 3.5.3–4. Origen argues that since God has been active from eternity and never sleeps, there must be an infinite series of worlds both before and after the present world.

25. Plutarch records Alexander the Great as saying that there were only two times when he felt like a man and not a god: one of these was when he was sleeping (Plutarch, *Alexander,* 22).

26. One of Cicero's interlocutors mockingly asks whether the gods had not created the universe earlier because they were reluctant to get to work. He asks whether they decorated the universe with stars because they became bored with darkness. In other words, motives we find in humans are attributed to the gods (Cicero, *The Nature of the Gods,* 1.22. The vigorous attack on anthropomorphism of the gods is picked up again at 1.76–84.)

27. Cicero, *The Nature of the Gods,* 1.22–23.

28. Cicero, *The Nature of the Gods* (trans. McGregor) 1.23.

29. Cicero, *The Nature of the Gods,* 1.25–43.

30. Cicero, *The Nature of the Gods,* 1.62.

31. See L. Jacobs, *Principles of the Jewish Faith,* Commentary Classics (New York: Basic Books, 1964), 37.

32. Solomon ibn Gabirol "Keter Malkhuth" ("The Royal Crown"), in *Selected Religious Poems of Solomon ibn Gabirol,* trans. Israel Zangwill and ed. Israel Davidson (Philadelphia: Jewish Publication Society of America, 1952), 8.

33. Gibbon, *Decline and Fall,* vol. 1, chapter 2, writes:

> The Greek, the Roman, the Barbarian, as they met before their respective altars, easily persuaded themselves that, under various names and with various ceremonies, they adored the same deities. The elegant mythology of Homer gave a beautiful and almost a regular form to the polytheism of the ancient world.

He adds in a note that within a century of their conquest, the Gauls applied Roman names to their gods.

34. Among them was the sixteenth-century Dominican bishop of Chiapas, Bartolome de las Casas, who wished to fend off the criticisms of the New World peoples who committed human sacrifice. He argued that the sacrifice showed the belief in a supernatural source who wished public recognition of its kindness and that humans wished to give their finest possessions as thanks. (Thanks to Professor David Lupher, who wrote about de las Casas in a note to the Classics Internet List on 10 August 1998.)

35. As Aristotle says, we deliberate about means, not ends (*Rhetoric,* 1362a15).

36. Cicero, *The Nature of the Gods,* 2.83ff. Later, the late eleventh-century Jewish writer Bahya ben Joseph ibn Pakuda gives virtually the same example, substituting a sheet of paper on which there is writing (*The Duties of the Heart* [*Hovot ha-levavot*], trans. Yaakov Feldman [Northvale, N.J.: J. Aronson, 1996], chapter 6). No one would think that ink accidentally spilled on the paper in the form of the letters of an intelligible text. This is a much earlier formulation of the idea behind the story of the various monkeys at typewriters, typing out, in infinite time, all the works of literature. It would surely be a pleasant diversion to collect versions of this theme.

37. For further discussion of this aspect of apparent design, see chapter 14, p. 268.

38. Cicero, *The Nature of the Gods,* 2.160–61.

39. G. H. Joyce (*Principles of Natural Theology,* 3d ed. [London: Longmans, 1934], 134) is aware of the argument that a supreme architect is not necessarily God but dismisses it. He says that anyone who accepts a supreme architect will not doubt that he has proved the existence of God.

40. Cicero, *The Nature of the Gods,* 3.12–13.

41. See also Jacobs, *Principles,* 48.

42. Cicero, *The Nature of the Gods,* 2.163.

43. Cicero, *The Nature of the Gods,* 3.23.

44. Cicero, *The Nature of the Gods,* 3.24.

45. Although it has been traditionally believed that Plato's work presents a system, it cannot be authoritatively determined what the system is, for Plato's dialogues contain too many tentative hypotheses, or points that are rhetorical distractions whose purpose is to surprise the opponent totally (such as the use of the notion of recollection as a proof for the immortality of the soul in the *Meno*). See J. Arieti, *Interpreting Plato,* 1–11, 206–7. Of course, Plato is significant more for what he is believed to have said and for the tradition that developed out of his words than for the immediate purpose of those words.

46. See chapter 3, p. 64, for our discussion of the psychological and spiritual response to the political and social situation of the Hellenistic period.

47. See the section on Albinus by P. Merlan in *The Cambridge History of Later Greek and Early Medieval Philosophy,* ed. A. H. Armstrong (Cambridge: Cambridge University Press, 1967), 64–73.

48. See P. Merlan, "Atticus and Other Platonists of the Second Century A.D.," in *The Cambridge History of Later Greek and Early Medieval Philosophy,* ed. A. H. Armstrong (Cambridge: Cambridge University Press, 1967), 70–78; L. Liebeschütz, "Boethius and the Legacy of Antiquity," in *The Cambridge History of Later Greek and Early Medieval Philosophy,* ed. A. H. Armstrong (Cambridge: Cambridge University Press, 1967), 540; and R. Walzer, "The World, Man, and Society," in *The Cambridge History of Later Greek and Early Medieval Philosophy,* ed. A. H. Armstrong (Cambridge: Cambridge University Press, 1967), 658.

49. This is the judgment of E. R. Dodds, *Select Passages Illustrating Neoplatonism* (Chicago: Ares, 1979), 21.

50. Augustine quotes long passages from the *Enneads,* for example, which he read in a Latin translation. See Augustine, *Confessions,* 9.10, where he paraphrases Plotinus, *Enneads,* 5.1.2, and Augustine, *On the Immortality of the Soul,* where he paraphrases Plotinus, *Enneads,* 4.7.3.

51. Even the most valiant attempt of the atomists, as we discussed in chapter 4 (pp. 84ff.), left too many problems unresolved.

52. Plotinus, *Enneads,* 6.9.9, 5.1.3, 5.1.5–7.

53. The analogy is defective because in fact the torch would be affected, at least at the quantum level, by the photons it emits.

54. Plotinus, *Enneads,* 5.4.1, 5.1.6, 5.2.1.

55. He may be likened to Hesiod, who gives varying accounts for evil in the world. In one account, Hesiod describes the natural process of descent from a splendid Golden Age of long ago to the wretched Iron Age of now. In a second account, he tells the story of Pandora. Each story is given as the sole cause of evil. One might excuse a poet like Hesiod, who is not bothered by inconsistency. It is harder to forgive a philosopher like Plotinus.

56. See *Encyclopedia of Philosophy,* s.v. "Plotinus."

57. Augustine, *Confessions,* 7.10.

ing outside of." Philo (*Who Is the Heir?* 249ff.) distinguishes four kinds of ecstasy—a classification in itself suggestive of how seriously were taken attempts to separate one's soul from
one's body while living. For the great literary critic Longinus, ecstasy can be brought about
by speeches and writings that are sublimely beautiful. In his discussion of ecstasy, Philo says
that the best of the four kinds is an inspired state of being possessed and is a kind of madness
as well, the kind prophets make use of. This desire to feel one's mind as a thing separate from
the body (or at least to imagine that one is feeling it so) is probably responsible for the human
interest in seeking the sensation of ebriety or a "high." This feeling may be obtained most immediately and harmfully with alcohol or other mind-altering drugs, a fact that explains their
ubiquity. Today we also believe that it may be obtained by vigorous athletic exercise, by religious frenzy, by discovery, or by the beauty in nature, music, literature, and art.

59. For Aristotle, by contrast, although a person's intellect is the core part of his soul, a human being is nevertheless a composite of form and matter, soul and body. In the particular
composite, a person achieves individuality. The Neoplatonists follow the Stoics in identifying
a person with his soul and considering the body only so much excess baggage. The Aristotelian and Stoic conceptions of happiness also differ. Although, for Aristotle, the core of human happiness is an activity of the soul in accordance with virtue, he acknowledges (*Ethics,*
1099b1–10) that good birth, health, a sufficiency of wealth, and good appearance are required
as well. The Stoics disagree, teaching that a good man can be happy "even on the rack." In
other words, they wholly dismiss the need for external goods. The constant theme of the spiritual philosophies and heaven-aiming religions is disdain for the body and things physical;
nevertheless, human nature rebels against such asceticism and asserts, in agreement with Aristotle, its composite character.

60. The "somehow" is very well explained by S. Pinker in *How the Mind Works* (New
York: Norton, 1997), 220–33.

61. We find the same love of allegorizing and punning in the nineteenth-century New
England transcendentalists. It is impossible to read a paragraph of Thoreau's *Walden,* for
example, without seeing deep meaning conferred on the humblest speck of nature. It is no
surprise that Thoreau was very fond of Plato and quotes him frequently, along with similarly poetic Indian and Chinese philosophers.

62. See A. Altmann, *Studies in Religious Philosophy and Mysticism* (Ithaca, N.Y.: Cornell University Press, 1969), 54–55.

63. Gibbon, *Decline and Fall,* vol. 1, chapter 13, *ad fin.*

64. In fairness to Plato, we must repeat the above claim that Plato himself did not think
that he was pronouncing truth from the skies. Throughout the dialogues he tells us that he
is making things up out of his head, joking, poking fun at his contemporaries. Despite his
warnings, his words have been taken literally, almost like pronouncements from heaven—
nay, in many cases, *as* such pronouncements. Rather than alter their literal reading of
Plato, some scholars even prefer to take as jokes only those passages in which Plato has
Socrates say that he is not to be taken literally.

65. Despite the favoring of that philosophical tradition by the Church, not all Catholics
approved of the infatuation with Platonism. Savanarola is said to have told the illustrious
members of the Platonic Academy of Florence that an old woman of his acquaintance
knew more of faith than Plato did.

66. ibn Gabirol's poem "Keter Malkhuth," for example, shows the deep spirituality and
religiosity of Neoplatonism.

II

RECONCILING SCIENCE AND RELIGION

6

General Considerations Concerning the Reconciliation of Science and Religion

A man brings some very fine material to a tailor and asks him to make a pair of pants. When he comes back a week later, the pants are not ready. Two weeks later, they are still not ready. Finally, after six weeks, the pants are ready. The man tries them on. They fit perfectly. Nonetheless, when it comes time to pay, he can't resist a jibe at the tailor.

"You know," he says, "it took God only six days to make the world. And it took you six weeks to make just one pair of pants."

"Ah," the tailor says. "But look at this pair of pants, and look at the world!"

—Joseph Telushkin

Our primary concern in this chapter is to consider briefly a few of the major questions that come into consideration in the attempts to reconcile various religious conceptions of God with philosophical knowledge. Before addressing specific attempts to reconcile science and religion in the bulk of part 2 of this book, we shall examine a few problems that have arisen from the qualities attributed to the deity either by tradition, such as the deity's invisibility, or by philosophy, such as the deity's infinite goodness, omnipotence, omniscience, and pure incorporeality. The questions arising from these qualities concern the various implications of invisibility, how absolute goodness and divine might can be reconciled with the apparent presence of evil, how the deity's omniscience might be reconciled with the apparent freedom of the human will, and how humans should deal with their own corporeality when only pure spirit can be divinely excellent. The reason for introducing these questions here is to give a foretaste of the kinds of problems reconcilers of science and religion face.

GOD'S INVISIBILITY

Although most people have never had a direct, personal encounter with a deity, they nevertheless wish to believe that a deity works somehow in their lives. The inference must be that God, except on the rare occasions on which he reveals himself to someone, works in unseen ways.

In earlier times, much more was unseen than is unseen now. For example, ancient peoples were ignorant of the true causes of disease. They did not know about viruses, bacteria, cholesterol levels, or vitamin deficiencies, and these invisible *natural* causes never entered their consciousness. When a person became sick, his affliction seemed to be a visitation of an invisible *supernatural* power—either a deity or an evil spirit. Hence the cure might include a prayer to a god for intervention or might involve various efforts to ward off the effects of evil spirits. Divine intervention in human health is pervasive both in the Bible, where plagues are sent by God, and in Greek literature, where diseases and cures are similarly sent by the gods. The invisible cause of illness and health is the divine power. In the same way, the invisible cause of lightning, earthquakes, storms, sunshine, the movements of the planets and stars, and all other phenomena was attributable to the divine. Three distinct questions arise from the deity's invisibility: (1) How can the deity communicate with humans or operate in the world while preserving his invisibility? (2) Why does the deity wish to work invisibly? and (3) How may we know of God despite his invisibility?

While communication with God by humans has always been seen as a simple matter (since one can pray from anywhere), communication from God with humans is more controversial. Given the fervent wish to hear from God, a way had to be devised that would preserve God's need for invisibility along with people's wish to know. The perfect solution, which capitalizes on human beings' notorious propensity to misinterpret statistical matters, was to attribute a divine voice to matters that would otherwise seem due to chance. For example, in the Book of Jonah, when a storm is raging on the sea, the captain draws lots to learn whose guilt has caused the terrible punishing of the storm. In Greece, the flight of birds in augury and the position of entrails in divination were regularly used. The Delphic Oracle was also consulted, where a priestess would speak in gibberish the will of the gods, while a priest translated her noise into dactylic hexameter verse. In these ways, people managed to receive communication with their deities while their deities remained unobtrusive. For ancients, the deity was able to work his way invisibly through natural events such as lightning and storms, whose causes were wholly unknown. Even today, some who attempt to deal with God's invisible intervention in the world find the possibility of divine action in the quantum fluctuations that are beyond humankind's ken.

The question of why the divine would prefer to operate invisibly does not seem to be considered by the ancient pagans, but there has been Jewish speculation on the subject. If God were visible everywhere, this speculation goes, people would not be spontaneously good, but would be so from fear of immediate detection and punishment. Just as people tend to slow down and drive within the speed limit when the police are visible because of a desire to avoid a traffic ticket, so, if God were visible, would people behave virtuously to avoid divine retribution.[1] If the police or God is not visible, then those who are good are presumably so because of freely chosen virtue. Of course, this speculation ignores one of the powerful religious motives to good behavior: that God is watching everywhere, like a ubiquitous radar speed trap or like the cameras placed on British streets to record potential nefarious deeds.

The question of how we might know of God despite his invisibility is not of course a problem for pagans or for those who believe that the deity or deities *are* visible. The pagans saw gods everywhere: the sun, the moon, the stars, the various bodies of water from tiny rivulets to giant oceans were all gods, as were intersections of roads, the winds, and things like the impulse to sexual intercourse, drunkenness, weaving, metalwork, and on and on. But, as Augustine illustrates agonizingly in the opening pages of the *Confessions,* the question of invisibility is a concern in those religions in which God is believed not to have a body. As we have discussed earlier, science mostly deals with things in the corporeal world, with matter and the forces that work on matter. God, if he does not have a body, would clearly not fall under the province of this kind of science. But, as we have also discussed, logic and mathematics do not have to deal with the world of matter. Thus if God can be known despite his invisibility, it would have to be through these disciplines. Hence among those reconcilers of science and religion who hold the concept of an incorporeal deity we tend to find attempts to prove the existence of God by means of logical arguments.

EVIL IN THE WORLD

Unless we follow Pseudo-Dionysius and Augustine in stipulating that evil is non-being, and by thus denying its existence dissolve the problem of accounting for it, we must admit that there is in fact evil and suffering in the world. The problem for the religious believer arises when we try to account for the existence of both evil and an omnipotent, all-good deity. If God is wholly powerful, wholly good, and wholly knowing, why does he not simply vanquish evil altogether, or at least much more of it than he has? Apart from denying the existence of evil, philosophers have found one answer for the suffering in the world in human free will. Because God in his power gives humans the great good of free will—thus enabling them to live moral lives by making moral choices and to love him freely—he cannot be blamed if his gift is abused. Indeed, the very logic of freedom allows for the possibility of abuse. In the case of natural evil, such as the suffering attributable to natural disasters instead of to human choice, philosophers say that God allows matter to obey its own laws for the sake of an orderly universe or that the free choices of supernatural beings, such as fallen angels, are responsible for this sort of evil. Matter — because of the inherent necessities of its nature — does not enjoy the perfection of spiritual things. Asked why God did not make matter and the laws governing it free from all evil consequences, one might suggest the reasonable possibility that in attempting to do so God would have to eliminate a greater quantity of good and hence end up with a world that would be, on balance, worse than it is. The goods gained by having free creatures and orderly natural laws are thus two of the justifications one might offer for a perfect God's having created a world containing evil and suffering.

In some mythological accounts we find a different explanation for evil, with stories about how human beings started out perfect and then descended by their own error into their current lowly state. This doctrine of the fall of humankind is of course familiar in many religious traditions as well. Sometimes mythology speaks of this deterioration as a descent from a golden age, passing through various levels of degeneracy, to the present evil age. Hesiod tells both stories in *The Works and Days* and finds them not incompatible.[2] In one story, Hesiod describes the five ages of mankind, beginning with an Age of Gold, then an Age of Silver, then a Heroic Age, and coming at last to the present miserable Age of Iron. In other versions, such as Hesiod's story of Pandora, a mistake is made and results in the presence of evil. With Hesiod, if a person does not fancy one story, he can choose another to explain the same thing. A story of a mistake also occurs in the Bible, where we find the disobedience of the first man and woman to their only negative commandment. (There is no record that they were disobedient to their only positive commandment, to be fruitful and multiply.)

These stories exonerate God from responsibility for evil by placing the blame on mankind. Mankind sinned and was punished. Since the causes of the everlasting punishment are supernatural, the account of a fall and its consequences is not scientifically satisfying; it is nevertheless *intellectually* satisfying, for it allows God to remain a good creator unsullied by any taint of evil and at the same time maintains evil and misery as very real facts of our lives.

A more specific, and certainly more psychologically urgent, problem of evil concerns the fact that the world apparently contains much *unjust* or *gratuitous* suffering. Innocent and gifted children contract horrid, debilitating diseases; wicked people murder their brothers and then go on to live long and prosperous lives; malevolent nations, motivated by greed, conquer and enslave peaceful, well-ordered agricultural communities; worthy causes are defeated by wicked ones; honest poor are subjected to the lust, cruelty, and whim of dishonest rich; indeed, very often the meek are exiled from the earth and peacemakers suffer unspeakable torments. To this world's injustices religions all over have found an intellectually and emotionally satisfying answer. If justice is not achieved here in this world, it will be found in another, better, long-lasting world. Malefactors will go to hell, or they will be reincarnated as lowly animals crawling with their faces in the muck, or they will have to endure long eons in purgatory or some other miserable way station experiencing cruel punishments before they can move on, or they will be doomed to float forever as restless ghosts without the benefit of peace. Similarly, those who suffer unjustly on earth will get their due reward in the afterlife. In other words, justice for all awaits another life, and the world conceived in its entirety contains no unjust suffering. The hypothesis of heaven and hell, of reincarnation, of a day of judgment, is a non-philosophical way of finding moral order in the universe and of thus vindicating God's ultimate goodness.

A different solution accepts the presence of both God and evil. According to this solution, evil exists as an external force along with God. Far from God's being able to eliminate evil from creation, God and evil are locked in an eternal struggle for dominance. This view, which sees struggle as a constant force in the world, is also satisfying in its own way—for it accounts for the dynamic we actually see in nature. Of course, this dualism of good and evil achieves its goal by diminishing the uniqueness and power of God, who is unable to vanquish evil once and for all. But if one can accept the principle of a diminished God—not a principle that any of the revealed biblical religions can accept—the view also offers an intellectually satisfying accommodation of God and evil.

GOD'S OMNISCIENCE AND HUMAN FREE WILL

The question of whether God's omniscience is compatible with free will arises from the view that God must be perfect in every possible respect. Being perfect includes perfect, complete knowledge of everything that has happened, is happening, or will happen. If God knows what will happen, how then can the will be free? For example, if God knows that a person will be shopping for toothpaste next Wednesday at 3:00 P.M., how would it be possible for the person to be doing anything else? If it is not possible for the person to be doing anything else, how can his will be free?

Obviously, the simplest solution to the dilemma would be either to deny that God's omniscience extends to the future—a limitation of God's power that is anathema to those who wish God's majesty to be without any limit whatsoever— or to deny human free will—a solution that demolishes any possibility of human morality and also questions the moral rightness of God in punishing sin or rewarding virtuous behavior.

Augustine and Boethius, two Christian philosophers, have shown great ingenuity in their reconciliation of the two positions.[3] Their solution posits the existence of a special "eternity." While human beings live in time, where events succeed one another in a linear fashion, one after the other, God dwells in this eternity, gazing on all time as a simultaneous present. For God, past, present, and future merge into a single point. Thus, though an action seems future to us, it is always in the present to God, for future, present, and past are one in God's vision. By positing this type of eternity, Augustine and Boethius find a consistent solution to the problem of free will and divine omniscience: the will is free because humans choose their own course of action in the temporal world; that same will is foreknown from God's vantage point in eternity.[4]

Though one might admire the logical consistency of this reconciliation and the clever means by which the apparent contradiction is converted into a paradox, one might nevertheless question the plausibility of the solution. One might very well inquire into the seeming "ad hocness" and unfalsifiability of the concept of eternity in solving paradoxes about God's nature. What the Augustinian-Boethian solution does illustrate is the stunning ingenuity that can be employed in working out the compatibility of religious and philosophical/scientific beliefs.

HUMAN CORPOREALITY

In the Platonic tradition, the world of ideas represents perfection. The idea of a perfect table, however, cannot be manifested in any particular material table. The idea of a table is timeless, but the particular material table exists in a world of change and decay. As we shall see in the next chapter, in the Platonic scheme, matter has by its very nature limiting constraints. The world of ideas is immaterial; the actual world we inhabit is — in the Platonic point of view — irremediably material.[5]

Philosophical traditions that trace their views to these parts of Platonism, traditions such as Stoicism and the monotheistic religions of the West, have all been influenced by this division of matter and spirit and have all placed the divine or God in the dimension of spirit. To be like God, to imitate God, is to become as spiritual as possible. The problem, of course, is that humans, unlike God, are made at least partly of matter and do have bodies.

The question here, then, is more practical than theoretical. What is a person to do, given the brutish fact of a body? The solution in the early centuries of the Christian era was to abuse the body. E. R. Dodds reports:

> Pagans and Christians vied with each other in heaping abuse on the body; it was "clay and gore," "a filthy bag of excrement and urine"; man is plunged in it as in a bath of dirty water. Plotinus appeared ashamed of having a body at all; St. Anthony blushed every time he had to eat or satisfy any other bodily function. Because the body's health was the soul's death, salvation lay in mortifying it; as a Desert Father expressed it, "I am killing it because it is killing me." The psychophysical unity was split in two not only in theory but in practice; one half found its satisfaction in tormenting the other.[6]

Disdain for the body was manifest as well in sexual renunciation. Many Christians proudly abstained from sexual relations their entire lives. Virginity was acclaimed as the "supreme achievement"; self-castration, as highly commendable.[7]

Hatred of the body was expressed in contempt for women, who were believed to be inferior, because of their lower body temperature (and hence lesser possession of the more spiritual element fire) and polluted, because of menstruation (which occurred because they could not burn up the surpluses coagulating in their bodies).[8] The Desert Fathers report numerous forms of self-torture: living for years on the tops of pillars, total abstinence from food throughout Lent, remaining perpetually in a standing position, and so on.[9]

Disdain for the body and the subjugation of the physical to the spiritual have been, for most of western history, the practical means by which religious people have reconciled themselves with the philosophical division of body and spirit. The struggles with sexual morality, the worry over priestly celibacy, the periodic flirtation with asceticism, and the continuing attention to dualistic theorizing are other enduring consequences of this dichotomy. Since Plato's influential remarks are responsible for much of this history, it is appropriate that we turn to him in the next chapter.

DISCUSSION QUESTIONS

1. How does God's invisibility affect belief in God? Are people more inclined to attribute supernatural powers to something they can see or to something they cannot see? Are there ways in which invisibility allows greater scope for belief than visibility?

2. There are all sorts of explanations to account for evil in the world despite the existence of a perfectly good and powerful deity. One ancient Greek solution proposed by Aeschylus says that "in suffering comes wisdom." This is, of course, easily recognizable as fitting into the "good out of evil" class of arguments. There are many versions of the argument: a little suffering is good for the soul; adversity toughens; and, in parental advice, "Spare the rod and spoil the child." Milton takes the story of the evil in Adam's fall and converts it to a good by making the fall the cause of the greater happiness that will accompany the coming of Christ. How successful is this class of solution? Does it address the problem of the sometimes overwhelming price paid for the resulting good? How valid is the analogical argument to justify human evil? For example, some people have defended the American practice of enslaving Africans on the grounds that the evil of slavery produced for the Africans themselves the great good of life in a Christian world where they could attain the eternal salvation of their souls. Is there a calculus by which the suffering of those who died during the passage to America or in their initial capture can be shown to have been worthwhile?

3. Is it necessary for there to be the possibility of choosing evil in order for there to be free will? Could God have arranged for *both* free will and the choice of only goods? When one goes to a grocery store and has the choice of buying perhaps eight or nine different varieties of apples, all of which are

tasty and nutritious, he thus has a free choice of a variety of goods. Is it conceivable that God could have arranged the world similarly, with a free choice from among a variety of good choices? Is free choice different when it involves the possibility of choosing evil? Must there be a possibility of choosing evil for there to be moral choice? Are lesser goods equivalent to evils? If so, what effect would this interpretation (i.e., of lesser goods being equivalent to evils) have on the proposed solution to the problem of evil?

4. Some philosophers say that a philosophically consistent explanation, i.e., one without any contradictions, is plausible (perhaps an explanation like the Augustinian-Boethian theory of eternity). What does the term *plausible* mean? Is consistency enough for plausibility? Is consistency enough for truth? Can something be philosophically plausible in the sense of being consistent and at the same time self-evidently *untrue*?

5. Can we apply the "good out of evil" argument to the Platonic dualism that distinguishes body and soul? Can all the abuse heaped on bodies be justified on the basis of the enlightenment that has come from the distinction of mind and body? How might the history of the world have been different if Aristotle's concept of living creatures as inseparable composites of form and matter had been the only available theory?

NOTES

1. On this view see Dennis Prager and Joseph Telushkin, *The Nine Questions People Ask about Judaism* (New York: Touchstone, 1975), 20.

2. See H. Frankel, *Early Greek Poetry and Philosophy,* trans. M. Hadas and J. Willis (Oxford: Blackwell, 1975), 116–21.

3. Augustine in *On Free Will* and Boethius in book 5 of *The Consolation of Philosophy.*

4. For a sympathetic discussion of the Augustinian-Boethian conception of eternity as an immutable, atemporal duration, see Stump and Kretzmann, "Eternity."

5. The dichotomy between body and spirit begins in Greek culture, even in Homer. Plato is perhaps just one of the most influential developers of the notion. The origins of the dichotomy and the development of the idea are traced by E. R. Dodds, *The Greeks and the Irrational* (Berkeley: University of California Press, 1964), chapter 5.

6. Dodds, *Pagan and Christian,* 29–30.

7. Dodds, *Pagan and Christian,* 32.

8. Peter Brown, *The Body and Society: Men, Women, and Sexual Renunciation in Early Christianity* (New York: Columbia University Press, 1988), 10.

9. Dodds, *Pagan and Christian,* 33.

7

Plato

The Lady Angela. How purely fragrant!
The Lady Saphir. How earnestly precious!
Patience. Well, it seems to me to be nonsense.
The Lady Saphir. Nonsense, yes, perhaps—but oh, what precious nonsense!

—Gilbert and Sullivan

The most influential effort the world has ever witnessed to reconcile naturalistic and religious viewpoints is that of Plato, as put forth in his dialogue *Timaeus*. Despite the book's influence, Plato himself may have meant it as a satirical critique of his rivals and contemporaries, the Pythagoreans. The long account of how the world came into being, which seems to be a way of reconciling the gods with the latest and most up-to-date science, is put into the mouth of Timaeus, a physician from Locri and a member of the Pythagorean school. His account, as well as the whole dialogue, is full of all sorts of jokes, nonsensical explanations, extravagantly wild claims, puns, and all manner of silliness. Plato's purpose is to warn his readers about scientific know-it-alls, scientific hucksters and charlatans who are convincing because they can develop a tale persuasively but whose claims, when examined carefully, turn out to be hollow persiflage.[1] Nevertheless, with one or two exceptions, the dialogue was not understood in this way in antiquity. In fact, its influence as a literal—rather than tongue-in-cheek—description of reality has been enormous on Western culture and, through Western culture, on the whole world. Diogenes Laertius, an ancient biographer of the philosophers, goes so far as to say that Timaeus is one of only four characters in the dialogues who expound Plato's own views.[2] In what follows we shall therefore discuss the dialogue as though it were a serious and straightforward attempt to reconcile religious and scientific views, exiling to the desolate wasteland of endnotes a few skeptical comments. The names *Plato* and *Timaeus* will be used interchangeably.

The pre-Socratics competed with one another to provide the most persuasive account both of cosmogony, how the universe came into being, and of cosmology, how it operates. Each philosopher noticed certain problems in a predecessor's theories and addressed himself to those specific problems, seemingly oblivious to the new problems he was generating in his own theories. Of course, the pre-Socratic models were developed out of their inventors' heads wholly by reflection rather than being based on any experimentation. What is remarkable, as we have observed, is how insightful were both their questions and their solutions. We observed that while our modern solutions are quite different from theirs, in broad outline both the questions and the solutions are similar. (For example, the question of whether the universe is made from one underlying substance or from many was an ancient question and continues to be a modern one.)

For Plato, or Plato's successors, the object of knowledge is not the changing material nature of the world, as it was for most of the pre-Socratics, but the unchanging abstractions known variously as the "Ideas" or "Forms" or "Platonic Archetypes." In this Platonic view, because these ideas are universal, unchanging, and eternal, they are all that can be known. They alone possess permanence and certainty; they alone are intelligible. These ideas have an actual existence in the *World of Being,* to which humans gain access by possession of ideas. The model sciences are mathematics, logic, and geometry, for in these there is no admixture of change and dynamism to muddy things up, as there is in biology or any of the other physical sciences that cannot yield absolute knowledge because the object of their studies does not stand still.

According to the Platonic scheme, to repeat what we have observed earlier (p. 47), the physical world is a world of continuous change. To this physicality and change the Platonic school gives the name *World of Becoming.* In postulating the simultaneous existence of both these worlds, Plato stands as one of the great synthesizers of philosophy. His dualistic system combines, in effect, the Parmenidean world of unity and being with the Heraclitean world of change. The *Timaeus* proposes a solution to the problem that any dualism faces—how the two realms are connected—by providing a detailed account of the connection.

Timaeus immediately warns his listeners (as we must refer to those who in the dramatic context of the dialogue are actually present as the audience of Timaeus's speech) that because he is going to be talking about *becoming,* his tale will be as likely as any other.[3] Here Timaeus (or Plato) seems to invite comparison with his predecessors who explained the universe according to various theories. He announces that he will give us a *model* or a hypothesis and that he is not proposing to give us the truth, the whole truth, and nothing but the truth, as he has been supposed to have done by his later readers.

Elsewhere, Plato's Socrates has complained that the early natural philosophers give accounts of the physical universe without really explaining how the universe's rational and intelligible order comes about.[4] In the *Timaeus,* though, we seem to have just such an account as Socrates demands, one that relies on the existence and activity of what Plato's speaker calls a Craftsman. (In Greek, as well as in many accounts of the *Timaeus,* the Craftsman is called a *Demiurge.* Here, however, we shall use the English word *Craftsman,* so that the sense of the term will be more apparent.) The visible world in which we live, this physical world, says Timaeus, was made by the Craftsman as a likeness of an eternal pattern.

Perhaps a bit of elaboration on Plato's notion of an eternal pattern will help. Let us imagine that a carpenter wishes to make a table. After conceiving the table in his mind, he will proceed to construct it. His mental image, drawn from some conceptual repository of things a carpenter can make, is the pattern. In the case of Plato's divine Craftsman, the mental image is of the ideas that exist in the World of Being—a heavenly repository of the perfect and eternal and unchanging ideas. In the case of our familiar human craftsman, it is very easy to understand how he has a picture of a table in his mind.

In presenting a Craftsman, Timaeus or Plato says that the world came into being the way any fabricated product comes into being. A thinking, rational individual begins with an idea. Using the materials at hand and constrained by their limitations, he makes an object. Just as the carpenter is constrained by the kinds of wood available and by the limitations of that wood, and just as he must accommodate his wishes to what is actually possible using the available materials, so must Timaeus's Craftsman of the universe. Like any artisan, the divine Craftsman had a purpose and designed each element of his product with a specific purpose in mind. Just as the carpenter might make the various parts of his table to serve subsidiary purposes—for instance, making the top flat to keep objects from slipping off, making the legs equal so that the top will not wobble, allowing the table to be fitted with a removable leaf so that a large group can enjoy a meal together, or using wooden pegs instead of iron nails so that there will be nothing to rust—so too the Craftsman of the universe made every part to serve some subsidiary or ultimate purpose. The basic quality of the universe that Timaeus describes is that it is *teleological,* that is, that everything in it serves a purpose.

The universe of the pre-Socratics, who focus on material and efficient causes, arises by physical forces alone and does not work towards any purpose or have any final cause. For Plato, the idea of a purposeless universe simply makes no sense. Timaeus's account therefore begins by asking the broad question, Why create the world at all? The answer is that the Craftsman is good and desires that all things be as much as possible like him, i.e., as good as possible.[5] In the Craftsman's mind, it would not be appropriate for the matter of the universe simply to lie around inert, devoid of the good qualities that the Craftsman might form in it. This desire by the Craftsman to make the world resemble his own goodness is a remarkable concept for a pagan author to have. Indeed, it resembles the Christian God's desire to create the world as an extension of his love. The Craftsman's motives thus raise familiar questions: Why was the universe not made still bigger, that it might contain even more goodness? Why were not all things made at the same highest level of goodness? Or are we to suppose that the totality of higher and lower goods is somehow greater than a totality of uniformly higher goods?

Although neither the Christian nor the Platonic conception of a good creator becomes compelling without answers to these questions being given, we need not
digress to discuss them now.

Like any artist, no matter how good his intentions are, the Craftsman must
work with the materials at his disposal, materials that have their own, sometimes
recalcitrant and limited natures. Plato calls these natures the facts of necessity. In
other words, the motions and potencies of matter itself, the material with which
the Craftsman must work, are not the result of some prior design but are the result of the inherent, innate nature of matter. Anyone who has engaged in carpentry or plumbing or gardening is familiar with the "darned cussedness" of matter.
Timaeus says that where things appear not to have worked out for the best, it is
not because of some defect in the will or goodness of the Craftsman, but because
of the inherent limitation of the materials. Here we have a foreshadowing of an
enormously influential idea that dogs Western intellectual and religious life—that
matter is somehow defective and unworthy of the minds that should by all rights
control it. As we shall see later, this idea develops into a disdain for all things
bodily and fleshly and an exaggeration of the conflict between the material and
the spiritual or divine.

According to Timaeus, then, the world is made by intelligence operating upon
a necessity in the materials. The Craftsman's intelligence, gazing at the divine
pattern in the World of Being, imitates the pattern as well as he can, given the materials at his disposal. Earth, air, and water are arranged in due proportions; the
universe is made round because, he says rather arbitrarily, roundness is the perfect shape,[6] the perfect idea; soul is attuned according to various mathematical ratios, ratios that exist as ideas in the World of Being.

Matter in a state of disorderly motion seems to have existed before the creation
of the universe.[7] The purpose of making the universe was to put this matter into
an order as much like that of its maker as possible, i.e., an order that is good and
rational. Since—presumably by definition—reason cannot exist apart from soul,
the Craftsman made the universe as a living creature with a reasoning soul. The
cosmos, like a human being, is "a living thing endowed with soul and reason."[8]

The similarity between man and universe is expanded in Timaeus's claim that
the cosmos is made in the image of all the other living animals. What that image
is, Timaeus does not clearly state. If, like Pico, we may assume that man has the
potential of becoming all other creatures (a view given credence later in the dialogue, in the discussion of how all the other animals are created from degenera-
tive versions of man), it is likely that the "man-universe" is intended to be similarly malleable.[9] This interpretation that man includes all the other creatures is
also supported by the statement that the god wanted to make the cosmos "resemble most closely that intelligible creature which is fairest of all and in all ways
most perfect."[10]

The claim that the universe resembles the one fairest creature leads Timaeus to
one of the questions posed by the atomists—whether there is one or an infinite
number of worlds. The question is resolved by Timaeus very easily. If, as

Timaeus asserts, the universe is framed after a pattern that includes everything, there must be one cosmos—otherwise it would not contain everything.[11] The idea seems to be that a cosmos—a beautiful and orderly whole—would simply not be a cosmos if it were incomplete.

Continuing his discussion of the universe, Timaeus explains the necessity for the four elements with the assertion that the two most unlike elements, fire, which is necessary for sight, and earth, which is necessary for the solidity required by touching, require a bond between them and that "the fairest of bonds is the proportion."[12] Because a proportion requires four terms, there need to be two middle terms, or middle elements, in addition to fire and earth. When we recall that the Craftsman is constructing the universe from a divine pattern, we see here how the idea of mathematical ratios is translated into the number of elements present in the World of Becoming. Implicit in Timaeus's scheme is the principle that various mathematical truths are reflected in the physical reality of the world. Because cubic numbers, which have two mean terms, reflect solidity, there must be two elements corresponding to the two mean terms.[13] Later on in the dialogue, Timaeus discusses the mathematical ratios according to which the various rotations of the soul move. Still later, he describes in geometric terms the various kinds of triangles from which all matter is formulated. It is thus clear that in Timaeus's scheme mathematics is a central preoccupation of the divine mind and that the universe is the physical manifestation of that mind. Religion and mathematics turn out to be parts of the same subject.[14]

Timaeus goes on to say that the cosmos's body is harmonized according to mathematical proportions. From the harmony comes amity (*philia*), which ensures that the cosmos is indissoluble except by its maker. "Amity" or "friendship" was used in physics earlier, by Empedocles, to describe how the elements were brought together, only to be separated later by strife (*eris*).[15] Here, however, Timaeus suggests that only the maker can dissolve the proportions by which the cosmos is bound together. Timaeus perhaps is implying a correction of Empedocles—that it is not strife but the Craftsman alone who can undo creation.

The next subject Timaeus takes up is the Craftsman's creation of time as a "movable likeness of eternity."[16] The phrase seems to indicate that the motions of the heavenly bodies will be orderly, taking their rhythm from eternal numbers. The nature of time is thus another way in which the World of Becoming reflects eternity. The climax of this discourse occurs in the revelation of the Craftsman's purpose for making the moon, the sun, and the planets: so that we can tell time! The heavenly bodies move at different velocities so that it will be possible to measure relative speeds and so that "all the living creatures entitled thereto might participate in number, learning it from the revolution of the Same and Similar."[17]

The Craftsman himself constructs the gods, making them mostly of fire, "to be a true adornment embroidered in the whole."[18] These gods have two motions, forward motion and motion on their own axes (so that they might always have identical thoughts about the same things—an anticipation perhaps of the mind of Aristotle's

Prime Mover).[19] As for the gods of mythology, those descended from Zeus, Earth, and the others, Timaeus dismisses them offhandedly, saying that we might as well believe the stories about them. Besides, dealing with them would be "too big" a subject. Of course, in the light of all the trouble one might get into by questioning the gods, perhaps this concession to traditional piety should be understood as an ironic disclaimer intended to avoid the liability invited by a charge of atheism or impiety.

The Craftsman, says Timaeus, addresses both kinds of gods—the created, "scientific" gods who revolve as Timaeus has just described, and the mythic gods. The Craftsman tells both kinds of gods that they can be destroyed only by his will but that he has no intention of destroying them because they were well made. His will, he says, is even stronger than the physical bonds with which they were made. He then tells the gods about the three kinds of creature still to be made (presumably those who will dwell in the air, the water, and the earth). If he, the Craftsman, were to make them, they would be perfect, but, for a motive which is not revealed, he does not want them to be equal to the gods. Therefore, the created gods are to make them. He, however, will make the immortal part of the creatures and bring it to the gods to weave together with the mortal part that they are to make.

It is impossible to overemphasize the historical influence of this particular passage. As we shall see (p. 148), Philo understands it as an explication of Genesis 1.26, where God says, "Let us make man in image, after our likeness." God first made the likeness, the *logos,* and then patterned men after it. For Christians—for whom Philo was a Father—the Platonic passage appears to confirm Christian views about angels and about Christ's participation in the creation of man.[20]

The longest part of the *Timaeus* deals with the construction of man. There is no danger of sexism in this use of the word *man,* for Timaeus makes clear that he is discussing *males.* (In a later passage, which is almost certainly satirical, he says that women are the reincarnation of degenerate males.) The discourse begins with an account of the senses, which, like the rest of the cosmos, are explained as the work of mind on recalcitrant materials. As the next step, according to Timaeus, the Craftsman assists his sons the gods in making mortal things by giving them the immortal soul that he himself has made and around which they are to construct bodies. In addition to this immortal soul, the gods also place into bodies a mortal kind of soul, which contains all the passions. From these premises come an array of anatomical conclusions. To avoid polluting the divine soul, the gods put the mortal soul in the chest and separate it by an isthmus. The gods make the heart a bodyguard to tell all the organs (by circulating the blood) when an unjust deed has been done. To relieve the leaping of the heart, the gods make the lungs, the coolness of which enables the heart to be subservient to reason in times of passion. All these anatomical features are created for the sake of mind, for the sake of philosophy.[21]

The gods put the appetitive part of the soul in the area of the stomach, so that it will be as far away as possible from the reasoning part of the soul.[22] So that the stomach might receive instructions from reason, the gods place the liver nearby, for it is bright and shiny and can thus serve as a mirror for the thoughts of the mind. It is made with some bitterness, too, so that it can frighten the stomach.[23] Long intestines prevent food from being digested too quickly, which would leave men too hungry to engage in philosophy.

There follows a marvelous passage on why we have little flesh to protect our skulls, yet an abundance of flesh on our hips.[24] Because the bones that contain the most marrow are those in which the greatest degree of intellection takes place, and because an abundance of flesh in these places would make these parts more forgetful and obtuse, the gods put little flesh on these. A greater amount of flesh on the head, however, would have given man a life twice as long or many times as long as our present life, and one free from pain.[25] But the gods decided that man ought to have a shorter but superior life rather than a longer but inferior one. We have here, in essence, the choice of Achilles — the long but dull life as opposed to the short but glorious life — applied to human anatomy!

The generation of the rest of the animals is explained by Timaeus as the reincarnation of men who have lived less than exemplary lives.[26] Cowardly and unjust men return as women. Birds derive from light-minded men, who, when they were studying meteorology, put their trust in sight instead of in reason. Wild animals who go on foot derive from those men who never studied philosophy. Therefore, these animals always look down at the ground, with the more foolish ones creeping lower and lower until the quintessentially foolish ones wriggle on the earth. Utterly stupid men return as fish. Timaeus adds that the creatures continue to pass one into another according to their gain or loss of reason during their lives. With this last remark, Timaeus announces the end of his speech: mortal and immortal creatures have filled up the cosmos.

The *Timaeus* itself is not light reading. It is full of analogies between mathematical shapes and physical objects, and a great many of its scientific accounts are laborious to follow. But the book merits careful study, if only because it has been so enormously influential. It becomes the pattern for numerous subsequent attempts to reconcile mind and nature. The genius of the dialogue is in its powerful explanation — even if that explanation is satirical — of how the mind of God, the eternal pattern of ideas, is translated into the physical world. A core problem that finds its first expression in this work is the development of a changing, concrete material world from the fixed, immutable abstract truths in God's mind. When modern physicists from Galileo to Stephen Hawking assert that the material world reflects a divine mathematical pattern, they echo the sentiments of Timaeus of Locri.

DISCUSSION QUESTIONS

1. In the *Timaeus* we find the idea of a craftsman who has an *idea* of a physical thing and then, using materials subject to the limiting qualities of matter,

manufactures that physical thing. In what ways is this idea anthropomorphic? Are there any ways in which Plato's Craftsman is not anthropomorphic?

2. Does the idea of a single craftsman with a single controlling pattern represent a revolutionary departure from polytheism? How does the character Timaeus try to accommodate polytheism into his system? What are his possible motives for doing so?

3. Does Plato satisfactorily account for the prior existence of a pattern of the universe? Is it intellectually satisfying to posit the pattern as a *given?* Or must it be accounted for in some other way?

4. How important is it to science today that the universe be subject to mathematical laws? Does the fact that mathematics reveals patterns in nature suggest design? What would a universe be like that was not subject to mathematical regularity?

5. In what ways is the *Timaeus* a mélange of profound insight and total nonsense? As we look at the panoply of human genius, we often find insight and nonsense residing in the same souls. For example, Johannes Kepler, who showed that the planets orbit the sun in elliptical orbits, believed in witchcraft; even Isaac Newton's superstitions are legend. Is creative genius a close relative of irrational fancy?

NOTES

1. See J. Arieti, *Interpreting Plato,* 19–53.
2. Diogenes Laertius, *Life of Plato,* 52.
3. Plato, *Timaeus,* 29C–D.
4. Plato, *Phaedo,* 97C–98D.
5. Plato, *Timaeus,* 29E.
6. The arbitrariness of the perfection assigned to the shape is mocked by Cicero in *The Nature of the Gods,* 2.47.
7. Plato, *Timaeus,* 30A. The existence of this disorderly motion has, with good reason, troubled Platonists since ancient times. If, as appears in Plato, the soul is the cause of motion (*Phaedrus,* 245C-E), how can there be motion before the existence of soul and cosmos? Of course, if we do not take the Timaeus as representing Plato's own views, the difficulty dissolves.
8. Plato, *Timaeus,* 30C.
9. Plato, *Timaeus,* 30C–D.
10. Plato, *Timaeus,* 30D.
11. For possible fallacies in this position, see the discussion by D. Keyt, "The Mad Craftsman of the *Timaeus,*" *The Philosophical Review* 80 (1971): 230–35.
12. The metaphor of the bond as an actual cosmic force is taken quite literally by R. J. Mortley, who writes, "The numbers that could be used in a proportion such as this would not represent relations between elements, but cosmic forces existing as Forms affecting the sensible world in the same way as other Forms" ("The Bond of the Cosmos: A Significant Metaphor (*Tim.* 31c ff.)," *Hermes* 97 [1969]: 372–73).

13. Cubic or "solid" numbers include two mean terms for a continuous proportion. For example, $x^3 : x^2y :: x^2y : xy^2 :: xy^2 : y^3$. In this proportion, x^2y and xy^2 are the mean terms. Perhaps it is easier for moderns to understand if written as fractions: $x^3/x^2y = x^2y/xy^2 = xy^2/y^2$.

14. For the rotations of the soul, see Plato, *Timaeus,* 36ff. For the kinds of triangles, see 53C–55C. Critical discussion on this latter passage has chiefly concerned the extent to which Plato borrowed the idea of the different solids from Philolaus and Pythagoras. See, for example, J. E. Raven, *Pythagoreans and Eleatics* (Cambridge: Cambridge University Press, 1948), 150ff.; and M. T. Casridini, "Il cosmo di Filolao," *Rivista Critica di Storia della Filosofia* 3 (1946): 322–33. According to the view described above that the Platonic dialogues are not to be taken literally, the whole structure of the physical universe given by Timaeus is based on analogical fancy, which Plato meant to be parody. Plato's real intention is to display some of the methodological errors of the Pythagoreans, whom Timaeus represents. Thus Plato would be drawing the very same criticism as Aristotle does when he says that the Pythagoreans try to make numbers represent everything (*Metaphysics,* 985b ff.). Even if the two mean terms in Timaeus's proportion exist in the physical world, there are no grounds for saying that one mean is water and the other air. That these elements correspond to the means is in fact asserted (32B), but the assertion merely illustrates the folly of considering numbers to be physical objects. It entirely possible—indeed, likely—that the same criticism Aristotle lays out in the *Metaphysics* is made here dramatically by Plato.

15. On the satirical purpose of the passage, including a satirical mockery of Empedocles, see J. Arieti, *Interpreting Plato,* 48n25.

16. Plato, *Timaeus,* 37D.

17. Plato, *Timaeus,* 38C–39C.

18. Plato, *Timaeus,* 40A.

19. Plato, *Timaeus,* 40B.

20. For discussions of the confirmation of Christian views by Plato, see W. J. Burghardt, *The Image of God in Man According to Cyril of Alexandria* (Woodstock, Md.: Woodstock College Press, 1957); and H. A. Wolfson, *Philo: Foundations of Religious Philosophy in Judaism, Christianity, and Islam* (Cambridge, Mass.: Harvard University Press, 1947), esp. 271ff. For the identification of these subordinate, intermediary deities and *logos* in Philo, see, as one of many examples, *On the Confusion of Tongues,* 147.

21. Plato, *Timaeus,* 70B–D.

22. Plato, *Timaeus,* 70E.

23. Plato, *Timaeus,* 71B.

24. Plato, *Timaeus,* 74E.

25. Plato, *Timaeus,* 75B.

26. Plato, *Timaeus,* 90E–92B.

8

Philo of Alexandria

> After practicing detailed comparisons of names and definitions and visual and other sense perceptions, after scrutinizing them in benevolent disputation by the use of question and answer without jealousy, at last in a flash understanding of each blazes up, and the mind, as it exerts all its powers to the limit of human capacity, is flooded with light.
>
> —Plato, *Seventh Letter*

Aristotle remarks that "it would be absurd for a man to say that he loved God."[1] The gods of Aristotle and Plato, however different they may be in other respects, share one fundamental trait: neither is what we call a personal god. Each philosopher, to be sure, was able to penetrate beyond anthropomorphic characteristics and beyond the characters of the pagan pantheon—beyond Zeus and Athena and Aphrodite and Dionysus—to some sort of monotheistic unity. But that unity, however sublime, is not lovable. The Prime Mover and Timaeus's Craftsman are computer-like minds, a thinker thinking about itself in the former case, pure intelligence shaping matter in the latter case. Opposed to the view of an unlovable god stands the Hebraic notion, enshrined in the *shema:* "Thou shalt love the Lord thy God with all thy heart, with all thy soul, and with all thy might."[2] Philo of Alexandria (fl. 40 c.e.) made it his task to show that the God of the *shema* is in fact the same deity as that of Platonic philosophy, that there is no irreconcilable difference between the two, and that indeed Plato's work and the work of the Pythagorean numerologists is indispensable for elaborating the sacred text.

Of Philo's life not very much is known. Philo's brother Alexander, a wealthy banker, and his nephew, Alexander's son Tiberius Julius Alexander, are better known from historical sources.[3] Philo's only historically recorded action is to have led a delegation of Jews from Alexandria on a mission to the emperor Caligula. We do not know of any other travels except for a pilgrimage to

Jerusalem. The writings of Philo, which, he says, come from his own soul,[4] show him to have been well educated in contemporary science and philosophy. It is not clear whether he knew Hebrew, for his references to the Bible are to the Septuagint, the Greek translation.

Perhaps the best way of approaching Philo and his attempt to reconcile science and philosophy will be to take a look at his commentary on Genesis, *On the Creation,* for it is an epitome of views that are found throughout his corpus. In the main, Philo's program is to show that Timaeus's explanation—Philo takes Timaeus completely as Plato's mouthpiece—sheds light on the meaning of Genesis. He demonstrates this thesis by expatiating on the similarities between the two cosmological accounts, by explaining the biblical text in Platonic terms, and by disclosing where the mythological outward form expresses an inner spiritual truth. The process is most fascinating. While Philo's work was not influential in the history of Judaism, it was profoundly influential in Christianity.[5]

On the Creation begins with a contrast between the work of other lawmakers and that of Moses. Other lawmakers, Philo says, either have simply drawn up a code of laws or have surrounded their codes with a good deal of irrelevant material. Moses, however, gave as an introduction to his laws an account of the creation of the world. Thus it is clear that

> the world is in harmony with the law, and the law with the world, and that the man who observes the law is constituted thereby a loyal citizen of the world, regulating his doings by the purpose and will of nature, in accordance with which the entire world itself is administered.[6]

Philo's claims here are quite remarkable. As a Jew he gives consummate importance to the law, the commandments. Rabbinical Judaism has always made its focus the study and refinement of the law; the Talmud is a commentary on the law. Philo is simultaneously very Greek. As a Greek, he looks at the Bible as a rhetorical composition.[7] The account of creation is the "exordium," the first part of a speech, and as such receives the highest praise for putting the law into the context of the entire universe. The law is not written by a single prominent citizen, like those devised by Solon and Lycurgus for Athens and Sparta. It is written by the creator of the entire cosmos. Jewish law is thus infused with a significance that lifts it out of any local setting and removes from it the limitations it would have as a purely man-made object. The person who follows the Mosaic law is a citizen of the world, not a citizen of Judea or Alexandria or a Jewish community somewhere, but of the *world*. In this way Philo embraces the Hellenistic, Stoic idea that the entire human race is one brotherhood, where the differences between Roman and Greek, Jew and Gentile evaporate. God created the universe for everyone, and his law is for everyone. Moreover, the law is said to be in accordance with nature, so that there is a merging of the Torah and natural laws. In short, we see Philo adopt the philosophical view of mainline Greek philosophy that there is no divorce between the nature of the universe and its laws—physics—on the one hand, and the human world and its laws—ethics, on the other. Ethics and physics are in harmony because the universe is a place of order.

This idea of a harmony between human ethics and the physical laws of the universe is fundamental to the spirit of the Hellenistic Age. The harmony is most easily observed in Epicureanism and Stoicism, the two most prominent philosophical systems of the period. For Epicureans, the world consists of atoms falling in a void, a view that reduces the universe to a place devoid of transcendental meaning. The ethics derivable from this physics consists of making the best of a world where nothing ultimately matters. If nothing matters, the best one can do is avoid pain; hence, avoidance of pain became the primary ethical goal of Epicureans. Stoics had as the basis for their physics the passive principle of matter, a kind of cosmic stuff lacking in any quality whatsoever, and an active principle, god or *logos*. A human being consists both of the passive principle—his body—and the active principle—his divine *logos*. Stoic ethics aimed at maintaining the order and excellence of the active principle. What we wish to stress here is that Philo too sees a harmony between physics, which for him is expressed in the story of creation in Genesis, and ethics, which is expressed in the laws of Moses in the other four books of the Pentateuch. For a man of the Hellenistic Age, ethics and physics are simply different notes of a harmonious chord. If we might be allowed to translate Philo's point into modern terms, it would be as though the American Constitution and the law books of the United States were to be preceded by an account of Newtonian and Einsteinian physics. A commentator like Philo would then say that the civil laws were based on and harmonious with the laws of physics, that this harmony gives them their validity so that they are really laws not just for the citizens of the United States but for all people, and that by following them all people are united as citizens of the cosmos. This claim that law harmonizes with physics is the bold claim that Philo makes for the Bible at the introduction of his discourse, an introduction as bold perhaps as the one he attributes to the Torah itself.

Philo cautions, however, against emphasizing the physical world at the expense of its creator.

> There are some people who, having the world in admiration rather than the Maker of the world, pronounce it to be without beginning and everlasting, while with impious falsehood they postulate in God a vast inactivity; whereas we ought on the contrary to be astonished at His powers as Maker and Father, and not to assign to the world a disproportionate majesty. Moses, both because he had attained the very summit of philosophy, and because he had been divinely instructed in the greater and most essential part of Nature's lore, could not fail to recognize that the universal must consist of two parts, one part active cause and the other passive object; and that the active cause is the perfectly pure and unsullied Mind of the universe, transcending virtue, transcending knowledge, transcending the good itself and the beautiful itself; while the passive part is in itself incapable of life and motion, but, when set in motion and shaped and quickened by mind, changes into the most perfect masterpiece, namely this world.[8]

Here Philo clearly responds to the kind of philosophers criticized in Cicero's *Nature of the Gods*. They praise nature but not God, to whom they attribute inactivity. Philo seems to be attacking especially the Epicureans, who admire the nature they see as having arisen from chance collisions of atoms and who, while acknowledging that there are gods, say that they too are made of atoms, do not bother themselves with our woes, and live carefree lives of idleness and joy somewhere far removed from the world. It is God we ought to praise, Philo says, not the world.

It is important to observe that Philo expressly calls Moses a philosopher. No one would have been more startled by such an appellation than Moses, but for a learned Greek of the Hellenistic period there is no greater possible compliment. When we recall that Philo was a Platonist-Pythagorean and that according to the views of these schools the entire universe was designed for the very purpose of allowing some people to become philosophers, we understand that the term *philosopher* is clearly the highest praise.

As a philosopher, Moses could not help knowing that the world consists of both an active and a passive principle. The active principle is God, whom Philo describes as wholly transcendent, a pure mind that goes beyond goodness, virtue, and beauty. Now for the Platonic school, transcendence stops with the eternal ideas. The highest philosophic success to which one could aspire was a glimpse of the idea of the good itself or of beauty itself. For Philo, God is at least one level of transcendence beyond the eternal ideas. Beyond the ideas themselves lies ineffability, the *via negativa* that we have heard about before, the concept that it is impossible to describe the unlimited deity in limited language. The Judaism of Philo here surpasses his Platonism as he extends the distance from humanity to the divine beyond the measure Plato had delineated. In the last part of the quoted passage, Philo expresses the views that we have seen in the *Timaeus*. This world is the masterpiece created by mind working upon the passive principle, matter. Matter by itself cannot move and cannot be alive; life and motion come from mind, and this mind is God.

Now God did not create the world directly. First he made a pattern. In the *Timaeus,* the Craftsman looked upon the eternal pattern and formed the world after it. But there was no discussion in the *Timaeus* of where that pattern came from. For Philo, Judaism provides the answer—God. He writes,

> For God, being God, assumed that a beautiful copy would never be produced apart from a beautiful pattern, and that no object of perception would be faultless which was not made in the likeness of an original discerned only by the intellect. So when He willed to create this visible world He first fully formed the intelligible world, in order that he might have the use of a pattern wholly God-like and incorporeal in producing the material world, as a later creation, the very image of an earlier, to embrace in itself objects of perception of as many kinds as the other contained objects of intelligence.[9]

Timaeus's Craftsman has been replaced by God, and the origin of the pattern has been found to be in God's mind. Philo elaborates on the idea of a pattern and its extreme theological importance. Just as a city that a king constructs exists all at once in the king's mind, so the universe existed all at once in God's mind. God's creative work occurs in the simplicity of the moment—the vision of the pattern. The six days of creation were needed only for the matter to be settled in order.[10]

Why does Philo include a *pattern* in his explanation of creation, and on what basis does he think that the Bible sanctions the pattern? In the answer to these very questions lies Philo's influence on Christianity. To answer the questions, it is best to skip to Philo's discussion of Genesis 1.26, where God decides to create humankind: "And God said, 'Let us make humankind according to our likeness and according to our image.'" In another work, Philo emphasizes that Moses did not say that man *is* "the image of God" but that man is made "*according* to the image."[11] Thus, says Philo, God first made an image of himself, which Philo calls *Logos,* reason. Man, he continues, "is third-hand from the Maker, while between them [man and God] is Reason, which serves as a model for our reason but is itself the effigy or presentment of God."[12] Philo finds evidence for the "pattern" in the very words of the Bible. It is pleasant to imagine Philo as he sat in his study in Alexandria, perhaps with a window looking out onto the bay with its famous lighthouse, when he discovered—or recognized—this echo of the Platonic idea. Perhaps he leapt from his chair and, Archimedes-like, shouted "Eureka!" Here lay before him the key to rendering revelation scientific; here lay a correspondence between the very best science as represented by Plato and the Torah as composed by the consummate philosopher Moses.

Philo calls the pattern *Logos*—reason—and makes the commonness of God and man the immortal part of the soul, just as Timaeus did when he assigned to the Craftsman the making of the immortal part of the soul but to the lesser gods the making of the mortal parts. That reason is the image of God and the essence of man is a central tenet of the Platonic school, which holds that the divine part of the soul is reason. Here then Philo introduces the concept of *Logos* as the pattern for the universe, a view that finds its way into the Gospel of John, which begins with a parallel notion: "In the beginning was the Logos [Word], and the Logos was with God." As H. Chadwick writes, for Philo, "The Logos is 'the idea of ideas,' the first-begotten son of the uncreated Father and 'second God,' the pattern and mediator of creation, the archetype of human reason, and 'the man of God.'"[13]

The discussion of Genesis 1.26 in *On the Creation* contains one of the greatest passages in Philo's corpus and one of the noblest anywhere. It is worth quoting at length.

> After all the rest, as I have said, Moses tells us that man was created after the image of God and after His likeness. Right well does he say this, for nothing earth-born is more like God than man. Let no one represent the likeness as one to a bodily form; for neither is God human in form, nor is the human body God-like. No, it is in respect of the Mind, the sovereign element of the soul, that the word "image" is used; for after the pattern of a single Mind, even the Mind of the Universe as an archetype, the mind in each of those who successively came into being was molded. It is in a fashion a god to him who carries and enshrines it as an object of reverence; for the human

mind evidently occupies a position in men precisely answering to that which the great Ruler occupies in all the world. It is invisible while itself seeing all things, and while comprehending the substances of others, it is as to its own substance unperceived; and while it opens by arts and sciences roads branching in many directions, all of them great highways, it comes through land and sea investigating what either element contains. Again, when on soaring wing it has contemplated the atmosphere and all its phases, it is borne yet higher to the ether and the circuit of heaven, and is whirled around with the dances of the planets and fixed stars, in accordance with the laws of perfected music, following that love of wisdom which guides its steps. And so, carrying its gaze beyond the confines of all substance discernible by sense, it comes to a point at which it reaches out after the intelligible world, and on descrying in that world sights of surpassing loveliness, even the patterns and the originals of the things of sense which it saw here, it is seized by a sober intoxication, like those filled with Corybantic frenzy, and is inspired, possessed by a longing far other than theirs and a nobler desire. Wafted by this to the topmost arch of the things perceptible to the mind, it seems to be on the way to the Great King himself; but amid its longing to see Him, pure and untempered rays of concentrated light stream forth like a torrent, so that by its gleams the eye of understanding is dazzled.[14]

In studying this passage, one might agree with many of the Church Fathers, who joked that either "Plato philonizes or Philo platonizes." Philo's use of the mystical language of the dialogues was to become a theme much revisited in the Christian and Neoplatonic traditions. The sentence following the quotation says that because images do not always correspond to their patterns, Moses has added the words "after the likeness" to "after the image" in order to show that God intended to make an accurate copy.[15] The additional sentence brings us down to earth and to philology and makes it clear that Philo has intended his hymn to reason as a purple passage in his discourse. The idea of the soul flying out of its human confines and glancing at the eternal ideas is found in Plato's *Phaedrus,* among other Platonic works, and is especially common in the Neoplatonists. Philo's imagery deliberately links the Platonic ideas to the Bible.

The Bible seems to have two accounts of the creation of man, one in the first chapter of Genesis and one in the second. Philo is just as aware of the fact of two accounts as are the "Higher Critics" of nineteenth-century Germany. But his theory is uniquely Philonic. The man discussed in chapter 1 of Genesis, he says, is the idea. The man made in chapter 2 is the actual man in the physical world, a composite of earth and divine breath. Thus man is immortal in the invisible part, mortal in the visible.[16] Let us see what Philo has done in developing this hypothesis. First, of course, he notices that there is the "all at once" creation of humankind in Genesis 1.26. Then, in 2.4, God seems to begin all over again to create the world, as the text announces (2.5) that God has not yet caused it to rain and that there is no man to till the ground. In 2.7, God forms man of dust from the ground. When God breathes into his nostrils the breath of life, man becomes alive. Philo must at this point have experienced another of those "eureka" moments: here is biblical confirmation for the bipartite division of man into matter and soul, the matter from the ground, the breath directly from God.

The rest of chapter 2 in Genesis shows the continued creation of man in time. The physical man, completed in 2.7, is not, of course, the *whole* man, for man must have something to do. Work for man (tilling and keeping the garden) is not created until 2.15. Even then, man is not yet fully man until he has a moral code, which requires prohibitions. God creates man as a moral being in 2.16, with the commandment about not eating a particular fruit. Nor is man complete unless he is also a social and parental being. From verses 2.18 through the rest of the chapter, God, with the first man's help, creates woman and thus completes the *process* of making man into a physical, moral, and social creature. In conformity with the *Timaeus,* woman is made only *after* man.

In Genesis, Philo thus finds confirmation of the Platonic scheme. God, like the Craftsman, looked upon the pattern, whose existence, as well as the fact of God looking at it, is recorded in Genesis 1. The actual process of molding matter in accordance with the pattern takes place in time, a process the Bible records in Genesis 2. What might appear to "Higher Critics" as a problem with the biblical text—the apparently divergent accounts of the creation of man—turns out to be a key to reconciling science and religion, to showing how the finest science, the Platonic theories expressed in the *Timaeus,* is analogous to or even parallel with the truth expressed in the Bible.

Philo applies many other Platonic considerations to his exegesis of Genesis. There are, he says, three proofs for the excellent fabrication of man. First is the purity of the original material. This purity has several causes: its original supple freedom from alloy, God's selection of the best clay from all the globe, and the skill of the Creator "to bring it about that each of the bodily parts should have in itself individually its due proportions, and should also be fitted with the most perfect accuracy for the part it was to take in the whole."[17] A bit later, Philo observes that all mortal things are subject to change and that it is woman who is the cause of a blameworthy life. To show the influence of sexual desire on man's degeneration, Philo refers to Aristophanes' speech in the *Symposium,* taking the speech as literally true. Philo writes:

> Love supervenes, brings together and fits into one the divided halves, as it were, of a single living creature, and sets up in each of them a view to the production of their like. And this desire begat likewise bodily pleasure, that pleasure which is the beginning of wrongs and violation of law, the pleasure for the sake of which men bring on themselves the life of mortality and wretchedness in lieu of that of immortality and bliss.[18]

In the first two lines of the quotation we have, in addition to the Platonic reference, a submerged reference to Genesis 2.24: "Therefore a man leaves his father and his mother and cleaves to his wife and they become one flesh." Again, the genius of Philo brings together the Bible and Plato in an attempt to marry them, as it were, and make them, if not one flesh, one text. It was, perhaps, fortunate for Judaism that it ignored this aversion to matter with its accompanying denigration of sex. Christianity was not so fortunate.

In the conclusion of *On the Creation* (170ff.), Philo points out the five lessons of the Genesis story of creation: God *is* and is from eternity; God is one; the world came into being; the world is one (because God used up all the available material); and God used forethought for the world. All of these are Platonic in their formulation, even while all can be supported by the biblical text.

In considering Philo, one must wonder what audience he was aiming at, even though it is impossible ultimately to know his intentions. On the one hand, perhaps he was attempting to be a proselyte for philosophy to Jews. Extremely well educated in philosophy, Philo might have wished to show his co-religionists that there is much in Greek philosophy of profound value. Of course, in so far as Jewish tradition for the most part rejects Greek philosophy—indeed, derogatorily referring to all philosophers as *Epikouroi,* after Epicurus, whose philosophy could be easily, even if wrongly, dismissed as merely pleasure-seeking and God-denying—Philo failed. On the other hand, if he was attempting to render Jewish ideas acceptable and esteemed by the Pagan world, he also failed, for there is no direct evidence that he was ever read by a pagan.[19]

Though Philo failed to spread philosophy to Jews and also failed in his mission to spread the truths of Judaism to the Pagan world, he nevertheless uncovered notions that would be developed into full-scale doctrines in Christianity. He stands as a model of an enthusiastic attempt to reconcile the best scientific theories of his era with revealed religion. His enterprise was taken up again in the Middle Ages in Islam, Judaism, and Christianity with the most established, most highly respected science of *that* era—the science of Aristotle. As we shall see in later chapters, the attempt goes on today too, as some theologians and scientists hope to find a reconciliation of the Bible and science in the most respected science of our day, e.g., in physics, cosmology, and biology.

DISCUSSION QUESTIONS

1. Since ethics deals with how to live in the world, it is important to understand the nature of the world so that we might figure out how to live in it. Though from antiquity on there have been radically different accounts of the physical nature of the world, similar ethical systems have been derived from these systems of physics. Is the similarity of the ethics surprising? What might account for the similarity?

2. What features of the Book of Genesis lend themselves to analysis in Platonic terms? Is Philo taking advantage of built-in similarities in the metaphors inherent in human language to develop his reconciliation of philosophy and religion?

3. On the one hand, Philo takes the account of creation to be a prologue, a kind of drum roll and introduction, to the Mosaic laws. On the other hand, he subjects the account of creation to a very close analysis. Can he have it both

ways? If the account of creation is a poetic flourish to lend dignity to the law, is it appropriate to interpret it hyperliterally and to claim for it scientific validity?

4. *Consilience* is the term used when evidence from one field in favor of a theory confirms evidence from another field in favor of that same theory. Both anatomical and genetic evidence, for example, independently confirm the evolutionary relationships between humans and chimpanzees. Can a similar consilience have given confidence to Philo that Plato and the Book of Genesis shared the same theory of the world's nature and origins? Is there any difference between consilience in science and consilience in philosophy and religion?

NOTES

1. Aristotle, *Magna Moralia,* 1208b27–31.

2. Deut. 6.4.

3. Tiberius Julius and his father are best known from the accounts in Josephus. Tiberius became a military official for the Roman emperors. He was appointed prefect of Egypt by Nero, where he ordered his soldiers to suppress a rebellion that left fifty thousand Jews dead. Later, as the second highest ranking officer in Titus's army in Judea, he is said to have voted in council to destroy the Temple. But these events occurred long after Philo's death.

4. Philo, *Cherubim,* 27. At the same time, he refers to his predecessors and uses ideas borrowed from others. See H. Chadwick, "Philo," in *The Cambridge History of Later Greek and Early Medieval Philosophy,* ed. A. H. Armstrong (Cambridge: Cambridge University Press, 1967), 138.

5. On the important effect of Philo on Origen, see H. Chadwick, "Origen," in *Cambridge History,* ed. Armstrong, 183; on the effect of Philo on Clement, see H. Chadwick, "Origen," *The Cambridge History of Later Greek and Early Medieval Philosophy,* ed. A. H. Armstrong (Cambridge: Cambridge University Press, 1967), 179.

6. Philo, *On the Creation,* 3.

7. The examination of all works of literature according to rhetorical theory is a feature of Hellenistic Greek thought. In a commentary on Longinus's *On the Sublime,* James A. Arieti and John M. Crossett have argued that even this treatise about literary criticism is designed as a speech (New York and Toronto: Edwin Mellen, 1985), xi–xv.

8. Philo, *On the Creation,* 7–8.

9. Philo, *On the Creation,* 16.

10. Philo, *On the Creation,* 12–13.

11. Philo, *Who Is the Heir?* 231.

12. Philo, *Who Is the Heir?* 231.

13. Chadwick, "Philo," 143.

14. Philo, *On the Creation,* 68ff.

15. Philo, *On the Creation,* 68ff.

16. Philo, *On the Creation,* 133ff. In the *Legum Allegoriae* (1.31) Philo adds that the two accounts—the creation of the earthly man in Genesis 2.4 and the creation of the heavenly in 1.26 correspond to the sensible and intelligible worlds.

17. Philo, *On the Creation,* 136–37.

18. Philo, *On the Creation,* 152.

19. E. Goodenough, *The Politics of Philo Judaeus with a General Bibliography of Philo* (New Haven, Conn.: Yale University Press, 1938), 250, and A. D. Nock, "The Loeb Philo," *The Classical Review* 75 (1943): 77–78, argue that no pagans knew the work of Philo. Wolfson, *Philo,* 158, believes that he finds echoes of Philo in various works. Arieti and Crossett have suggested that Philo is the unnamed philosopher in the last chapter of Longinus's *On the Sublime,* but they also suggested that Longinus was perhaps a Hellenized Jew.

Reconciling Science and Religion in Medieval Islam

I have tried in my time to be a philosopher, but, I don't know how, cheerfulness was always breaking in.

— Oliver Edwards (in Boswell's *Life of Johnson*)

PRELIMINARY COMMENTS

The story of science and religion in Islam is a microcosm of the story in the entire western world. At its start a religion exclusively of the book—the Qur'an, a revelation from God through his prophet Mohammed—Islam soon became acquainted with Greek rationalism. The caliphs who ruled Syria discovered that Greek culture, with its myriad books and schools, was thriving in their lands. Excited by the promise of this learning, they commissioned translations into Arabic. In 830 C.E., the Caliph al-Mumun established an academy in Baghdad and hired a legion of Greek scholars to translate scientific works. Through these translations, a great many Greek astronomical, medical, mathematical, and philosophical texts entered into the Muslim tradition.

Greek philosophy, like Greek literature, was believed, at least by the Greek academic community, to have passed its prime. Scholars were not engaged in the creative work of Aristotle and Plato but in the less original, more plodding work of writing commentaries. Differences between Aristotle and Plato, as well as the attempt to reconcile them, constituted one of the principal philosophic programs, as it had for Boethius in the Christian world. In a way, the effort was parallel to the modern attempt to reconcile the theory of relativity with quantum mechanics in order to form a complete "Theory of Everything." In the second half of the first millennium of the Christian era, the philosophies of Plato and Aristotle were both held to have penetrated to the deepest mysteries of reality but were also perceived as significantly different from each other. To some degree, the Neoplatonists had strained to formulate a metaphysics combining Plato's world of ideas with the peculiar qualities of the Prime Mover that Aristotle had laid out in the twelfth book of the *Metaphysics*. When Aristotle's work first reached the Muslim philosophers, it reached them in the form of what might be called a Neoplatonized Aristotelianism. A work known as *The Theology of Aristotle,* for example, which was believed to be by Aristotle although it was actually a Neoplatonic treatise, was quite influential.

Among the first Muslims stirred by the possibilities of philosophy were those known as the Mutazilites, founded, according to tradition, in the mid-eighth century.[1] Their central view, the all-pervasive nature of God's justice, was less remarkable for its novelty than for the Mutazilite method of defending it philosophically. The argument is that God cannot act contrary to reason and cannot act in disregard for the welfare of his creatures, since to do so would undermine his justice and wisdom. In other words, God is constrained by definition to be the highest good—a Greek notion—and, as the highest good, is constrained to behave in accordance with reason. Traditionalist Muslims, however, believed that God, being omnipotent, could do whatever he wants; he could "act in total violation of all the precepts of justice and righteousness, torture the innocent, and demand the impossible, simply because he was God."[2] The Mutazilite view of God's absolute justice contradicted as well the complete predestination of all human actions, for predestination would remove the personal responsibility of men for their own suffering in hell. In addition, Mutazilites maintained the absolute oneness of God and rejected any anthropomorphisms whatsoever. Where the Qur'an could not be understood to agree with the precepts of reason, it must be interpreted allegorically. On this matter the Mutazilites anticipate one of the strategies for scriptural interpretation that Galileo defends in his letter to the Grand Duchess Christina, as we shall see later.[3] Yet another view of the Mutazilites was that the Qur'an itself was created in time and had not always existed in the mind of God. These controversial views were not without response from the traditional Muslim community. In the generation after the liberal al-Mumun, the Mutazilites were persecuted, and the eternity of the Qur'an was established as an article of law.

AL FARABI

The first prominent Arab philosopher was Ya'qub ibn Ishaq al-Kindi, who died sometime after 870 C.E. Although he was certain that revelation and human wisdom were different means to the same ultimate truth, he was willing to yield to Scripture where it seemed incompatible with philosophy. He also affirmed creation in time, unlike al Farabi (878–950), who would accept neither the subordination of philosophy nor creation in time. Al Farabi was educated in Baghdad, where he took up philosophy and Greek science. He studied Aristotle especially, claiming to have read the *Physics* forty times and *On the Soul* two hundred times. Despite this concentration on Aristotle, his views were distinctly Neoplatonic. He identified the Neoplatonic First Being (or One) with the Islamic God. In Neoplatonic fashion he maintained that all other existent things emanate from God in hierarchical order. From what he considered to be this fact of nature, he drew his political philosophy. Just as the universe is designed as a hierarchy in which all things draw their being from God, so in a polity all parts descend in a hierarchical orderly progression from the head of state, in whom all authority resides. As the heavens have various levels and as each level is controlled by the celestial sphere closer to God, and in turn controls those farther away, so all the ranks of society control and are controlled—all except, of course, for the head, who controls but is himself not controlled. (The head thus resembles Aristotle's Prime Mover, who moves but is not himself moved.)

According to al Farabi, God is perfect, necessary, self-sufficient, eternal, uncaused, immaterial, without any existence of the same rank, different from everything else, and unable to be defined.[4] God in his essence is intellectual rather than material.[5] He is thought thinking itself, just as Aristotle said.[6] God generates the universe by a "necessity of his nature" from his superabundance of being and perfection. Because this emanating goodness (also called the "active intelligence," from which come bodies and soul—a view that seems inspired by the *Timaeus*) is a necessity of God's nature, it is independent of God's choice or desire. Despite the difficulties of understanding such a deity, al Farabi says that mankind's greatest efforts should be aimed at knowing God. As the universe flows from God and returns to God, so should mankind strive to return to God, after mankind has been enlightened by God.

Al Farabi, like Philo, tries to bring together the best philosophy of his day—the blend of Neoplatonism and Aristotelianism that he inherited and that he thinks to be pure Aristotelianism. The role of revelation in his worldview is less than obvious, as is any distinctively Islamic character in his thought.

AVICENNA

The rationalism of Avicenna (980–1037) led him also into a philosophic distancing from religion. Where al Farabi claimed to have read the *Physics* forty times, Avicenna claims to have read the *Metaphysics* forty times without understanding it—surely one of the greatest acts of faith in the value of Aristotle that the world has known, a faith that must have been generated by Aristotle's reputation. When, with the aid of al Farabi's commentary, he finally understood it, he ran through the streets, not crying "Eureka" à la Archimedes, but spreading alms.[7] The anecdote is perhaps itself a symbol of Avicenna's reconciliation of science and religion: the marriage of intellectual understanding and religious, ethical practice. And it is in ⌐mony with the story that he memorized both the Qur'an and the *Metaphysics*.[8]

Avicenna undertook to elucidate the nature of God for philosophers, the few wise men who study the highest matters using only reason. His hope was that these few could then teach their own students. For the multitudes, however, traditional popular religion would have to suffice. Popular religion requires prophets who can talk to people in language they can understand, explaining the laws of morality necessary for social harmony. Even some of the doctrines that were part of the core teachings of Mohammed, such as the eventual resurrection of the body and the sensuality of heaven, were aimed only at the common people, who could not readily understand the spiritual truths comprehensible to the philosopher. Indeed, if Mohammed had spoken the truths that Avicenna and other philosophers enunciated, there would have been no possibility of uniting believers into a unified and powerful nation. In short, Avicenna's view of religion was like that attributed to philosophers in Gibbon's *Decline and Fall of the Roman Empire:* religion's usefulness lies in controlling the people. As we shall see shortly, these views provided fodder for al Ghazali's powerful attack on philosophy. Yet, for Avicenna, the form of Mohammed's teaching is consistent with Aristotle's political philosophy. Aristotle teaches that man is a political animal, a social animal who can fulfill his nature only in society, in which men must associate with one another in a way aimed at justice. For justice there must be a lawgiver and laws, both of which must be at the same time comprehensible and inspirational. Hence, Scripture must be written in a form suitable for these purposes.[9]

What are Avicenna's "scientific" views? Are they incompatible with religion? Avicenna looks at problems in the philosophy he has inherited and tries to solve them by applying ideas from monotheism. That the particular monotheism is not specifically Islamic does not seem to matter to Avicenna, so long as it is not obviously opposed to Islamic principles. For example, one of the old problems of philosophy concerns the question of whether, as the Platonists believed, there is a separate world of ideas, where the ideas have some sort of actual independent existence, or, as Aristotle believed, ideas are "immanent" in things themselves, with no independent existence. Avicenna "solves" the dilemma by saying that ideas do exist separately from things—they exist logically prior to things in the mind of God, where they are the pattern for actual things in this world; the ideas, he says, also exist as abstract ideas in the human mind. But in the natural world (as distinct from the supernatural world of God) the ideas do not exist apart from things themselves. Here, then, is a reconciliation of Aristotle and Plato, and, by the participation of God in the scheme, of religion as well. If the solution seems vaguely Platonic or Aristotelian, or more Neoplatonic than Islamic, well, no matter. The majority of people, says Avicenna, have never been interested in the debate about ideas and probably never will be—so if the Qur'an does not deal with the subject, it is because its purpose is to communicate with the masses.

Perhaps Avicenna was right. The debate about science and religion is one for philosophers, and not even for all of them. Philosophers who reject God will not bother trying to reconcile science and religion; fervent believers will care about what science has to say insofar as it conflicts with their religious beliefs. The debate will be of interest only to those who feel a struggle in their souls, who want to have both religious faith and rational, scientific belief. Philosophers will deal with the rather esoteric questions that concern philosophers, such as the logical consistency of God's nature. Even the striking consistency among philosophers about the nature of God, even in diverse traditions around the world, has not impressed the believer. Though reason, as if with mathematical clarity, or at least as much as the subject allows, has led philosophers who are Buddhists and Hindus and Muslims and Jews and Christians to pretty much the same general conclusions about God—oneness, stability, goodness, incorporeality—the force of this intellectual consensus seems to have no persuasive power. But let us return to Avicenna.

In Avicenna's opinion, metaphysics deals with existence in both its necessary and contingent forms. Given that contingent beings are those that can be brought into existence only by something else and that there cannot be an actually infinite chain of contingent beings, there must be a noncontingent, necessary being such as we conceive God to be. There must be a cause external to the chain, a necessarily existent being, which, of course, is God.[10] This first cause is free from matter, is one, and is simple.[11] Hence God has no genus or species and admits of no definition. Since the first cause is immaterial and since matter is the source of evil, God is purely good.[12] Here one can see a mingling of Aristotelianism and Neoplatonism, in the Aristotelian rejection of an actual infinity and in the Neoplatonic denigration of matter.

For Avicenna, as for Aristotle, the world did not come into being, but is eternal, and for Avicenna, *eternal* includes the attribute of unchanging uniformity.[13] Hence, a great problem for Avicenna is how to reconcile an eternally existing world and an eternally existing God with the apparent fact of a changing world full of a multiplicity of things. In other words, how does an absolutely unchanging, static, simple, undifferentiated, and undifferentiating God affect a dynamic world? This is one of the perennial problems of philosophy, first given expression by Parmenides. It is the dilemma implicit in the question of God's foreknowledge versus human free will and the question of creation ex nihilo in time. (As Cicero put it, why did God suddenly wake up?) Avicenna's solution, not unlike that of Philo and the Neoplatonists, involves the interposition of layers of insulation between God and the world. Where Philo places the *Logos* or pattern of ideas between God and the world—for God made the world "after the pattern"—Avicenna places spiritual substances, "intelligences," between God and the world of generation and corruption.[14] God "emanates" the world by an emanation of the first intelligence. Although this mystic notion defies complete understanding, perhaps it can be understood analogously. Let us take a painting, say the *Mona Lisa,* and let us agree for the sake of the analogy that it is beautiful. As the beauty of the *Mona Lisa* emanates from the painting, so does the world emanate from God. Where the analogy works best is in the obvious fact that the painting exercises no thought or choice in emanating the beauty. And it is totally unaffected by the beauty it emanates. Once it has been hung on the wall and begins its emanation, it does nothing actively to affect the course of events. If someone comes to see the painting and is so stirred by the beauty emanating from it that he decides to become a painter himself, it is not because of any active intervention on the part of the painting. In just the same way, the universe emanates from God without God intervening in it. Like the painting, *he* is one and unchanging, yet the cause of everything else. Unlike the painting in the analogy, however, God and the emanation were never hung on the wall, so to speak, for both God and the emanation are eternal. What Avicenna wants to say is that there is a priority that is not temporal. Another example might be logical priority, of which a syllogism is an example. In the syllogism "All men are mortal; Socrates is a man; Socrates is mortal," the priority of the major premise ("All men are mortal") is logical, not temporal, for all the claims are simultaneously valid. Now such a view will not be without its problems for religion. If the emanations are posited as an eternal and unchangeable given, what becomes the point of prayer or ritual? Why should one bother with a God who need not be persuaded or appeased or feared? Avicenna's philosophically pleasing God seems definitely at odds with the God of the Qur'an (or Bible), who can at will destroy and bring back the world. Indeed, the view of an eternal God who simply emanates and takes no active role in the actual changing world would either render false all the accounts of God in Scripture or, at best, render them all metaphorical, salvageable only by allegorization or some such device. Indeed, regarding the Qur'an's treatment of the religiously central matter of resurrection—an article of faith for Muslims—Avicenna declares the language figurative, explaining that what was really meant was the resurrection of the *soul,* which alone can be immortal. In a similar way, Averroës says that, because absolute destruction is impossible, the term *destruction* is used metaphorically; when something is said to be "destroyed" it merely changes into something else.[15]

Avicenna's philosophical scheme is consistent with the fundamental and essential Islamic idea of one transcendent God. Perhaps, if this idea alone makes one a believer, Avicenna may be considered a faithful believer. The identification of goodness with existence—and both of these with God—is another point of connection between Islam and Avicenna's philosophy. But there is no meeting of the Qur'an and philosophy on the questions of God's knowledge and participation in the world. The Neoplatonic philosophy that Avicenna embraces says that God does not participate directly in the world; the Qur'an says that God is aware of and controls, even at the level of the smallest, most insignificant things in the world, all that happens in heaven and on earth. These positions are not easily open to reconciliation, even though Avicenna attempts to achieve it by granting to God a complete knowledge of the order that emanates from him to all existent things.[16] Such positive knowledge, however, is far from equivalent to active control.

Many of the familiar ancient questions recur in Avicenna's thought. For example, his question of *when* creation took place reveals the kind of controversy at issue in *Euthyphro* 10B. There the question is whether something is pious because God wills it, or whether God wills it because it is pious. On the matter of when creation took place, the Mutazilites said that the world was created at the most suitable time, that is, that God made the world when he did because it was the suitable time to do so. The Ash'arites (followers of Abu'l-Hasan al Ash'ari, who broke away from the Mutazilite school and advocated the supremacy of revelation and the prophetic tradition), on the other hand, said that the best time for creation is determined only by God's will—in short, that God's will alone defines suitability. Avicenna says that both are mistaken, for no one time can be more suitable than another; instead, God could not have created the universe at some good time, because if the time were good, it would have to be for some purpose or profit for the creator—and for God to act out of such motives would be incompatible with the unity and unchangeableness of his being.[17] Thus the world has always been, with the relation of God and creation being one of *logical,* not temporal, priority.

Of Philo it has been asked whether he was more Jewish or more Platonic. About Avicenna it might be asked whether he was more Muslim or more that blend of Neoplatonism and Aristotelianism that late antiquity bequeathed to the early Middle Ages. Clearly, al Ghazali thought the latter, branding Avicenna an infidel philosopher.

AL GHAZALI

After having asked what Athens has to do with Jerusalem, Tertullian answered "nothing." Al Ghazali might be said to have come up with the same answer for Mecca, Rome, and all other cities identified with religion, not just Jerusalem. Though in his youth he authored scientific treatises on the motion and nature of stars, as well as a summary of astronomy,[18] al Ghazali is best known for his works against philosophy, *Intentions of the Philosophers (Masqasid al-Falasifa)* and the more famous *Incoherence of the Philosophers (Tahafut al-Falasifa),* in which he aims to show that the Islamic scholastics, especially al Farabi and Avicenna, are heretics subject to the penalty of death. Although Muslims believe in creation in time, those philosophers teach that the world is eternal; whereas Muslims believe in the omniscience of God, those philosophers teach that God's knowledge is limited; and while Muslims believe in the resurrection of the body, those philosophers teach that only the soul is immortal. Al Farabi and Avicenna were of course already safely dead by the time of al Ghazali (1058–1111), but al Ghazali's work was so powerful that it caused the virtual disappearance of philosophy from the Islamic world, despite Averroës' attempt to answer the arguments in *The Incoherence of the Incoherence.*

The question for al Ghazali, as for all the others who came in touch with Aristotelian philosophy, was whether to reject that philosophy outright or to reach some sort of accommodation with it. Al Farabi and Avicenna chose accommodation; al Ghazali chose rejection. Al Ghazali endeavors to use the arguments of the philosophers against them, showing that their arguments do not meet their own philosophical standards. Apparently a convert himself, his work is animated with all the zeal of one. In his early career he was an academic at Baghdad and reputedly a popular lecturer.[19] He then suffered some kind of internal struggle while studying the philosophies of al Farabi and Avicenna, philosophies he understood so well that his summary of them in *Intentions of the Philosophers* was renowned in its Latin translation for its clarity. In his spiritual crisis, he left the university and found solace in mysticism (sufism). He concluded that syllogisms can persuade the mind but that only divine light can persuade the heart; in the end, he felt, true knowledge could not be separated from certainty of a sort that only revelation can provide.

Al Ghazali maintains, despite Avicenna's theory of eternal emanation, that philosophers have not *proved* the eternity of the world. Here Thomas Aquinas will agree with him, maintaining that the question of whether the world is eternal or created in time cannot in principle be answered by philosophy. Aquinas says, moreover, that it is better for philosophers not to try to prove creation in time because if the arguments should be found wanting (as he thinks they will be) the entire Catholic faith will be undermined.[20] Perhaps Aquinas had the arguments of Avicenna in mind and found their proofs for the eternity of the world unsatisfactory. Perhaps, as a result of the persuasiveness of al Ghazali's arguments, Arab Aristotelianism—and with it, Arab philosophy—died in Islam. The more agnostic position of Aquinas concerning creation and his consequent avoidance of bad arguments to support creation in time may have helped to avoid a similar fate for philosophy in Christianity.[21]

If the world is eternal, says al Ghazali, there can be no action on the part of the eternal deity to create it in time, for action requires a result that is later than the cause, and for an eternal God there can be no "later." An eternal world would not merely relegate God to a distant cause; it would eliminate the need for him altogether. If God had ever willed the world to come into being, this would have been a change, and so there would have been the need for something to have caused God to will the change. But if there is nothing external to God (because, since nothing has yet been created, God is all there is), then the philosophers will find no cause to move God. For al Ghazali, the view that things cannot be other than what they are would limit God. God can, after all, do whatever he wants. If he wishes to will the world into existence at a later time, he can do so. The philosophers would reply that there must be some reason for God to will what he wants; but for al Ghazali, God's will is its own master.

The philosophers maintained that the emanation from the One could not be different from what it is. Because the One with its emanation is a necessary existent, the world is necessarily as it is. But Islam believes in an omnipotent God who freely creates everything in the world as he desires it to be. When something changes, Islam teaches, its atoms are being continually re-created in a new form by God. The results of this creation do not follow from any logical or causal necessity but from God's will alone. Anticipating Hume, al Ghazali challenged philosophers to show that there is any logical connection between cause and effect. He maintains, for example, that it is wrong to assume that cotton will necessarily catch fire when a flame is applied to it. Although the philosophers maintain that cotton catches fire because of the flame, al Ghazali says the cotton burns independently of the flame and because of the will of God alone. As al Ghazali puts it,

> The philosophers have no other proof than the observation of the occurrence of the burning, when there is contact with fire, but observation proves only a simultaneity, not a causation, and, in reality, there is no other cause but God.[22]

Although al Ghazali's point is nothing less than the Humean dictum that correlation does not equal causation, he draws the distinctly non-Humean conclusion that God's will provides the causal connection between correlated events. Thus, what we normally think of as causality is actually the operation of God's perfectly sovereign will. With this view, al Ghazali also anticipates Malebranche's occasionalism by over half a millennium.

By no means limiting God's causal activity to cases of correlated events, al Ghazali gives God back his divinity in a big way. Everything that happens—everything—results from the will of God. No events whatsoever are independent of God's will. A crucial implication of al Ghazali's attributing everything to God's sovereign will and nothing to natural causality is that the possibility of natural science, with its predictions and explanations grounded in natural law, is eliminated. Because God can act however he wishes, and because violations of apparent laws of nature are therefore always an open possibility, there is no natural foundation on which science can be based. All a human being can do is submit—that is, be a Muslim, for "Islam" means "submission." This is piety triumphant. Although we may talk as if things cause other things to change, in reality "there is a power which does not exist in the things themselves but ultimately in God and which makes possible the transformations which we can see in the world."[23]

One important religious consequence of al Ghazali's removal of natural causality is that God's power to work miracles is made manifest, although miracles must be thought of as special divine interventions rather than violations of natural law. When the philosophers denied to God any power to intervene in the world, when they asserted that creation was an unchanging emanation of the One, when they took from God the ability to make a decision about any present circumstances, they also eliminated God's power to work miracles. To be sure, philosophers could account for scriptural miracles by calling them allegories or by finding some natural cause that explained them or by declaring that they flowed from the eternal emanation as pre-programmed effects. But all of these explanations render miracles nonmiraculous and deny another essential power of God. How powerful, after all, is a God who cannot intervene in the world at his discretion?

Al Ghazali makes an even broader attack on the philosophers for their frequent reference to God and the Qur'an. Their attempt to overlay their theories with a veneer of orthodoxy, he says, is merely an attempt to provide protective camouflage for impious views. Whereas Avicenna declared that the highest truths were reserved for the philosophers and that the Qur'an was written as it was for the sake of inspiring the unlettered masses to correct social behavior, al Ghazali adopts the opposite view, granting to the Qur'an utter supremacy over philosophy and vouchsafing little respect for attempts to reconcile the two as equally respectable avenues to truth.

The question of how to communicate with "the unlettered masses" (a group less odiously called "the many" in the Platonic corpus but seldom, if ever, afforded much respect by Plato or Greek philosophy generally) is pervasive in the western world. To what extent should religion be used to control the masses? To what extent may the texts of religion be truly considered the word of God? To what extent are they to be considered as speaking to different audiences and with different levels of meaning all at the same time? And to what extent may deception or lies ever be used to good purpose? Plato seems to condone lying for a good end in the *Republic* (388) when he allows the use of lies to deceive an enemy or an insane man. In the *Phaedo,* Socrates says that taking the risk of believing tales about the afterlife, tales he has just himself invented, is noble, for an afterlife that rewards virtue will inspire good behavior and also a good end. Aristotle himself suggests that the great-minded man might use irony in talking to the masses so that they will be inspired to obey him.[24] Later, Livy shows how the laws King Numa gave Rome were a pious fraud. Livy approvingly says that to inspire the rough Romans with a fear of the gods, "he [King Numa] prepared them by inventing some sort of marvelous tale; he pretended, therefore, that he was in the habit of meeting the goddess Egeria by night, and that it was her authority which guided him in the establishment of such rites as were most acceptable to the gods."[25]

Al Ghazali is no lax Livy, willing to sacrifice truth to expediency. Al Ghazali says that when the philosophers say that Mohammed wrote the Qur'an so as to deceive and trick the masses into conformity and belief, so as to conceal the truth and to claim things that were not true, they degrade the holy prophet and demean the sacred texts. For al Ghazali, the line between allegory—converting the literal meaning of the Qur'an into lessons for living—and lies is invisible. Why, he asks, should the hard truth be reserved for the so-called philosophers while everyone else must be contented with soft allegory? Here he puts his finger on one of the great problems for those who seek to maintain the rational truth of a sacred text. Statements that appear false when taken literally must somehow be interpreted as true, typically by considering them to be metaphors or paradoxes, i.e., by taking the text in which they appear as a rhetorical or poetical document. For fervent believers of the literal truth of every word of Scripture, when a sacred text is declared to be a rhetorical document—one which tells tales or uses any form of deceptive artifice, including metaphorical and allegorical language—it is entirely undermined.[26]

The question of which parts of a text are metaphor and which are straightforward is a continuing problem for those who accept texts as sacred and authoritative. Christianity, like Islam, has from the very beginning had to contend with these issues. Is the divinity of Jesus, for example, to be understood as a symbolic or a literal truth?

Is the transubstantiation of the bread and wine into the flesh and blood of the Messiah to be understood as a literal transformation? This question of scriptural interpretation is one to which we shall return often.

Al Ghazali's rejection of philosophy in *The Incoherence of the Philosophers* was answered by Averroës in *The Incoherence of the Incoherence*. But to be answered is not to be silenced. In fact, it was philosophy that was silenced in the Islamic world. Al Ghazali's forceful arguments must resonate with all who wish to affirm the truth of both the traditional conception of God and the sacred texts. The God of philosophy is a pale shadow of the traditional God; it is a deity that is comparatively weak and unfree and impersonal, a deity totally unable to inspire religious feeling. It is no wonder that al Ghazali found his academic career anemic and sought the lifeblood of religion in a direct, mystic relationship with the transcendent. Philosophers of course might ask whether in seeking an emotionally satisfying spiritual fulfillment he was practicing an objectionable sort of self-deception and self-delusion, or, perhaps like Cicero or Pascal, was engaging in a worthwhile sort of deception.

AVERROËS

About the life of ibn Rushd (1126–1198), known in the West by the inexact Latin transliteration "Averroës," not very much is known for sure, beyond his birth into a prominent family in Cordoba. He represents the last burst of Islamic philosophic endeavor. With his death, the attempt to reconcile science and religion comes to an end in the Muslim world. At just about the same time, Aristotle is translated directly into Latin, and philosophy is energetically pursued in the Christian West.

As we study Averroës, we are reminded of the inexorable logic of Parmenides struggling against the world of apparent change and diversity. The average man of the Middle Ages must have viewed the world as al Ghazali did, a world with an active deity, actual miracles, and the possibility of personal immortality providing an incentive to virtue and piety. The "incoherent" world of the philosophers, with their emanations and their distant, unchanging God, would have been utterly alien. God and his agents called the faithful to prayer five times a day. Ritual affirmed the ever-present deity. The "always existent One," if mentioned at all, was highfalutin jargon. Nevertheless, Averroës devoted his efforts to defending philosophy and has certainly become the Islamic philosopher best known and most quoted in the West, the one to whom Aquinas refers as "the Commentator."

The great work of Averroës, of course, is his commentaries on Aristotle, the goal of which is to remove from Aristotle the Neoplatonic influences that contaminated the work of al Farabi and Avicenna. In particular, the notion of the emanations of the Existent One had to go, so that the resulting science would be more purely Aristotle's. Obviously, if Averroës had not believed Aristotle's work to represent the highest truth, he would not have devoted his life to studying the Greek philosopher. Al Ghazali's attack on philosophy was a real threat to the value of the philosophic enterprise itself and a matter of great practical consequence as well, especially since al Ghazali decreed death for infidel philosophers. Al Ghazali's work demanded a vigorous and authoritative reply. In attempting that reply, Averroës claims that *theologians,* among whom he counts al Ghazali, as distinct from *philosophers,* like himself, are not capable of understanding the highest truths of metaphysics.

Perhaps the best way to treat Averroës is to look at his responses to the various problems that al Ghazali raised concerning creation in time and the related questions of the nature of causality, the omniscience of God, the resurrection of the body, and the language of religion, that is, whether there is one truth for both science and religion.

Al Ghazali devoted about one-fourth of *Incoherence* to the philosophers' assertion of the eternity of the world. Aristotle, the primary source of the view, theorized that there was no absolute beginning of the universe but that, like motion, the universe is continuous and eternal. Al Ghazali objected that if one posits an infinite series of causes, as Aristotle did, then it is contradictory also to posit a first cause, as Aristotle did with his Prime Mover. Al Ghazali argues that a first cause would have to be inspired by some determinant (for causes do not act or occur without a reason), but in the vast emptiness before the creation there can be no such motive (because before creation there is nothing in which such a determinant can occur) and hence no such cause. Therefore, said al Ghazali, the philosophers cannot account for the world, for by their arguments it would be absurd to think that the world exists at all. Since, however, there is such a world, clearly the philosophers positing an eternal world are wrong.

Averroës' defense of the philosophers in response to al Ghazali turns on a crucial difference between human and divine action. Whereas humans act and react, as al Ghazali says, to some stimulus, some external determinant or cause of their action, God's will is independent of any such cause like need or desire, for he is perfect and as such neither needs nor desires anything. Moreover, God is not faced with choices, for to choose means to be faced with the possibility of choosing the less good, which is of course impossible for God. Thus, says Averroës, it is doubly false to say that God chooses to respond to some determinant in creating the world, because God is not faced with choices and because no external determinants can affect him. Hence, God does not respond, and the claim implicit in al Ghazali—that there would have to be some precipitating cause for creation—is invalid.[27] The philosophers' belief in the eternity of the world, for Averroës, thus survives the flawed critique of al Ghazali.

The Neoplatonic Aristotelians whom al Ghazali was refuting wanted to show not only that the world is eternal, but that it is nevertheless dependent on God. This was the goal of their theory of God's emanation. In his refutation, al Ghazali responds to all the possible variations on this doctrine:

> Is this circular movement [of the most distant heaven] temporal or eternal? If it is eternal, how does it become the principle for temporal things? And if it is temporal, it will need another temporal being and we shall have an infinite regress. And when you say it partially resembles the eternal, partially the temporal, for it resembles the

eternal in so far as it is permanent and the temporal in so far as it arises anew, we answer: Is it the principle of temporal things, because of its permanence, or because of its rising anew? In the former case, how can a temporal proceed from something because of its permanence? And in the latter case, what arises anew will need a cause for its arising anew, and we have an infinite regress.[28]

Al Ghazali's questions go to the heart of the connection between the eternal, conceived as a totally immutable, atemporal duration, and the temporal.[29] It is our old question of how to reconcile the worldviews of Parmenides and Heraclitus. Plato's solution, we recall, was to posit two worlds, the World of Being and the World of Becoming. But that solution led to a problem as least as serious as the one it solved, for it explained the connection of the two worlds by having the World of Becoming somehow "participate" in the World of Being, where the nature of the "participation" remained inscrutably mysterious, as Aristotle rightly pointed out. How does Averroës respond to al Ghazali's questions? He writes:

> This argument is sophistical. The temporal does not proceed from it [the eternal] in so far as it is eternal, but in so far as it is temporal; it does not need, however, for its arising anew a cause arising anew, for its rising anew is not a new fact, but is an eternal act, *i.e.,* an act without beginning or end. Therefore its agent must be an eternal agent, for an eternal act has an eternal agent, and a temporal act a temporal agent. Only through the eternal element in it can it be understood that movement has neither beginning nor end, and this is meant by permanence, for movement itself is not permanent, but changing.[30]

Averroës' rejoinder to al Ghazali's criticisms of the purported interface between eternal and temporal realms is less convincing than his rejoinder to al Ghazali's criticisms of arguments for the eternity of the world. Here Averroës seems to be claiming that the temporal "rising anew" is an eternal act, because movement itself is permanent—because, as it were, change is the only constant. But surely al Ghazali's criticisms can be rephrased as an equally unanswerable dilemma: how can *particular instances* of motion proceed from something eternal without incoherence or from something temporal without an infinite regress?[31]

Another of the philosophical arguments of Averroës for the eternity of the world is similar to those he used to defend the philosophers against al Ghazali. It proceeds by showing the absurdity of conceiving of a beginning. If the world had a beginning, he says, then there would have been empty time before, and nothing could have happened in the emptiness to "wake God up," to move him to create the world. This view of God's action contrasts sharply, of course, with that of al Ghazali, who wrote that God's will is entirely free and would be undetermined by any kind of precipitating event. Averroës, however, replies that if there is no precipitating event and if God creates the world because of a whim on his part, then neither intelligence nor goodness can be attributed to God, for we do not consider good or intelligent those beings that operate by whim. Averroës, in other words, thinks that al Ghazali buys God's freedom at the price of God's goodness and intelligence—a price that Averroës himself is loathe to pay.

Al Ghazali's and Averroës' disparate views on whether God can create a temporal world follow largely from their disparate views on causality. The only real causality, said al Ghazali, is God's conscious will; what philosophers and people generally think of as causal relations between events are merely correlations. Although the burning of cotton is strongly correlated with its being placed in fire, for example, al Ghazali maintains that God can make cotton either burn or not burn—solely according to his will and not in obedience to any natural necessity—when it is placed in fire. Averroës, on the other hand, defends a view of causality more in accordance with common sense—namely, that strong correlations really do point to causal relations—and more conducive to scientific investigation of the world. He makes his point without mincing words: "To deny the existence of external causes which are observed in sensible things is sophistry, and he who defends this doctrine either denies with his tongue what is present in the mind or is carried away by a sophistical doubt which occurs to him concerning this question."[32]

In contrast to al Ghazali's commonsense appeal to the notion that infinite causal chains are just as impossible to traverse as are infinite distances—a notion still much debated by philosophers of religion and of science—Averroës offers a truly subtle distinction:

> You must understand that the philosophers permit the existence of a temporal which comes out of a temporal being *ad infinitum* in an accidental way, when this is repeated in a limited and finite matter—when, for instance, the corruption of one of two things becomes the necessary condition for the existence of the other.[33]

Averroës' point seems to be that since matter is finite, there is no infinite generation of new temporal or material causes, just an infinite repetition of existing causes operating on the same finite matter. Any particular event has an accidental cause in the infinitely preceding sequence of temporal events. But the process as a whole is caused essentially by the eternal God. If, for example, a given cup of water were alternately frozen and thawed infinitely many times, each instant in the infinite sequence of freezing and thawing is an accident, as distinct from, say, the continuous creation of infinitely many new cups of water. And the whole process of freezing and thawing would be caused essentially by God. However valid this distinction might be, Averroës simply fails to answer al Ghazali's question about how *any* temporal infinity can be traversed.[34]

According to another of al Ghazali's arguments, if, as his opponents maintain, the world had no beginning in time, then every event and every object would have had an infinite causal history. Every tree and every person would be the result of an infinite series of discrete causes. But such an infinite series cannot actually be traversed. If a tree has an *infinitely* long chain of causal prerequisites, we would simply never end up with a tree. Al Ghazali invited his reader to consider standing by a river whose source is infinitely distant. The water of such a river would never pass by, for it cannot traverse an infinite distance. Al Ghazali used this argument, which is similar to one of Zeno's paradoxes designed to show the impossibility of motion, to prove that there *must* have been a beginning in time and that the universe cannot be eternal.

Given Averroës' loyalty to Aristotelianism, it is unsurprising that Averroës defends Aristotle's cosmology and metaphysics against the attacks of al Ghazali. For Aristotle, there is no absolute coming into being, for everything comes from something else, as it does for the atomists. Coming into being always involves the actualization of a pre-existing potentiality. Thus a statue comes into being when the potentialities of the marble slab are actualized, and so forth. Aristotle's distinction between potentiality and actuality was his answer to the Parmenideans, who asserted that either a thing *was* or *was not.* Al Ghazali rejected Aristotle's answer, affirming that every coming into being involves an entirely new thing wholly created by God without any other determinant or any actualization of an eternally pre-existing potentiality. A statue is not potentially in the marble, as Aristotle would have said; it is an entirely new creation of its maker.[35]

Averroës defends Aristotle's conception of causation and assertion of an eternal world against al Ghazali's alternative views:

> There must, therefore, be an eternal movement which produces this interchange in the eternally transitory things. And therefore it is clear that the generation of the one in each pair of generated beings is the corruption of the other; otherwise a thing could come into being from nothing, for the meaning of "becoming" is the alteration of a thing and its change, from what is potentially, into actuality. It is not possible that the privation itself should change into the existent, and it is not the privation of which it is said that it has become. There exists, therefore, a substratum for the contrary forms, and it is in this substratum that the forms interchange.[36]

The differences between the views of Averroës and al Ghazali reduce to the two philosophers' fundamental intuitions about the world, in particular about whether causal processes are naturalistic or not. If they are, then coming into being can be adequately explained in terms of the actualization of perhaps eternally existing potentialities. If causation is essentially a matter of God's original, free action, though, then no natural process is independent of God and nothing existed before God's act of creation. The possibility of such a stark difference in worldview, brought into focus by a consideration of these two medieval Islamic thinkers, pervades debates about science and religion to the present day.

There is a striking similarity, though the language is rather different, between Averroës' concept of God and that of the pre-Socratic philosophers. In both, God is the eternal unchanging law of nature rather than an anthropomorphized mover and shaper of everything that happens. Here, perhaps, we may speculate that al Ghazali, with his powerful defense of an understandable, human-like God, like the one that appears in Scripture, was far more likely to be received favorably by traditional Muslims than Averroës with his multiplying distinctions, difficult arguments, and purely philosophical conception of God. Moreover, as we have seen, some of Averroës' arguments are less than compelling and still vulnerable to the objections of al Ghazali. When we consider a few additional matters, besides causality and the creation of the world, we shall find still more reasons to understand the failure of Averroës to overcome al Ghazali.

According to the Qur'an, God knows everything about the world, including the thoughts of every human being and things that seem wholly insignificant: "No leaf falls without his noticing it."[37] Following the sacred text, al Ghazali says that the philosophical claim that God knows only universals but not particulars contradicts revelation and is therefore heretical.[38] According to Aristotelians, however, in order to have sense-knowledge one must have senses. Indeed, Aristotle says specifically that if God had sense perceptions he would feel pleasure and pain—feelings incompatible with his divinity.[39] The difficulty, of course, is that if God's knowledge extends to the transitory world of human and animal pain and suffering, that knowledge would profoundly affect a feeling God; hence the stunning idea of Aristotle and the philosophers who followed him, that God is thinking about himself thinking and has no knowledge of particulars.

Al Ghazali responds as follows. If God does not know particulars,

> God cannot know Mohammed's proclaiming himself a prophet at the time he did, nor can God know this of any definite prophet; He can only know that some people proclaim themselves prophets and that they have such-and-such qualities, but any individual prophet he cannot know, for he [i.e., the individual prophet] can only be known by sense-perception.[40]

God's not knowing particulars would involve a serious diminution of God indeed! Averroës replies that al Ghazali is engaging in sophistry by applying to divine knowledge limitations that correctly apply only to human knowledge.[41] He adds (461):

> And his [Ghazali's] second objection, that those philosophers who affirm that God knows universals must, by admitting in His knowledge a plurality of species, conclude that a plurality of individuals and a plurality of conditions of one and the same individual is permissible for His Knowledge, is a sophistical objection. For the knowledge of individuals is sensation or imagination, and the knowledge of universals is intellect, and the new occurrence of individuals causes two things, a change and a plurality in the perception; whereas knowledge of species and genera does not imply a change, since knowledge of them is invariable and they are unified in the knowledge which comprehends them, and universality and individuality only agree in their forming a plurality.[42]

Averroës seems to "solve" the problem by defining sensation and the things known by sensation, namely particulars, out of the province of knowledge. To know a particular is not to have knowledge at all, for knowledge is of universals. He concludes that God's knowledge is different from human knowledge, for human knowledge is knowledge of the effects of God, but God's knowledge is of the causes.[43]

Even if Averroës can convince us, against al Ghazali's objections, that God's knowledge is complete, his conception of God is of a being so different—and distant—from humans as to be religiously uninspiring, a fact that is perhaps the real reason for Averroës' failure to convince Muslims that a philosophically coherent version of God can at the same time be spiritually satisfying. Again, we can see that Averroës has failed to reconcile science and religion. A God who sees only the abstract principles, the universals, and does not see our individual crying hearts is not the god of revealed religions. One interesting corollary of Averroës' view is that no knowledge that modern scientists would consider knowledge—namely of data arrived at through the senses—actually constitutes knowledge, for it is all of particulars!

The questions of bodily resurrection and the language of religion are considered by Averroës together in the last section of *Incoherence.*[44] Al Ghazali said that in denying a literal interpretation of the Qur'an's explicit statement of resurrection of the body (e.g., 36.77–82, 75.1–4, 81.7), the philosophers placed themselves out of Islam.[45] Averroës takes a windy approach to addressing this particular charge, expatiating on the universal belief by religious persons in some bliss beyond the grave and the sort of activity necessary to achieve it. He says that the learned classes, presumably the philosophers, must participate in life with the masses and must subscribe to "the general doctrine" in which they were brought up or they will deserve the name "unbeliever" and will be liable to the appropriate penalty. He then says that the learned must choose the best religion available to them. All religions, he adds, are a blend of inspiration and reason. In fact, if there were a natural religion based on reason alone it would be less perfect than the religion that is a blend. Lawgivers, he continues, have laid down the "principle as praiseworthy which most incites the masses to the performance of virtuous acts"[46]—a clear statement of the utility of religion. Finally, he identifies the doctrine of the afterlife as an example of that utility, for the promise of an afterlife encourages virtuous actions. A material description of heaven, he maintains, is more appropriate and more stimulating of virtue than a spiritual one. But then, warming up to his subject, he accuses of heresy those who believe that paradise consists of sensual enjoyment, despite very clear references in the Qur'an to sensual delights (e.g., 55.56–58, 78.33, 37.48).[47] He commits himself to the immortality of the *soul* but denies immortality to the body, explaining that only likenesses of the body can arise but not the bodies themselves:

> that which has perished does not return individually. . . . Therefore the doctrine of resurrection of those theologians who believe that the soul is an accident [i.e., that there are distinct souls for individuals] and that the bodies which arise are identical with those that perished cannot be true.[48]

In the end, then, Averroës does not affirm the doctrine of resurrection unless it is understood nonliterally. In his mind, rational considerations—e.g., the rejection of the sensuous depiction of paradise—prevent the literal form of the doctrine, i.e., individual bodily immortality, from being true.

Averroës' philosophical rejection of the literal resurrection of the body shows that he does not take the Qur'an as the literal word of God. Where it does not agree with the dictates of philosophy and demonstrable conclusions, he says it should be interpreted metaphorically or allegorically or should be declared to be a rhetorical statement for the masses. He does not hold to a theory of "double truth" — as has been often attributed to him but is denied by everyone who writes about him. There is only one truth, and it is expressed either explicitly by science or metaphorically by religion.

The difficulties that al Ghazali raises are profound ones for all who wish to hold on to their Holy Scriptures while at the same time reaching some accommodation with philosophy. Despite Averroës' valiant attempts to vindicate Aristotle, as he understands Aristotle, to confute the arguments against philosophy, and to reconcile reason and religion, al Ghazali is more than Averroës' match. With brilliant acumen he focuses on the gravest problems inherent in the philosophers' theories, revealing both their internal inadequacy and their inability to enjoy a harmonious marriage with religious beliefs. As al Ghazali rejected philosophy, so, ultimately, did the Muslim world. Many in the West have bemoaned the withdrawal of Islam into fundamentalism and have lamented the too-brief flowering of Islamic philosophy, which was abandoned after Averroës' death.[49] But if the arguments of the relevant thinkers are carefully considered, the intellectual respectability of al Ghazali's decision to eschew the philosophical arguments of the Aristotelians and instead seek inspiration and mystic union with the received text becomes amply evident.

DISCUSSION QUESTIONS

1. Although the Mutazilites attributed only goodness and justice to God, their views were proscribed after just one generation. What are the dangers, intellectual or political, that might arise from the belief that God cannot be other than the highest good?

2. Avicenna "reconciles" Aristotle and Plato by asserting two realms, the supernatural, where ideas have a separate existence in the mind of God, and the natural, where ideas do not exist apart from the things of which they are ideas. Can this kind of dualism account for why ideas, which are perfect *supernaturally,* are imperfect when embodied in nature?

3. Avicenna, like many before him and after him, declares that the language of Scripture is figurative. Declaring that a statement is figurative means, of course, that the statement is not saying what it seems to say, but something else. The usual motive given for the figurative language of Scripture is the inability of the masses to understand the truth. For a "thought experiment," let us assume that the figurative language of Scripture is in fact converting a difficult truth, one only philosophers can understand, into a comprehensible

but ultimately false formulation for the ignorant masses. Would an alternative strategy, one of stating things in a form true but incomprehensible to the masses, have been successful? As an analogy, we may observe that though Einstein probably realized that the mass of modern people would not understand the equations of his theory of general relativity, the incomprehensibility (for the masses) of the equations did not nevertheless persuade him to express the theory in solely figurative language. Could God, who is after all the reputed author of Scripture, have used Einstein's alternative approach? Could he have expressed religious truths in a way that only trained philosophers, and not the ignorant masses, could understand? Or is there some reason that God would not have worried lest the figurative language be misconstrued? Or, as fundamentalists have asserted, is the whole concept of figurative language to be rejected in favor of literalism?

4. Al Ghazali showed his keen understanding of philosophy by his pellucid summaries in his early book, *Intentions of the Philosophers*. Doubts of the explanatory success of all the philosophers afflicted him and he saw as the only alternative a rejection of philosophy and, instead, a wholehearted embracing of the literal truth of the Qur'an. Was his choice the best alternative open to him? Is there a difference between affirming the truth of a philosophy that breaks the rules of intellectual legitimacy when the philosophy's deficiencies are revealed, and affirming the doctrines of a religion that merely asserts the truth of those teachings but does not make logical rigor and consistency the standard of legitimacy? Is al Ghazali's choice the same one that Augustine made earlier, when Augustine preferred the Catholic to the Manichaean faith because the Catholic faith did not claim to *know* but only to *believe?*

5. Is al Ghazali's bluntness attractive? When al Ghazali attacks philosophers for putting a glossy veneer of orthodoxy atop their teachings as a cover for their impious views, and when he attacks them for claiming the utility of Scripture's deceptive language for controlling the masses, do these criticisms ring true? Would al Farabi or Avicenna blush at these charges? How would they defend themselves?

6. Al Ghazali identified a serious problem in Aristotle's metaphysics: the contradiction between the idea of an infinite series of causes, an idea that led to the conclusion of the eternity of the world, and the idea of an unmoved mover, or first cause. Averroës' defense of both views rests on the difference between human and divine action and the notion that humans respond to a stimulus whereas God never responds because no external stimulus can affect him. Is Averroës' response a *philosophical* response, or does it depend on an assertion that requires faith—namely faith in God's attribute of not responding to external stimuli? Would an acceptance of this attribute of not responding to stimuli make God more or less attractive as God? Would such a God be able to respond to prayers?

7. Many problems arise in reconciling science and religion on the subject of whether the world was created in time or is eternal. Problems also arise over

the world's age. In debates over these problems, partisans of one side or the other try to make their case by showing that the arguments of their opponents are absurd. (Perhaps by now readers of this book are concluding that *every* possible position has been shown to be absurd.) Is there in fact a measure of absurdity in the various arguments about these problems? Is there a measure of reason in them? Is the measure of reason enough to keep alive the hope that the view might be right? What does it mean for an argument to be absurd? Are the standards of absurdity the same in science and religion?

8. Averroës tries very hard to defend natural causality against al Ghazali's claim that the only causality is God's will. Does al Ghazali have a point? Are our notions of causality based on correlation? What are some examples of confusing correlational evidence with causality? Can there be a priori knowledge of causes in nature? Has later philosophy effectively solved the problem of causality?

9. How successfully does Averroës defend the doctrine of resurrection? Does he have to compromise his philosophy to accommodate it? How successfully does he defend philosophy against al Ghazali's charge of incoherence?

NOTES

1. The Mutazilites were founded by Wasil b. "Ata." See M. Fakhry, *A History of Islamic Philosophy* (New York: Columbia University Press, 1970), 59.

2. M. Fakhry, *Islamic Occasionalism and Its Critique by Averroës and Aquinas* (London: Allen and Unwin, 1958), 68ff.

3. See pp. 221–22.

4. Al Farabi, *Mabadi' Ara Ahl Al-Madinah al-Fadilah* (trans. Walzer), 1.1–8.

5. Fakhry, *History,* 136.

6. Al Farabi, *Mabadi' Ara Ahl Al-Madinah al-Fadilah,* 1.1–8.

7. D. Saliba, *Étude sur la métaphysique d'Avicenne* (Paris: Les presses universitaires de France, 1926), 21.

8. S. Inati, "Ibn Sina," in *History of Islamic Philosophy Part I,* ed. S. H. Nasr and O. Leaman (London: Routledge, 1996), 231.

9. M. Afnan, *Avicenna: His Life and Works* (Westport, Conn.: Greenwood, 1958), 178.

10. Avicenna, *Al-Najahr,* 271–72.

11. Avicenna, *Al-Najahr,* 264–65.

12. Inati, "Ibn Sina," 241.

13. Avicenna seems to subscribe to the Augustinian-Boethian conception of eternity as a timeless present, a notion that is not found in Aristotle. See the discussion of the Augustinian-Boethian conception, p. 131.

14. O. Leaman, *An Introduction to Medieval Islamic Philosophy* (Cambridge: Cambridge University Press, 1985), 34.

15. Averroës, *Averroës' Tahafut al-tahafut (The Incoherence of the Incoherence),* trans. S. Van den Bergh (London: Trustees of the "E. J. W. Gibb Memorial," 1978), 86. All references are to this edition. Henceforth, the work will be referred to simply as *The Incoherence of the Incoherence.* Averroës' point, of course, is also the point of Plato's *Sophist.*

16. Afnan, *Avicenna,* 172.

17. Afnan, *Avicenna,* 177.

18. G. Sarton, *A History of Science* (Cambridge, Mass.: Harvard University Press, 1952), 1:753.

19. W. M. Watt, *Muslim Intellectual: A Study of Al-Ghazali* (Edinburgh: Edinburgh University Press, 1963), 115.

20. C. Vollert, *St. Thomas Aquinas: On the Eternity of the World and Selected Miscellaneous Texts* (Milwaukee: Marquette University Press, 1964), 16.

21. On Aquinas's nontemporal version of creation, according to which God creates the world by *sustaining* it in being, see p. 208.

22. Al Ghazali, *Incoherence of the Philosophers (Tahafut al-Falasifa),* 317.

23. Leaman, *Islamic Philosophy,* 78.

24. Aristotle, *Nicomachean Ethics,* 1124b30.

25. Livy, *Ab Urbe Condita,* trans. A. de Sélincourt (New York: Penguin, 1971), 1.19.

26. Plato has Socrates banish Homer and other poets from his imaginary republic for the same reason, that they fail to tell the truth (*Republic,* 595Aff.).

27. Averroës, *Incoherence of the Incoherence,* 37ff.

28. Al Ghazali, quoted in Averroës, *Incoherence of the Incoherence,* 62. A strikingly similar argument, quoted by E. Stump and N. Kretzmann ("Eternity," 448) is made by N. Pike (*God and Timelessness* [London: Routledge and Kegan Paul, 1970], 104–5):

> Let us suppose that yesterday a mountain 17,000 feet high, came into existence on the flatlands of Illinois. One of the local theists explains this occurrence by reference to divine creative action. He claims that God produced (created, brought about) the mountain. Of course, if God is timeless, He could not have produced the mountain *yesterday* [emphasis in the original]. This would require that God's creative-activity and thus the individual whose activity it is have position in time. The theist's claim is that God *timelessly* brought it about that yesterday a 17,000 feet high mountain came into existence on the flatlands of Illinois. . . . [But] the claim that God *timelessly* produced a temporal object (such as a mountain) is absurd.

29. See the discussion of Augustine's and Boethius's view of eternity on p. 131.

30. Averroës, *Incoherence of the Incoherence,* 63.

31. On other problems with Averroës' theory of time, see Leaman, *Islamic Philosophy,* 48–49.

32. Averroës, *Incoherence of the Incoherence,* 519. For the views of J. S. Mill on correlations and causality, see the discussion on p. 66.

33. Averroës, *Incoherence of the Incoherence,* 56.

34. Leaman, *Islamic Philosophy,* 46, also understands the point this way.

35. Al Ghazali's argument (presented in Averroës, *Incoherence of the Incoherence,* 100) is actually more sophisticated than we have represented it. He says that according to the philosophers, what becomes is only matter, and that whatever something becomes must be either impossible, necessary, or possible. It cannot be impossible, for the impossible will never exist; it cannot be necessary, for the essentially necessary will never be in a state of nonexistence. Therefore it must be essentially possible. But matter, the passive, formless, inert substrate (see p. 99) cannot possess either the cause of its own actualization or an ability to acquire form. Since the philosophers whom al Ghazali is refuting deny that God suddenly wills a change (for the act of willing would be a change in him and they deny that any change is possible for an immutable, eternal God), the matter could not change from its primal state. In short, matter cannot change itself; only God could change

it; but God himself does not change matter because to change matter would involve a change in God, and God does not change.

36. Averroës, *Incoherence of the Incoherence,* 102.

37. Qur'an 34.3, 50.15, 35.12. The quotation is from 6.59.

38. Al Ghazali, *Munqidh* (trans. McCarthy), quoted in Leaman, *Islamic Philosophy,* 108n1.

39. Aristotle, *On the Soul,* 414b4.

40. Al Ghazali, *Incoherence of the Philosophers,* as quoted in Averroës, *Incoherence of the Incoherence,* 457.

41. Averroës, *Incoherence of the Incoherence,* 460.

42. Averroës, *Incoherence of the Incoherence,* 461.

43. Averroës, *Incoherence of the Incoherence,* 468.

44. Averroës, *Incoherence of the Incoherence,* 582–85.

45. Al Ghazali, *Incoherence of the Philosophers,* 355.4.

46. Averroës, *Incoherence of the Incoherence,* 584.

47. This is one of the accusations Aquinas makes against Islam in *Summa contra Gentiles.*

48. Averroës, *Incoherence of the Incoherence,* 586.

49. "All these events—the death of Averroës, the abrupt decline of Arab intellectual dynamism, the translation into Latin of Aristotle (notably the *Metaphysics* and the *De Anima* about 1200), and the exponential acceleration of Western philosophizing—occurred virtually within two decades. These are perhaps neither radically causative nor dependent events, but their close association is historically remarkable" (*Encyclopedia of Philosophy,* s. v. "Averroës"). Surely the failure by the most reputed Islamic scholar to refute al Ghazali effectively had much to do with the decline of Arab philosophical enthusiasm.

Reconciling Science and Religion in Medieval Judaism

In truth it is a puzzle to me
Why people study philosophy.
It is such tedious and profitless stuff,
And is moreover godless enough;
In hunger and doubt their votaries dwell,
Till Satan carries them off to hell.

—Heinrich Heine

SAADIA GAON

In our modern vanity we often think that everything under the sun is new, and, like adolescents who fall in love for the first time and think that no one in the history of the human race has ever felt or ever will again feel such intense passion as they now feel, we think that the conflict between religious orthodoxy and religious innovation and accommodation to contemporary events is something novel. Of course, even a cursory glance at history will give the lie to this sense of newness, if we are open-minded enough to give the glance. Thus in the ninth century arose the fundamentalist Karaites, who, like the Sadduccees before them, insisted that Judaism should look for authority only in the Bible. Rabbinical Judaism, which through its tradition of the law, the Talmud, was endeavoring to accommodate Jewish practice to contemporary life, was to be rejected, said the Karaites, and only a fundamentalist biblical Judaism allowed. Where, for example, Rabbinical (or Pharisaic) Judaism allowed a non-Jew to light candles for a Jewish home on the Sabbath, the Karaites insisted on living the holy seventh day in darkness.

Into this milieu Saadia ben Joseph Al-Fayyumi (882–942) was born, later known simply as Saadia Gaon, given the surname Gaon by posterity from his title as head of the academy in Sura, in Babylonia. Saadia's intellectual life involved treading a path with Karaites on one side of him, Aristotelian philosophers on the other. An active and energetic man, an eager participant in the affairs and controversies of his day, Saadia was also, as we shall see, a deep thinker, willing to confront some of the knottiest problems of science and religion. Already at twenty-three he wrote a treatise against Anaan, the founder of the Karaite sect, and a little later, engaged in a heated debate with Ben Meir over the calendar, a debate that involved the rival claims of supremacy of the Jewish schools in Babylon and Palestine. His philosophical views, which are what concern us here, are described in his *Al-Amanat Wa-l-I 'tiqadat (Book of Beliefs and Opinions)*.[1]

Saadia's underlying faith was that the part of the Bible known as the Torah could not contradict what is known by science. Like all holding this view, Saadia believed that there was an underlying order in the universe that man could study and come to know, that God does not introduce red herrings into the system to test our faith (as is the view of those who believe that God planted dinosaur bones that look millions of years old to test our faith in a recent creation), and that revelation is a legitimate means to truth. If there appears to be some contradiction between science and Scripture, the appearance has arisen either in a faulty process of reasoning or in a faulty interpretation of the Torah. The faulty reasoning may also have resulted from faulty sense perceptions, for, he says, there are three sources of philosophical conviction: the data collected by our senses in direct observation, our pure reason acting by itself (i.e., the intuition of the intellect), and what reason may deduce from logical necessity.[2] This explanation of faulty reasoning is, of course, recognizable as the commonsense view that Aristotle introduced in the *Metaphysics*. A fourth means to conviction, which corroborates the validity of the first three, is the tradition passed down in the Torah, the truth of which was established by thousands of witnesses to the miracles performed by God in the desert, particularly the manna that fed Israel in its wanderings.[3] The manna, he jokes, was so clever a scheme for feeding the people for forty years that it could not have been thought up by philosophers.

Saadia's work is also an apologetic for Judaism, for Saadia believes that his scientific examination of the world will confirm the views given assertively, that is to say, dogmatically, by the prophets and will answer the critics of the religion. It is also a polemical work, for it will show that Judaism is true and consistent with reason, while other religions are inconsistent with reason and thus to be rejected. It is, finally, the duty of the philosopher to confirm the truths of religion by reason. Nothing will be more persuasive than reasoned arguments, and nothing will serve God more than winning for him more worshippers. Of course, worshipping God and obeying his commandments is the highest and best activity for human beings—the means by which they attain perfect happiness.[4] To the question of why, if reason is sufficient to understand the truths of the world, we should need divine revelation, Saadia provides an ethical answer. Because the progress of science is very slow and very gradual, in the meantime we need guidance.[5] Perhaps an analogy may be made with the rearing of children: until the children are old enough to be able to reason about good and evil, it is essential for parents to give them guidance in the form of commands. As they grow and mature and become more and more amenable to reason, the "revealed" guidance can yield to reasoned arguments. What chaos would plague us if children had to grow without any guidance until they could think for themselves! What a misfortune it would have been, says Saadia, for the human race to be without a divine guide while working its slow way to reasoned truth.

Here we shall look principally at Saadia's views on creation and the nature of God, to which, since we cannot have any help from the senses, Saadia argues, only rational arguments will apply.[6] Then we shall take a brief look at some of the "dogmatic" subjects, such as resurrection and the afterlife, for which his proofs are less philosophically persuasive.

Saadia's views on the existence of God are mingled with his view of God as creator of the world in time. Taking aim at the Neoplatonists and their confidence that by their theory of emanation they have proven that the eternity of the world and its creation by God are compatible, Saadia shows that if the world were eternal, we would have to give up on a proof of God's existence. If the world and the matter in it are eternal, he says, then God's existence cannot be proven, for if matter always existed in its present form and so never came to be, there would be no need for God to create it—and hence there would be no way of knowing about God, and no proof of God's existence.[7] If, however, we say that the world either was made out of primitive matter or was created out of nothing—a claim he seeks to prove separately—then the world cannot have made itself, for neither matter nor nothingness have within themselves the requisite principle of change. Hence, we do need God. What is particularly brilliant in this part of Saadia's proof of God's existence is the use of Aristotle's conception of matter to help establish an un-Aristotelian doctrine, namely, that God created the universe at a beginning in time. As we recall from our earlier discussion of Aristotle (see p. 99), primitive matter—*hyle*—is simply the stuff of matter without any form—and this is what Saadia says cannot effect a change in itself. Thus, for Saadia, the proof of the world's beginning in time is intermingled with the proof for God's existence. Once a beginning in time is established, as Aquinas similarly realized, God's existence follows immediately, given the inability of both primitive matter and nothingness to bring about the present world. And, without a beginning in time, there can be no proof of God's existence.

Saadia's goal, then, is to prove demonstrably and deductively that the universe had a beginning in time. We should note at the outset that this question was much debated in the Middle Ages, with many of the same arguments recurring frequently. In this book, we shall concentrate on the points of significant difference among such arguments. In Saadia, we have some quite original arguments.

The first of his four proofs against the Aristotelian view of the eternity of the world depends on the finitude of the earth itself.[8] That the earth is finite is obvious, he thinks, from the fact that it is surrounded by heavens. An infinite earth could not be surrounded. The heavens also are finite, he says, for they make a revolution of the earth in twenty-four hours; if they were infinite, they would take an infinite time to revolve around the earth or they would have to move at an infinite speed—and both of these possibilities are absurd. In addition, a finite body like the heavens cannot have infinite power. (One might think of a steamship. So long as it is powered by coal, it will sail, but since the ship is finite, it can carry only a finite amount of fuel and will eventually stop.) Hence the world's own force must be finite and cannot have gone on for infinite time. Because it cannot have gone on for an infinite time, the universe had to have come into being. Implicit in the proof is of course the ancient system of the celestial spheres that, in conformity with what we observe, make a daily rotation around the earth. Also implicit is the pre-Newtonian idea that a moving force moves only so long as it is carried along by some motive power. The argument requires very little in the way of sensory data, perhaps only the observations that were obvious to people of the Middle Ages—that the heavens revolve nightly around the earth and that a moving body moves only because of the force by which it is moved. Moderns, of course, reject both of these "self-evident truths"—and so for us the argument is far from compelling. Yet, given the medieval view of science, and especially Saadia's epistemology and its four sources of conviction, this argument stands as an intellectually respectable monument in the attempt to reconcile religion and science on the issue of creation. Given the limited goal of the argument to show that the world had a beginning in time—and thus to lay the groundwork for a proof of God's existence—it does very well.

Saadia's second argument that the universe had a beginning has to do with the fact that the actual world is made of parts, as well as with the composition of those parts. Sometimes the parts are joined and sometimes they are separate. In the Aristotelian concept of pure matter with no form, among the essential qualities that matter does *not* include are combination and separation. But since matter does in fact combine to produce the parts of the world (there are several heavens and the celestial spheres are full of separate stars), an external force must have been applied in order to make the compositions. Thus the universe cannot be eternal, and we have another Aristotelian conception being used in the service of an un-Aristotelian conclusion. Perhaps the atomism that was an accepted part of the Islamic view of the material world also figures in the reasoning. The most difficult feature of Democritus's theory was the explanation of how atoms came to combine; atomists simply postulated that an occasional swerve caused the collisions out of which the universe, from numerous chance collisions, came to be. The swerve was the weakest part of atomic theory and is omitted entirely by Saadia, whose outside force is God.

Saadia's third argument rests on the concept that matter always contains accidental qualities. Again we must recall that matter separated from any form whatsoever is prime matter. We never actually find prime matter because it is always attached to qualities such as color, shape, motions, and the like. These accidental qualities are always changing; hence, accidents themselves are not eternal, for they are constantly coming into being and going out of being. Since accidents are temporal, says Saadia, the substances bearing the accidents must also be temporal. If matter is temporal and the world is made of matter, the world is not eternal. Here the argument seems to rely on the impossibility of an eternal substrate's being somehow joined with changing accidents. Because this, of course, was just what Aristotle denied in his concept of matter, it is clear that Saadia does not analyze the argument very deeply.[9]

Saadia's last argument is one that appears in Islamic philosophy and that we have already considered in our discussion of Avicenna (see p. 158). Past time, says Saadia, cannot be eternal because if it were, an infinite time would have passed before the present. But an actually infinite time is impossible. Thus time, and the world with it, must have a beginning. The argument does not apply to God, of course, who alone is not subject to time.

Once it has been proved that the universe is not eternal and that no matter existed before the world, the only reasonable alternative, says Saadia, is that there *is* an author of the universe, and that he is intelligent and alone eternal. Whether this author, God, made matter and then made the world or whether he made the world outright is irrelevant. Saadia rejects the Neoplatonic position—God and the universe are both eternal because the universe is an emanation—on the grounds that it is not likely that an eternal substance having none of the categories (which are all accidents) should change, even by emanation, into bodies having accidents.[10] Adding even more scorn to the theory of emanation and pointing out that it is the Neoplatonists themselves who posit that matter is evil, Saadia asks why a perfect being would emanate evil. Although he admits that creation out of nothing is an extremely difficult concept—perhaps inconceivable to human minds—he points out that such creation is attributed to God alone.[11] To demand to know the exact method of creation out of nothing would be to demand that we be God. The alternative, believing in the eternity of matter, is, in his view, more absurd than believing in a God whom we cannot comprehend.[12] And as for the nature of God, Saadia does not differ from the other philosophers. Because God is incorporeal and unique, all anthropomorphic descriptions of him in Scriptures are to be taken figuratively, not literally.

Of course, the reconciliation of science with a religion like Judaism, where observance of the commandments is of central importance, requires an analysis of the scientific basis for those rules. Here, alas, the difficulty of coming up with demonstrable proofs is insurmountable. Although there are no a priori arguments for ritual, Saadia nevertheless tries the best he can. He claims that the evidence of the multitudes who saw the miracles accompanying the reception of the law at Sinai is proof of the reality of the miracles. That the law should have been bestowed upon mankind is essential given human nature and human limitations, for no one could live well by relying on his senses alone.[13] Information for living may be received by a tradition or acquired through reason. And while either is subject to error, the possibility of error is eliminated when the tradition is af-

firmed by a whole nation, as in the case of the Jewish tradition. As for man's fee-
bleness and the dangers of disease and natural disaster to which man is subject,
Saadia says that these keep man humble and God-fearing and thus encourage man
to fulfill the commandments and achieve the happiness that is possible only to
him, as the only creature possessed of reason.[14] Since man is punished or rewarded according to his behavior, he must have free will; therefore, the passages
in the Bible that seem to deny free will must be interpreted allegorically. The
most famous such passage, where in Exodus 7.3 it is written that "God hardened
Pharaoh's heart," Saadia understands as saying not that God took away Pharaoh's
free will, but that he gave Pharaoh extra strength to endure the plagues without
giving in.[15] Thus God is not actually taking away free will but is enabling
Pharaoh to be true to his own determination.

Saadia believes that the existence of an afterlife in which a man is punished or
rewarded can be proved by reason.[16] His argument depends on God's justice, the
disproportionate relation between virtue and its reward in this life, the reward of
a soul for abstaining from things forbidden by the commandments, the inequali-
ties of punishments in this world, and so on. The question that so plagued
Boethius in the *Consolation of Philosophy,* namely, why the wicked seem to pros-
per while the righteous are miserable, is answered by the claim that a righteous
man suffers for his bad deeds in this world but is rewarded for his numerous good
deeds in the next, while a wicked man is rewarded for his few good deeds in this
world and is punished in the next.[17]

On the matter of bodily resurrection, Saadia says that since a man is a composite of body and soul, it is reasonable that his future reward or punishment
should involve the composite.[18] He gives as a possible objection to bodily resurrection the hypothetical observation that when a person dies his body decays and
may give rise out of its matter to a new body; hence, two people might be resurrected from the same original matter. Saadia rejects this scenario as untrue to nature, explaining that when a body decays its matter never becomes part of another
person but instead returns to nature, where it awaits use in the resurrection.[19] Il-
lustrative of Saadia's reasoning is the discussion of the resurrection of someone
devoured by an animal:

Should someone ask, however, how someone who has been devoured by lions or
other animals can be resurrected, seeing that he has been metamorphosed into other
bodies, our reply would be that the maker of this assertion assumes that the bodies
that are devoured lose their identity by assimilating with the bodies into which they
have entered. We must, therefore, answer him on two points at the same time by citing to him a basic principle that we, the congregation of monotheists, profess and acknowledge; namely, that no body of any creature can in any way bring about the extinction of another body. Aye, even if the former were to burn the latter with fire, it
could not cause it to be extinct forever, because no one is capable of so annihilating
things as to render them nonexistent other than He that created them *ex nihilo* and
brought them into being. So far as all creatures are concerned, however, they can
only separate the parts of material bodies. Even when fire is enkindled in a certain

body, its sole effect is to produce a resolution of its component parts into their original elements.[20]

All of Saadia's conclusions about the afterlife are in accord with reason—so long as one accepts his crucial and far from self-evident premises about God's active participation in rewarding or punishing every man.

Saadia's worldview is a combination of some forceful and some very weak arguments. Perhaps he felt that once he had proven God's existence he could let down his guard and dabble in less defensible views. Perhaps he felt that having persuaded his readers of God's existence, they would not demand as rigorous of proofs for his ethical propositions and his traditional pronouncements. The leap, certainly, from metaphysics to commandments is analogous to the shift from assessing the accuracy of grocery scales to judging contestants in a beauty contest: the degree of possible accuracy is not commensurable. The problem for Saadia is that when he is most Jewish he is least a philosopher; and when he is most philosophical he is least Jewish. That is to say, his defense of particularly *Jewish* doctrines is based not on natural reason but on revelation.[21]

ABRAHAM IBN DAUD

Ibn Daud (1110–1180), celebrated as the forerunner of Moses Maimonides, was the first to attempt a reconciliation between Aristotelianism and Judaism.[22] Saadia had attempted a general reconciliation of Judaism with philosophy, but as time passed, and as it was discovered that the original version of Aristotelianism was heavily corrupted by a mystical, magical, irrational Neoplatonism, there was, in the Jewish intellectual world, as in the Islamic, an attempt to discover the virginal, pure Aristotelianism, where the chaste, unsullied, purely rational truth lay. We moderns, with our more adventurous view of the scientific process, may lament the fact that the thinkers of the Middle Ages did not dream of directly exploring nature itself for discoverable truths but instead looked to the ancient past, to the finished product of a Greek mind that had blazed magnificently a millennium and a half earlier. This earlier philosophy was not a "burden of the past" but a challenge. The first task was to uncover as much of the Aristotelian treasure as possible and then to reconcile any of its apparent contradictions with the revealed truth of the Bible. A deep faith animated their hearts that such a reconciliation would reward their efforts with what today we call a "theory of everything." This was their "holy grail," in the quest for which they were as confident as are the modern physicists who believe that one day a general theory will show the simple unity of nature and the harmony of nature's forces. Where in modern times the attempt has resulted in what seems to a casual observer to be a confusing multiplication of particles, strings, and dimensions, so in the Middle Ages there was what might seem to the unzealous outsider a confusing hair-splitting and casuistry. Yet, as today we might ask, "Is not an additional dimension or one more string a small price to pay for a unified theory?" so a man of the thirteenth century might have asked, "Is not a fragile and thin distinction that may seem invisible to the untutored eye a small price for showing that God and Aristotle agree?"

It is the consensus of historians of medieval Jewish philosophy that the work of Maimonides is a brilliant and successful continuation of ibn Daud's work.[23] We shall therefore postpone a more thorough look at the reconciliation of Aristotle and Judaism until the discussion of the later thinker. Here, however, we might note some of the particular contributions of ibn Daud.

For ibn Daud, the acquisition of metaphysical knowledge is the purpose of human life. Once the necessities for survival and the requirements of an ethical life have been met, man's highest aspiration lies in understanding the secrets of being, the secrets of God, and the secrets of the invisible—angels, soul, the divine intellect. The Torah and the entire Bible are in complete agreement with philosophy, said ibn Daud, and all philosophy after the Bible is already implicit in it.

All his work assumes this premise of total harmony. Every chapter of his book *Al-'Aquida al-Rafi'a* (in Hebrew *Ha-Emunah ha Ramah [The Exalted Faith]*) begins with an exposition of philosophical ideas that are followed by supporting verses from the Bible. For example, he recalls Aristotle's discussion of substance or matter (*hyle*), the formless material substrate to which various accidents, which the ten categories comprise, attach themselves. These ten categories (substance, quantity, quality, relation, place, time, being in a position, possessing [state], acting, and being acted upon) are implicit, he says, in Psalm 139. Here is a part of ibn Daud's exposition (with ibn Daud's identification of each category in italics).

[What] Scripture Testifies concerning Concepts and Grades of Lights

David, peace unto him, already enumerated substance and most of these accidents. He alluded to the wisdom of God, may He be exalted, comprehending them by saying,

"O Lord, You searched me and You knew me." This [verse] speaks about his substance, which is a *substance*.

Then [David] said, "You know when I sit down and when I rise up," which is a *position*.

Then he said, "You understand my thought from afar," which is a disposition of the soul, which is one [kind of] *quality*.

Then he said, "You measure my going about and my lying down," which speaks of the knowledge of God, may He be exalted, comprehending his ends, which is a *quantity*.

Then he said, "You are acquainted with all of my ways," which are the remaining kinds of *quality*.

Then he said, "In back and in front You hemmed me in and You set [Your] hand upon me," which says that God, may He be exalted, gave him a figure, which is a notion that is a composite of *quality and quantity*.

Then he said, "Where shall I go from your sprit?" through his saying, "Even there Your hand will guide me and Your right hand will take hold of me," which speaks about every where at which it is possible for a man to be, all of which is comprehended by the knowledge of God, may He be exalted.

Then he said, "You knit me together in my mother's womb," which speaks about *relation*.

Then he said, "When I was made in secret, [and] I was formed in the lowest parts of the earth," which speaks about *action and affection*.[24]

That matter is itself without form and that matter may be formed and change its form, ibn Daud finds to be the metaphysical import of Jeremiah 18.3–4:

> We say that there is no clear explanation in the books of prophecy of what [in this case] is understood by true philosophy, so that the understanding of the people who are the masses of men would not be slow. Rather, [Scripture] alludes to [the topic] and arouses the unique individual to understand the secret meanings of those allusions.
>
> [Thus, that individual] knows that wisdom is included in the books of prophecy, while the masses are satisfied with their literal senses. The [following] statement from Scripture is one of the allusions to matter and [the claim that] forms consecutively befall matter:
>
> "The word that came to Jeremiah from the Lord saying, 'Arise and go down to the house of the potter and there I will cause you to hear My words.' Then I went down to the house of the potter and, behold, he made an artifact on the wheels. And [when] the vessel that he made in clay was marred by the hand of the potter, he again made another vessel, as seemed right to the potter to do."[25]

That every body needs another to move it, for nothing except the unmoved mover can move itself, ibn Daud finds in, among other places, in these lines from Job 38.37, Proverbs 30.4, and Isaiah 40.13:

> Who can number the clouds by wisdom? (Job 38.37)
> Who established all the ends of [the] earth? (Proverbs 30.4)
> Who meted out the spirit of the Lord? (Isaiah 40.13)[26]

The Aristotelian idea that the universe is finite rather than infinite in size, ibn Daud finds in Isaiah 40.12:

> Thus it is clear that it is not possible that a body is infinite, a line is not infinite; and ordered, infinite entities do not exist in actuality.
>
> [How] Scripture Alludes to the Preceding [Claims]
>
> Concerning all bodies being infinite, [Scripture says], "Who measured in the hollow of His hand the waters, and with the span meted out [the] heavens, and comprehended with a measure the dust of the earth, and weighed in the scales mountains, and the hills in a balance?"[27]

One will find ibn Daud's discovery of philosophy in the Bible, as illustrated by the foregoing quotations, either ingenious or mad, according to one's personal faith.

The question of whether the Bible contains *all* wisdom or only that which concerns how to live a holy life or how to achieve salvation will come up again for us. Galileo will quote approvingly a witty clergyman who says that Scripture deals with how to go to heaven, not with how the heavens go.[28] Ibn Daud, however, thinks that the Bible contains the truth about *everything,* and he employs his intelligence in showing that there is no conflict between the Bible and Aristotle because the Bible says everything that Aristotle said—when the Bible is read correctly.

MAIMONIDES

Maimonides (1135–1204) writes in *The Guide of the Perplexed* that "the things about which there is perplexity are very numerous in divine matters, few in matters pertaining to natural science, and nonexistent in matters pertaining to mathematics."[29] His book is aimed, naturally, at those who are perplexed about divine matters. After reading *The Guide,* however, one remains perplexed, albeit perhaps in a Socratic way: one knows that one is perplexed and that one is right to be perplexed, for divine matters are inherently perplexing. To claim to know about an area in which knowledge is not possible is to be truly ignorant. To avoid such ignorant claims, Maimonides uses his Aristotelian understanding of science to show the limits of science and human reason. On the greatest controversies of his day, in the end, he admits his human frailty and acknowledges his own ignorance. To various commentators through the ages, he has seemed to affirm one position or another—and his text supports even contradictory interpretations.[30] But the confusion about where Maimonides stands probably results chiefly from his commendable ability to see the merits in opposing arguments. Though an Aristotelian, he was perceptive enough to recognize that there were problems even with Aristotle, a recognition gained from Maimonides' vantage point both as a Jew who believed in the truth of the Bible and the Talmud, *and* as an Aristotelian scientist who could see internal inconsistencies in Aristotle's scientific views.

As a thinker of the twelfth century, Maimonides could not have been a serious scientist without also being an Aristotelian. Any other science was so far inferior to the coherence of the largely recovered pure Aristotle that it would have seemed "quack" science. Indeed, Hasdai Crescas (d. 1410), who was at pains to refute Aristotle's physical and metaphysical doctrines, was taken about as seriously as someone who today denies the standard model of atomic theory. For his efforts he survives as nothing more than a footnote in most histories of philosophy. Maimonides was, despite his Aristotelianism, true enough to the non-dogmatic spirit of Aristotle himself and astute enough to see some of the problems that lie beneath the surface of that school of thought. He was not so slavish an Aristotelian as to have considered the Greek the master of all knowledge.[31] Before exploring some of Maimonides' views about the common questions of the medieval attempt to reconcile religion and science, perhaps it would be useful to glance at what the Jewish thinker understood as the limitations of science, i.e., the received body of Aristotelian thought.

In book 2, chapter 9 of the *Guide* Maimonides observes that in Aristotle's day the exact number of celestial spheres had not been agreed upon.[32] Moreover, mathematicians debated where to place the spheres of Mercury and Venus. Although some ancients placed these spheres above the sun, Ptolemy placed them below the sun, "on the basis of the greatest likeness to natural order."[33] In his system, three bodies were above the sun and three below. The debate over the locations of the planetary spheres, explains Maimonides, was continued by Spanish mathematicians and ibn Aflah (whose son Maimonides says he met), who supported Ptolemy's view, and by Abu Bakr ibn al-Saigh, who argued for the opposite position. Maimonides himself says that the debate cannot be resolved by demonstration, i.e., by the "strong proof" from causes that Aristotle describes in the *Posterior Analytics*. Later on, in chapter 11, he makes it clear that some astronomical matters *are* in fact known, such as the fact that the sun's path is inclined with respect to the celestial equator, while other matters, such as whether the sun's motion requires an eccentric sphere or an epicycle, are not known.[34]

In chapter 24 he draws a conclusion about the impossibility of reconciling Aristotle's system of concentric spheres with Ptolemy's scheme of numerous eccentric orbits and epicycles:[35]

> Consider now how great these difficulties are. If what Aristotle has stated with regard to natural science is true, there are no epicycles or eccentric circles and everything revolves round the center of the earth. But in that case how can the various motions of the stars come about? Is it in any way possible that motion should on the one hand be circular, uniform, and perfect, and that on the other hand the things that are observable should be observed in consequence of it, unless this be accounted for by making use of one of the two principles [i.e., epicycles or eccentric circles] or of both of them? This consideration is all the stronger because of the fact that if one accepts everything stated by Ptolemy concerning the epicycle of the moon and its deviation toward a point outside the center of the world and also outside the center of the eccentric circle, it will be found that what is calculated on the hypothesis of the two principles is not at fault even by a minute. The truth of this is attested by the correctness of the calculations—always made on the basis of these principles—concerning the eclipses and the exact determination of their times as well as of the moment when it begins to be dark and the length of time of the darkness. Furthermore, how can one conceive the retrogradation of a star, together with its other motions, without assuming the existence of an epicycle? On the other hand, how can one imagine a rolling motion on the heavens or a motion around a center that is not immobile? This is true perplexity.

Here Maimonides points out significant limitations in Aristotle's conception of concentric spheres, which make intuitive sense but do not allow for accurate predictions of such phenomena as eclipses and planetary retrogradations. Yet Ptolemy's system, despite its predictive accuracy, has the heavenly bodies revolving around imaginary points that are themselves moving—enough of a departure from perfect circular motion to strain the imagination of any Aristotelian scientist.

What can one conclude from this perplexity? Maimonides' answer is worth quoting at length.

I have already explained to you by word of mouth that all this does not affect the astronomer. For his purpose is not to tell us in which way the spheres truly are, but to posit an astronomical system in which it would be possible for the motions to be circular and uniform and to correspond to what is apprehended through sight, regardless of whether or not things are thus in fact. . . . Now the truth is that Aristotle was not aware of [eccentricity] and had never heard about it, for in his time the mathematics had not been brought to perfection. If, however, he had heard about it, he would have violently rejected it; and if it were to his mind established as true, he would have become most perplexed about all his assumptions on the subject. I shall repeat here what I have said before. All that Aristotle states about that which is beneath the sphere of the moon is in accordance with reasoning; these are things that have a known cause, that follow upon one another, and concerning which it is clear and manifest at what points wisdom and natural providence are effective. However, regarding all that is in the heavens, man grasps nothing but a small measure of what is mathematical; and you know what is in it. I shall accordingly say in the manner of poetical preciousness: *The heavens are the heavens of the Lord, but the earth hath He given to the sons of man* [Ps. 115.16]. I mean thereby that the deity alone fully knows the true reality, the nature, the substance, the form, the motions, and the causes of the heavens. But He has enabled man to have knowledge of what is beneath the heavens, for that is his world and his dwelling place in which he has been placed and of which he himself is a part. This is the truth. For it is impossible for us to accede to the points starting from which conclusions may be drawn about the heavens; for the latter are too far away from us and too high in place and in rank. And even the general conclusion that may be drawn from them and for the grasp of which they have no instrument, is a defect in one's inborn disposition or some sort of temptation. Let us then stop at a point that is within our capacity, and let us give over the things that cannot be grasped by reasoning to him who was reached by the mighty divine overflow so that it could be said of him: *With him do I speak mouth to mouth* [Num. 12.8]. That is the end of what I have to say about this question.[36]

The passage is remarkable in many respects, not the least of which is that it gives us a paradigm of how Maimonides deals with the puzzling problems that confront those who seek knowledge of both scientific and religious matters.

First, we gain some insight into the title of the work, *The Guide of the Perplexed.* Maimonides is himself one of the perplexed, and the title is surely meant to be understood in this way. It is not a guide that will lead us out of our perplexity, but rather a guide for coping with the perplexity that we feel. It has been observed that the *Guide* is a difficult work whose meaning is not clear and whose teaching lends itself to vastly different interpretations.[37] Perhaps Maimonides is deliberately difficult so that we shall realize that there is no simple solution to the perplexities with which he is dealing. This teaching would in itself be startling to his contemporaries, who thought that Scripture was evidently true, or that science could give answers to everything, or even that the truths of faith and of science are self-evidently consistent. Maimonides' world, however, is one of uncertainty and perplexity, perhaps even of the existential loneliness that comes from looking up at the heavens and realizing one's own incapacities.

The passage begins by pointing out that astronomers are aiming not at absolute truth but at giving an accurate account of what we observe. Underlying this view is the common assumption that appearance may not exactly reflect reality. Later on, during the Copernican Revolution, the same claims will be made that a mathematical model might not reflect reality, that it might be devised for its predictive ability or convenience rather than for its truth. As for the anomalies in the motion of the sun that led Ptolemy to posit an eccentric circle, Maimonides observes that Aristotle could not know of the eccentric, which had not been developed by the mathematicians of his day. Maimonides suggests that if Aristotle had heard of the eccentric and been convinced of its real application to the sun's motion, he would have been as perplexed as Maimonides. Maimonides then makes one of his bold concessions to human smallness: what Aristotle said about things under the sphere of the moon—things sublunary—is true and can be proved by demonstration through causes; but of things above the sphere of the moon man grasps little other than a few mathematical facts. This point will perhaps not surprise the modern cosmologist, who is quite familiar with the concept of "horizons" beyond which scientific investigation cannot proceed. For if we substitute "observable universe" for Maimonides' "lunar sphere," similar conclusions might be drawn: asked what might lie beyond the observable universe, or what might have happened before the Big Bang, a cosmologist will reply that answers to these questions lie beyond our ken, as Maimonides says about what lies above the lunar sphere. Where Maimonides might disagree with a modern theorist, however, is that the medieval Jewish philosopher would say that knowledge of the heavens belongs to God alone. As the angel Raphael will tell Adam in *Paradise Lost,* man's place is to be "lowly wise," to know about the things of earth, his dwelling place.[38] Maimonides concludes by saying that we should leave to Moses (with whom God speaks face-to-face, "mouth to mouth" in the quotation from Numbers) the things that cannot be grasped by reasoning. In other words, we should be concerned with the matters of our lives, the matters directed by the Torah.

The point, then, is that except in matters related to mathematics (such as logic), we shall always have some perplexity. We can have some demonstrative knowledge about the science of mathematics, and perhaps a very little about God (perhaps that drawn from logic alone). One of the aims of the *Guide* is to comfort us in our perplexity, to assure us that perplexity is the proper condition for the reasoning man. There is something heroic in the submission to perplexity, in resigning oneself to not ever knowing the most important truths, to accepting, as Job does, the impossibility of satisfying the desire to know.

Still, there are some things that we can say even in our perplexity, for reasoning is possible and can take us part of the way towards truth.[39] For example, reason is able to show what can and cannot be said of God. Of the five kinds of attribute,[40] Maimonides rules out four as not being applicable to God.[41] The first kind of attribute, which has its definition predicated of it, is merely an explanation of a term;

since no predicate can be the logically prior formal cause of God's existence, God admits of no definition. Nor can one assign to God the second kind of attribute, where the predicate is partial, as when it is predicated of man that he is living or rational, for to do so would suggest that God's essence is a composite, which is absurd. The third kind of attribute is that which describes accidents, such as tallness in a man; this kind is ruled out because accidents are not applicable to God, all of whose properties are presumably necessary. The fourth kind of attribute concerns relations. Because every relation implies something in common between the terms of the relation, and because there can be no relation between the necessary existence of God and the contingent existence of a created thing, no relational predicate can apply to God. We are left, then, with attributes of action, which are not predicated directly of God but of his actions.[42] To say, for instance, that God is merciful, means that he *acts* mercifully; to say that God is just, means that he acts justly.[43] But no positive statement can be made about any of God's essential qualities, for such a statement would limit God.[44] Hence, any positive attributes that are assigned to God really mean the denial of the opposite attribute; in other words, the so-called positive attributes must be understood as negations. If God is said to be existent, it means, really, that he is not nonexistent. To know God at all, then, is to know in the weak sense of knowing his actions and knowing them a posteriori, or from effects of, say, his merciful or just actions. Furthermore, man is not able to know God in his essence,[45] for that essence is immaterial in itself, and man, who is made of matter, is not able to escape the material limits of his mind.[46]

The science of mathematics helps us to know what we *can* know about God. It teaches us to know that God's unity, whatever it is, is *not* like the unity of a number, for it is not subject to addition. Physics and astronomy are useful for teaching us about God's actions—that is, that he moves the spheres by the intermediary of the separate intellects. And this knowledge of God is not purely negative, for we are led to understanding something of the gulf that separates us from God.[47] The anthropomorphisms of the Bible must be understood in this light, as metaphors helping the unphilosophical many to understand God.[48]

Like many others that we have discussed, Maimonides believes that Scripture is written for the ordinary person, the person untutored in metaphysics, the person who lives in civil society without realizing the highest good for mankind, philosophic endeavor. According to Maimonides, there are in fact five reasons that the secrets of metaphysics should not be divulged to the vulgar crowd:[49] the inherent difficulty of the subject, the inability of most people to fulfill their potentiality for the highest wisdom, the long and tiresome preparatory period needed for such studies (the need first to study logic, mathematics, and the natural sciences), the need first to perfect a moral and dignified character, and finally the need to perfect one's body so that it will not distract one from the leisure of theoretical studies. All people, however, must be taught that the anthropomorphisms of the Bible are to be understood figuratively and that God is noncorporeal, for otherwise they will not worship correctly.[50] Luckily, there is a religious tradition that teaches the many the minimum number of truths necessary for a good life.

Here we find one of the ways of reconciling science and religion, or natural and revealed knowledge. Metaphysics, as an example of naturalistic knowledge, leads to a more abstract view of God than does traditional religion—to a more exact, though still imperfect, comprehension of God as he relates to creation. Consider an analogy to modern university education. Occasionally two versions of undergraduate classes on calculus are offered. The majority of students, who are planning a practical career in economics or the other social sciences, are required to memorize only the received formulas that will enable them to compute and solve problems when particular values are substituted for the generalized terms. A minority of students, who are particularly gifted or intrigued by mathematics, study also the long and somewhat tedious proofs that lead to the same formulas. These latter students are analogous to Maimonides' philosophers: the philosophers study logic and the other subjects that enable them to grasp the difficult metaphysical truths reached by the long and tedious process of deductive reasoning. The former students are analogous to the vulgar many, who learn the commandments, the rules for living a civic life, and then act as though the formulas (here the laws of the Torah and Talmud) were bestowed directly by God. Both groups are able to cope and to solve the problems of practical life, but the philosopher, like the student who has learned the proofs of calculus, has a deeper, richer understanding of the physical and spiritual universe and has fulfilled more of the innate human potentiality for wisdom (as the student has fulfilled an innate scholastic potentiality for learning mathematics). The analogy is not of course perfect. For Maimonides, as for ibn Daud, the truths of philosophy are contained in the Torah. Any contradictions with the Torah result from seeing only the surface, literal meaning of the sacred text. A philosophical exegesis of the Bible will remove all contradictions and show that the Torah contains in it the highest philosophical truth.[51]

For Maimonides, God, when correctly understood by metaphysics, is essentially Aristotle's Prime Mover, a unity consisting of Intellect, Intellecting, and Intelligible.[52] In other words, in what to readers of this book (but not to the "vulgar crowd") are more familiar terms, God is thought thinking about itself. One way to glimpse what God is like, says Maimonides, is to examine human thought. When a person (to use his example)[53] sees a tree, he might reflect that it is made of wood and eventually might come to the abstract concept of wood—not the wood of the particular tree, but the idea of wood itself. At a certain point, he discards the actual matter and thinks only about the qualities of wood. When his mind is wholly fixed on the abstract concept, the individual is no longer in a sense himself; his thinking and the subject of his thinking—the abstract concept of wood—have been united, and the thinker himself is united with his thinking and with the content of the thinking. This is a crude image of the unity that is God and his thought ("thought" understood here as both the *process* of thinking and the *subject matter* of the thinking). Of course, God's subject matter is exclusively himself, a circumstance that constitutes a huge gap between man and God. In fact, this gap, and the inability of human language to describe this gap, is another source of human perplexity.[54]

Given this conception of the deity, the question for Maimonides, as for the principal thinkers of the Middle Ages, is how to account for God's work as creator. Saadia Gaon said that to prove the existence of God, it is necessary to establish creation in time by proving that the world is not eternal. Maimonides says that even if the world is eternal, the existence of God as creator can be shown.[55] His four proofs for the existence of God are those common to his day and rely on the impossibility of an infinite regress (though not, of course, on the impossibility of an infinite past for the universe). Through the proofs, he works his way to an incorporeal Prime Mover that exists outside and apart from the celestial sphere. Although he says that human reason is not able to decide the issue of the eternity or temporal creation of the world, nevertheless, the arguments for the incorporeality of God flow by a necessary demonstrative argument from the premise that the world is eternal.[56] Therefore, Maimonides says, he will speak of the world *as though* it were eternal in order that the deity may be known to be incorporeal. This view, that the world is eternal, a view Maimonides says he is merely assuming for the sake of reiterating the key concept of God's incorporeality, is what led most early commentators to conclude that Maimonides actually believed the world to be eternal.[57] Shem Tov Ben Joseph Falaquera, for example, objected that it was highly dubious to demonstrate a matter so central as God's incorporeality on the basis of a premise that was untrue—the eternity of the world.[58]

It is said by critics that Maimonides actually believes in the eternity of the world but thinks that if this truth were revealed it would destroy religion, which is indispensable for human society. Thus, for the sake of maintaining civil society, the human population must be deceived into believing in creation in time.[59] Perhaps a more plausible interpretation of Maimonides is that the truth of God's existence—though it can be shown demonstratively from the unprovable premise of the eternity of the world—and the truth of creation in time—though it cannot be proved by reason—are both perplexities resulting from the great gulf between man and truth itself. The philosopher who has studied metaphysics will understand the perplexities; the majority of mankind will not be aware of them. Those individuals who do not understand that it is the highest wisdom to be perplexed about these matters—with its concomitant humility like that of Job after his conversation with God—will simply be confused, as readers of Maimonides have been. The point is that it is right to be confused, and the confusion that Maimonides creates is a reflection of the true confusion that must afflict humankind when trying to understand the relation of God to the world. Perhaps it is here that the traditional idea that "The beginning of wisdom is fear of the Lord" and the Platonic Socrates' observation from the *Theaetetus* that "Philosophy begins in wonder" come together.

Maimonides discusses additional perplexing matters that arise from the debate over the eternity of the world.[60] He suggests that if it ever were proved that the world is eternal—and he reiterates that there has been no such proof—we would have to interpret figuratively the Bible's statements about creation in time and about the temporality of the world. It has been adequately demonstrated, according to

Maimonides, that God does not have a body like man's, so anthropomorphic references to God must also be understood figuratively. If a similarly adequate demonstration were made about eternity, we would also have to interpret figuratively the Bible's comments about the temporality of the world. But, Maimonides reiterates, the eternity of the world *has not* been so demonstrated. Moreover, the physics of Aristotle, as mentioned before, applies accurately only to the sublunary world, so his metaphysics is really just a conjecture.[61] As a consequence, we do not know about the celestial spheres, let alone about God. Here Maimonides asserts his independence from Aristotle and the monolithic system that others accepted as a whole. In *not* taking Aristotle as the final word, Maimonides was truer to Aristotle than most others, for Aristotle understood himself to be in the tradition of those who worked toward greater understanding, as one in a continuing process of scientific discovery. That Aristotle wrote such good arguments and thus stifled rather than encouraged debate and discovery is one of those unintended consequences to be most lamented in the history of philosophy. In any case, in Maimonides, with his willingness to concede the impossibility of knowing many things and with his confession that he does not know the answers, we have a tower of intellectual honesty.

An answer to the question about the eternity of the world, for example, is beyond human capacity. Moreover, either an affirmative or a negative answer would be problematic. If, on the one hand, the world is eternal, then it is difficult to see how God is not reduced to a Neoplatonic machine wholly uninvolved with the world, a God whose work of creation is an unchanging emanation. Such a conception, even if it facilitates an argument for incorporeality, destroys the Torah and religion. If, on the other hand, the world has been created in time, the desirable arguments of the philosophers about the impossibility of creation out of nothing and about God's incorporeality fall apart. So if we accept one answer, we destroy religion; if we accept the other, we destroy philosophy, man's greatest gift. As a Jewish thinker of the Middle Ages, Maimonides must find his way between this Scylla and Charybdis. His way was to accept perplexity.

Another of the familiar problems about God concerns his knowledge of individual events. Does God, as the Qur'an says, know about every atom in the universe at every moment, about every leaf, or does he know only the most abstract general truths? If his activity is exclusively self-contemplation, as the philosophers say, how can he know about individuals, as Scripture says? According to Aristotelian science, all particular things arise from matter, which is inseparable from accidents. But knowledge is of what is common, of what is intelligible, and thus cannot be of the constantly changing accidents attached to matter. Maimonides discusses the five possible solutions to this problem. The atomists said that everything was chance, and so God would know nothing and problems concerning God's knowledge would not even arise. Aristotle (according to his commentator Alexander of Aphrodisias) said that the *fixed* laws of nature, such as the movement of the spheres, are made and known by God. The Asharites claimed that everything came from God and that there were no laws of nature whatsoever, that if a person wrote a letter, it was a coincidence that his hand moved while he thought he was moving it, for the movement actually came from God. Next is the view that God fixes laws that conform to his divine wisdom and grants rewards to deserving individuals in the world to come. Finally, there is the law of Moses, which states that man has an absolute free will, for it is God's will that men and animals have free will.[62] And here Maimonides will make a distinction between animals and men with respect to God's providence for them.

Maimonides says that his own view concerning this distinction does not arise from a philosophical demonstration, but from the Bible and, in particular, from the books of the prophets.[63] When he explains the source of his opinion, he emphasizes that the matter resides outside of philosophy. Given his views about the nature of God and the impossibility of humans comprehending the celestial spheres, it is not at all surprising that he places insights about God's knowledge of the world outside the realm of demonstration. His opinion, then, is that as far as plants and animals are concerned, Aristotle is correct, and whatever they experience or suffer is the result of chance. But whatever human beings experience or suffer is in accordance with their deserts as God judges (and with his providence, which watches over human individuals).[64] *How* God judges cannot be fully understood by human intellects. So when it comes to individuals, God is not concerned with every atom or every leaf but with human individuals, and especially philosophers—most of all when they turn their thoughts to God. Maimonides adds that the divine intellect illuminates the mind of the philosopher like flashes of lightning, which are manifested in proportion to their degree of connection with the divine intellect.[65] Each flash has a permanent effect, leaving its recipient improved. When Maimonides leaves the area of demonstrable conclusions, he thus perhaps allows himself some Platonic poetry.

What Maimonides offers, then, is a license to be perplexed. Perplexity is the right and respectable position for a learned thinker who understands the limits of human reasoning, who understands what yields to and what resists reason. Alas, as we pointed out in chapter 2, the human mind—at least the mind of the average person, one of the many—is not content to dwell in perplexity. The philosopher for whom Maimonides is writing is surely not content with perplexity either. But perhaps he can grow accustomed to it and, like Socrates, reach some sort of accommodation knowing that he is wise because he knows he is not wise, because he knows that he does not know.

It is no wonder that when its greatest philosopher could offer only perplexity instead of solutions Judaism withdrew from philosophy and retreated to the mysticism of the Kabbalah, which promised immediate and direct access to the ineffable. Averroës, as we argued in the last chapter, was unable to meet the challenge of al Ghazali's powerful logic: a reasonable Muslim would have been convinced that the philosophers *were* incoherent. Maimonides in turn showed that philosophy could not offer a more coherent or more accessible vision of God and the world than could Scripture. Why continue to follow so unpromising a road as philosophy, when the broad and inviting avenue of religion beckons?

DISCUSSION QUESTIONS

1. Saadia Gaon argues that there can be no proof of God's existence unless the world had a beginning in time. He adds that since we deduce the qualities of God from the world God has created (i.e., qualities deduced a posteriori), we could not have knowledge of God unless he created the world. Both conclusions, that we deduce God's qualities from his creation and that unless he created the world there could be no knowledge of him, concern our ability to know about God. Would the same conclusions apply to non-Western religions or to religions that do not hold a creator-deity as central to their belief?

2. Are there echoes in the second law of thermodynamics of Saadia's view that the world's energy cannot be infinite? Are there echoes in the notion of an initial singularity (prior to the Big Bang) of Saadia's view that the world's forces cannot have gone on for an infinite amount of time? While it is unlikely that the majority of people in the Middle Ages would have reflected on the nature of infinity in such a fashion as to have come to the conclusion of a beginning in time, would Saadia's reasoning have given Saadia himself a satisfying glimpse of consilience from which he would have felt confident of being on the right path?

3. In Saadia, as in so many Western thinkers, we see the irresistible hold of the Parmenidean principle that perfection and change are incompatible. Saadia concludes that believing in the eternity of matter is more absurd than believing in an incomprehensible deity. Is this claim valid? If one view is shown to violate the laws of reason and the other view is shown to be incapable of being understood, and if the views exhaust the alternatives (that is, they are the only views there are, so one *must* be true), is it legitimate to reject the one that violates the laws of reason and to accept the view that is incapable of being understood? How can we be sure that the second view is merely "incapable of being understood" and is not itself absurd? Is it legitimate to declare that the first view only *appears* to violate the laws of logic, but somehow—in ways we have not *yet* understood—is actually paradoxical and hence ultimately true? In other words, is there a way to be absolutely certain that a view violates the laws of logic? Is there a way to be absolutely certain that a view is incomprehensible and that the claim of incomprehensibility is not simply a smoke screen for preferring the second alternative?

4. Saadia's metaphysical views are more intellectually rigorous than his ethical views or his views in support of a specific religious doctrine like res-

urrection. Are already-religious believers likely to be more convinced of their beliefs because of metaphysical arguments like Saadia's? Are irreligious people likely to accept his less ably argued religious views because of the excellence of his metaphysical arguments? Is Saadia an example of those who "preach to the choir," that is, who are persuasive to those who already hold the same opinions as the "preachers"? How pervasive in the attempt to reconcile science and religion is the phenomenon of accepting enthusiastically those scientific arguments that can be shown to support one's firmly held religious views?

5. One can imagine that Saadia argued his theories with a host of litigious individuals. His discussion of how the resurrection of someone devoured by animals takes place suggests that Saadia had been challenged on this question by a pesky interlocutor. Are there other clever questions that would tax the ingenuity of a believer like Saadia? How does Saadia's ingenuity compare to that of ibn Daud in his discovery of the various Aristotelian categories hidden within Psalm 139? What purpose, if any, do clever questions like the one about the resurrection of a devoured person serve in the arguments about science and religion?

6. Maimonides rejects four of the attributes that are assigned to God on the basis of Parmenidean considerations of oneness. He does not, however, reject the fifth attribute, the attribute of action. God's actions, he says, can be known only from effects (a posteriori). Can Maimonides successfully avoid Parmenidean difficulties in this way? Or does any action—action being understood as a kind of motion that involves change—violate absolute oneness?

7. Many Western philosophers seem fond of the *via negativa*, that is, describing God in terms of what he is not. Can such a description by negative attributes appeal only to the religiously faithful?

8. Maimonides gives five reasons that metaphysics should be kept from the "vulgar crowd." Are his reasons valid? Do they have a modern analogue in the public schools?

9. Maimonides concludes that Aristotelian science applies only to things below the sphere of the moon, that is, to things *sublunary*. About God and things above the sphere of the moon, things *superlunary*, we humans can only speculate. He believes that if we do not accept perplexity about certain superlunary matters, such as the infinity of the world and creation, we shall destroy philosophy and religion, and, he argues, perplexity is a much better choice than such destruction. Is the modern world so changed from the medieval world that perplexity is no longer an attractive option? Are there dangers in choosing perplexity? Can one actually *choose* to be perplexed? Is one more likely to adopt one of the alternative views than to adopt perplexity?

10. Saadia argued that philosophy should be put in the service of religion, for he believed that nothing is so persuasive as philosophical arguments and

that if arguments could be used to prove the teachings of religion, philosophy would win more worshippers—and worshipping God is the highest possible human activity. Ibn Daud believed that the purpose of human life is the acquisition of metaphysical knowledge, understanding the secrets of being, God, the angels, soul, and the divine intellect. He took as an assumption a total harmony between the philosophy of Aristotle and these secrets. Unlike his predecessors, Maimonides believed that philosophers had to reconcile themselves to perplexity. Does this sequence of medieval Jewish philosophers represent a *development?* Would philosophy appear to be more attractive or less attractive as a discipline by the time Maimonides had finished his work?

NOTES

1. References are to the translation by S. Rosenblatt (New Haven: Yale University Press, 1948).

2. Saadia Gaon, *Book of Beliefs and Opinions,* 16. As an example of the second source of knowledge, notions that "spring up solely in the mind of a human being," Saadia gives "approbation of truthfulness and disapproval of mendacity." A moment's reflection exposes the brilliance of the example: only human beings are capable of truth and lies—and no one needs to be taught to respond, as Saadia says.

3. Saadia Gaon, *Book of Beliefs and Opinions,* 29–30.

4. The summary in this sentence is drawn from I. Husik, *A History of Mediaeval Jewish Philosophy* (Philadelphia: The Jewish Publication Society of America, 1916), 38.

5. Saadia Gaon, *Book of Beliefs and Opinions,* 87, 89.

6. Saadia Gaon, *Book of Beliefs and Opinions,* 38.

7. Here he is like Maimonides (see p. 178) in suggesting that God can be known only a posteriori. Aquinas, in the discussion leading up to his proofs for God's existence, also says that God can be known only a posteriori, that is, from his effects (*Summa Theologica,* 1.2.2).

8. The four proofs can be found in Saadia Gaon, *Book of Beliefs and Opinions,* 41–44.

9. See C. Sirat, *A History of Jewish Philosophy in the Middle Ages* (Cambridge: Cambridge University Press, 1985), 24, who says that Saadia derived this and the other proofs from the *Mutakallimun.* She adds that Saadia "used his sources without considering them deeply or criticizing them. He was profoundly convinced that only the infinite action of God is able to sustain and explain the constant alteration of the corporeal universe, the perpetual generation of a finite world in space and time."

10. Saadia divides his account into seventeen refutations (*Book of Beliefs and Opinions,* 58ff.).

11. Husik, *Jewish Philosophy,* 31.

12. Saadia Gaon, *Book of Beliefs and Opinions,* 53.

13. Saadia Gaon, *Book of Beliefs and Opinions,* 138. See also Husik, *Jewish Philosophy,* 40.

14. Saadia Gaon, *Book of Beliefs and Opinions,* 137.

15. Saadia Gaon, *Book of Beliefs and Opinions,* 199.

16. Saadia Gaon, *Book of Beliefs and Opinions,* 327.

17. Saadia Gaon, *Book of Beliefs and Opinions,* 214, 216.

18. Saadia Gaon, *Book of Beliefs and Opinions,* 336.

19. Saadia Gaon, *Book of Beliefs and Opinions,* 412–13.

20. Saadia Gaon, *Book of Beliefs and Opinions,* 413.

21. He is like the modern theologians who will be examined later, in chapter 14, whose science is sound but whose extrapolations to particular religious doctrines are dubious. See, e.g., our discussion of A. Peacocke, pp. 284ff.

22. See ibn Daud, *The Exalted Faith,* trans. N. Samuelson (Rutherford, N.J.: Fairleigh Dickinson, 1986), 9.

23. E.g., Husik, *Jewish Philosophy,* 198; Sirat, *Jewish Philosophy,* 143; Samuelson, *The Exalted Faith* (Rutherford, N.J.: Fairleigh Dickinson, 1986), 9.

24. Ibn Daud, *The Exalted Faith,* 17b17–18b11.

25. Ibn Daud, *The Exalted Faith,* 29b13–30b6.

26. Ibn Daud, *The Exalted Faith,* 53b12–13.

27. Ibn Daud, *The Exalted Faith,* 44b3–8.

28. See chapter 12, p. 221.

29. Maimonides, *The Guide of the Perplexed,* trans. S. Pines (Chicago: University of Chicago Press, 1963), 2:66. All references are to this edition.

30. Sirat, *Jewish Philosophy,* 175ff.

31. We are referring of course to Dante's phrase for Aristotle, "il maestro di color che sanno." In the opening sentence of chapter 54 of *The Guide of the Perplexed,* Maimonides refers to Moses as "the master of those who know." One can only wonder whether Dante knew the phrase in the *Guide* and was deliberately applying it to the pagan philosopher.

32. Maimonides, *The Guide of the Perplexed,* 268.

33. Maimonides, *The Guide of the Perplexed,* 268.

34. Maimonides, *The Guide of the Perplexed,* 273.

35. Maimonides, *The Guide of the Perplexed,* 325–26.

36. Maimonides, *The Guide of the Perplexed,* 326–27.

37. E.g., *Encyclopedia Judaica,* s.v. "Maimonides, Moses"; and J. Guttmann, introduction to *Maimonides: The Guide of the Perplexed,* ed. J. Guttmann and trans. C. Rabin (Indianapolis: Hackett, 1995), 5–7.

38. The following passage from *Paradise Lost,* 8.70–84, perfectly captures Maimonides' point about the limits of man's knowledge of astronomy.

> Whether heav'n move or earth,
> Imports not, if thou reckon right; the rest
> From man or angel the great Architect
> Did wisely to conceal, and not divulge
> His secrets to be scanned by them who ought
> Rather admire; or if they list to try
> Conjecture, he his fabric of the heav'ns
> Hath left to their disputes, perhaps to move
> His laughter at their quaint opinions wide
> Hereafter, when they come to model heav'n
> And calculate the stars, how they will wield
> The mighty frame, how build, unbuild, contrive
> To save appearances, how gird the sphere
> With centric and eccentric scribbled o'er,
> Cycle and epicycle, orb in orb.

39. Perhaps Dante, in having Bernard as his last guide, was in a way suggesting that only the mystic could get close to God. Still, Dante, like Maimonides, believed that reason could go part of the way.

40. The kinds of attributes are discussed by Aristotle in *Posterior Analytics,* 73a21–74a3.

41. Maimonides, *The Guide of the Perplexed,* 114–19.

42. Maimonides, *The Guide of the Perplexed,* 124 ff. See Sirat, *Jewish Philosophy,* 180–81.

43. Maimonides, *The Guide of the Perplexed,* 125–26.

44. Maimonides, *The Guide of the Perplexed,* 135–37.

45. Maimonides, *The Guide of the Perplexed,* 322–31.

46. Maimonides discusses the connection of the mind to the body in *The Guide of the Perplexed,* 257. For a discussion of what Maimonides means when he talks about the physicality of the soul, see O. Leaman, *Moses Maimonides* (London: Routledge, 1990), 110–14.

47. These remarks will agree with those of Leaman (*Maimonides,* 34–36) but not those of L. Strauss (introduction to *The Guide of the Perplexed,* by Maimonides, trans. S. Pines [Chicago: University of Chicago Press, 1963], xlviii–xlix).

48. A very clear statement by Maimonides against anthropomorphism is found in sections 11 and 12 of *H. Yesodei ha-Torah,* as quoted by M. Fox, *Interpreting Maimonides: Studies in Methodology, Metaphysics, and Moral Philosophy* (Chicago: University of Chicago Press, 1990), 41:

> Since it has been demonstrated that He is not a body, it is clear that none of the accidents of matter can be attributed to Him. This being so, the expressions in the Pentateuch and books of the Prophets already mentioned, and others similar to these, are all of them metaphorical and rhetorical.

49. Maimonides, *The Guide of the Perplexed,* 72–79.

50. Maimonides, *The Guide of the Perplexed,* 79–81.

51. Guttmann, introduction to *Maimonides,* 11.

52. Sirat, *Jewish Philosophy,* 183.

53. Maimonides, *The Guide of the Perplexed,* 163–64.

54. Leaman, *Maimonides,* 165. S. Pines, "The Limitations of Human Knowledge According to Al-Farabi, Ibn Bajja and Maimonides," in *Studies in Medieval Jewish History and Literature,* ed. I. Twersky (Cambridge, Mass.: Harvard University Press, 1979), 1:94, suggests that the "probable" doctrine about the celestial spheres provides philosophers with "a system of beliefs, somewhat analogous, as far as the truth function is concerned, to the religious beliefs of lesser mortals."

55. Guttmann, introduction to *Maimonides,* 13–14.

56. Maimonides, *The Guide of the Perplexed,* 181–82. Here is Maimonides' argument:

> If, however, the world is eternal, it follows necessarily because of this and that proof that there is an existent other than all the bodies to be found in the world; an existent who is not a body and not a force in a body and who is one, permanent, and sempiternal; who has no cause and whose becoming subject to change is impossible. Accordingly he is a deity. Thus it has become manifest to you that the proofs for the existence and the oneness of the deity and of His not being a body ought to be procured from the starting point afforded, for in this way the demonstration will be perfect, both if the world is eternal and if it is created in time.

57. Sirat, *Jewish Philosophy,* 189.

58. Shem Tov Ben Joseph Falaquera, *Moreh ha-Moreh,* 43, quoted in Sirat, *Jewish Philosophy,* 189.

59. This seems to be the view of Strauss, introduction to *Guide,* xiv. For a critique of Strauss, see D. H. Frank, new introduction to *Maimonides: The Guide of the Perplexed,* ed. J. Guttmann and trans. C. Rabin (Indianapolis: Hackett, 1995), xi–xii.

60. Maimonides, *The Guide of the Perplexed,* 327–28.

61. Maimonides, *The Guide of the Perplexed,* 319–20.

62. Maimonides, *The Guide of the Perplexed,* 469.

63. Maimonides, *The Guide of the Perplexed,* 471–72.

64. Maimonides, *The Guide of the Perplexed,* 472.

65. Maimonides, *The Guide of the Perplexed,* 624–25.

11

Reconciling Science and Religion in the Christian Middle Ages

And now I have my answer to the man who says: "What was God doing before He made heaven and earth?" Someone once, evading the force of this question, is said to have made the jesting reply: "God was making hells for people who look too deeply into things." This is not my answer. To make a joke about something does not mean that one understands the subject. No, that is not my answer. Personally I would rather say: "I don't know," when I don't know, than make the kind of reply which brings ridicule on someone who has asked a deep question and wins praise for an inaccurate answer.

—Augustine, *Confessions*

From nearly its beginning, Christianity was more open to Greek science than either Judaism or Islam. The underlying reason for Christianity's greater openness probably lies in the fact that Christianity and science spoke the same language: Greek. Where Jews spoke Greek, in Alexandria, Egypt, Philo had attempted to marry his revealed religion with Platonic science. But for the most part the language of Jews was Aramaic or Hebrew; the center of Talmudic studies was in Babylonia; and Plato and Aristotle were distant, foreign writers. In the ninth century, when the *lingua franca* of the educated world was Arabic, the language into which the Greek philosophical texts were translated, those texts became accessible to Jews and Arabs, who, as we have seen, made various attempts to reconcile the truths of science and faith. But the Christian gospels themselves were composed in Greek, and Christianity had grown up in a Greek milieu, where the entire educational system depended on Greek texts. Thus Greek science had been accessible to Christianity from Christianity's very beginnings.

It must be said, too, that Christians had the advantage of reading Philo, who had brilliantly demonstrated the compatibility of the Bible with Plato's ideas—

especially those expressed in the *Timaeus*—such as the idea of creation in time by a Craftsman who looked out for the good and constructed the world in accordance with an image of himself. Of course, a Christian war cry against everything pagan, including Greek philosophy, had been powerfully raised by Tertullian, who asked what Athens had to do with Jerusalem. His answer was that the philosophers were charlatans, hucksters of wisdom and eloquence, and that the ideas of the philosophers, including Aristotle, were the source of heresy.[1]

In its climb up the ladder of intellectual respectability, Christianity rejected Tertullian. Origen and, after him, Augustine argued that while the gospels were at one level accessible to the common, unlettered masses, they could be read at a higher, more abstract level by the more sophisticated leaders of the Church. The discovery of this "more spiritual" way of reading the Bible, developed in Alexandria during the second and third centuries in the Christian school of theology and apologetics under Clement, contributed greatly to Augustine's conversion. Augustine concluded that much of the seeming nonsense of Scripture, when read figuratively, disclosed a profound reality. Augustine, moreover, showed what a really fine mind could do when it got hold of philosophy, especially Neoplatonic philosophy, namely, that it could devise numerous arguments for the truth of Christianity. Augustine praises the Neoplatonists as superior to the pagan gods. All of Scripture could be rendered rationally acceptable when analyzed with the aid of Neoplatonism or Philonic Platonism, or, where either of these failed, by allegorization.

The debate about whether, as Tertullian wished, classical culture should be abandoned altogether gave way by the fourth century to a debate over how, and how pervasively, elements of classical culture should be included in Christian culture. Basil, in his *Octavius* or "Letter to Young Men," suggested that as a bee flits from flower to flower collecting only the nectar, so should Christians pluck only the nectar of Greek literature, choosing the parts that are unquestionably good and leaving aside the rest. But Basil himself was enthusiastically pro-Greek and perhaps showed how outrageously Greek culture could be used to illustrate Christian virtue when he claimed that the laurel wreath given to victors in the Olympic Games showed, by the modest simplicity of its value (as distinct from, say, a gold medal worth a lot of money), how humble the athletes were! Gregory Nazianzen insulted the unsophisticated boorishness of Christians who looked down on Greek culture. By the time of Chrysostom in the early fifth century, classical education was being hailed as a good in its own right, not simply a means to Christian truth.

Greek learning survived through late antiquity in the work of the encyclopedists, of whom perhaps the greatest was Isidore of Seville. It survived also in the monastic schools established by Cassiodorus, where ancient texts were copied. Among these texts, the most important was the work of Manlius Boethius, "the last of the Romans," as Gibbon puts it, "that Cato or Tully [i.e., Cicero] could have acknowledged for their countryman."[2] The magnificent project of Boethius was to translate into Latin all the works of Aristotle and Plato and then reconcile them. Theodoric's execution of Boethius cut off the project after only Aristotle's logical works had been translated and commented on. This translation was in itself a major accomplishment, though, one that made these works available in a way that none of the other Aristotelian works were available. The familiarity and excellence of these logical works no doubt prepared the ground for a favorable reception of the rest of Aristotle when it would become available in the eleventh and twelfth centuries.

Rationalism never died in the Christian West; it enjoyed (though not without sorrow) a few buds in the wintry centuries before springtime brought Thomas Aquinas. There was Jean Roscelin and his controversial work on the trinity; there was Anselm, whose *Monologion* argued the need for an absolute standard, God, to make relative qualities meaningful, and whose *Proslogion* put forth the famous ontological argument for God's existence; there was Abelard, with his refined logic and respect for pagan philosophy. But, as in the Islamic and Jewish worlds, the most sustained efforts to reconcile science and faith came only once Aristotle was rediscovered in all his fullness.

It is a familiar story that when Aristotle's writings reached Paris at the beginning of the thirteenth century, they were at first banned, for it was believed that Aristotelian doctrines, which represented a brilliant and complete—but non-Christian—view of the world, would destroy faith. In 1210, a Church council in Paris banned Aristotle's physics and metaphysics, as well as commentaries on these works. The Fourth Lateran Council (1215) allowed the reading of Aristotle's works on logic and ethics. In 1231, Gregory renewed the bans, as did Urban IV in 1263. None of these bans seems to have worked, however; hence their renewal. In fact, if human nature has not changed since those days, the bans probably only served to increase the reading of Aristotle, a ploy we ought perhaps to use in our own time.

There were, of course, many philosophical controversies in the thirteenth century. Averroës was adored and loathed as the promulgator of a dangerous Aristotelianism. Siger of Brabant, teaching the eternity of the world while affirming his orthodoxy, was condemned in 1277 by the Inquisition. Because Peter of Albano (1250–1316) attributed causality not to God but to the stars, the Inquisition condemned his corpse to be burned at the stake, despite the fact that he himself escaped the fury of the Inquisitors by dying of natural causes. Still, in the mid-thirteenth century, the Church felt that some accommodation with philosophy needed to be attempted. The two greatest attempts were those of Bonaventure and Thomas Aquinas.

BONAVENTURE

John Fidanza, later known as Bonaventure, was a friend and colleague of Aquinas. It is perhaps a testimony to the good nature of both that they could disagree on the most urgent philosophical issues of their day yet remain friends. Dante, in his travels through *Paradiso,* finds Bonaventure enjoying a status equal to that of Aquinas. If we may grant wisdom to Aristotle's theory of friendship— that it is best among equals—we can imagine a strong friendship that both men found intellectually stimulating.

The effort to elevate Platonism in order to lower Aristotle breathes through Bonaventure's work. We suggested earlier, in the section on Maimonides, that being a serious philosopher in the high Middle Ages meant being an Aristotelian. Although, in the middle decades of the thirteenth century Aristotle was certainly ascendant, and although in the early 1250s Bonaventure, in his *Commentary on the Sentences of Peter Lombard,* could forgive many of the ideas attributed to Aristotle as well-meaning errors that might be corrected, nevertheless, by the late 1260s, Bonaventure concludes (in *Hexaemeron*) that the errors had virtually reached the level of heresy among the Averroist Aristotelians of the University of Paris, Bonaventure's own school. This Averroism, he said, leads to three fundamental mistakes: that the world is eternal, that there is one intellect for all human beings, and that a mortal cannot attain immortality.

According to Bonaventure, the fundamental cause of these errors is the failure of Aristotle, the great philosopher himself, to accept the reality of the Platonic Archetypes, the world of Ideas, and their place in the World of Being. Plato, though superior to Aristotle in Bonaventure's mind, was not without error either, for although he did look upwards to the eternal ideas, he did not adequately look downwards to explain the natural world. Aristotle looked *only* downwards and thus did not see how divinity or spirituality could operate in the world. But Augustine, says Bonaventure, got it right—the Augustine who lamented in the *City of God* that Plato had come so close, but, lacking the revelation of Scripture, could not reach the goal. Augustine, says Bonaventure, showed exactly (more or less) how the Platonic Ideas are the models that God used to make the world.

What Bonaventure does in his explanation is, essentially, to Christianize Philo. Philo, drawing his inspiration from Plato's *Timaeus,* said that God created the ideas after his own image then used these ideas as the pattern for creating the world. Bonaventure, borrowing from Augustine, explains how the world of ideas is connected with the Son, the second person of the Trinity. Philosophy, says Bonaventure, can discover the existence of the World of Ideas, as Plato had done; only Revelation, however, can show that the Father begets the Son by an eternal self-knowledge. The idea of eternal self-knowledge is essentially Aristotle's notion of the activity of God; what makes the idea Christian is the claim that the eternal self-reflection is nothing other than the begotten Son of the Father. Bonaventure adds that the Son, as the Wisdom of the Father, expresses in his person the creative faculty of God. The Son as *Logos* is hinted at by the best philosophers, he says, and is fully revealed at the beginning of the Gospel of John. To this rather poetical or mystical view of God, Bonaventure appends the Aristotelian conception of knowledge.[3] According to Aristotle, he says, knowledge, insofar as it is knowable, is eternal. (Bonaventure is, of course, using *knowledge* and *knowable* in the strong sense of a priori knowledge, that is, knowledge through causes—the kind of ahistorical knowledge we have about things mathematical. See our discussion on p. 24.) So if anything is known in this strong sense, it is known "through that Truth which is unshaken, immutable, and without limit," in other words, through God, in his person of the Son.

This World of Ideas, then, is distinct from God the Father, in the same way as the Son is distinct from the Father. If it were not distinct, and if God lacked the Ideas, which Bonaventure calls "exemplar ideas" because they are the exemplary patterns God uses in making the world, Aristotle would be right and God would not be the Creator. What God would know, if there were no World of Ideas, would be himself alone, and the deterministic, eternally unchanging world that had so troubled the Arab critics of Avicenna and al Farabi would be the reality. Then Aristotle would be right and the Prime Mover would move only in the sense of being a final cause, in stirring up our desires, but would not himself act as an efficient cause in the universe. If he did not act, there would be no miracles, prayer would be vain, and there would be no heaven or hell (for there would be no divine justice, which requires actions). Bonaventure says that the World of Ideas, with nature made according to their pattern, implies that nature is God's mirror. The mirror reflects God's perfection in varying degrees, and man, by studying nature, might in this way begin to approach God. The operative word is "begin," for to progress closer to God requires the truth of revelation.

Aquinas, as we shall see, agreed with Maimonides in believing that creation in time is not subject to a demonstrable proof (see p. 210). Bonaventure, however, believes that the arguments for the creation of the world in time *are* philosophically provable. He begins his argument against an eternal universe by saying that one cannot add to an infinity. If the world is actually infinite, there can be no addition to it. But the new days and months and years that come into being are additions. Hence, the world cannot have existed from eternity in the first place.[4] Bonaventure offers as an additional argument for the same conclusion that, although an infinity cannot be traversed, the world will have had to traverse an infinite number of revolutions, on Aristotle's view, in order to arrive at the present moment. This contradiction entails that the world is not eternal.[5] He then argues that since the world would not have been without men in its infinite duration, there would have to be an infinite number of rational souls. Bonaventure writes:

> If an eternal world is posited, some one of these consequences follow necessarily: either there is an infinite number of souls since men would have been infinite in number, or the soul is perishable, or there is a transition from body to body, or the intellect is one in all men, the error attributed to Aristotle by the Commentator [i.e., Averroës].[6]

But, according to Bonaventure, none of these possibilities is acceptable; an infinity of rational souls is impossible; and the world cannot have existed forever. He concludes his discussion with what he feels is his strongest argument, the "evident contradiction" that arises from the view that the world is eternal. He writes:

> The last argument to this effect [i.e., that the world cannot be eternal] is: *It is impossible for that which has being after non-being to have eternal being,* because this implies a contradiction. But the world has being after non-being. Therefore it is impossible that it be eternal. That it has being after non-being is proven as follows: everything whose having of being is totally from another is produced by the latter out of nothing; but the world has its being totally from God; therefore the world is out of nothing. But not out of nothing as a matter (*materialiter*); therefore out of nothing as an origin (*originaliter*). It is evident that everything which is totally produced by something differing in essence has being out of nothing. For what is totally produced is produced in its matter and form. But matter does not have that out of which it would be produced because it is not out of God (*ex Deo*). Clearly, then, it is out of nothing. The minor, viz., that the word is totally produced by God, is evident [emphasis by the translator].[7]

Referring to his last, and, to his mind, best argument, he concludes:

> It has to be said that to maintain that the world is eternal or eternally produced by claiming that all things have been produced out of nothing is entirely against truth and reason, as the last of the above arguments proves; and it is so against reason that I do not believe that any philosopher, however slight his understanding, has maintained this. For such a position involves an evident contradiction.[8]

Everything has its natural place. For Bonaventure, apparently, Aristotle's place was to study the natural world. Aristotle's problem, as Bonaventure sees it, was not only that he rejected the Platonic forms but that he based all of his investigations on nature alone, paying no heed to what is above nature. For Aristotle there was only natural motion, laments Bonaventure, and no divine initiatives. Although a naturalist is right to draw his conclusions from nature, such conclusions can be only partial. A Christian, however, can know the workings of supernature through faith and revelation.

One might wonder how Bonaventure's ideas represent a reconciliation of science and religion. One might call Bonaventure's conclusions a reconciliation perhaps in the sense that a subordinate (in this case, philosophy) comes to recognize his subordinate place and resigns himself to rest content in it. So long as philosophy recognizes that its job is only to start one on the road to God—to serve the function of Cicero's dialogue *Hortensius* in Augustine's life—then science and religion might be considered to be reconciled.[9] Science should know its place, and earthbound philosophy should yield pride of place to heaven-bound theology, for any study that is devoid of revelation will fall far short of Truth.

Bonaventure's system was, we may conjecture, too imprecise, too poetical, too (for all its splendor) Platonic to win adherents. The discovery of Aristotle promised adamantine rigor, steely discipline, iron logic. Familiarity with these tools of logic allowed medievals to envision a natural theology that could withstand the strongest of assaults. It was not about to be surrendered for a sweet but feeble rigor, for a mystic irrationality incompatible with the concept of man the rational animal, whose reason, when triumphant over superstition, would show that he is indeed the image of God. If Aristotle was going to be beaten down by scholastics, it would have to be by logicians like Scotus and Ockham, who would match Aristotle's own logical tools with equally powerful philosophical resources.

THOMAS AQUINAS

Thomas Aquinas (1224–1273) spent his short adult life thinking and writing about the great issue of his day, whether faith and reason contradict each other. His enormous efforts involve some significant differences with respect to others working in the same field. For this book we shall focus on those differences and limit our discussion to the following questions: (1) Aquinas's relation to Aristotle; (2) Aquinas's first two proofs of the existence of God and the relation of those proofs to the question of creation; (3) how Aquinas deals with the immutability of God and the mutability of creation; (4) the general significance of Aquinas's conclusions on the immutability of God and creation in comparison to those of Maimonides; (5) the next three proofs for the existence of God; and, finally, (6) the degree to which science can explain God. Thus limited, the discussion here in no way pretends to do justice to the extraordinary range of Aquinas's thought on other subjects.

Aquinas's Relation to Aristotle

Bonaventure objected to several of the concepts associated with the Aristotelians. First was what he believed was Aristotle's concept of a self-sufficient nature, that is, the idea that the things of this world can be explained in terms of natural causes. He much preferred the Platonic scheme of participation in the world of ideas, because this scheme was more spiritual and emphasized the role of immaterial entities. A consequence of this exaltation of the spiritual was a denigration of the material, with man himself viewed as a soul corrupted and pulled downwards by his body. In part, perhaps, Bonaventure's views represented a lingering reaction to the Albigensians of the twelfth century, who had resuscitated the Manichaean view of eternal forces of good and evil, with the good responsible for all things spiritual, the evil responsible for things bodily.[10]

Aquinas, however, argues that to denigrate the natural, material world is to denigrate the work of the Creator. To claim that matter is in itself evil would be to claim that God had created evil. If God made nature, nature must be good, and all of God's created world should be praised. The attempt by the Platonists to protect essences and intellect from pollution by matter results, thought Aquinas, from a failure to see the whole picture—how all reality, corporeal and incorporeal, is united in a harmonious unity. By making only the ideas true being, Plato implied that man could know them only by becoming a pure mind—a mind wholly liberated from the imperfect, sensible matter. The problem with Plato's system, for Aquinas, is that it ignored the reality that the world and man are at least in part physical; a metaphysics that excludes such a large part of reality cannot be right. For Aquinas man is not a soul imprisoned in a body but is one composite thing, an embodied soul. Man's work as an embodied soul is to know in his capacity of composite of body and soul.[11] Moreover, if the matter composing bodies is hopelessly evil, where would be the grace in resurrection? For resurrection, held by religion to be man's final destiny, is where the whole man—as a composite of soul and body—finds his final complete happiness. If matter is evil, why should a bodily resurrection involve a recomposition with matter? The natural world, says Aquinas, has a dignity that comes from being God's handiwork and that legitimizes Aristotle's emphasis on sensible things. The sensible world, to which man belongs, is an important part of divine creation, one from which man can ascend to spiritual truths using his particularly human gift of reason.

Moreover, one and the same God is responsible for both Scripture and the natural world. If they were not harmonious—if they were at all contradictory or if Scripture were false—then God would be responsible, in contradiction to his nature. Revelation, in the form of Scripture, completes what reason, as an investigation of the natural world, begins.

The arguments about God, says Aquinas, thus begin in the world of natural reason. Because God cannot be known directly through causes, at least not by human beings, and because humans exist in the natural world, we must come to know about God from his effects. Aquinas's arguments for the existence of God therefore all begin with what Aquinas takes to be perceived facts of the world. While he discusses the proofs of the existence of God in various places in his work,[12] his most famous discussion is in question 2, article 3 of the first part of his *Summa Theologica,* a passage known as "The Five Ways."

Aquinas's First Two Proofs of the Existence of God

Aquinas's first two proofs of the existence of God, which he himself thought to be the clearest, most easily show the relation between such proofs and Aquinas's proposed solution to the philosophical problem of creation, which we take up in the next section. The first proof restates Aristotle's argument for a Prime Mover and makes use of Aristotle's notions of potentiality and actuality. Beginning with what Aquinas takes to be the uncontroversial observation that things in the world are in motion, he proceeds to track down the ultimate cause of motion. Because being put in motion involves a transition from potentiality (i.e., potential motion) to actuality (i.e., actual motion), because only something actually in motion can cause something potentially in motion to become actually in motion, and because a given thing cannot be both potentially and actually in motion, it follows that everything that is in motion was put in that state by *something else,* i.e., by something that was already in motion. There cannot be an infinite regress of such movers, however, because that would mean that there is no first mover and hence no motion at all — contrary to the original observation of motion in the world. To use a Thomistic example, if a stone is moved by a staff that is moved by a hand, the stone will not move if the hand does not move: the issue is not which moves first, but whether the whole series has a first mover (the hand, in this example). To avoid an infinite regress in the case of the world as a whole, every instance of motion in the world must be traceable to a mover that is itself unmoved. This, says Aquinas, everyone calls God.

Whereas the first argument concerns motion, the second, very similar argument concerns efficient causation in general. Aquinas begins with the uncontroversial observation that the world contains causes and effects. As above, he argues that an effect cannot be *its own* cause, for that would make it prior to itself, which is impossible. Yet the chain of causes cannot be infinite, for if there were no first, uncaused cause, there would be no intermediate, and hence no ultimate, effects, which is contrary to the original observation. This first, uncaused efficient cause is what Aquinas thinks everyone takes to be God.

As in the argument from motion, the temporal priority of causes to their effects is not relevant here, even though most of the time when we think of causes, we think of them as prior in time to their effects. When we consider a baseball breaking a window, for example, we have a clear temporal succession of efficient causes: bat, ball, breakage. But Aquinas's argument in no way depends on causes preceding their effects in time. The argument applies equally well to causes that are simultaneous with their effects, such as the falling temperature that causes the mercury in the thermometer to drop or the rising sun that causes the flagpole's shadow to shorten.[13] The mercury would not drop and the shadow would not shorten if their causes ceased to operate. Perhaps another example will clarify the idea. Let us imagine a skyscraper with a radio antenna on its roof. The radio antenna is supported by the roof, which is thus the efficient cause of the antenna's standing several hundred feet off the ground. The roof itself is being held up by the superstructure of the building upon which it rests. The superstructure of the building is being held up by the substructure, which in turn is held up by the earth beneath. But the earth beneath is not being held up by anything. It is, so to speak, an unheld holder. Now the roof is the efficient cause of the location of the antenna, the building's superstructure of the roof, the substructure of the superstructure, and the ground of the substructure. All these are different levels of efficient cause and all take place simultaneously as far as the antenna is concerned. Yet every efficient cause is dependent on another until we arrive at the unheld holder. Aquinas would of course say that the ground too needs an efficient cause, and this is God, who sustains creation through a continuously operating efficient causality.

Aquinas's conception of creation may be understood in the light of this sustaining causality. Creation does not have to involve a coming into being from what was not. It does not have to involve a succession of new things. To look at creation as a temporal succession is to be bound by a kind of anthropomorphism, for succession is the way of human creating. Creation by God, says Aquinas, should be thought of as sustained and enduring dependence on the Creator. This dependence must be understood as the moving and efficient causes acting in the here and now and at every moment. The priority of God to creation is the *ontological* priority of the earth to the building that depends on it to remain upright; it is not a *temporal* priority. Creation so understood means that God continues as creator in the world at every moment. If he should somehow cease to create in his capacity as first mover and first efficient cause, then nothing would be, for everything depends existentially on God at every moment. This, of course, is very different from human creation. If someone writes a poem, he finishes the poem at a certain point in time and then may go do something different without the poem's ceasing to exist. The poem does not depend on the poet for its continued existence. But the poem, like everything else in the world, *does* depend on God for its continued existence.

The Immutability of God and the Mutability of Creation

The question of whether divine creation, understood in the above sense, occurred in time becomes a side issue to the question of how God creates the world. Augustine said that it is an error to think of time as existing prior to creation, because time came into being along with creation. For Augustine, time is a measure of mutability, of change, which did not exist before the world came into being. Of course, Augustine also believed that eternity is the continuous possession of everything in an instant with no successive moments. Aquinas argues that this type of eternity is for God alone. When we talk of the world's eternity, we mean a continual duration, with either no beginning, or no end, or neither beginning nor end. Whether or not the world is eternal in one of these senses does not affect the issue of whether God is the creator of the changing universe. And it is to establish the proposition that God exists and that he is creator of the universe that Aquinas says is the important matter, an important matter than *can* be established by reason, by the argument just presented.

The question now is whether Aquinas is successful in finessing the question of creation in time. Is the idea of a continuously sustaining efficient and moving cause merely a variant of Neoplatonic views and subject to the same difficulties? Let us assume, as Aquinas does, that God is simple, and that the simplicity of God means that he is a unity and immutable, that he is his properties, and so on. Then, as we have seen, God's activity must somehow be identical with himself, the divine nature subject to no alteration (lest it be more divine in one form than another). It will be obvious that an unchanging God cannot change. If, then, God cannot be other than what he is, it follows that God is restricted by his nature to be God, determined by his divinity to be just what he is without ever changing. And if God's continuous creation of the world is identical to God's nature, then it would seem that the world proceeds by necessity from the necessary and immutable nature of God. Where, then, comes God's freedom to act? Where can God exercise free will to create? How is God not a wholly determined machine?

Aquinas's Difference with Maimonides
on the Immutability of God and Creation

Aquinas's faith asserts both the simplicity of God, with all its Parmenidean and Neoplatonic implications, and the free will of God, without which there can be no religion. If the world exists eternally, Aquinas says it would have to have been created freely from eternity; if it was created in time, it would have to have been created without any change in God, so it would have to be the effect of an eternal and unchanging will. Now the claims that creation is a willed act, that is, a chosen act, and that the one who willed or chose has never undergone an alteration cannot be made compatible even by Aquinas, by any effort of reasoning or casuistry. Aquinas realizes this and concludes that the set of propositions is a *mystery,* not a contradiction. Creation, as it applies to God, is a *supernatural* activity, but human reason is *natural* reason, and in the end cannot comprehend God's activity. Aquinas does not believe it his job to answer all the questions; his job, like that of Maimonides, is to show how far reason may go and the point at which the questions do not yield to reason. Regarding the issue of whether the world always existed or was created in time, for example, Aquinas writes:

> That the world did not always exist we hold by faith alone: it cannot be proved demonstratively; which is what was said above of the mystery of the Trinity [*Summa Theologica* q.32.a.1]. The reason for this is that the newness of the world cannot be demonstrated from the world itself. For the principle of demonstration is the essence of a thing. Now everything, considered in its species, abstracts from *here and now;* which is why it is said that *universals are everywhere and always.* Hence it cannot be demonstrated that man, or the heavens, or a stone did not always exist. Likewise neither can the newness of the world be demonstrated from efficient cause, which acts by will. For the will of God cannot be investigated by reason, except as regards those things which God must will of necessity; and what He wills about his creatures is not among these, as was said above [*Summa Theologica* q.19.a.3]. But the divine will can be manifested by revelation, on which faith rests. Hence that the world began to exist is an object of faith, but not of demonstration or science. And it is useful to consider this, lest anyone, presuming to demonstrate what is of faith, should bring forth arguments that are not cogent; for this would give unbelievers the occasion to ridicule, thinking that on such grounds we believe the things that are of faith.[14]

Now when a *philosopher* is confronted with a contradiction, as we observed earlier, he *knows* absolutely that he has made a mistake and that the model he is presenting of the nature of things is false. He does not opine the theory's falsity, or "feel" that it is false, or "worry" that it may be false. He knows beyond a shadow of a doubt that it is false. Aquinas, however, as has been frequently pointed out,[15] does not call himself or the Christians to whom he refers "philosophers," perhaps because "philosopher" is reserved for those who seek truth exclusively by reason. For Aquinas, when a matter appears contradictory and yet must be held, it need not be abandoned or held to be a kind of "double truth," where there is one truth for religion and another quite incompatible truth for science. Aquinas can declare the matter a "mystery" and affirm his faith in the truth of both competing claims. Aquinas believes that in philosophy one reasons from prior knowledge, the attainment of which requires no *willed* assent. For example, one must assent to the fact that a whole is greater than a part or that one of a pair of contradictory statements must be false. In matters of faith, however, the intellect operates differently. The inclination to believe comes from God as a gift, which one either has or does not have. Thus, while the reduction of a question to a mystery will perhaps strike the nonbeliever as laughable, the believer will submit in humble faith. What we can assert, however, is that Aquinas's pointing out where faith and reason conflict is quite distinct from his having *reconciled* them. To end with an assertion of mystery is no more than a concession to human ignorance or intellectual limitation. Where Maimonides ended in an admission of profound perplexity, Aquinas ends in a declaration of faith in the truth of the unresolved "mystery."

Perhaps the difference between Aquinas and Maimonides is a reflection of a difference between Christians and Jews. In Christianity, faith is one of the cardinal virtues. Indeed, faith in Jesus is necessary for salvation. In Judaism, faith does not play so significant a role. Indeed, the rabbis teach that one need not even believe in God to be a Jew, so long as one does not deny God and so long as one practices the commandments.[16] So as a Jew Maimonides might feel that he could end in perplexity without a definitive assertion of how things are. For Aquinas, an unequivocal assertion of faith is paramount.

Aquinas's Final Three Proofs for the Existence of God

Let us look briefly at Aquinas's other three arguments for God's existence, after which we shall consider the knowledge of God that Aquinas thinks is actually compatible with science.

His third argument for the existence of God begins with the observation that in nature we find contingent things, i.e., things whose nonexistence is possible. A dog, for example, exists but does not have to exist. For every such contingent being, Aquinas believes, there is a time at which it does not exist. If *everything* were contingent, he concludes, then there would have been a time at which nothing existed. Because nothing can come from nothing, it would have been impossible for anything to have begun to exist at such a time. After all, there would have been nothing around to cause anything to come into being. Hence, nothing would exist *now*, which is absurd. We must therefore deny the assumption that *everything* is contingent and conclude that there exists a self-caused necessary being, which everyone calls God.

One of the more interesting aspects of this proof is Aquinas's move from the statement "For every contingent being, there is a time at which that being does not exist" to the statement "There is a time at which every contingent being does not exist." Any modern logician will recognize here the fallacy of composition. Aquinas might as well argue that the statement "For every professor at the college, there is a student at that college whom he has not taught" implies the statement "There is a student at the college whom no professor at the college has taught."

The fourth argument develops from the obvious fact of nature that there is a gradation in things: some things are better, truer, nobler, and so on, than others. Now none of these degrees would be recognizable if it were not for a standard of perfect goodness, perfect truth, or perfect nobility. We call something hotter than something else, for example, because it more closely resembles what is hottest. At this point comes the heart of the argument. Aquinas, referring to Aristotle's *Metaphysics,* says that the highest condition of something is that which has the most being and that the maximum in any genus is the cause of all that is in the genus. (This equality of being and perfection is, of course, the core of the Augustinian solution to the problem of evil: evil is simply the falling short, the privation, of a thing from its perfect state.) Aquinas says that the perfection that is the cause of every other goodness is God. This fourth argument, while interesting, is perhaps more Platonic than true, and seems to suggest that the standard of perfection is somehow the cause of goodness in other things because the other things "participate" in the idea of the standard.[17] But Aquinas does not actually explain the kind of causality he has in mind here; if it is one of the four Aristotelian causes, it is not clear which. One might wonder, moreover, about not-so-noble standards. Does there exist some divine or Platonic ideal of, say, sewage, in the perfect stench of which earthly sewage merely participates? Is there a maximally ugly being that stands as the cause and standard of human ugliness?

Aquinas's fifth way is the familiar argument from design, which we shall discuss at length in its modern form in chapter 13 (see pp. 251ff.). Aquinas begins with the observation, which most modern scientists would adamantly deny, that even inanimate objects in the natural world act for an end, because they act always or almost always with a regularity that will achieve the best result. In Aquinas's view, they so act not by chance but by design. But because they themselves are without intelligence, Aquinas concludes, they must all be directed towards their ends by a single intelligent being, which we call God.

Whether regular action, such as stones generally falling downward, requires a divine designer, we shall leave to the reader to decide. Similarly, we leave it as an exercise to show that the being who directs rocks to their "best result," i.e., falling downward, is the same being who directs every other inanimate object to its best result—nay, the same being that the third proof concludes is a self-caused necessary being and the fourth proof shows is the standard of all goodness, etc. We might conclude by noting that only when Aquinas reaches the idea of a designer, in his fifth proof, has he reached a deity in the common anthropomorphic sense, a deity to whom one might be comfortable praying. Working backwards through the other four arguments, we find increasingly more removed from common notions the concepts of God as standard of perfection, as necessary being, as first efficient cause, and as first mover.

The Degree to Which Science Can Explain God

Aquinas addresses the next issue—the nature of God—in the prologue to the question immediately following his proofs of God's existence:

> When the existence of a thing has been ascertained, there remains the further question of the manner of its existence, in order that we may know its essence. Now because we cannot know what God is, but rather what He is not, we have no means for considering how God is, but rather how He is not.[18]

This is, of course, a very lucid statement of the *via negativa,* the doctrine that God can be explained only by negatives, since any positive claim about God would limit the unlimitable. Aquinas points out that the negative path is well and good when it is used to deny God qualities that ought to be denied to him, such as mutability, corporeality, and temporality.[19] But when we wish to affirm a quality that God has, such as goodness or wisdom or justice, he says we must predicate the terms of God by analogy. Because humans can know God's qualities to only a very limited extent, when we predicate any quality of God we need to recognize that the quality applies to God only in some infinite and supernatural way that we cannot fully understand.[20] We humans can have only a dim sense of perfection, for example; when we call God "perfect," we are using the strongest term we have, but even the strongest term is of necessity far removed from the truth.

For Aquinas, then, the *summa,* or sum of human knowledge about God, is not very much. The subtlest truths about the deepest subjects can be affirmed only by faith. Reason itself shows the limits of reason, at which point one must rely on faith, if one is fortunate enough to have it as a gift from God.

Perhaps it is not difficult to see why Aquinas's favor should have waxed and waned in the history of the Church. In periods of uncertainty and crisis, when men's souls were crying out for assurances of certitude, the mystic extravagance of a Neoplatonism promising the ability to traverse the sphere of the moon to a celestial union with God would have been very appealing. Philosophies like those of Aquinas and Maimonides, which point out the limits of faith and reason, would have been deficient to this need. In periods of tranquility and security, however, when there were few perceived threats, a degree of philosophical uncertainty would have been tolerated. In such calm times—too few, alas, in the tumultuous history of the world—one could abide the candid acknowledgment that some things are simply not accessible to reason. In such times, one could be content with the lower degree of certitude found in faith. But if a doctrine that is affirmed by *faith* is proven to be a falsehood, the proof of its falsehood would, as Aquinas says in the passage quoted earlier, render the religion affirming the doctrine as laughable.

CONCLUSION

While he lived, Bonaventure was a loyal follower of the papacy. When the pope allowed the Franciscans to depart from Francis's original teachings concerning poverty and thereafter to own property, Bonaventure accepted these changes. After his death in 1274, however, a group of Franciscans known as "the Spirituals" began aggressively to reiterate the importance of their order's poverty and, further, to insist on the apostolic poverty of the whole Church, thereby questioning the power and property of the papacy itself. It is not surprising, perhaps, that a group that espoused Platonism, with its apparent aversion to materiality, would oppose the materiality of possessions.

Those who are driven by the purity of their principles to hate material wealth will naturally seek lives like Thoreau's at Walden Pond, aiming at the simple existence of a hermitage. Those whose motives are less spiritual will seek a life of material comfort and worldly power. Hence it is again not surprising that the party opposed to the Spirituals, the more worldly "Conventuals," sought and obtained control over the Franciscan Order. Significant work to support the position of the Spirituals was being done at Oxford, by the Franciscans Duns Scotus (1266–1308) and William of Ockham (1285?–1350). Scotus and Ockham, both keen logicians, attempted to show that between the finitude of the human mind and the infinity of God there can be no proportion. Hence human beings cannot understand the actual nature of God in any complete way. Unlike Thomas Aquinas, Scotus did not think that sense experience could lead by the rungs of some heavenly ladder to knowledge of God—the gulf between the limited human mind and the infinite being of God is too great to be bridged by human thought. The only source of knowledge about God is revelation.

Ockham went even further, declaring that logic could not pierce the veil to metaphysical truth. Like modern mathematicians who say that their conclusions are valid only within their systems of mathematics—and bear no actual relationship to reality—so Ockham said that logic deals only with its own terms. The universals towards which logic works are intellectual creations, far removed from ultimate reality, having only a noetic existence, an existence as thought, while they are in our minds. A Catholic al Ghazali, Ockham, like Scotus, was using the principal tool of philosophy—logic—to destroy logic's ability to discover ultimate truths about religion. Instead, he exalted revelation, intuition, and even mysticism, thereby liberating God from the limiting prison of human reason, the deterministic, mechanistic universe of Thomistic Aristotelianism. Here in Ockham and Scotus were views that would bring the Church to the simple faith of the early Franciscans, so different from the crude secular materialism of the day.

Perhaps then it was inevitable that when Ockham attacked the temporal power of the papacy and asserted the need for the entire church to embrace poverty, he aroused the ire of Pope John XXII. To escape that ire, Ockham sought refuge with King Louis of Bavaria. In 1323 the pope declared the doctrine of apostolic poverty a heresy. In Bavaria, Ockham responded that both the pope and general

Church councils could err. The claim had serious implications: if the Church could err, if it had no special hold on truth, why should the pope rule the secular world? For that matter, if pope and council were fallible, why should the Church, rather than the individual conscience of every Christian, be the ultimate authority in religious matters?

If the Averroists were right that science and revelation are two different roads to knowledge of God, perhaps human reason can ascend to such knowledge without the need for the Church. The conclusion, of course, would be that the intellectual elite would have less need for the Church. If the Oxford Franciscans were right, and simple faithful can reach God through a mystic revelation, or through revelation directly, and if the individual's own conscience has as great a claim to know the divine will as the worldly and wealthy Church, the power of the Church would be seriously undermined. The assault on the Church began in the schools of philosophy, with the diverse camps taking inspiration from Plato (the "Spiritual" party of Franciscans and, later, through Augustine, Martin Luther, and the Protestants) or from Aristotle (the Dominicans and, later, when Thomism was readmitted and made the core of Catholic teaching, the entire Catholic Church). That assault continues to affect the history of Christianity to the present day.

DISCUSSION QUESTIONS

1. Christianity arose in a Greek milieu, and, of course, the books of the New Testament were originally written in Greek. The two most significant possibilities open to Christianity in meeting Greek culture were rejection and adoption. In an arduous process involving much examination and debate, adoption was chosen. Are there any features of the Christian faith, as distinct from Islam or Judaism, that make a marriage of philosophy and science especially difficult? Do the faith claims of the Incarnation, transubstantiation, the Trinity, and redemption put a stress on attempts to reconcile science and religion that does not appear in the other religions of the book?

2. By adopting the Platonic World of Ideas as God the Father's eternal self-knowledge, and the Son as God's creative faculty, has Bonaventure successfully resolved the difficulty of having God move and act as an efficient cause without spoiling his perfection? Has Bonaventure successfully overcome the difficulties of Parmenidean oneness? Has he resolved Platonic dualism simply by *fiat,* that is, by positing as premises the Father's World of Ideas and the Son's World of Action? How philosophically plausible is his solution? Is faith in the Trinity any different from philosophy's unprovable first principles? If so, how?

3. Bonaventure's belief in the demonstrability of the creation of the world in time is based on his various notions of infinity—that an infinity cannot be added to, that an infinity cannot be traversed, that if the world were infinite,

there would be an infinite number of rational souls. Why do reconcilers of religion and science so often base their claims on an understanding of infinity? If the concept of infinity is a purely mathematical concept, why are there so many different ideas about it? Do the various thinkers who discuss infinity use the term in the same way?

4. Aquinas argues that since God created the world, the world is good, and that by applying the gift of reason to the world humans can ascend to spiritual truths. Yet there seems to be something about Christianity that has prompted it since its early centuries to flirt with a Manichaean dualism that denigrates the physical while exalting the spiritual. What are these features of Christianity?

5. Aquinas's conception of God's ontological priority to creation avoids the problem in the Neoplatonic theory of emanation that involves corruption as the emanation moves from the source. What other advantages does Aquinas's theory have? What are some of the problems that it does not solve?

6. Whereas some of Maimonides' reflections ended in perplexity, some of Aquinas's end in the assertion of faith in "mysteries." What is the practical difference between perplexity and mystery? How would the research program of two individuals differ, where one affirmed the seemingly contradictory propositions of a mystery, and the other acknowledged his perplexity?

7. Two of Aquinas's proofs for the existence of God are based on motion and efficient cause. Is Aquinas himself caught in the net of Greek philosophy, of having to think about God à la Aristotle, Plato, and Parmenides? Does Greek philosophy interpret God most persuasively by metaphysics? Has philosophy so shaped the discussion that the term *supernatural* has come to mean *metaphysical* rather than *magical* or something else?

8. Are there some periods when there seems to be a greater societal desire for certainty? The Middle Ages were a time of political fragmentation, sudden fatal disease on a massive scale (the Black Plague), rigid hierarchy, and pervasive religious influence in everyday life. What sorts of conditions might have affected the reception of philosophies that acknowledged their limitations as distinct from those that proclaimed complete knowledge? Are the same sorts of conditions applicable today?

9. It had been the plan of Boethius to reconcile the philosophies of Aristotle and Plato. Boethius's death forestalled the project, if such a reconciliation were even possible. As the centuries have passed there have been periods when Plato has been ascendant, and other periods when Aristotle has. In what ways do contemporary debates among Catholics and Protestants continue to reflect differences in the philosophies of Plato and Aristotle?

NOTES

1. Tertullian, *Apology,* 46. Though one can find abuse hurled on philosophers throughout the work of Tertullian, he is particularly dramatic in *de Praescriptione,* 7.

2. Gibbon, *Decline and Fall,* vol. 2, chapter 39.

3. Bonaventure, *In Hexaemeron,* 1.13, in *Opera Omnia* (Quaracchi: Ex Typographia Collegii S. Bonaventurae, 1882–1902).

4. Bonaventure, *In II Sent.,* 1.1.1.2.1., in *St. Thomas Aquinas, Siger of Brabant, St. Bonaventure: On the Eternity of the World,* by C. Vollert, L. H. Kendzierski, and P. M. Byrne (Milwaukee: Marquette University Press, 1964). Subsequent references are to this edition.

5. Bonaventure, *In II Sent.,* 1.1.1.2.3.

6. Bonaventure, *In II Sent.,* 1.1.1.2.5.

7. Bonaventure, *In II Sent.,* 1.1.1.2.6.

8. Bonaventure, *In II Sent.,* 1.1.1.2.6, *conclusio.*

9. *Science* should be understood in the premodern sense discussed on pp. 49ff.

10. When, in 1215, the Fourth Lateran Council declared that God alone is an eternal, the declaration had not settled the question about the eternity of matter—a question that for Christian thinkers, because of the connection they made between perfection and immutability, was related to the value to be placed on matter.

11. See A. Pegis, *Introduction to St. Thomas Aquinas* (New York: Modern Library, 1948), xx–xxiv.

12. E.g., *Summa contra Gentiles* 1.9. For a survey of Aquinas's arguments, see F. van Steenberghen, *Le problème de l'existence de Dieu dans les écrits de S. Thomas d'Aquin* (Louvain-La-Neuve: Editions de l'Institut supérieur de philosophie, 1980). See also J. F. Wippel, "Metaphysics," in *The Cambridge Companion to Aquinas,* ed. N. Kretzmann and E. Stump (Cambridge: Cambridge University Press, 1993), 102–5, 113–16.

13. Here and in similar cases we are ignoring, of course, the denial by modern physics that simultaneity exists over space.

14. Aquinas, *Summa Theologica,* 1.46.2.

15. E.g., B. Davis, *The Thought of Thomas Aquinas* (Oxford: Clarendon, 1992), 10–14. But on Aquinas as a philosopher, see Kretzmann and Stump, *Cambridge Companion,* 10.

16. Consider the statement of Prager and Telushkin (*Nine Questions,* 18):

The Talmud attributes to God a declaration which is probably unique among religious writings: "Better that they [the Jews] abandon Me, but follow My laws" (for, the Talmud adds, by practicing Judaism's laws, the Jews will return to God, Jerusalem Talmud Haggigah 1.7). According to Judaism, one can be a good Jew while doubting God's existence, so long as one acts in accordance with Jewish law.

17. Can it be that a blush of Platonism leads Aquinas into error? As Pegis writes (*Aquinas,* xv), "There are not many philosophical aberrations that were either inherited or developed by the thirteenth century that St. Thomas does not trace to the Platonic metaphysics, psychology and epistemology."

18. Aquinas, *Summa Theologica,* 1.3, introduction.

19. Aquinas, *Summa Theologica,* 1.13.2.

20. According to C. H. Lohr, "The Medieval Interpretation of Aristotle," in *The Cambridge Companion to Aquinas,* ed. N. Kretzmann and E. Stump (Cambridge: Cambridge University Press, 1993), believing in "the existence of truths revealed in the Bible which transcend human understanding" is what characterizes the theologian.

Reconciling Science and Religion from the Renaissance through the Enlightenment

Faith is a fine invention
For Gentlemen who see;
But microscopes are prudent
In an emergency!

—Emily Dickinson

As we have seen, the basic problems concerning accommodating a working, active deity with the natural world were already formulated in their dizzying complexity by ancient and medieval thinkers, with various solutions being proposed. As the conception of science shifted in the Renaissance from an emphasis on logic and metaphysics to investigation of the physical world, the focus of the discussion altered. Nevertheless, we shall see in some early modern philosophers, such as Leibniz and Spinoza, an ingenuity that resembles the ingenuity and resourceful inventiveness of the ancient pre-Socratics, as one thinker responds directly to the theories of another, pointing out the defects in his predecessor's theory while oblivious to the defects in his own. When we approach modern times with its super-sophisticated science, we shall observe the attempts to reconcile a traditional deity with this science too.

THE SCIENTIFIC REVOLUTION

Francis Bacon

The title page of Francis Bacon's *The Advancement of Learning* (1605) depicts a ship in full sail as it makes its way through the Pillars of Hercules to the great unknown ocean beyond. The symbol announces that, like the explorers who braved uncharted seas to discover worlds new to them, so science would take risks for knowledge. If the heroes of exploration could go where even mighty Hercules dared not go, the heroes of reason would be no less intrepid. To the geographical explorers of the fifteenth century, Hercules represented the limit of an adventurer's possibilities. To adventurous scientists, the limit to be breached was Aristotle's work, which appeared to be inscribed on rock more adamantine than Gibraltar.

The sixteenth century saw the Protestant Reformation as well as the exploitative colonization of the New World. But it was not an age of scientific discovery. There was no attempt to reconcile science and religion, because essentially there was no science. The work of Galileo and Napier and Kepler, of Harvey and Newton awaited the seventeenth century. Quite the contrary, the sixteenth was a century of witchcraft and fearsome supernatural torments. In the forty years before 1600, eight thousand women were burned in Europe as witches, and the 1597 work of James VI of Scotland, *Demonologie,* describes the powers and practices of witches. (James VI later became James I of England, the same of the "King James" translation of the Bible.) Men of science were as susceptible to superstition as anyone else: Napier, the inventor of the system of logarithms, believed the world would end between 1688 and 1700; Kepler fretted about witches; Newton, about the impending Apocalypse. Astrology was taught in the universities and was not to be eliminated from the curriculum until nearly the nineteenth century, even at some famous universities. (The University of Salamanca offered it until 1770.) In 1623, Pope Gregory XV demanded the death penalty for those convicted of killing a person by sorcery. A few who bravely—or rashly—denounced the mania of such superstitions, were themselves subject to imprisonment.[1]

At the beginning of the seventeenth century, then, the world was ready to be shaken up. A century of geographical discoveries had alerted Europeans to the possibility that the old limits were man-made and that vast territories were open to those with the will to search. The Protestant Reformation had shown that the world might go on even if obedience to the Catholic Church was no longer a virtue. Francis Bacon (1561–1626), perhaps the most original British thinker since Ockham in the mid-fourteenth century and a paradigm Renaissance man in the diversity of his interests, planned to write the syllabus for a new age of scientific inquiry. He invited James I to serve as patron for the enterprise. Bacon planned to classify the sciences, correct Aristotelian logic and scientific method, describe the phenomena of the universe, provide models of scientific inquiry, lay out his own discoveries, and, in short, write a complete philosophy based on natural science.

The title of Bacon's magnum opus announces his rejection of Aristotle. As a replacement for Aristotle's *Organum* of logical works, Bacon authored a *Novum Organum* for the new, mechanistic, and technologically fruitful science of the seventeenth century. As we saw previously (p. 50), Aristotle's "strong" knowledge requires necessary and universal causes and therefore applies in the strict sense only to mathematics and logic. Although "lower" orders of knowledge—of contingent things, those true "for the most part"—lack the perfection of mathematical and logical knowledge, they are legitimate forms of knowledge nonetheless. At the beginning of the *Metaphysics,* Aristotle praises sight as the sense through which we most learn. Indeed, Aristotle himself was a keen observer, as his works on embryology and animals attest. Though Aristotle held up syllogistic logic and mathematical deduction as the ideal, he nevertheless strongly advocated observation. Bacon's caricature of Aristotle as a medieval scholastic obsessed with logical quibbles thus misleadingly sharpens the contrast between the two thinkers.

Bacon envisioned science as free of illusions, inductive, practical, and separate from religion. He classified the numerous illusions and fallacies, preconceptions and assumptions—including those of the venerable ancient philosophers—from which he wished to free all thought into four categories of Idols. Idols of the Tribe comprise common human prejudices, such as wishful thinking. Idols of the Cave refer to individuals and derive from the peculiarities of their education and temperament. Idols of the Marketplace stem from the limitations and ambiguities of language. Finally, philosophical systems, such as Aristotelianism, lead to the prejudices of Idols of the Theater. Even though these sorts of prejudices are deeply ingrained in our thinking, true science can proceed only after they have been recognized and eliminated.

The hallmark of Baconian science is induction. Far from attempting to derive empirical information from first principles, a scientist should systematically collect all observations pertaining to a given phenomenon and, by a process of rejecting hypotheses in conflict with those observations, eventually come to understand the underlying essences and laws relevant to the phenomenon. The systematic nature of the observations was supposed to be proof against superstitious thinking and the aforementioned four Idols. Furthermore, Bacon believed his inductive method was essential to the technological applications that he saw lacking in Aristotelian science and that he trusted would improve human life. There is a fine line, it seems, between Bacon's Idol of the Tribe and his own faith in the improvement of the human condition.

Although Bacon's rejection of superstition and illusion might seem to tell against religion as well, Bacon circumvented any conflict between science and religion by sharply distinguishing the two spheres. In this strategy he followed his British predecessor Ockham, shared the view of his contemporary, Galileo, and prefigured the modern view of S. J. Gould and many others. Bacon's rationale for the methodological distinction can hardly be faulted: science appeals to empirical evidence and mechanistic explanations; religion, to revelation and the final causes inherent in God's designs. It thus comes as no surprise that Bacon was a devoted Churchman and believed that faith should rule where science and philosophy find no evidence.[2] He also advocated the argument from design, and, like Boethius, could not believe that "this universal frame is without a mind."[3]

Galileo

Also taking up arms against Aristotle, Galileo (1564–1642) boasted that he had disproved the Aristotelian claim that the speed of a falling body is proportional to its mass.[4] One need not even observe two falling bodies with different masses to test this claim, according to Galileo, for a thought experiment is sufficient. If two identical bodies fall at the same rate even when they are close enough together that they touch, then surely they will fall at the same rate when they are actually connected and in effect make up a single body with twice the mass. Although Galileo conceived of decisive refutations of other aspects of Aristotelian mechanics as well, the historical Aristotle, who "loved Plato but loved truth more," would readily have adopted Galileo's rigorously demonstrated conclusions.

The Catholic Church, on the other hand, which had embraced a Thomistic unification of Aristotelian principles and religious doctrines, would be far more hostile to doctrinal challenges. The Church realized full well the implications of the Copernican view that the earth, like the other planets, orbits the sun: not only did the view challenge all of Aristotelian physics, including the fundamental separation of earthly and celestial spheres, but more importantly it raised the issue of the spiritual centrality of man in the cosmos, questioned certain interpretations of the Scriptures, and challenged the teaching authority of the Church itself. That Galileo's telescopic observations provided powerful empirical support for Copernicanism, and that they were observations that any layman could make for himself, if he bothered to observe, made the issue even more urgent for a Church still reeling from the Protestant Reformation. Because the Church knew how dangerously upstart challenges could develop, perhaps it felt it safest to nip such innovations in the bud.

The Galileo affair is among the most notorious and complex in the history of the relations of science and religion, and its details are covered at length elsewhere. Perhaps it will suffice for our purposes to examine the key points with which Galileo defended his position on science and religion as he lays them out in his "Letter to the Grand Duchess Christina." He presents two seemingly incompatible views in the letter. The first is a claim of independence, embodied in his quotation of a witty Italian theologian, that religion deals with "how to go to heaven, not with how the heavens go."[5] This sentiment is of course a restatement of Bacon's idea that religion deals with matters in the realm of the unseen nonphysical world, like salvation, while science deals with the observable physical world. The two cannot conflict because they deal with different subject matters. Galileo's other main view, a claim of accommodation, is one he loosely adopted from Augustine, whom he quotes. Because there can be no contradiction between science and the Bible—in areas where they share a common subject matter, presumably—if science has presented a demonstrable proof, then it is necessary to interpret the Bible either metaphorically or in some other way so that it agrees with the scientifically demonstrated conclusion.[6] The inverse of this principle of accommodation also holds: if demonstrable scientific evidence is lacking on a subject, one should accept, at least provisionally, a literal reading of the Bible. We should note that where Augustine used the term *demonstrable* as the ancients used it, in the sense of "logically demonstrated," Galileo uses the term in the weaker, Baconian sense of "proven by the evidence of the senses"—the sort of evidence for which both he and Bacon claim primacy in scientific inquiry. Galileo wittily mocks his opponents for acting as though *he* put the objects in the sky with the aim of upsetting nature and overturning the sciences.[7] He challenges them to look for themselves. If we might be allowed to compare this epistemological claim with the claims of religion, the Galilean claim is rather akin to Protestantism: whereas for Luther the individual's *conscience* is the arbiter of what is right, for Galileo, the individual's *senses* are the arbiter of scientific truth. "Don't believe what *my* eyes tell *me*," says Galileo. "Look for yourself and believe your own eyes."

It is impossible, of course, to know what the physicist and astronomer believed in his heart, and one might incline to some doubt about his religious reverence, especially when at the end of his letter, in a marvelously comic *tour de force,* he endeavors to show that the biblical account of the sun's stopping in its course in response to Joshua's prayer to finish the Battle of Jericho before the commencement of the Sabbath is more readily understood on the Copernican than on the Ptolemaic theory! If, however, we take Galileo as sincerely religious, he finds the compatibility of science and faith in their different aims—for science, truth about the physical universe; for religion, understanding the means to achieve salvation. In the few cases of apparently direct conflict, either the scientific evidence is nondemonstrative or a different interpretation of the religious views is appropriate.

Johannes Kepler

Johannes Kepler's creative insight, arrived at after Kepler had analyzed Tycho Brahe's careful and abundant observations and had organized them by numerous mathematical hypotheses, was that Mars orbits the sun in an elliptical course. From antiquity it had been assumed that celestial objects move in perfect circles. The idea of elliptical orbits was perhaps a break with the past even more radical than the Protestant Reformation, which had rejected an institution a mere millennium and half old. This insight, quickly tested by Kepler on the recorded observations of planets besides Mars, was truly revolutionary. The perplexity that Maimonides had seen in the multiplication of epicycles around arbitrary invisible points was dissolved. Kepler noted as well that planets move more quickly when they are close to the sun than when far away. He followed these conclusions of 1609 with a third law in 1619, which showed a fairly complex mathematical relationship between a planet's revolution around the sun and the planet's distance.[8] Kepler, as one might imagine, delighted in having discovered the mathematical order of these cosmic bodies. He also thought that he had discovered the true music of the spheres: each orbit is like a note on a musical scale, and all the orbital motions together form a celestial harmony of the spheres, a symphony that could—alas—be heard only by the soul of the sun.

Kepler achieved a union of observable astronomy with what the Platonic schools had only dreamed of—an understanding of the way the world was ordered by numbers. For Platonists, numbers represent the most exquisite form of abstraction. If, as Galileo wrote, "the grand book of the universe is written in the language of mathematics,"[9] then the writer of that grand book, God, is a mathematician. In the early seventeenth century, a new era of mathematics seemed to dawn. Some of Galileo's uncontroversial physics (e.g., his work on the center of gravity in solids and his laws of uniformity and of parabolic fall), the reform of the Julian calendar on the basis of more accurate observation of the solar year, the publication in 1585 by Simon Strevinus of *The Decimal* and the introduction into Europe of that useful system for computing, the invention by John Napier of logarithms, the new instruments made possible by optics, the invention of the thermometer, which made possible numerical quantification of temperature and, of course, the work of Kepler, all suggested that mathematics was the means to understand the universe. If one could understand the mathematics, one could read God's script.

Perhaps a few words would be appropriate about Kepler and the "music of the spheres" he felt he had discovered.[10] While the notion of celestial music may at first seem rather silly to moderns, it was a common view throughout Western history, commencing with the Pythagoreans, who, like Kepler, held as an unquestioned first principle the reality of mystical connections between mathematics, music, and the universe. For the deeply religious Kepler, the idea reflected his majestic view of the deity. Kepler discovered that the relationship between the average distance of each planet from the sun and its orbital period is not random but appears to obey a harmonious formula, i.e., that the square of the orbital period of a planet is proportional to the cube of its average distance from the sun.[11] Kepler announced this discovery, known to science as Kepler's Third or Harmonic Law, in his book *The Harmony of the World* (1619). Inasmuch as even today physicists do not know whether or not this law results from some deeper principle, it was not irrational for Kepler to look at the pattern as the work of a designer. Since the pattern in planetary orbits resembles (at least in Kepler's mind) a musical scale, he was able to assume, in view of a general ignorance of how sounds are formed, and in accord with his absolute belief in "music of the spheres," that the celestial bodies create harmonic noise—music.[12] That humans cannot hear the music is obvious. But there would be no point to music without a hearer; hence the speculation about the soul of the sun. Kepler was thus wedded to teleology in his inability to conceive of sound without its being intended for a hearer.

René Descartes

Like most great thinkers of his time, René Descartes (1596–1650) was a devout Catholic with every intention of using his intellectual talents to bolster the position of the Church. Though well aware of the risks in his day of meddling in scientific matters that had any bearing on religion, he hoped to become the Aquinas of the modern period by reconciling Church teaching with the new science. The reason he is widely considered the father of modern philosophy, though, has more to do with his strict mind/body dualism and skeptical methodology than with his attempted reconciliation of science and religion.

In addition to achieving immortality in mathematics with the invention of analytic geometry—the synthesis of geometry and algebra in a system of coordinates on a plane—he endeavored to extend mathematical certainty to an entire philosophical system. His strategy was to adopt, for purposes of argument, as extreme a skepticism as he could conceive, to call into question all of his previous beliefs, then to rebuild the edifice of knowledge on rock-solid foundations.

Because his senses sometimes deceive him, all sensory knowledge is subject to doubt. He calls into question even the most immediate sensory knowledge, such as his sitting in a chair writing, on the grounds that he could be dreaming. After having cast into doubt all empirical knowledge, even about his having a body, he considers mathematical truths. These too fall prey to doubt, for several reasons. If the world was created, God could be deceiving him. If, on the other hand, the world formed by random chance, deception is even more likely. Furthermore, other people are often deceived about what they think they know best. Finally, there might exist an evil genius intent on deceiving Descartes about even a priori, mathematical truths. Hence, everything he once believed, no matter how certain, is subject to doubt.

The one truth he hits upon that cannot be touched by any of the above skeptical arguments is that he must exist in order to think at all. The claim "I am thinking; therefore I am" is indubitable. Even if one is dreaming, the dreamer must exist. Even if one is being deceived, there must be someone who is the object of deception. In addition to the truth of his own existence, there is another sort of truth that cannot be doubted. When Descartes thinks he is in the street it is possible that he is deceived. But that it *seems* to him that he is in the street is certain. Certainty is thus found in the mind, in the seeming to the mind. Since mental images are not the same as the reality of which they are images, what we really know are the mental images. For example, when a person looks out the window and believes he sees a puddle of water, he *may* be seeing a mirage or an illusion or a high-definition projection of water on a screen. The mental image may not accurately reflect anything in the real world. The mental image may be of nothing whatsoever that actually exists, like the mental images of the imagination or of dreams. The question that Descartes then takes up is how we can be sure that the sensations and mental images correspond to some reality. He finds his answer in God.

Descartes offers three proofs for God's existence, two cosmological and one ontological. Even though he cannot know anything about the external world, if there is one, before he has proved God's existence, he does have among his many ideas the idea of an infinitely powerful, knowing, and benevolent God. Because the idea of God contains far more content than Descartes himself could have conjured up, and because only God himself could have put such an idea into Descartes's mind, God must exist. The second proof is similar: the only being capable of sustaining the existence of Descartes, complete with his idea of God, is God himself. Both cosmological arguments answer a question about where something came from, whether it be Descartes himself or Descartes's idea of God. The third proof is an ontological argument, based solely on the content of the idea of God. Just as a triangle contains the idea of three sides as part of its essence, Descartes claims, so too part of the very essence of God is that he must exist.

Having proved that God exists, Descartes can bridge the gap between his mind and the external world. Because he has a natural tendency to believe his sensory and intellectual faculties, and because a perfect God would not systematically deceive him, his faculties must be reliable and he must for the most part be correct in what he thinks about the external world. Thus, the intelligibility of the world and the very possibility of science are attributable to God's benevolence. God is the indispensable link between the material and mental worlds.

Descartes's true self—the "I" of "I am thinking; therefore I am"—is of course an immaterial thinking thing, whereas his body and the material objects in the world are of an entirely different class of entity. This Cartesian dualism of indivisible, immaterial, and immortal minds joined with mortal bodies subject to mechanistic laws is the key to Descartes's attempt to reconcile science and religion. Like his contemporaries, Bacon and Galileo, Descartes defends a claim of independence for both science and religion, an independence fully consistent with his dualism. Physical bodies are subject to physical laws and scientific scrutiny, whereas minds lie beyond the reach of empirical enquiry. Hence, scientific inquiry cannot bear on religious matters or vice versa.

As we have observed again and again, the *bête noir* of dualism is the problem of interaction. How does the immaterial affect the material in human beings? Descartes speculated that the mediation occurs in the pineal gland, and he offers some mumbo-jumbo to explain how the mediation occurs. Locating the point of interaction in a gland whose real function was unknown was of course very convenient, quite analogous to the process of attributing all unknown causes to God. Indeed, such ad hoc hypotheses constitute one of the chief ways to maintain both religion and science rationally. For where something is unknown there is no definite *contradiction* in maintaining a proposition that depends on the unknown but asserted notion. After all, it *might* be true. A rational mind *can* live with a hypothesis, no matter how fanciful or ad hoc; it *cannot* live with contradiction.[13]

For all its philosophical implausibility, dualism meshes neatly with religious beliefs in an autonomous, immortal soul. But, despite the meshing, the mechanistic mode of explanation Descartes championed in science has matured into a serious competitor to religion. Aristotelianism at least already embodied teleology, and Copernicanism introduced no fundamentally new method of explanation. Although Descartes himself clearly believed in God and the immortal soul—indeed, for him they were the two most important subjects on which philosophy could support religion—the other, mechanistic half of his system—a mechanism that is very close to the atomism of the ancient Greeks—proved to be a minefield of future threats to the religious beliefs he cherished.

Baruch de Spinoza

Baruch (Benedictus) de Spinoza (1632–1677) was fortunate to live in a place where he could profess (without being a professor) his own thoughts in relative freedom. Though banned from the Jewish community of Amsterdam, and though his views were antithetical also to the doctrines of orthodox Christianity, he was able to work as a lens grinder and to think as an independent philosopher. His fundamental views remind one of the pre-Socratics, especially of the monists, for Spinoza thought that all things are in reality mere modifications of one infinite substance that has an infinite number of attributes, of which thought and extension are the two attributes perceptible by humans.

Spinoza finessed the problem of science and God in a way similar to that of the pre-Socratics. He was able to do so because of his rejection of biblical revelation, rejecting, among other things, such notions as Moses' authorship of the Pentateuch and the reality of Adam as the first man. Once the Bible has been eliminated as the official word of God, one is free to look for God in other places. Spinoza found God in one underlying infinite substance. This substance is God, and the laws of nature are God's will. The more one studies nature, the more one understands God's will and hence God himself. For Spinoza, God's love is an intellectual understanding, without feeling or passion, of the necessity that rules everything. In this way, Spinoza translated the supernatural into the natural: there are no miracles, because miracles would be incompatible with God's will, and God's will is natural law. Dualism does not exist in Spinoza's thought, for there is only God, and everything in the universe is a manifestation of God, the mental and physical but two aspects of the same substance. God is nature, and nature is everything. By this view, whatever happens follows logically from God's nature, and everything is as it should be and cannot be different.

It is obvious that Spinoza could seem both "God-intoxicated"[14] and an atheist. His doctrines are perhaps no more satisfying to those with religious cravings than is Aristotle's impersonal Prime Mover. To someone mourning the death of a loved one or tormented by a painful disease, it is surely no comfort to learn that God is aware of the suffering without compassion or any feeling whatsoever and, furthermore, that the suffering is, like everything else, in accord with natural law and hence is God's will. Nonetheless, Spinoza eliminates all contradictions between God and science by identifying the two, essentially defining God as nature and nature's laws. Armed with this definition, Spinoza could consider himself a religious man. If one studies Spinoza's life and examines the decency of that life, one will conclude that the thinker lived more tranquilly and more charitably than many who made the daily or weekly trek to church or synagogue.

Isaac Newton

Samuel Johnson is reported to have said "that if Newton had flourished in ancient Greece, he would have been worshipped as a Divinity."[15] The invention of calculus, as well as the discovery of the law of universal gravitation and numerous other laws of physics, would justify Johnson's claim. Relevant to this book are the attempts of Newton (1642–1727) to use his discoveries to find a place for God even in a mechanical scheme of things. He introduces God extensively in the *Principia Mathematica,* the principal source for the discussion here.

Newton followed Bacon's program of a science based on observable phenomena. When Newton said "I don't imagine hypotheses" (*non fingo hypotheses*) he meant that he was not going to speculate beyond what he could accord with observations. He was able to describe how gravity functioned, how it decreased by the square of the distance from its source, how this law of gravity affected the planets' elliptical orbits, and how it worked compatibly with Kepler's laws of planetary motion. He could not, however, explain *why* gravity worked, especially through empty space and over vast distances. This was a perplexity for Newton as it was for those who doubted his theory. Indeed, it probably seemed to his contemporaries as bizarre as our contemporary theory that says how at a quantum level what happens in one part of the universe might affect something at a very distant part—at the same moment.

As we have repeatedly noted, where there is perplexity, there is an opportunity to find God. In the second edition of the *Principia,* Newton addresses the question of God. Mechanics, he says, can describe but cannot explain the objects in the sky. Astronomical systems, he asserts, are proof of a non-mechanical, of a divine, cause. That the planets all move in ellipses, in roughly the same plane, that the six planets have ten moons in similar kinds of orbits, in virtually the same plane, and that objects like comets can fly spectacularly into the solar system without disturbing the entire order are all testimony of an intelligent and powerful creator.[16] In addition—in a foreshadowing of the "anthropic principle"—he observes that if the various suns with their possible planetary systems were not located at such vast distances from one another, they would feel the effects of one another's gravitation and the whole universe would be compressed into a single huge mass.[17] The stars are where they are because of a divine plan. Mechanics is unable to explain *why* these things are as they are; mechanics can merely describe *how* they are. Mechanics, like metaphysics, describes continuous, unchanging processes that operate by blind necessity. But the actual variety in the phenomena cannot be explained by such laws. Only a non-mechanical, voluntary, intelligent being could devise the universe with its actual variety.[18]

In another work, Newton elaborates his argument for God's existence from the design of the universe.[19] That the sun is hot but the planets cool, that the sun is in the center so as to provide light to the planets, that the largest planets are furthest from the sun so that their gravity won't disrupt the entire solar system—these are all evidence of a voluntary and intelligent deity. For Newton, God is the originator of the laws of physics and of the entire universe, the designer of the structures that compose the solar system, the engineer who determines the mathematical relations and order of everything. For Plato's Timaeus, God was a philosopher; for Newton, he is a mathematician. God sets up the coordinates of space and time,[20] and God intervenes as needed to keep mechanical systems operating regularly. Since mechanical things slow down on account of the resistance of fluids, God needs to give things a little push from time to time to keep them going (a view not too different from Aquinas's notion of God as efficient cause). Also, because there are various irregularities in the behavior of the solar system, God corrects them when the need arises.[21]

To the reader who has persisted up to this point, it will be apparent that Newton has added nothing substantially new to the attempts of his predecessors to reconcile science and faith. What little is new is deriving design from the specific discoveries about gravity. God is handy for Newton when no other explanatory cause is available. Though he was able to admit that he did not understand the nature of gravity itself, Newton could not bring himself to say he did not know how the order of the cosmos arose. Instead, in a classic "god of the gaps argument," he attributed the cause to God.

Gottfried Leibniz

Like Descartes, Gottfried Leibniz (1646–1716) strove for mathematical precision in philosophical matters. But, like Spinoza, he deemed the defects of Descartes's dualism irremediable. As so often in things mortal, an attempt to repair one problem results in the creation of a different problem. Aristotle's theory of excess and deficiency applies to philosophy as much as it does to the practice of virtue. Spinoza avoided the problem of how immaterial thought and physical matter affected one another by reducing everything to one substance—God—and by claiming that thought and matter are two aspects of the same underlying reality, in a way analogous to the idea in modern physics that matter and energy are the same underlying stuff, convertible into one another. Of course, Spinoza's monism differs from that of modern physics because "energy" in physics is a material phenomenon, a kind of material "substance." Energy is not a spiritual substance, and the ability of one form of matter to be transformed into another is not nearly so difficult to imagine as the ability of thought to transform itself into matter. Spinoza could offer no persuasive mechanism separating nature, man, and God. Like a pre-Socratic, Leibniz set out to correct the defects of his predecessors with a novel hypothesis, a unique way of unifying mind and matter, teleology and mechanism. Perhaps also like the pre-Socratics, he was oblivious to the defects of his own hypothesis.

Instead of a world composed of atoms, the small irreducible bits of matter proposed by Democritus and Epicurus, Leibniz proposed that the world is constructed of assemblages of "monads," spiritual atoms. Being immaterial and indivisible, Leibniz's monads avoid the question of why divisibility would stop at any particular size of material atom. In Leibniz's mind, because there could be no sufficient reason for one level of divisibility rather than another, all forms of material atomism are arbitrary. Another problem with material atoms, according to Leibniz, is that there is no way to account for their spontaneous motion, for material objects need to derive their motion from something else. The problem of how a material object could generate movement was troublesome to the ancients; indeed, self-motion was one of the principal arguments for the soul (see p. 101). In Newton's mechanistic scheme, every bit of matter exerts a moving force on everything else, a force called gravity.[22] This force of universal attraction, however, is quite different from the motion Leibniz conceived of, the ability of a thing to move itself. Leibniz proposed that monads, bits of self-moving energy or soul, are the true substance. Monads combine to make everything in the world, including material objects, and so everything is full of life. The theory is reminiscent of the founder of science, Thales, who said that everything is full of gods and may have been referring to a similar principle of self-movement.

In addition to being immaterial, each monad possesses an extraordinarily complete nature. As Aristotle observed that the predicate of a true proposition is contained in the subject (i.e., when one says that a circle is round, "roundness" is implicit in "circle," so that if one knows what a circle is, one also knows the predicate roundness), so too Leibniz held that monads come complete with predicates. Indeed, the nature of a given monad includes properties that relate it to everything else in the universe. The monad of Julius Caesar, for example, includes the property of having crossed the Rubicon at a certain point in time, of viewing the world from a body located at a certain distance from the Andromeda galaxy, etc. A monad, in short, implicitly contains the whole universe, albeit from a single perspective. Leibniz's rationale for this astounding claim rests on the principle of sufficient reason, namely, that there must be a reason for every contingent fact. The only sufficient reason, he held, for monads containing all these predicates is that they *necessarily* contain them and contain all of them.

God's decision as to which monads to create follows from God's benevolent nature and from the same principle of sufficient reason. God chose to create this world, i.e., this particular assemblage of monads, precisely because he knew it to be the best possible combination. It is important to realize that, "before" creation, God knew the complete nature of every monad, including what we would call its past and future history, as well as exactly how the entire collection of monads would fit together. Thus each monad independently unfolds its existence in a sequence foreknown by God. The harmonious interrelationships among monads stem not from any real interaction—there is none, for monads are entirely self-contained—but rather from the universal harmony established by the creator.

The principle of sufficient reason leads not only to this picture of a best possible world but to a proof of the existence of God himself, a proof reminiscent of Aquinas's Third Way. Even if every contingent step in a causal chain is explained by some other step in the chain, perhaps ad infinitum, the causal chain itself is contingent and requires a sufficient reason for its existence. Hence there must be a necessary being whose rational choice grounds the existence of all contingency. This being is, of course, God, the creator of the optimally harmonious assemblage of monads.

Claiming that the actual universe is the best of all logically possible universes might seem to fly in the face of our knowledge of the profound suffering of billions of sentient creatures throughout history and of the seemingly suboptimal design of, especially, biological systems. For Leibniz, as for Augustine, Aquinas, and many others, perfection applies to the whole, not the parts. Suffering and other apparent imperfections are negligible phenomena in the vast scheme of things. Just as a small enough portion of a masterpiece of Michelangelo might look like a few meaningless colors or shapes when taken out of context, so a person looking at his own suffering might not understand how his private misfortune fits into God's perfect plan. Leibniz thus presented a standard response to the problem of evil and thereby opened his views to the mockery of Voltaire, who wondered whether noses were made to hold up eyeglasses and whether the culinary satisfaction of cannibals compensates for their victims' suffering.

Leibniz's view that divine authorship governs the world and every substance in it echos that of al Ghazali, who assigned to God the entire authority for everything that happens (see p. 162). How then is freedom possible? Leibniz attempted to preserve human freedom by asserting, famously, that our motives incline but do not necessitate our actions. What he means is that, although the chocolate-eater chose to eat the chocolate for good reason, his not having chosen to eat it would not have constituted a logical contradiction. Small consolation for the dieter—especially one who takes seriously Leibniz's inviolable principle that every contingent action has a sufficient reason for its occurrence or one who believes in Leibniz's view of the all-encompassing nature of both monads and God's knowledge of them. Not eating the chocolate may have been a logical possibility, but God knew from all eternity that that person would eat that particular piece of chocolate at that precise time. In effect, the person was a prisoner of his own desires and reasons, of God's knowledge, and of his own nature.

Another concern that immediately arises regarding Leibniz's metaphysics is how even an infinity of nonphysical monads can add up to a physical substance. Is Leibniz's substitution of monads for atoms really an improvement? Because, for Leibniz, matter is on a par with mind (in the sense that matter is divisible into mind and in the sense that matter amounts to mind without memory or full awareness), he seems ultimately to resolve the mind-body problem with a monism like that of Bishop Berkeley: ultimately, only mental substances exist. Although Leibniz would thereby avoid problems associated with how mental and physical substances interact, his solution to the problem of how monads themselves interact—that God harmonizes them—is strikingly similar to the occasionalists' solution to the mind-body problem, where God too coordinates the interaction (see note 13).

If bodies ultimately reduce to spiritual monads and if the principle of sufficient reason calls forth teleological explanations, in what sense is mechanistic explanation valid? Leibniz tries to have it both ways: mechanism governs particular explanations, such as why a particular body falls at a particular rate, whereas teleology accounts for the actuality of this particular world, with the particular mechanisms it embodies. This strategy, common to Newton, of viewing physical processes as ordained by God constitutes an effective denial of empiricism and evinces a desire to let God fill in whatever explanatory gaps there are. In contrast to Descartes, Leibniz fails to give due credit to mechanistic explanations or indeed to the very existence of a material world.

FINAL THOUGHTS ON THE SEVENTEENTH CENTURY

As one glances over the prominent seventeenth-century thinkers discussed here, one may note that as a group they resemble the ancient pre-Socratic philosophers, not of course in their precise views, but in the wide range of imaginative ideas and in the way they generated their theories about God and nature. The pre-Socratics started with a creative insight that sprang from their imagination. Then they worked out the logical consequences of the insight and built it into a system. The men of the seventeenth century followed the same procedure. Whether the theory was Kepler's music of the spheres, or Spinoza's pantheistic infinite underlying substance, or Leibniz's monads, or Descartes's non-deceiving deity, the ideas flash like a bursting firework and, also like a firework, provide a brilliant spectacle. But, almost instantly, as the theory is gazed at, the colored sparks fade in the darkness of the night sky, and the theory seems fanciful at best, loony at worst. Human beings are resourceful creatures, and when one theory fails, they will devise another.

THE ENLIGHTENMENT

David Hume

Far from attempting to reconcile science and religion, Hume (1711–1776) was openly hostile toward popular religion, dismissing it as unworthy of refutation, and highly critical of natural religion, i.e., the enterprise of bolstering religious beliefs with empirical and rational arguments. His skeptical arguments—in particular his decisive refutation of the eighteenth-century argument from design— bear directly on historical attempts to find empirical, even scientific, evidence of God's existence and are well worth considering.

In his *Dialogues Concerning Natural Religion,* Hume presents compelling criticisms of both a priori and a posteriori arguments for God's existence. After dismissing a priori proofs on the grounds that no proof of existence can proceed a priori, he turns to cosmological and teleological arguments, both a posteriori. In contrast to Descartes's and Leibniz's endorsements of cosmological arguments,

Hume held that there is no further need of a cause of a series if each member of that series has an established cause.

The principal a posteriori argument to which Hume therefore directs most of his attention is the teleological argument, or argument from design. Design arguments, he believes, constitute unfounded inductions, since we have no experience of universe-making and hence no sample on which to base an inductive argument. They also rely fundamentally on weak analogies between human and divine design. Because the universe is finite and imperfect, it can never furnish evidence for an infinite and perfect creator. Furthermore, the creator might have been competent enough to create *this* universe but might still rank lower than the intelligent creators of other universes. An exact analogy between human and divine work might in fact lead one to conclude that our creator was mortal or that there was a committee of creators. Indeed, the universe might just as well have sprung from a seed as from a personal creator. What is more troublesome, if the creator is personal, we should, in light of the presence of evil and suffering in the world, assume him to be either malevolent or indifferent. In addition to these analogical weaknesses, design arguments are subject to the same regress of explanation that their proponents are trying to escape. The question, Where did the designer come from? is just as valid as the question, Where did the universe itself come from? Finally, there are alternative explanations to a divine creator, such as the ancient atomist hypothesis, which has the universe forming by chance processes over vast stretches of time.

Hume has even less respect—if that is possible—for the testimony of miracles. Because accounts of miracles involve violations of the laws of nature, it will always be more likely that such an account is false for some reason (inaccurate reporting, wishful thinking, prior bias, vested interest, the lure of sensationalism, etc.) than that a law of nature, for which we have the greatest possible evidence, was actually violated. In practice, Hume notes, reports of miracles overwhelmingly come from primitive or uneducated people, capitalize on the human hunger for both telling and hearing sensational news, and are, in addition, contradicted by the reports of miracles of competing religions.

Immanuel Kant

Throughout his life, science and religion absorbed the philosophical hours of Immanuel Kant (1724–1804). Perhaps the religious devotion that marked his childhood education—where every day school began at 5:30 A.M. with a half hour of prayer, followed by an hour of instruction in religion, and where each subsequent hour ended with a prayer—was so imprinted in his soul that he was unable wholly to leave it behind. Indeed, he originally studied theology before changing his focus to philosophy and natural science. Nevertheless, by the time he was sixty-nine and had published *Religion within the Limits of Reason Alone* he had come a long way towards setting aside the religion of his ancestors. Although in later life he refused even to enter a church, he remained a deeply moral person and did not abandon religion; instead, he redefined it so as to be compatible with his philosophy.

Here is not the place for a lengthy exposition of Kant's philosophical views or of their development. Suffice it to say that a study of their development would expose a fluid mind ready to revisit issues again and again in an effort to understand them better. For example, in 1755, when he was thirty-one, in *General History of Nature and Theory of the Heavens,* Kant claimed that the world operates by magnificent mechanical laws and that this system could not exist were there not a supreme divine intelligence at work. But later, in *The Critique of Pure Reason,* as we shall see, Kant explicitly rejected the arguments from design for the existence of God. Abandoning the argument from design, however, was not without risk, said Kant many years later in 1790, in *The Critique of Judgment.*[23] He concludes there that the world is in fact without design. But he adds that if we abandon the belief of design in nature, life loses meaning for us, and that, moreover, if we do not believe in a deity's design of the universe, we are very likely to go mad. Perhaps he thought that without some such concept we would be like the fallen angels in *Paradise Lost,* who, engaging in philosophical reflection, went round and round and "found no end, in wandering mazes lost."[24]

In *The Critique of Pure Reason* (1781), Kant concludes that pure reason, i.e., the mind's faculty for drawing knowledge from a priori principles, cannot prove the existence of free will, immortality, or God. All three classical arguments for God's existence—teleological, cosmological, and ontological—he finds defective. Teleological proofs fall prey to Hume's criticisms that the designer cannot be shown to be one, immaterial, or immortal. Hence, such proofs rely on cosmological proofs to the effect that there must be a necessary being who grounds the existence of the contingent world. But such proofs beg the question, argued Kant, i.e., they work only if there really is such a necessary being. Hence, cosmological proofs depend on the ontological argument that God's very nature includes existence. Kant's critique of this argument is twofold. First, existence, unlike wisdom, power, and beneficence, is not a predicate. To use a Kantian example, a real million dollars is no larger a sum than a merely possible million dollars. Second, the ontological argument works at best only for a stipulated definition of God as a "being that must exist," but not for any actual divine being. This argument is therefore circular as well: its conclusion follows only if the assumption that there exists a divine being meeting the stipulation is assumed to be true.

Although Kant sought to refute decisively the arguments of the natural theologians, he never sought to prove the tenets of religion false. Far from it: he adopted religious principles, such as the existence of God and the freedom and immortality of the soul, as regulative principles, needed in order for us to make sense of the world. The world is unintelligible unless it is the product of a higher intelligence; morality presupposes freedom; moral perfectibility assumes immortality (or something close to it); and just moral deserts require divine justice.

Faith in these matters is allowable insofar as science cannot disprove them. The very structure of our minds gives rise to these "ideas of reason," which are unavoidable attempts by our minds to unify our knowledge even if such knowledge is inapplicable to things in themselves. The ideas don't constitute knowledge proper; they are instead practical postulates that allow us to apply reason to its proper sphere. In his denial of natural theology but acceptance of practical postulates, Kant resembles Parmenides, who, having shown in *The Way of Truth* that motion is impossible and that the entire world is a homogeneous, unmoving, and unchanging One, in *The Way of Seeming* wrote a treatise more compatible with conventional views. In his postulation of divine justice, Kant reminds us of Boethius, who claims in *The Consolation of Philosophy* that there must be a God to be the source of moral standards.[25]

Two of Kant's four famous antinomies of pure reason are worth mentioning. The first concerns the question of the universe's finiteness. If one supposes that time applies to things in themselves rather than just to the objects of possible experience, then it would be possible to show both that the world had a beginning in time and that it did not. It can be shown to have had a beginning by Bonaventure's argument that an actual temporal infinity cannot be traversed, by the very definition of infinity. It can be shown not to have had a beginning by the argument of Parmenides and others that nothing could have come from the empty time that would have had to precede the initial point in time. Kant's solution is that both horns of the dilemma are false because time applies only to the objects of possible experience. Both arguments fail because they attempt to go beyond spatial and temporal experience, and the antinomy is solved by realizing the proper domain of our faculties. The third antinomy involves the freedom of rational agents. In this case both horns are true: natural causality applies to the spatio-temporal, phenomenal world, whereas freedom applies to the rational, noumenal world.

In 1791, in *On the Failure of All Philosophical Attempts at Theodicy,* Kant despaired that reason could provide insights into the relation between the world and God's wisdom. Here too, after nearly a lifetime of study and reflection, he seems to have come to the conclusion of Simonides' lament quoted by Cicero,[26] that the more he pondered the various questions, the more unable he became to answer them.

Kant's last major work on religion, published in 1793, is *Religion within the Limits of Reason Alone*. In response to the work came a letter from King Frederick William II accusing the thinker of misusing philosophy to "undermine and debase many of the most important and fundamental doctrines of Holy Scriptures and Christianity" and threatening him with "unpleasant consequences"[27] if he continued to cause offense. Prudently unwilling to let Germany sin against philosophy, Kant promised the king that he would refrain in the future, in his writings and lectures, from making comments about religion, either natural or revealed.

In *Religion within the Limits of Reason Alone* itself, Kant took up some of the principal questions of Christianity and rejected the traditional views. On the origin of evil, for which the Christian answer was Adam's original sin of disobedience,

Kant found an anthropological explanation: early man needed to develop certain skills to survive in primitive conditions, skills that civilization and its moral sensibility later came to deplore, but the tendency for these skills persisted and is the source of the evil in human nature.[28] He also rejected Christianity's claim to a special revelation from God: the best religions, he said, would not base themselves on revealed commandments, but upon that sense of duty that is the most divine element in human nature.[29] Nor should religion require a person to affirm a faith in miracles—one of the traditional proofs for the validity of Christianity. Nor should proper religion require anyone to believe in the divinity of Christ—though not believing in Christ's divinity was heretical for Christians from before the Council of Nicea. Nor, indeed, was it necessary to believe in what Paul had affirmed as the essence of Christianity, the belief that Christ atoned for the sins of all mankind through his execution on the cross and that as a consequence the possibility of salvation for believers was established. Nor was it necessary to believe what Martin Luther had asserted to be the central claim of his Protestant Reformation, that God predestined heaven or hell for every individual regardless of anything that he did in his life, regardless of any works, however noble or base.[30] Nor, despite the prayers he was compelled to deliver in his school days, did Kant grant any validity at all to petitionary prayer. Such prayers, he said, are illusions.[31] He boldly proclaimed that when a church compels belief or worship or when it claims for itself the sole right to determine what is morally right or to interpret the Bible or when it introduces magic into its rituals or when it establishes a priesthood with exclusive claims to God's grace or when it works with the state and suppresses intellectual and academic freedom—when a church does any of these things, a free mind will rightly reject the church altogether.[32] In short, he rejected just about everything that Christianity stood for and that the Christian Churches had been demanding for eighteen hundred years. He concluded that the free man who rejects such a church will seek a religion of reason, whose main purpose is the pursuit of a moral life. To the man who asked Rabbi Hillel whether he would teach him the Torah standing on one foot, Rabbi Hillel assented and taught, "Do not do to others what you would not have them do to you. This is the essence of Torah. All the rest is commentary." Hillel's ethical goal is identical to Kant's goal for religion. It is no wonder the German king was annoyed.

Kant's genius lay in articulating the limits of reason. Adopting, after his fashion, Aristotle's strong requirements for knowledge, Kant accepted that very little could actually be known about God as creator of the universe. In accepting ignorance about God, he was in agreement with the soundest of medieval thinkers. At the same time he embodied the Enlightenment in not requiring people to accept a view of God or practices of organized religions that were incompatible with reason. For Kant, God was to be found in moral goodness. Moral goodness was both proof that God exists and the goal to be sought in seeking godliness. Gibbon wrote in *The Decline and Fall of the Roman Empire* that for the politician all religions are equally useful. Kant would agree that religion was useful, not, however, for the purpose of keeping people politically subservient, but for the purpose of making political association possible, for only in communities where people value virtue is life worth living. Kant reconciles science and religion by establishing religion as the means to ethical conduct. On the more metaphysical doctrines concerning God, he acknowledges the incapacity of reason. In the end, the arbiter of religious truth for Kant is reason, not faith, and the reconciliation is effected when religion sits obedient at the feet of philosophy.

CONCLUSION

With his commitment to reason, Kant perhaps exemplifies the acme of Enlightenment thinking, and his death just four years into the nineteenth century is appropriate for a man whose affinity is with thinkers of the eighteenth century. In the nineteenth century, at the same time that there are extraordinary advances in science, not least of which is Darwin's algorithm for explaining how there might be design without mind, there is a revival of religious feeling and belief in a superintending personal creator. As we shall see in the next chapter, attempts to accommodate traditional notions of the deity with the developing science of the nineteenth century continue the pattern that we have seen since the birth of science in the millennium before the Common Era.

DISCUSSION QUESTIONS

1. Although Bacon actually has much in common with Aristotle, the Renaissance thinker exaggerates his differences with the Greek, emphasizing his own novelty. What possible motives might have stirred Bacon? Does a scientist in general do more harm or more good to his program by stressing his differences with his predecessors rather than by showing how he stands on their shoulders?

2. If you had been alive in the seventeenth century, when mathematics finally seemed capable of precise quantitative descriptions of phenomena, would you have been persuaded that God was a mathematician who had written his blueprint in numbers? What evidence, if any, might have caused you to doubt this inference about God?

3. How successfully does Descartes put his proofs of God's existence beyond the reach of doubt?

4. Could any established religion accept Spinoza's views without condemning itself? What in Spinoza's views would be the most objectionable to established religions?

5. Why do you suppose that Newton chose to introduce God to deal with anomalies in the system of celestial mechanics rather than acknowledge that he himself did not know how to explain the anomalies?

6. To what extent do philosophers such as Spinoza and Leibniz seem to have abandoned the Baconian research program?
7. Kant suggests that the value of religion lies in its incitement to an ethical life. Aristotle devised an ethics from an understanding of human nature, on the principle that the human good must be based on the uniquely human quality of reason. Hence, Aristotle worked out an ethical principle the core of which is that happiness is a life of virtuous activity. Aristotle's theory does not invoke religion at all. Why might *Kant* wish to employ religion in the service of ethics?

NOTES

1. The example of Cornelius Loos will serve. He was about to publish an attack on witch-hunting but was imprisoned and forced to recant before the book could be published. P. Smith, *History of Modern Culture* (New York: Holt, 1930), 1:453.

2. Francis Bacon, *Concerning Arguments*, 9.1.

3. Francis Bacon, "Of Atheism," in *The Essays* (Mount Vernon, N.Y.: Peter Pauper, n.d.), 65.

4. Galileo makes this boast in a biography by his friend Vincenzo Viviano, as quoted by Lane Cooper, *Aristotle, Galileo, and the Tower of Pisa* (Ithaca, N.Y.: Cornell University Press, 1935), 26.

5. Galileo, "Letter to the Grand Duchess Christina," in *Discoveries and Opinions of Galileo,* trans. S. Drake (New York: Doubleday, 1957), 186.

6. Galileo, "Letter," 186.

7. Galileo, "Letter," 175.

8. The square of the period of a planet's revolution around the sun is proportional to the cube of its mean distance from the sun.

9. Galileo, "Il Saggiatore," in *Discoveries and Opinions of Galileo,* trans. S. Drake (New York: Doubleday, 1957), 237.

10. For a good account of Kepler's fixation on the concept, see J. L. E. Dreyer, *A History of Astronomy from Thales to Kepler,* revised by W. H. Stahl (New York: Dover, 1953), 406–11.

11. About Kepler's discovery, A. Koestler writes (*The Watershed: A Biography of Johannes Kepler* [Garden City, N.Y.: Anchor, 1960], 214):

> What exactly does he mean by "harmony"? Certain geometrical proportions that he finds reflected everywhere, the archetypes of universal order, from which the planetary laws, the harmonies of music, the drift of the weather, the fortunes of man are derived. These geometrical ratios are the *pure* harmonies which guided God in the work of Creation; the *sensory* harmony which we perceive by listening to musical consonances is merely an echo of it.

12. Dreyer (*History,* 408) describes how Kepler arrived at a tune for each planet and reproduces the musical score.

13. A theory known as "occasionalism" was established by Descartes's followers Arnold Geulincx (1625–1669) and Nicholas Malebranche (1638–1715). They maintain that God has created two independent series of events, one mental and one material. God

has timed the two series to work together so that it *appears* as though one affects the other. The two series are like the visual and sound tracks of a film, which are synchronized so that the image on the screen seems to be speaking and making noise; in fact the noise comes from a strip of tape. Those accepting "occasionalism" would say that if parents receive a telegram informing them that their son has died in battle and they then become emotionally saddened, their sadness is wholly coincidental to the news, for the news that is communicated in the physical realm is wholly unconnected from their mental state. Their sadness *seems* caused by the news but is actually simply timed to appear so.

14. W. Durant attributes this epithet to the Catholic poet Novalis (F. von Hardenberg). See *The Story of Philosophy* (New York: Simon & Schuster, 1926), 149.

15. Boswell, *Life of Johnson,* 2:144n1. Others had almost as lofty a view of Newton. Leibniz said that Newton's contributions to mathematics were equal in value to all previous work combined (D. E. Smith, *History of Mathematics* [Boston: Ginn, 1923], 1:404), and Hume said that Newton was "the greatest and rarest genius that ever rose for the adornment and instruction of the species" (David Hume, *The History of England: From the Invasion of Julius Caesar to the Abdication of James the Second, 1688.* [Philadelphia: J. B. Lippincott, 1865], 5: 433).

16. Newton, *Principia Mathematica,* 527.

17. In *Opera Omnia,* 4: 430, 441, Newton says that if the universe were finite (although he thinks it infinite), a deity would be necessary to keep the matter from merging into a big spherical mass. (Shades of Parmenides!)

18. The brilliance of Darwin was to conceive of a mechanical algorithm to explain diversity.

19. Newton, *Opera Omnia,* 4: 430, 441.

20. Newton, *General Scholium,* 528.

21. Newton, *Principia Mathematica,* 677.

22. For an account of this natural motion in Newton, see J. E. McGuire, "Natural Motion and Its Causes: Newton on the 'Vis Insita' of Bodies," in *Self-Motion from Aristotle to Newton,* ed. M. L. Gill and J. G. Lennox (Princeton, N.J.: Princeton University Press, 1994), 305–29.

23. Immanuel Kant, *Critique of Judgment,* trans. J. C. Meredith (Oxford: Clarendon, 1952), 2:89.

24. Milton, *Paradise Lost,* 2.561.

25. Boethius, *The Consolation of Philosophy,* 3.10.

26. Cicero, *The Nature of the Gods,* 1.60.

27. King Frederick William II, quoted in W. Durant, *Rousseau and Revolution* (Simon & Schuster, 1967), 546.

28. Immanuel Kant, *Religion within the Limits of Reason Alone,* trans. Theodore M. Greene and Hoyt H. Hudson (Chicago: Open Court, 1934), 35.

29. Kant, *Religion,* 142–43.

30. Kant, *Religion,* 57, 134.

31. Kant, *Religion,* 183–85.

32. Kant, *Religion,* 153, 164–65, 168, 112.

Science and Religion in the Nineteenth and Twentieth Centuries

The brain is wider than the sky,
For, put them side by side,
The one the other will include
With ease, and you beside.
The brain is deeper than the sea,
For, hold them, blue to blue,
The one the other will absorb,
As sponges, buckets do.
The brain is just the weight of God,
For, lift them, pound for pound,
And they will differ, if they do,
As syllable from sound.

—Emily Dickinson

A FEW PRE-DARWINIAN VIEWS

Perhaps it would be worthwhile to take a brief look at the intellectual world, especially in England, in the years when Darwin was working out his theory of natural selection. It was an era of energetic hope that science would come to the aid of religion, aid especially urgent because of the shadow cast by Hume's powerful critique of the argument from design. The eighth earl of Bridgewater, commissioned (in his will) the Bridgewater Treatises, scholarly works that would show how God's "power, wisdom, and goodness" were revealed in creation.[1] The method of the Treatises is a repetitive description of how only a designer could have produced works where form so perfectly follows function. The evidence of design no doubt seemed overwhelming, whatever Hume might have said.

239

Part of the impetus for this energetic defense of God's work was the new science of geology with its exciting discoveries. In early nineteenth-century England there were just the two universities, Oxford and Cambridge, whose chief function was to serve the state religion by producing ministers. The gentlemen who attended the universities and were not planning clerical careers amused their youthful idleness by taking classes in the novel sciences from professors who were truly absorbed in their work. Extraordinary from a twentieth-century point of view though entirely conventional in the nineteenth, the professors were all ministers. William Whewell, Professor of Mineralogy at Cambridge; Adam Sedgwick, Professor of Geology at Cambridge; William Buchland, Reader in Mineralogy and Geology at Oxford; Baden Powell, Professor of Geometry, were all ministers. Devout men of the cloth, they were predisposed to see the handiwork of God in the material they studied, and see it they did.

William Whewell seems to have embodied a particularly peculiar mix of religious and scientific sentiments. Darwin honors him by citing his work in the first of three epigrams facing the title page of *On the Origin of Species* (for his view of the universal rule of nature's laws):

> But with regard to the material world, we can at least go as far as this—we can perceive that events are brought about not by insulated interpositions of Divine power, exerted in each particular case, but by the establishment of general laws.

At the same time, Whewell believed in a supernatural continuing creation of species. Perhaps he had in mind God operating as in the quotation from Augustine in chapter 1, where, after the flood, God created new animals on islands far out at sea. As a scientist, Whewell, like Leibniz, believed that everything that occurred in geological history had a cause, but he admitted supernatural causes in addition to natural ones.[2] He believed that miracles could also be invoked to explain the adaptations of living creatures. Science and religion are not at odds, he claimed, because in invoking miracles as explanations he was *going beyond* science, not violating it. There is a logic to his view, which may be illustrated by analogy to the behavior of kings. A tale is told in book 3 of Herodotus's *History of the Persian Wars* about King Candaules of Persia, who wished to marry his sister. Since it was unlawful for Persians to marry their sisters, Candaules asked his advisers what he should do. A clever adviser pointed out that Candaules might marry his sister without violating the law because of another law, which conveniently stated that a king may do as he pleases. In other words, the king's actions were *outside* the province of the law and thus could not constitute a *violation* of the law. For Whewell, the situation of God and nature was like that of the Persian king and the law: whatever God does is *beyond* science; it takes place in a parallel realm and so does not fall under the jurisdiction of science.

Another form of reconciling the new geology and science was by the familiar method of interpreting the Bible as meaning something other than what it literally says, i.e., by granting it a liberal use of figurative language or "poetic license." For example, since humankind is the matter of most vital concern, the Bible speaks of time accurately when speaking of the periods that refer to human activities, but everything before the creation of man can be said to have taken a very long time—even eons—consistent with the understanding of the geological record.[3] Thomas Chalmers (1780–1847) suggested that between the "beginning" recorded in Genesis and the six days of creation there was a gap of undetermined length and that the changes recorded by geology took place in this time—a view identical to that of some fundamentalist sects today.[4] An analogous reinterpretation of the Bible's language that eliminates any possible conflict is that of Hugh Miller in his 1856 book *Testimony of the Rocks; or, Geology in Its Bearings on the Two Theologies, Natural and Revealed.*[5] He maintains that the geological record accords well with Genesis, so long as one understands the Bible's use of "days" as long periods of time. Sir John Herschel (1792–1871), writing to Charles Lyell (1797–1875), suggested no difficulty in believing that the patriarchs lived to be fifty thousand years old, yet he was willing to extend each of the Bible's "days" to fifty thousand million years![6]

CHARLES DARWIN

Darwin's religious journey is best left to his biographers.[7] Here we may note that Darwin (1809–1882) was fully aware that his theory of evolution would have deep religious implications. In the last few pages of *On the Origin of Species,* he acknowledges the revolutionary nature of his work by comparing it to Newton's work in physics.[8] That Newton's theory cannot explain the essence of gravitation, he says, is no more a refutation of it than that his theory cannot explain the origin of life is a refutation of the process of natural selection. Discussing the potential religious impact of his views, he again draws a comparison with the theory of gravity. He observes that people eventually recovered from the shock of the law of gravity, a law that—he quotes Leibniz—was "subversive of natural and inferentially revealed religion."[9] The implication is that the same people will manage to recover from their shock over his theory of evolution too. Then, in a most revelatory confession of his views of science and religion, he approvingly quotes a "celebrated author and divine" who praised as very noble the conception of a God who created a few original life forms capable of self-development. His point, then, is that there need not be a God who creates every species in a once-and-for-all moment of creation. Darwin's God is deistic: he starts nature going in "the beginning" and then lets it take its course.

Perhaps it was reasonable to believe in the immutability of species before geology showed that vast expanses of time had passed on earth during which huge changes had taken place.[10] But, Darwin says, now that geology has shown the world to have been around a very long time, it is reasonable to suppose that species have come into being. Darwin is critical of those who hide behind such phrases as "plan of creation" or "unity of design," because these phrases are not explanations but mere restatements of the way things are! (Darwin himself uses the exclamation point to show how erroneous these critics are.) He mocks the naturalists who accept some species as variations on the original ones yet insist that other species are newly created.[11] They are unable to tell which are which or to give a coherent account of their views. "The day will come," he writes, "when this will be given as a curious illustration of the blindness of preconceived opinion. These authors seem no more startled at a miraculous act of creation than at an ordinary birth."[12] He jokingly asks how these new creatures were made, whether as eggs or fully grown, and whether mammals were made "with false marks of nourishment from their mother's womb"[13] (a witty, if periphrastic, way of asking about belly buttons).

In language perhaps deliberately resonant with religiosity, he predicts that "Our classifications will come to be, as far as they can be so made, genealogies, and will then truly give what may be called the plan of creation."[14] The plan, he adds, is benevolent: "And as natural selection works solely by and for the good of each being, all corporeal and mental endowments will tend to progress toward perfection."[15] In a way, this plan is better than the one described in Genesis. There God began with perfection, and the world deteriorated through time. With Darwin's version of the "plan of creation," things move from primitive forms *towards* perfection. He can claim that evolutionary theory is a more lovingly divine vision than the story in the Bible.

The last sentence of *Origin of Species* presents an assessment of evolutionary theory as an especially fine view of the scheme of life:

> There is grandeur in this view of life, with its several powers, having been originally breathed by the Creator into a few forms or into one; and that, while this planet has gone cycling on according to the fixed law of gravity, from so simple a beginning endless forms most beautiful and most wonderful have been, and are being, evolved.[16]

The language deliberately echoes Genesis 2.7, where God breathes into man the breath of life and makes him a living being. Darwin acknowledges that he is rewriting the Bible and challenges the religious establishment to deny that his conception of the divine role is majestic. He cleverly revisits the implied comparison between his work and the groundbreaking work of Newton on gravity. Evolution, he hints, is as surely a law as gravity. Darwin suggests, with his use of the word *planet,* that he has understood the big picture, and yet, with the use of the same word, he indicates that our planet is a part of the universe and subject to the universe's laws. The highly poetic language of the paragraph (the echo of the Bible, the submerged reference to Copernicus and Newton in the words "this planet has gone cycling," the juxtaposition of opposites in "beginning endless") and the evaluation of his own vision in the superlatives "most beautiful" and "most wonderful" show his sense of having created a new religious vision.

However fitting it might be for Darwin's God to operate in the world through the mechanisms of evolution in natural selection, two aspects of the theory of evolution contrast sharply both with a literal reading of the Bible and with central Aristotelian doctrines. Instead of viewing species as created originally by God in their present forms or as fixed Aristotelian categories, Darwin conceived of species as mutable, as continuously evolving entities. Secondly, the blind, mechanistic explanations provided by natural selection challenge the usefulness of teleology as an explanatory mode. Darwin presented a plausible alternative to explaining natural phenomena in terms either of God's designs or of the unfolding of innate tendencies. The challenge posed by Darwin, as we shall see, will generate a great deal of discussion among late twentieth-century reconcilers of God and science.

A FEW PROMINENT PHYSICISTS OF THE TWENTIETH CENTURY

Albert Einstein

The great inventor of the theory of relativity is famous for his comment that "God does not play dice with the universe." The anthropomorphizing of God into a human gambler is, however, a mere rhetorical conceit, for Einstein (1879–1955) repeatedly rejects any kind of anthropomorphic deity. Indeed, for him, God *is* the order that one finds exemplified in physical laws. When directly asked by Rabbi Herbert S. Goldstein, "Do you believe in God?" Einstein replied, "I believe in Spinoza's God, who reveals himself in the harmony of all being, not in a God who concerns himself with the fate and actions of men."[17]

Religion figures in Einstein's life and writing. Einstein says that though his family was irreligious, he grew up with the religion that he absorbed from his culture, and, at an early age, believed it.[18] But when he was twelve, he came to the conclusion that many of the stories in the Bible are not true. He says that this discovery was enormously liberating for him, for it freed him to think independently. Thus he claims to have entered into his freethinking way of life *because* of his rejection of traditional religion.

Einstein was born Jewish and identified more closely with the Jewish people as he grew older, perhaps because of the terrible persecution that he saw Jews suffering in Germany, perhaps because of his identification with the Zionist cause. But his views concerning Judaism were ambivalent. On the one hand, he saw it as a religion that stressed a moral attitude in life and, far from being a creed dictating what one must or must not believe, as a negation of superstition. On the other hand, he says that Judaism also includes a regrettable and disreputable attempt to base moral laws on fear.[19]

According to Einstein, the world's religions should concentrate on ethics, so that, as he wrote in his essay "Science and Religion," "the individual may place his powers freely and gladly in the service of all mankind."[20] He divided religion into three kinds. The first is the most primitive kind, which has an anthropomorphic God. The second is the kind in which moral principles dominate and the focus is the moral life of its adherents (this would be the ideal form of Judaism).[21] The third, which he prefers, is the religious feeling that comes over the scientist as he contemplates the majesty of the universe:

> The fairest thing we can experience is the mysterious. It is the fundamental emotion which stands at the cradle of true art and true science. He who knows it not, and can no longer wonder, no longer feel amazement, is as good as dead, a snuffed-out candle. It was the experience of mystery—even if mixed with fear—that engendered religion. A knowledge of the existence of something we cannot penetrate, our perceptions of the profoundest reason and the most radiant beauty, which our minds seem to reach only in their most elementary forms;—it is this knowledge and this emotion that constitute the truly religious attitude; in this sense, and in this alone, I am a deeply religious man. I cannot conceive of a God who rewards and punishes his creatures, or has a will of the type of which we are conscious in ourselves. That an individual should survive his physical death is also beyond my comprehension, nor do I wish it otherwise; such notions are for the fears or absurd egoism of feeble souls. Enough for me the mystery of the eternity of life and the inkling of the marvelous structure of reality together with the single-hearted endeavor to comprehend a portion, be it ever so tiny, of the Reason that manifests itself in nature.[22]

How very much he echoes Plato's Socrates, who declared that philosophy begins in wonder! Einstein identifies this wonder with religious feeling, and because he is suffused with it, he calls himself a religious man.[23] By excising from God the various qualities that religions have attributed to him, by denying a personal God, Einstein was able to feel free of superstition. He was solidly in the tradition of the Enlightenment philosophers, who "saved" God by defining him in a way wholly compatible with reason.

Max Planck

For Max Planck (1858–1947) religion and science occupy different realms. Science deals with the sequence of cause and effect in all external phenomena.[24] Religion is never specifically defined, though it seems to include "The Divine Spirit" and "spiritual happenings."[25] Concerning a rational exploration of religion, he writes:

> And so we arrive at a point where science acknowledges the boundary beyond which it may not pass, while it points to those farther regions which lie outside the sphere of its activities. The fact that science thus declares its own limits gives us all the more confidence in its message when it speaks of those results that belong properly to its own field. But on the other hand it must not be forgotten that the different spheres of

activity of the human spirit can never be wholly isolated from one another; because there is a profound and intimate connection between them all.[26]

Planck here seems to express the inconsistent, if understandable, wish to have science and religion both separate and yet connected. His confusion stands in the tradition of Western thought that has not been able to resolve the contradiction in its wishes.

Erwin Schrödinger

Schrödinger (1881–1961), the discoverer of the "wave equation" in modern quantum mechanics, believed that he proved each individual to be a deity. He says that as a scientist he knows that his body functions as a pure mechanism operating by the laws of nature. But he also knows from direct experience that he controls his body's movements. The obvious conclusion: "Therefore I am God Almighty." His theory, in a humbler version, is actually a view noted earlier, in Plato, when his character Socrates argued that all souls are self-movers (see p. 101). Schrödinger credits the Upanishads with the same insight and also the Christian mystics, who, celebrating their union with God, said, *"deus factus sum"* ("I have become God").

Werner Heisenberg

The hero of the Uncertainty Principle, Heisenberg (1901–1976) wrote on science and religion in, among other places, *Across the Frontier.*[27] Modern science, he said approvingly, represents a turning away from Aristotle to Plato. What Heisenberg does not like is the Aristotle who objects to the natural philosophers who make up theories out of their heads and then attempt to fit the facts of the visible world to the theories. Heisenberg argues that the facts of the visible world are actually misleading and that the attempt to find *mathematical* order, even when that mathematical order does not conform at first to what we perceive, leads to progress. He attributes the mathematical approach to Plato. Heisenberg gives several examples to support his view.

First, he says, it is clear to our senses that the earth stands still and the sun and planets move. But, as Copernicus understood, it made more *mathematical* sense to imagine the sun as the center of the planetary system. Again, he says that it seems clear that light bodies fall more slowly than heavy ones. But Galileo *speculated* that in a vacuum light and heavy bodies would fall at the same speed. Despite the empirical support he obtained from his experiments with inclined planes, Galileo *reasoned* to this conclusion, and since neither he nor anyone else had actual experience of a vacuum, the theory was based on laws that could be mathematically formulated. Similarly, Heisenberg points out that when Kepler deduced elliptical orbits—again a mathematical construct, not a phenomenon directly observable by the senses—Kepler thought he had for the first time in human history observed the beauty in God's works.

What these examples mean, according to Heisenberg, is that truth and beauty exist in a realm beyond the senses. The mathematical ordering that the physicists have discovered is God's work. But, he admits, this ordering God is not the God people turn to in times of trouble. Perhaps, he suggests, science has paid too much attention to the mathematical features of God, but the totality of God includes other areas of spirituality. These other areas are the religiously inspired ethical ideals that arise from the communal association of human beings. The ideals, like the mathematical ordering that physicists have discovered, do not come from the visible world but "from the region of structures lying behind it."

It is to be expected that the languages of science and religion differ. "Heavens" in the Bible, he says, are not the same heavens into which rocket scientists send their spaceships. He writes:

> Science tries to give its concepts an objective meaning. But religious language must avoid this very cleavage of the world into its objective and its subjective sides; for who would dare claim the objective side to be more real than the subjective? *Thus we ought not to intermingle the two languages;* we should think more subtly than we have hitherto been accustomed to do.[28]

Here we have a reconciliation of science and religion that assigns to each its own sphere. Religion concerns subjectivity, ethics, poetry, and the God who gives the world its mathematical order; science concerns objective sensory reality. It is a form of the old theory of "double truth" discussed earlier (see p. 171). What moves Heisenberg is the ordering cosmic religion that also moved his colleagues.

We suspect that Heisenberg and many of his fellow physicists are like the intellectuals of Plato's day who divided the world's people into the many and the few. The many were those who devoted most of their attention to their earthly needs. They are slaves to their bellies and their material desires. But the few, a group that always includes whoever is writing, are the more mathematically and spiritually minded people, the ones who rise to see the loveliness in ideas, the grandeur in the heavenly order, and who alone are able to seek union with the divine.

CONCLUSION

As far as the attempts to reconcile science and religion are concerned, the views of the twentieth-century physicists do not warrant lengthy study. The physicists are of course brilliant in their area of research, but brilliance in one area does not guarantee brilliance in another. A baseball player adept at hitting the long ball may not be able to pitch; it is even less likely that he could plot the trajectory of a spaceship. Nor does an ability to see mathematical relationships imply a similar genius in the other activities of life or learning. Mathematicians are not philosophers. Thus the work of those who have thought more about philosophical and theological subjects will in general reveal subtler insights. The medieval theologians whom we examined earlier devoted a good part of their thinking to the questions of faith and reason, exploring the subjects with admirable thoroughness and subtlety.

Modern physicists, for the most part, find exceptionally moving the rapture they feel when they see that their equations accurately portray the world. Their rapture is identical in kind, and perhaps also in degree, to that of a child who, looking at a checkerboard, notes that the process of multiplication tells him at once that there are sixty-four squares on the board and that it is not necessary to count each one, that he might quickly multiply the eight on each side to find the total. The child experiences a "eureka moment" in which he sees that mathematics works. Or the rapture may be as intense as the sense of awe a traveler feels when he visits the Grand Canyon for the first time, as he approaches from what appears to be ordinary dull flat ground and all of a sudden catches sight of the magnificent chasm. The mathematical awe of modern physicists is their religious feeling; it is the "natural high" that stirs them to imagine that they have seen the mind of God. They confidently believe that they have earned the right to make such grand claims for themselves, and perhaps they have. The same sense of awe is available to all of us, of course, if we take the trouble to reflect on the vastness of space and time and our own smallness. Whether this expression of rapture at the beauty of the ordering principle is the essence of religion or merely a sentimental effusion of joy, and whether it sheds light on the relationship between science and religion, are matters to be taken up in the following chapters.

DISCUSSION QUESTIONS

1. How many examples can you think of in which scientific explanations of a phenomenon have superseded religious ones? Can you think of any where religious explanations have superseded scientific ones? Are religious explanations of natural phenomena always temporary in the sense that they fill gaps in human understanding—but only until science provides more rigorous, naturalistic explanations?

2. Can a single phenomenon have *two* proper explanations, one religious and the other scientific? Are there natural phenomena for which a religious explanation is the only sort of explanation that can in principle be given?

3. Must modern scientists put aside their scientific training and beliefs when they go to religious services? Must they suspend their religious beliefs while working in the lab during the week? Has the potential tension between one's religious leanings and scientific beliefs increased or decreased since the days of Whewell and Sedgwick, given all the advances that science has made in the past two centuries?

4. If interpretations of the Bible need to be adjusted to accommodate advances in science, what independent authority does the Bible have? Indeed, what independent reason is there for deferring to the teachings of the Bible instead of, say, those of the Qur'an? Are there cases in which scriptural texts are definitive and unambiguous enough to trump scientific theories, however well supported the latter might be?

5. Recall that it took more than a century and a half for the subversive and unsettling effects of the Copernican Revolution to "sink in" to the consciousness of the common people. Might we now be witnessing the last stages of acceptance by nonscientists of the Darwinian Revolution? Are the reasons for doubts about Darwinism predominantly religious or non-religious? How does your answer to this question bear on the likelihood that conflicts between science and religion will ever be fully resolved?

6. Critics of evolution theory often point to disagreements among evolutionary biologists. Given that falsifiability is a pillar of scientific method, to what extent is such disagreement, especially on the cutting edges of research, to be expected, even applauded? At what level of discourse are the disagreements among biblical fundamentalists, young- and old-earth creationists, theistic evolutionists, and indeed adherents to various world religions? In other words, are the disagreements about first principles, data, interpretation of data, or something else?

7. Can you think of any good reasons for God's *preferring* to do his creative work through evolutionary mechanisms? If God does guide evolution, what evidence might there be to help you ascertain that *God* is behind the process? Can you think of reasons for God to shun such evolutionary mechanisms in favor of direct creation? Are your reasons primarily philosophical, scientific, or religious?

8. Is the theoretical elegance of modern scientific theories and the mathematical beauty of natural laws evidence for or against a divine designer? Do the world's elegance and beauty reveal to you its autonomy or its having been crafted by God?

NOTES

1. M. Ruse, *The Darwinian Revolution* (Chicago: University of Chicago Press, 1979), 70.

2. William Whewell, *Philosophy of the Inductive Sciences* (London: Parker, 1840), cited in Ruse, *Darwinian Revolution,* 89.

3. Whewell, *Inductive Sciences,* cited in Ruse, *Darwinian Revolution,* 67–68.

4. It is a view traceable to Origen. See the discussion on p. 104.

5. Hugh Miller, *Testimony of the Rocks; or, Geology in Its Bearings on the Two Theologies, Natural and Revealed* (Edinburgh: Constable, 1856).

6. Ruse, *Darwinian Revolution,* 70.

7. An excellent account may be found in Adrian Desmond and James Moore, *Darwin: The Life of a Tormented Evolutionist* (New York: Warner, 1991).

8. Charles Darwin, *On the Origin of Species by Means of Natural Selection; or, The Preservation of Favored Races in the Struggle for Life* (New York: New American Library, 1958), 442–43.

9. Darwin, *Origin,* 443.

10. Darwin, *Origin,* 443–44.

11. Darwin, *Origin,* 444.

12. Like Albert Einstein, who will be discussed shortly, Darwin seems to have lost a good measure of his faith when he lost his belief in miracles. Darwin had been brought up on Paley's *Evidences of Christianity,* in which Paley founds much of Christian belief on the genuineness of miracles. As Ruse writes, "Christianity without miracles was nothing (at least as a divinely inspired religion), and so his adherence to Christianity faded away" (*Darwinian Revolution,* 180).

13. Darwin, *Origin,* 445.

14. Darwin, *Origin,* 448.

15. Darwin, *Origin,* 450.

16. Darwin, *Origin,* 450.

17. Albert Einstein, "Autobiographical Notes," in *Albert Einstein: Philosopher-Scientist,* ed. P. A. Schilpp (New York: Tudor, 1951), 103.

18. Einstein, "Notes," 3–4.

19. Albert Einstein, *The World As I See It,* trans. Alan Harris (New York: Covici Friede, 1934), 143–44.

20. Quoted in A. P. French, *Einstein: A Centenary Volume,* ed. A. P. French (Cambridge, Mass.: Harvard University Press, 1979), 219.

21. Einstein, *World,* 263.

22. Einstein, *World,* 242.

23. Richard Feynman, another prominent physicist, like Einstein became disenchanted with religion when he discovered that stories his Rabbi was telling him were made up (*What Do You Care What Other People Think? Further Adventures of a Curious Character* [New York: Bantam, 1989], 25–28). But, also like Einstein, he found "religion" in science. He writes about his religious feeling in language strikingly similar to that of Einstein (243–44):

> The same thrill, the same awe and mystery, comes again and again when we look at any question deeply enough. With more knowledge comes a deeper, more wonderful mystery, luring one on to penetrate deeper still. Never concerned that the answer may prove disappointing, with pleasure and confidence we turn over each new stone to find unimagined strangeness leading on to more wonderful questions and mysteries—certainly as grand adventure!

It is true that few unscientific people have this particular type of religious experience. . . .

24. Max Planck, *Where Is Science Going?* trans. J. Murphy (New York: Norton, 1932), passim, but especially 111ff.

25. Planck, *Science,* 103.

26. Planck, *Science,* 105–6.

27. Werner Heisenberg, *Across the Frontier* (New York: Harper & Row, 1974).

28. Werner Heisenberg, quoted in K. Wilber, ed., *Quantum Questions: Mystical Writings of the World's Great Physicists,* ed. (Boston: New Science Library, 1984), 42–43.

14

Science and Religion at the End of the Twentieth Century

When I heard the learn'd astronomer,
When the proofs, the figures, were ranged in columns before me,
When I was shown the charts and diagrams, to add, divide, and measure them,
When I sitting heard the astronomer where he lectured with much applause in
    the lecture-room,
How soon unaccountable I became tired and sick,
Till rising and gliding out I wander'd off by myself,
In the mystical moist night-air, and from time to time,
Look'd up in perfect silence at the stars.

                —Walt Whitman

This is not piety, this oft-repeated show of bowing a veiled head before a stone;
this bustling to every altar; this kowtowing and prostration on the ground with
palms outspread before the shrines of the gods; this deluging of altars with the
blood of beasts; this heaping of vow on vow. True piety lies rather in the power
to contemplate the universe with a quiet mind.

                —Lucretius

This book is about the attempts to reconcile science and religion; hence, the views
of physicists and biologists who are atheists are not strictly relevant, except insofar as they serve to illustrate or help formulate the views of those who would propose such a reconciliation. Some scientists think the whole process of reconciliation a waste of time; others—and these tend to be those for whom Christianity is
a deep source of comfort—work earnestly at showing the compatibility of science
and religion. These are people for whom the achievements of science are too obvious to be denied yet for whom the truth of religion is deeply felt. As one might

imagine, there are numerous variations of the same general themes; it would be a gargantuan, not to mention redundant, task to discuss all of them. Just as at a paint store one might today find a sample sheet with seventy-five shades of white, so one might find every view about reconciling science and religion to have at least seventy-five slight variations. In this chapter, we shall discuss what appear to us to be representative views that reflect the thinking of many others. This discussion will show a continuity since ancient times in both the issues and the solutions. The exact theories may change, but the general questions, main themes, and even metaphors used by the scientists and theologians do not. The whole subject shows both the promise and the limits of human ingenuity.

In the first, and most substantial, section of this chapter, we discuss the intelligent design research program, which its proponents believe represents the cutting edge of contemporary research on science and religion, the most articulate and technically sophisticated attempt to detect evidence of a designer in the natural workings of the world. Our evaluation of the program will be highly critical and, we hope, equally sophisticated. From intelligent design, we turn to a survey of three prominent contemporary scientist/philosopher/theologians, whose ideas represent some of the available options for interpreting the nature of God and of religion in a scientifically respectable way. We conclude the chapter with a look at a contemporary debate over whether science and religion occupy entirely independent domains.

THE INTELLIGENT DESIGN RESEARCH PROGRAM

The lineage of attempts to prove the existence of a divine designer by a posteriori means is, as we have seen, ancient and, as a post-Darwinian might suspect, perhaps overdue for extinction. Yet the human tendency to see intelligence behind observational data often proves hardier than logical rigor. The latest version of the argument from design, a version vigorously contested in philosophical journals, in conferences on science and religion, and in well-publicized debates, is the brainchild of the "intelligent design" research program. Defenders of this new version claim that it avoids the standard—and persuasive—objections to traditional design arguments by achieving a higher level of scientific rigor than that of earlier arguments and by distancing itself from specific, and therefore controversial, claims about God's nature.

The most prominent and tenacious proponent of such inferences of design is William Dembski, a mathematician and philosopher whose book *The Design Inference*[1] lays out in meticulous detail the circumstances under which the intelligent design of objects, events, and phenomena can be inferred, and whose latest book, *Intelligent Design,* provides a further case for bridging science and theology and addresses key objections to the intelligent design research program. For many of his real-life examples, Dembski cites the work of biochemist Michael Behe, another theorist of intelligent design. Behe's book *Darwin's Black Box* makes the case that irreducibly complex mechanisms within living cells could have arisen only through intelligent design, a case Dembski thinks dovetails perfectly with his own analysis of the general structure of design arguments. In addressing Dembski's work, we shall be assessing the most articulate spokesman for "intelligent design." Criticism of his work applies to a greater or lesser extent to that of his colleagues.

Dembski is confident that design will emerge as the crucial link between science and theology and that his work will hasten the "impending collapse" of naturalism, especially in the biological sciences.[2] The key to destroying naturalism, argues Dembski, is that the detection of design is an empirical matter, worthy of the same respect accorded any serious scientific theory. He believes that "natural and intelligent causes can operate in harmony without doing violence either to science or to theology"[3] and that hence it is time for a scientifically rigorous continuation of the tradition of British natural theology in the two centuries prior to Darwin, the view exemplified in Paley, discussed earlier, that complex organization, like that in a watch found in the woods, is evidence of an intelligent craftsman.

To discern the extent to which Dembski's analysis of the structure of design arguments forces scientists to take design seriously, stirs philosophers to rethink the relationship between science and religion, and challenges naturalists to abandon their position, we shall first lay out Dembski's basic case. We shall then consider his technical refinements and assess his responses to objections to his position.

Dembski's Explanatory Filter

Dembski's central point is that design inferences have a common logical structure embodied in what he calls an "explanatory filter." The filter works by applying the process of elimination to what Dembski takes to be the three mutually exclusive and exhaustive modes of explanation: regularity, chance, and design. The aim of the filter is, put simply, to detect highly improbable patterns that neither regularity nor chance can explain.

The first step is to ask whether an event to be explained is highly probable. If it is, as in the case of getting heads at least once in a hundred tosses of a fair coin, then regularity—that is, the regular patterns associated with coin tossing—is identified as the proper explanation and there is no need for further questions. Dembski's point is that, because regularities explain probable events, design need not be invoked.[4] In the present example, design need not be invoked to explain getting heads at least once in a hundred coin tosses.

If an event to be explained is not highly probable, the next step is to ask whether the probability of the event's occurring by chance alone is high enough that chance should be taken as the proper explanation. In the language of probability, is the probability of the event, given some hypothesis of chance—P (E/H)—sufficiently high? The probability, for example, of getting heads at least sixty times in a hundred tosses is too low to attribute to any regularity or law of nature but not too low to rule out as a chance occurrence. Coin tossers occasionally do get heads sixty or more times in a hundred tosses by chance alone.

When, however, an event is of extraordinarily low probability (a notion to be elucidated below), we need to ask whether the event conforms to an independent pattern, or, in Dembski's terminology, is specified (another notion to be elucidated below). The reason for the specification requirement is that unspecified events of extremely low probability, such as a random sequence of one hundred coin tosses, also occur by chance. Indeed, every series of a hundred random tosses will result in an equally improbable sequence of heads and tails, but very few of these sequences will conform to any interesting pattern. Only events that are both highly improbable and specified pass through the explanatory filter, where regularity and chance are eliminated, and end up being attributed to design. If, for example, one had declared in advance that the hundred coin tosses would comprise twenty heads in a row followed by twenty tails, twenty heads, twenty tails, and twenty heads, and if the coin tosses came out exactly this way, we would have an event that is both highly improbable and specified. Again, the appearance of the first one hundred digits of pi in one hundred spins of a roulette wheel would be far too improbable to attribute to regularity and far too specified to chalk up to chance. Intelligent design alone, according to Dembski, can explain such occurrences. Dembski's explanatory filter thus detects what he calls "complex specified information," where specification is taken to be holistic in the sense that order matters. The digits of pi, for example, must come from the roulette wheel in a specific order, and the coins must come out heads or tails as prescribed.

For applications of these mathematically driven intuitions, Dembski turns primarily to "cosmic fine tuning" and to Behe's "irreducibly complex" biological systems. A commonly cited example of the first sort is the relative masses of subatomic particles. Protons, for example, are roughly 1,836 times more massive than electrons. If this ratio were even slightly different, there could be no stable chemistry and hence no life. A favorite biological example, discussed by Behe, is the blood-clotting mechanism, which involves a complex Rube Goldberg–like system comprising dozens of indispensable proteins that control, among many other things, the formation, strengthening, and eventual dissolution of clots. As Dembski puts it, "For an irreducibly complex system, function is attained only when all components of the system are in place simultaneously. It follows that natural selection, if it is going to produce an irreducibly complex system, has to produce it all at once or not at all."[5] Such a system exhibits the sort of holistic specification of information that, according to Dembski, is the hallmark of intelligent design. "The great myth of modern evolutionary biology," Dembski avers, "is that information can be gotten on the cheap without recourse to intelligence."[6]

Refinement of the Explanatory Filter

Whereas the main idea of the explanatory filter is straightforward—that highly improbable but specified events, ones that embody complex specified information, cannot be attributed to regularity or chance and can be explained only in terms of intelligent design—the notions of probability and specification themselves require elaboration. Dembski takes two different approaches to quantifying the sort of extremely low probability essential to inferences of design. The first approach capitalizes on the fact that an improbable event, such as winning a million-ticket lottery, becomes more probable as the number of opportunities for the event's occurrence increases, as would be the case if a person bought thousands of lottery tickets or entered thousands of different lotteries. Dembski's point here is that an event should be considered extremely improbable if the probability of the occurrence of an event of that type in the entire duration of the universe, given the hypothesis of chance, is less than one half. If a specified event meets this test of extremely low probability, Dembski rejects chance as an explanation in order to avoid the "probabilistic inconsistency" of believing a chance hypothesis that renders an event unlikely and then discovering that the event has actually occurred.

Dembski's other approach to quantifying low probability is quite different. It involves estimating the total number of patterns, or specifications, that can be generated in the duration of the universe. By estimating the lifetime of the universe, the number of particles in it, and the rate at which they can change, he comes up with a generous figure of 10^{150} as the maximum number of actual specifications and hence 10^{-150} as a universal upper bound on extremely low probability. This probability roughly corresponds to five hundred bits of information as a universal complexity bound.[7] Dembski issues an open challenge for anyone to come up with a specified event of probability lower than 10^{-150} (or complexity greater than five hundred bits) that can be explained without recourse to design.

In addition to quantifying the level of probability needed for making design inferences, Dembski also makes explicit the key requirements of specification. The first requirement is "conditional independence": the chance hypothesis H must render the event E probabilistically independent of background knowledge I. In other words, the probability of E given both H and I must equal the probability of E given H alone, i.e., $P[E/(H + I)] = P(E / H)$. Conditional independence simply means that one's chance hypothesis must include all of one's knowledge that is probabilistically relevant to E. Dembski's rationale for including this condition is that if one's background knowledge influenced the probability of an event, it would be too easy to come up with an ad hoc "specification" of the event and hence too easy to arrive at a false positive inference to design. If one knows in advance the result of a long series of coin tosses, for example, any pattern derived from that very knowledge cannot be the sort of pattern indicative of design. The conditional independence of the background knowledge from which a specification is derived, on the one hand, and the event to be explained, on the other, is therefore essential for preventing false claims to design.

Although the event E and the background knowledge I must be conditionally independent, they must be mutually related to a certain description of E—call it D—by the two remaining components of specification, tractability and delimitation. Tractability applies to the relationship between D and I: it must be a tractable problem for one to formulate D from I. It would be a tractable problem, for example, to derive the sequence 00, 01, 10, 11 from background knowledge of binary arithmetic. It would be an intractable problem, however, to derive the specific outcome of a series of five hundred coin tosses from background knowledge about coin-tossing: there are simply too many possibilities. Delimitation applies to the relationship between D and E: E must logically entail (or, in Dembski's terminology, "delimit") D. These last requirements close a loophole: if tractability were not an issue, a person could, for example, generate a list of all possible sequences of five hundred coin tosses and then in principle locate any particular sequence on that (very long) list. In fact, however, the specification by brute force of such truly improbable events as a sequence of five hundred coin tosses is "intractable," i.e., incapable of being formulated.

Such is Dembski's explanatory filter, complete with his technical refinements. On the surface it appears both commonsensical and mathematically rigorous. Our job of seeing how it stands up to the various objections that have been raised against it and against design arguments in general is made significantly easier by Dembski himself. Like Descartes, who published a whole volume of objections and replies to the central theses of his own *Meditations,* Dembski responds to nine key objections to his arguments. In what follows, we consider each of these objections, along with Dembski's response, then conclude with a look at some technical problems with the refinements to the explanatory filter.

God of the Gaps

Dembski's rendition of the classic "god-of-the-gaps" fallacy—that "design substitutes extraordinary explanations where ordinary explanations will do"[8]—reveals a preoccupation with methodological naturalism and a failure to address the *real* god-of-the-gaps fallacy, which might be phrased as the charge that design substitutes extraordinary explanations where ordinary explanations *are currently unavailable.* To commit the god-of-the-gaps fallacy is to assert (falsely) that the current incompleteness of a scientific explanation will be permanent. This vulnerability to false assertions of design is a problem about which Dembski himself is rightly concerned: "if things end up in the net [i.e., if things meet the complexity-specification criterion for design] that are not designed, the criterion will be worthless."[9] Dembski is well aware that the natural theology of the eighteenth century is rife with examples of claims about design, especially regarding the adaptations of organisms to their environments, that later science proved false. It is, perhaps, likely that the Large Hadron Collider currently under construction by CERN will advance our knowledge of particle masses or that the recently published explanations of the evolution of blood-clotting mechanisms will prove plausible—thus shrinking the "gaps" in naturalism available to design theorists.

To avoid the embarrassment of having a design inference supplanted by a future scientific explanation, Dembski must first show that a particular event is not rendered probable by *any* natural regularity, even a regularity that has not yet been discovered. He must do so because his explanatory filter works by the process of elimination: once an event is deemed too improbable to be attributed to a natural regularity, the issue cannot be revisited in light of newly discovered regularities. Because the design inference is said never to err in moving past regularity as a possible explanation, one had better be sure not to overlook any possible regularity while still at this first stage in the filter. Moreover, Dembski generously places no limit on the plausibility, independent confirmation, or prior probability of the sorts of regularity one might consider when estimating the value of $P(E)$. *Any* regularity one can dream up—no matter how improbable it might sound—is fair game. Dembski cannot close this loophole, because he disavows all estimates of prior probability in order to protect himself from having to estimate the prior probability of a designer and from having to do the one thing he is loathe to do, pin down the designer's identity. Design theorists therefore encounter a serious stumbling block at the very first stage of Dembski's explanatory filter. Because design theorists refuse to discuss the identity and prior probability of designers, their opponents have carte blanche to use the improbable regularity of their choice in order to drive the probability of any event high enough to stop the filter dead in its first track. Dembski cannot, for example, prevent a person from dreaming up a "regularity" that renders that person's last sequence of a hundred coin tosses probable. Even if someone cautious of hasty design inferences does not exercise this option and agrees to eliminate all regularities as possible explanations, the possibility always looms that future scientific discoveries will reveal that the elimination of regularity explanations was premature.

A parallel problem occurs, only more severely, at the second stage of the filter. Not only is there no limit on the prior probability of the chance hypotheses that can figure in to the conditional probability $P(E/H)$ and raise it arbitrarily high, but hypotheses that invoke natural selection, which Dembski classifies as a chance hypothesis, are readily available and often quite compelling. Well aware that natural selection is his chief explanatory competitor, Dembski wisely challenges such hypotheses in the biological realm on the grounds of low explanatory power rather than prior probability. His argument, that natural selection is unintelligent and undirected, and thus cannot explain the complex specified information evident in biological structures, is worth quoting at length.

> CSI [complex specified information] does not emerge by merely aggregating component parts. CSI is not obtained by arbitrarily stitching items of information to-

gether. Only if a specification for the whole is given can parts be suitably arranged to form CSI.

This fact severely limits the ability of selection and mutation to produce CSI. Because the Darwinian mechanism of mutation and selection is nonteleological, it cannot specify in advance the adaptations it will produce. Selection and mutation operate with no memory of the past or knowledge of the future—there's only the present organism with its ability to survive and reproduce given its environment. Consequently whatever CSI mutation and selection generate must be generated in a single generation. To suppose otherwise is to think that mutation and selection can sustain a specification over multiple generations until the adaptation that was specified comes to fruition. But this is teleology, and teleology is utterly inconsistent with the Darwinian mechanism. For mutation and selection to solve the information problem, they must do it in a single generation.[10]

In arguing that unintelligent, undirected selection cannot produce complex specified information, Dembski allies himself with Michael Behe, who makes exactly the same point in claiming that irreducibly complex biological mechanisms can never be selected for. Because Dembski and Behe ignore both functional multiplicity and eliminated redundancy, however, they exhibit a fundamental misunderstanding of natural selection. The fact that *multiple* functions may be selected for in a series of ancestral environments renders irrelevant the holistic or irreducible complexity of a current structure. A bird's wing, for example, might be considered irreducibly complex relative to the function of flying: if its surface area were reduced or its feathers rearranged, shortened, or removed, the wing would no longer serve that particular function. The catch is that parts of the wing may well have served *different* functions in different ancestral environments. Feathers, for example, may have served as heat-regulators before they became long enough for flight. Evolution is opportunistic. It takes advantage of available structures adapted for one function and co-opts them into a different service. None of this requires foresight, intelligence, or teleology. Just the contrary: it could be the result of blind forces working over eons to cobble together whatever happens to work, regardless of shifts in functionality.

Dembski and Behe also ignore eliminated redundancy of the sort nicely illustrated by a stone arch that supports itself even after its construction scaffolding has been removed. The arch is irreducibly complex insofar as every stone must be in place for the arch to stand and insofar as an arch cannot be built up one stone at a time without collapsing before completion. But arches *can* be built using temporary scaffolding that becomes redundant once the arch is complete. So too can biological structures capitalize on existing "scaffolding"—just another example of available structures being co-opted to serve a new function—which might be eliminated by subsequent selection. Gene duplication provides an apt and very common example of biological redundancy. While one copy of a gene performs its "scaffolding" role, selection can operate freely on its duplicate without compromising an organism's fitness. In time, the duplicate gene, like the stonework in an arch, can become adapted in ways that render the original gene obsolete.

Hence, consideration of how a structure might have developed through evolutionary history, including how functions might have shifted and redundancy been eliminated, presents a serious objection to Dembski's in-principle argument against the generation of complex specified information by natural selection. Dembski and Behe have attacked only the straw man of evolution stripped of functional multiplicity and eliminated redundancy.

Dembski supplements his argument that evolution cannot generate complex specified information with the claim that evolution cannot generate any information whatsoever, a claim that echoes the charge that evolution violates the second law of thermodynamics by purportedly increasing the order of a closed system. The flaw in such arguments lies in an equivocation of scope. Though it is true that selection cannot introduce new information into a system as a whole, it does not follow that selection cannot organize information at a local level, as, for example, when only those micro-organisms immune to penicillin survive in a person's body. Here again, Dembski's criticism reveals a fundamental misunderstanding of the operation of evolution. The key action of natural selection is the sifting of adaptive "information" through the sieve of differential reproductive success. Dembski misleadingly focuses on the organisms that survive this process rather than on the totality of organisms, including the vast number that do not make it through the sieve. Indeed, his act of focusing on a particular biological structure is an act of narrowing his scope to a high-information region—not a claim that information has been added to a system. Evolution adds no order or information to the whole system, any more than a person focusing on a string of five consecutive 5s in the digits of pi has added information to the entire sequence of digits.

Besides falling into an equivocation of scope, Dembski leaves himself open to two ad hominem rebuttals. First, because he himself accepts microevolution, he therefore must explain why his in-principle argument that evolution can generate no new information whatsoever applies only to macroevolution. Secondly, he needs to clarify his rationale for calculating a universal upper bound on $P(E/H)$ in the first place, if chance hypotheses (including natural selection) cannot explain *any* of the information in E. That total lack of explanatory power would seem to render chance hypotheses incapable of influencing the probability of an event. Yet the whole point of the 10^{-150} figure is to identify cases where a chance hypothesis renders an event less probable than that upper bound.

Thus Dembski's criticisms of selective hypotheses fail to prevent such hypotheses from raising $P(E/H)$ above the level needed for the design inference to work. Moreover, the conditional independence requirement for specification reinforces our assurance that no design inference will go through. In order for background knowledge I to be conditionally independent of E, I cannot include knowledge pertaining to ancestral environments, possible evolutionary routes, likely adaptive histories, plausible shifts in functionality, or anything else remotely relevant to the probability that E would occur. In short, an enormous amount of information must be lumped into the chance hypothesis H if conditional independence is to be satisfied and any specification is to be forthcoming.

Dembski then bears the burden of showing that $P(E/H)$, where H includes all present and future evolutionary information of the slightest relevance to E and of the slightest independent plausibility, is below 10^{-150}. As we have seen, this wealth of evolutionary information will certainly prevent $P(E/H)$ from being low enough for an inference to design. In short, Dembski's criticisms of selective explanations are misguided, for such explanations do in fact harbor ample explanatory power, especially in the biological realm. Moreover, given the lack of restrictions on prior probabilities, selection can always be invoked to raise $P(E/H)$ above 10^{-150} and thus prevent design inferences from ever being successful. If, therefore, Dembski is correct in asserting that the design inference yields no false positives, it is because the inference yields no positive results at all. And if it does, those results fall squarely into the god-of-the-gaps category.

As with god-of-the-gaps arguments generally, the strategy behind design inferences is methodologically suspect, because that strategy would stifle scientific research. Dembski's design inference is particularly culpable because of its eliminativist structure. Once naturalistic regularities and selective hypotheses are eliminated, they are gone for good. The only response Dembski offers is that, before ruling out naturalistic explanations, we should make "a full and efficient use of our empirical and theoretical resources for discovery."[11] This vague pronouncement hardly qualifies as a satisfactory identification of the point at which the search for traditional scientific explanations should be abandoned.

Explanatory Power

The second criticism Dembski addresses concerns explanatory vacuity, the charge that "design explains everything and so explains nothing."[12] Dembski again aims at a straw man and misses the real concern about explanatory power. He argues that the critic of the design argument's explanatory power confuses design with intentionality and thus fails to realize that while the intentional action of an intelligent agent *can* be invoked to explain anything, the notion of design arises only in connection with complex specified information. My casually placing a book on a desk is an example of an intentional action that involves no complex specified information. It is thus easy to see that any event whatsoever can be "explained" by reference to an intelligent agent intentionally bringing it about. But design, Dembski argues, is different, because it can be invoked only where complex specified information is evident. He concludes that design does not explain everything and hence does not lack explanatory power.

This response, however, overlooks the true problem of explanatory power, that design can be invoked to explain *any event that appears to embody complex specified information*—without the design theorist's having to identify the nature of the designer, estimate the prior probability of there being such a designer, or calculate the likelihood that such a designer would bring about the event in question. There are two problems that render such an explanation hollow. First, the totally unidentified designer stands as a mere placeholder for explanation rather than performing any real explanatory function. If such an argumentative move were permissible, then we could just as well explain any instance of complex specified information by reference to intelligent extraterrestrials about whose nature we refuse to speculate. How did complex biological structures arise? Extraterrestrials made them. How did the fundamental constants of the universe come to have their actual values? Extraterrestrials. As should be obvious, satisfying explanations are not so easy to come by. The invoker of extraterrestrials has to say something about the prior probability of their being such extraterrestrials and about the likelihood that they would and could bring about the event in question—and both probability estimates depend crucially on precise descriptions of the origins, abilities, beliefs, and intentions of the extraterrestrials. If ad hoc extraterrestrial hypotheses are not to be granted equal footing with design, and if design inferences are to perform any explanatory work of their own, the designer must be identified.

The second problem with the explanatory prodigality of design inferences also results from their failure to identify a designer. The problem concerns whether a designer is a more satisfying stopping point for explanation than naturalistic hypotheses. After all, for any given explanation, one can always ask what explains that explanation; hence, the ancient preoccupation with infinite regress. Dembski responds to this charge of explanatory regress—i.e., what explains the designer?—with the observation that the theoretical entities of science are subject to the same regress—i.e., what explains them? Fair enough. If explanatory regress cannot be avoided in either case, though, the only option is to compare the probabilities of design and naturalistic explanations. Without such a comparison, there would be no grounds for preferring design. But such a comparison again saddles the design theorist with the unavoidable task of identifying the designer, which is the only way he can estimate the probability that there is such a designer and that such a designer would bring about the event to be explained.

In discussing the god-of-the-gaps fallacy, we observed that Dembski's refusal to speculate about the identity and prior probability of the designer gave his critics carte blanche to dream up regularities and chance hypotheses capable of blocking any design inference. Here we have seen that an unidentified designer has no more explanatory plausibility than unidentified extraterrestrials and is incapable of circumventing the charge of explanatory regress.

Religious Status

The next two criticisms Dembski addresses concern the religious and scientific status of his design inference. His intention is to uphold both the religious neutrality and the scientific respectability of the inference. The first criticism, says Dembski, is that "design is nothing but scientific creationism cloaked in newer and more sophisticated terminology."[13] Dembski dodges this charge with the simple ruse of distancing himself from the specific literalist claims of creationism and asserting that intelligent design theory by contrast has no prior religious commitments. Creationism, however, is a red herring. The real issue is whether the designer of the design inference is a deity.

Dembski denies any implication of divine design, stating unequivocally that design theory is "devoid of religious commitments."[14] "Intelligent design is theologically minimalist. It detects intelligence without speculating about the nature of the intelligence. . . . Intelligent design is under no obligation to speculate about the nature, moral character or purposes of any designing intelligence it happens to infer."[15] The job of identifying the nature of the designer he leaves for theologians.[16] Here Dembski is reminiscent of the medieval theologians who held to the doctrine of negative attributes. Where these theologians feared that any given attribute would limit God and thus deny God's infinite nature, Dembski perhaps suspects that any specific identification of God would subject his theory to criticism. Like our contemporary politicians, he finds that the best way to avoid censure is to remain vague. In rejecting naturalistic explanations, Dembski is careful to say that he is not thereby accepting supernatural ones. The proper contrast, he claims, is between natural causes and intelligent causes. Of course, it is difficult to conceive of what sort of intelligent cause he could have in mind besides a supernatural one, given that the cause in question is responsible for the very structure of the universe.

Although Dembski seems to be proposing a conception of intelligent design so general and vague that it appears immune to philosophical and theological objections, he does claim that intelligent designers cannot have originated by naturalistic processes and that they must be nonphysical. He argues that the sort of intelligence responsible for design cannot have a naturalistic origin, on the grounds that only nonnaturalistic agents can generate complex specified information and that any other claim illicitly presupposes naturalism.[17] He also rules out physical designers: "No intelligent agent who is strictly physical could have presided over the origin of the universe or the origin of life."[18] In addition to being nonnaturalistic and nonphysical, we might also presume that the designer possesses adequate knowledge, power, and desire to preside over the origin of life and the universe.

Such a designer is of course "supernatural," even if Dembski eschews the word. Indeed, why would identifying the nature of the designer be a job for the theologian if the designer weren't supernatural? Why would the book *Intelligent Design* be self-consciously about reconciling science and theology? Because designers do not exist in the abstract, it seems fair to ask Dembski exactly how such a nonphysical being interacts with physical things in designing life and the universe (our familiar problem of dualism), what the probability is of there being such an entity in the first place, and why such a superior being would want to make its design work evident to advocates of the design inference. Although not a brand of "young-earth creationism,"[19] Dembski's design inference is clearly religious. While this in itself is no criticism, Dembski can at best postpone but not avoid the philosophical, theological, and probabilistic questions lying in wait for whatever sort of nonnatural, nonphysical intelligent designer he intends to infer.

Scientific Status

Other critics of design fault it not for being religious but for failing to achieve respectable scientific status. Dembski is particularly intent on rebuffing such criticism, because one of the distinctive features of the design inference, as he envisions it, is its empirical and mathematically rigorous character. Dembski's defense strategy is to consider a number of the usual features of scientific theories, e.g., falsifiability, predictive success, and tentativeness, and to argue that, for each feature, there are scientific theories that lack it. We do not wish to dispute this point, for scientific fields range from the highly mathematical (physics) to the historical (evolution) to the social (sociology), and many respected theories lack one of the above features. What Dembski fails to realize, though, is that his design inferences lack *all* the features of good scientific theories. Because his filter is purely eliminative and because Dembski refuses to identify the designer, design inferences amount to purely negative attacks on competing explanations. As such, they make no predictions, not even probabilistic—let alone quantitatively precise and falsifiable—ones. Indeed, their eliminativist structure renders them unfalsifiable and anything but tentative. They are empirical in the broad sense that they deal with observational subject matter, but not in the scientifically relevant sense of being subject to experimental confirmation. Despite appearances, they possess no quantitative precision, as we shall show later, in the discussion of the applicability of mathematics to design inferences, and can boast no widespread agreement on the probabilities with which they deal. And, as we have argued above, they show no explanatory power whatsoever.

Regarding the issue of testability, Dembski's claim that "intelligent design is indeed testable, and it has been confirmed across a wide range of disciplines, spanning everything from natural history to molecular biology to information theory"[20] amounts to a confusion between invoking design and actually testing it. Besides, Dembski's definition of testability—"sensitiv[ity] to new evidence and to further theoretical insight"—hardly qualifies as a scientifically rigorous test.[21] In short, Dembski's preoccupation with what he sees as a prejudice in favor of methodological naturalism blinds him to the failure of his design theory to achieve *any* of the merits of scientific theories, even if no scientific theory achieves all of them.

Suboptimal Design

The next criticism, that biology abounds with examples of less than perfect design, repeats one of the Epicurean arguments against divine creation. The criticism returns us to the issue of the designer's nature. Dembski argues that, unless one is dealing with a designer who is free to be a perfectionist, all design must involve compromise. Here, Dembski reminds us of Plato's Timaeus, who claimed that the Craftsman had to compromise between his idea and the necessary imperfection of his materials (see p. 138). Hence, apparently suboptimal designs might represent optimal compromises (as in Leibniz's best of all possible worlds) or, for that matter, intentional suboptimality. However plausible this response might be, it undermines Dembski's policy of refusing to characterize the designer. Any claim about a designer's motives—its desire for optimal compromise, intentional suboptimality, or lack of perfectionism—is a claim about the aesthetic and moral characteristics from which Dembski wishes to distance himself. Any claim about the trade-offs under which a designer must operate is a claim to knowledge of the environment in which the designer operated—presumably a quite tentative claim in the case of the designer of the universe. Yet Dembski must venture just this sort of claim, i.e., he must once again identify the designer, if he is to avoid the problem of the universe's imperfect nature. In addition, he must both estimate the likelihood that a designer whom he identifies as simultaneously superpowerful and subject to severe design constraints fashioned biological structures and show that the likelihood of a designer's doing so exceeds the likelihood that natural selection cobbled together these same structures.

It is interesting to note how puzzling a strategy Dembski has chosen in shouldering the problem of suboptimal design. Because evolution proceeds by cobbling together from available materials whatever works, regardless of its long-term benefits or its moral and aesthetic characteristics, evolutionary explanations of suboptimal design are particularly compelling. Suboptimality is exactly what one would expect from such a mindless process. More importantly, Dembski seems to be under no obligation to justify suboptimal designs in the first place. After all, he never claims that the complex specified information the explanatory filter detects must be in any way optimized. To accept a gratuitous burden of proof in an arena in which naturalistic explanations enjoy a distinct competitive advantage perhaps seems foolhardy.

Anthropic Selection Effect

The next objection to the design inference that Dembski considers is aimed at the cosmological instances of apparent design: "Design in nature is an anthropic coincidence. . . . It's incredibly improbable that nature should be organized just the way it is; but if it weren't, we wouldn't be here to appreciate that fact."[22] The objection claims, in other words, that a simple selection effect, not design, accounts for the apparent fine tuning of the universe. Dembski rebuts this anthropic selection effect argument by claiming that it relies on the assumption of multiple universes (from which our actual, life-supporting universe is selected) and thereby commits an "inflationary fallacy" of multiplying worlds that are in principle unobservable. The shortcoming of Dembski's response is that multiple universes are not the only way of making sense of the universe's apparent fine tuning without invoking design. A more parsimonious alternative is to claim that the current gaps in cosmological theories will be filled, as such gaps have been filled in the past, rather than that the various instances of apparent fine tuning are all the work of a divine designer. To argue otherwise is to run the risk of committing the god-of-the-gaps fallacy.

There are, moreover, effective criticisms of "anthropic fine tuning" arguments for design that have nothing to do with the multiple universes on which Dembski focuses and that he does not address.[23] Dembski's own distinction between "specificational" and "probabilistic" resources can be appropriated to clarify these criticisms. The distinction can be illustrated with a lottery example. Although one's chance of winning the state lottery might be tiny, one can increase one's chances dramatically by buying enough tickets, i.e., by increasing one's specificational resources. Alternatively, one can increase one's chances by entering multiple lotteries, i.e., by bolstering one's probabilistic resources. In short, both specificational and probabilistic resources must be taken into account to assess one's actual chance of being a winner. The probability of being a winner increases in direct proportion to any increase in specificational or probabilistic resources.

Design arguments based on fine tuning rely on the claim that the basic physical setup of the universe is highly improbable unless a designer created it. But, as Dembski's distinction teaches us, we need to consider specificational and probabilistic resources in order to assess the true probability in question. Unfortunately for Dembski, there are at least three reasons for thinking the relevant specificational resources high enough to preclude any argument of creation by design.

(1) The very omnipotence that enables God to create the entire universe and the laws governing it ex nihilo and then to violate those laws at will in the performance of miracles prevents him from being constrained by the tight requirements embodied in the fine-tuning argument. In other words, the traditional Judeo-Christian-Islamic theist's belief that God is not bound by physical constraints undermines the claim that the universe would not have been habitable if it had not been set up like it was. An omnipotent God can achieve habitability—and other equally significant outcomes—in myriad ways. Hence, the specificational resources are as great as God's power.

Another way of thinking about the tension between claims to fine tuning and belief in an omnipotent designer is to consider that fine-tuning arguments rely essentially on imaginative pictures of what the universe would have been like if certain parameters (such as the relative masses of the proton and electron) had been different—while everything else, including the laws that determine what is physically possible, is held constant. The theist, however, has no reason to limit himself to what is physically possible under current physical laws when he imagines the ways the universe could have been created. He has no reason to hold constant the laws of nature, for the creator of those laws is not restricted by them. The theist has no reason to hold *anything* (except perhaps the laws of logic) constant and hence no grounds for arguing that the universe is finely tuned relative to the constancy of various laws. Given the possibility that the laws of physics themselves could have differed in countless ways at the behest of their creator, it is impossible to limit the relevant specificational resources (i.e., the ways of getting a habitable universe or something equally interesting) and hence impossible to defend the incredibly low probabilities associated with fine-tuning arguments.

(2) The traditional theistic belief in conscious, intelligent, and moral—but nonphysical—beings (immortal souls, angels, God himself) runs counter to the argument that finely tuned physical conditions are necessary for the emergence of conscious, intelligent, and moral creatures. The whole issue of fine tuning concerns physical entities such as stars and galaxies and perhaps even human bodies, but has nothing whatsoever to do with souls. If, despite the stories of angelic beings as exemplars of both human excellence and human depravity, one insists that any imaginable universe without embodied intelligence is paltry compared with one with it, one has merely pushed the problem back a step and must resort to the questionable strategy of arguing that intelligence can be embodied (even by an omnipotent designer) only in "life as we know it" and only in a universe structured within the remarkably fine constraints on which the fine-tuning argument is based. In short, the innumerable possibilities of unfamiliar intelligent beings, embodied or not, increase the specificational resources enough to remove the original motivation for a fine-tuning argument.

(3) A third reason for thinking the specificational resources high has to do with the insignificance of the outcome of the fine tuning rather than with the multiple ways of obtaining equally significant outcomes. If merely getting close to winning the lottery (e.g., by purchasing a ticket in the right store) counts as significant, then specificational resources have in effect been increased, because the "target area" of significance has expanded. Now, the mere habitability of the universe, with no guarantee of any sort of life arising in it, is the true subject of the fine tuning and is a much larger target area of significance than would be the actual occurrence of intelligent life. Even if, contrary to what we have argued above, the designer must engage in extreme fine tuning to obtain a universe in which intelligence, embodied or not, is possible, it remains the case that a merely habitable universe is not particularly significant, especially when compared with an actually inhabited one. The ruling out of equally significant outcomes, which is part and parcel of probability arguments, will thus be exceedingly hard to accomplish. An uninhabitable world of exquisite beauty, for example, seems at least as significant as one that is ugly and lifeless, albeit habitable. The case for fine tuning thus reduces to this: if the universe had not been finely tuned for habitability, it would have lacked significance in all respects that are at least on a par with habitability. The ease of being on a par with habitability is the crux of this third argument that specificational resources are high enough to block any anthropic fine-tuning argument.

Unfortunately, there is no guarantee that probabilistic resources will be low enough, either, for the fine-tuning argument to go through. But first a point about the uncertainty of the probability figures themselves.

Just as one must know something about the administration of a lottery before determining the probability of a given ticket winning, so too one must know something about the range of values that the universe's various parameters can take on, about the processes in the very early universe that determine these values, and about the probabilities associated with each value in comparison with all the others in the range. But these are just the things we do *not* know about the early universe. Assuming that our ignorance of the probabilities makes them all equal, the proponent of the argument from design proceeds to claim that we have a one in ten-to-the-whatever chance of having galaxies and the like. This is like claiming that there is a one in fifty-two chance of drawing the ace of spades from a deck of cards—without any information on whether the deck is a standard one, how many cards are in it, whether it has been shuffled, how many aces of spades it contains, etc. To make such probability estimates in the first place is foolish; to dignify them with mathematical precision—which is the secret of their appeal— is plain flimflam.

Just as ignorance of the probabilities governing the values that various parameters can take on is no reason to assume that all those values are equally probable, so too ignorance of the total number of "trails" there have been in universe-formation is no reason to assume that there has been only one trail and hence that probabilistic resources are minimal. Cosmologists have proposed various multiple-universe hypotheses, as well as various scenarios in which the Big Bang was but a local occurrence in an unimaginably vast universe. Because the theist is the one making the probability assertions here, he bears the burden of ruling out these scenarios and of guaranteeing that probabilistic resources are low enough for his argument to work. If he cannot rule out these scenarios— and he does not seem able to—he will be like the man amazed to see a full house dealt in a game of poker because he has failed to consider the total number of poker games and the consequently rather high probability of full houses being dealt from time to time.

Applicability of Mathematics

Dembski's response to the next objection, that "specified complexity is a purely mathematical construct and therefore irrelevant to biology," also targets a red herring.[24] The problem is not that mathematics is irrelevant or that anyone harbors a disdain for mathematics, but rather that natural selection is resourceful enough to prevent the probability of a biological structure's having been selected for from being anywhere near as low as the design inference requires.

Dembski illustrates his basic intuitions about design with the easy cases of coin tosses, card games, and the like, which have little relevance to the probabilities associated with biological structures and which, incidentally, involve probabilities well above those necessary for design inferences. When he turns to calculating biological probabilities, he takes pure chance rather than selection as the relevant hypothesis on which his probability calculations are based, and hence he ends up with a calculation that is totally irrelevant, even if it is mathematically correct. The probability of getting various DNA or amino-acid sequences by chance alone, for example, has nothing to do with the probability of getting these same sequences by natural selection. Dembski's discussion of the functionality of amino acids and proteins—a matter crucial to his probability calculations—completely ignores functional multiplicity. His computations therefore falsely underestimate the probability of getting a specific function and are irrelevant to determining the likelihood that a particular amino acid or protein arose by natural selection. Dembski has failed to show that $P(E/H)$ is less than 10^{-150} given every possible chance and selective hypothesis.

A separate issue that hampers Dembski's calculations is the ambiguity of the event whose probability is being calculated. Defined generally enough, an event can be made as probable as one likes; defined narrowly enough, as improbable. What, for example, is the "event" of a bird's having a wing capable of flight? Should the blackness of the feathers or their length to the nearest millimeter be included in the description of the event? Should the event be defined more generally, as the occurrence of a wing that permits flight? Or should the description be even more general: that an organism has *some* adaptation relevant to its reproductive success? Nowhere does Dembski give a nonarbitrary, determinate definition to the events whose probability is critical to the design inference and whose scope of definition directly affects the relevant probabilities. Without such a definition, which it is incumbent on Dembski to provide, the applicability of mathematics to the elements of the explanatory filter remains ambiguous. This ambiguity in how events are defined leads to an interesting paradox[25]: the conjunction of several events may be improbable enough to reject chance, whereas each of the events may be probable enough not to reject chance. Hence, Dembski is in the awkward position of having to say that a group of events individually explainable by chance is itself a result of design, assuming of course that an event that is the conjunction of the several events is itself specified. Thus our consideration of the applicability of mathematics shows that Dembski underestimates the probabilities associated with natural selection and that ambiguities in his definition of the events to be explained undermine a mathematically rigorous science of design.

Hume's Objections

The final two objections Dembski treats are closely related. The first is derived from David Hume: "design in biology is either an argument from analogy or an inductive generalization based on a sample of size zero."[26] Hume meant that analogies drawn from human design and applied to divine design are always strained because we lack the experience of universe-formation from which we can formulate general principles. Dembski responds that design arguments are inferences to the best explanation rather than arguments from analogy or inductive generalizations.[27] But here Dembski creates a more difficult problem for himself than Hume's original one. Because, as Dembski notes,[28] inferences to the best explanation involve a direct comparison of competing probabilities, he commits himself to comparing the relative likelihoods of design and natural selection. The assessment of these probabilities draws on the very sorts of objectionable analogies and generalizations that Hume originally had in mind. By appropriating inference to the best explanation, Dembski combines Hume's problems with the new and significant problem of having to identify the designer in order to compare the probabilities associated with its work to the probabilities associated with the operation of natural selection.

We can now summarize the consequences of Dembski's refusal to speculate about the nature of the designer: the explanatory filter is blocked at either of its first two stages with arbitrarily improbable hypotheses of regularity or selection; design lacks explanatory power and hence scientific respectability; the charge is left standing that his design inference is intrinsically religious; there is no answer to the challenge of less than perfect design; and, finally, there is no way of appealing to inference to the best explanation in response to Hume's objections.

Transcendent Designers

The criticism that "we have no experience of transcendent designers and can make no scientific claims about them" is a restatement of the objection to arguments from analogy.[29] Dembski's response—that we have no direct access to a human's internal states either—misses the point, given that we do in fact have access to human but not to divine *artifacts*. The problem remains that the farther one goes from human agency, the weaker the design inference becomes. The reason we can conclude that artifacts of unknown purpose in the Smithsonian Institute were designed (a favorite example of both Dembski and Behe) is precisely that we are familiar with the work of human designers. We would have a much harder time identifying objects that only a superpowerful extraterrestrial or an omnipotent deity could design: we have very little idea of the likelihood of there being such agents, much less the sorts of things they might design.[30]

Conclusion on the Intelligent Design Research Program

Having now discussed the nine criticisms of the intelligent design research program that Dembski considers, we need hardly point out that we believe his efforts to defend intelligent design against its critics have not been successful. Indeed, the program faces intractable problems—not the least of which involves the identification of the designer. Although the invocation of intelligent design, in the manner in which Dembski invokes it, might well be a popularly cited method of harmonizing religion and science, it does not stand up to careful scrutiny or qualify as anything approaching a viable option. We turn now to three contemporary thinkers who suggest other options for reconciling God, religion, and science.

KEITH WARD

Keith Ward, Regius Professor of Divinity at Oxford, is the author of *God, Chance, and Necessity*,[31] which treats the two principal questions on which contemporary discussions tend to focus, the creation of the world and the theory of evolution that leads to—or results in, if "leads to" is too loaded a term—human beings. One might note in passing that these two subjects are of course both taken up in the opening chapter of Genesis, a fact that is no coincidence. Human beings perhaps naturally divide the world into two parts, themselves as one part, everything else as the other. Given the philosophical tendency towards dualism, we might equally see the distinction of two parts as one that contains conscious, rational thought and one that is wholly material. (For those to whom the essence of humankind is conscious rationality and not a composite of rationality and body, the division devolves into one of matter and mind, or, if mind is a form of spirit, into matter and spirit.) In other words, modern discussions, however much they may assert the independent novelty of their approaches, reflect the ancient formulation of the questions, in a way similar to how in evolution theory chimpanzees and human beings show a common ancestor.[32] Then again, the development of the universe and the appearance of conscious rationality present considerable challenges to the ability of humans to explain their surroundings.

Ward makes it plain at the beginning of his book that his enemies are those who adopt "a form of materialism which is entirely hostile to religion, and which mocks any idea of objective purpose and value in the universe."[33] He will take aim, in other words, at those modern Epicureans who reduce all of nature to atoms and the laws that govern physics. His targets will also include the physicists who think that the laws of nature make God superfluous and those who believe that evolution is a product of mere undirected chance. The scope of his criticism thus encompasses both metaphysical issues (materialism) and methodological ones (the adequacy of various forms of explanation). His thesis is that for the generation of the world and all living things there are three explanatory possibilities—chance, the necessity inherent in the materials used, and God. Of the three, he considers God the best explanation.[34] His formulation of the various possibilities is somewhat reminiscent of the character Timaeus whom Plato invents in his dialogue *Timaeus*. In the *Timaeus*, chance was rejected outright as an explanation of the origin of the universe, as it was for all the ancients except the atomists. Timaeus developed a theory that the Craftsman (i.e., the Demiurge) applied mind to the materials, working within the constraints imposed by the "necessity" of those materials (i.e., the physical laws inherent in the materials). Although Timaeus's "necessity" referred to the defects caused by the *corporeality* of the world, Ward speaks of "necessity" as a causal explanation, as the idea "that there is only one logically consistent set of quantum laws which, operating over some form of primeval energy, inevitably gives rise to a universe like this sooner or later."[35] Underlying both senses of necessity is a set of inevitable results flowing from what the physical substrate comprises.

Ward, like Timaeus, observes that the world conforms to laws. The Big Bang, too, conforms to laws, for even quantum events are described by rigorous laws of probability.[36] Scientists, he says, are willing to accept the reality of the laws; they are willing to accept the beauty in the laws and in the theories that describe the universe by means of those laws. But natural scientists are unwilling to accept God as the original author of the laws and of the beauty. They will acknowledge that everything *since* the Big Bang has occurred with an explainable cause; but the Big Bang itself, as well as the laws governing it and all its results, "just happened." Ward thinks it more likely that the Big Bang happened because of God. The discussion echoes that in question 2 of Aquinas's *Summa Theologica*.[37] The question there is whether everything can be explained in terms of nature alone or whether we need to invoke God. Aquinas points out that if we *define* God as nature or as the author of nature, then the problem evaporates. If we do not so define God, we remain with the problem of how nature came into being. Aquinas and Aristotle— and Ward—are content to attribute the first cause to God. Scientists might balk at the word *God,* but perhaps they would not balk too forcefully if God were acknowledged as a substitute for the words "just happened" or "for some unknown reason" as in "the Big Bang *just happened*" or "the Big Bang happened *for some unknown reason.*" But, of course, those who believe in God—including Ward— will not be content with such enfeebling identifications of God.

If scientists can be shown to operate on the basis of faith, Ward seems to feel that they will be persuaded to accept God. So he tries to show that indeed they *do* have faith (albeit not in God).[38] They have faith that the world can be comprehended by human minds; they have faith that the operations of physics will yield to reason; they have faith in truth and that humans can comprehend it; they have faith in the goodness of the universe, by which Ward means that the universe "is friendly to investigation." All these, he says, are examples of a faith that is "identical" to religious faith. As Ward puts it, "Faith in the comprehensibility of the universe is in fact faith in the ultimate truth, beauty and goodness of reality, in the virtue of pursuing them, and in the certain hope of eventually finding them."[39] It seems to us, however, that Ward is here indulging in rhetorical fancy, if not overstatement, in an effort to win over some who may not be firmly committed to the view that science and religion are different areas of investigation. The rhetoric is effective. Since he has just been discussing modern laws of physics, he seems to have established his scientific credentials. But of course he is wholly failing to distinguish the variations in degrees of certainty and belief that we discussed earlier (see p. 17). The faith that religions demand concerns matters that appear contradictory or are violations of nature or defy any known mechanisms. Among the great examples of men with faith in the Hebrew Bible are Abraham and Job, both of whom believed, or seem to have believed, matters quite self-contradictory. Abraham believed simultaneously that he would sacrifice his son Isaac and be the father of many nations through the same Isaac.[40] Job believed simultaneously that he has not sinned and that God does not allow sinless men to suffer. In the New Testament, Paul requires Christians to believe the extraordinary propositions that

Jesus was both man and God, that he died and came back to life, that his death atoned for sinful mankind, and that he was born of a virgin. These are quite unlike the subjects of the faith that Ward grants to scientists. A scientist's faith (even as Ward has described it) is more fittingly called "confidence," for it is more akin to saying, "Because I have successfully completed problem 1 on this examination, I have faith (i.e., confidence) that I can successfully complete problem 2." This is not *religious* faith. In other words, scientific faith is based on induction from past success and is *methodological*. It represents a confident pragmatism about successful methods. Religious faith, by contrast, involves belief without evidence, belief in the seemingly absurd, or belief much stronger than is rationally justified.

For Ward, as for Newton, the laws of physics are created by the mind of God. This view is quite different from saying that the laws of physics are the mind of God (as Spinoza said), for it makes God a separate entity, that is, separate from the laws. The notion has deep problems, however, problems that were observed of old and constituted the challenge of explaining how God could be eternal and unchanging yet create. The chief problem, of course, is that creation implies a change from nonbeing to being. This is Ward's discussion:

> The divine mind does not come into being, since it always exists, as the conceiver of all possibilities. If it has come into being, it would once have been merely possible. But then, *ex hypothesi,* it would already have to have been conceived in the mind of God, which cannot therefore have been merely possible. So the mind of God can never come into being. Like numbers, it must always exist, and it can be the source of any actual universe. The mind of God is not "nothing" (though one may well say that it is not a—finite—thing). It is a necessarily existing source of all actuality, which actualises a subset of possibilities by a contingent act of will. . . . [This argument] does not eliminate God at all. On the contrary, it provides a rather elegant way of getting at an important part of what is meant by the word "God."[41]

We can hear in Ward's words echoes of the ancient thinkers. In "it [the mind of God] must always exist" we hear Aristotle's always-existing Prime Mover who is pure actuality (see p.100); in "it [the mind of God] is a necessarily existing source of all actuality, which actualises a subset of possibilities by a contingent act of will" we hear the familiar vexing problem that led the Neoplatonists to their theory of emanation (see p. 111). In Ward's theory we can also detect Platonic notions, for Ward maintains, as does the Platonic school, that the ideas *reside* in the eternal mind of God, what Platonists called the "World of Being," but are *actualized* in the temporal actual universe, what Platonists call the "World of Becoming." But the mechanism by which the nonphysical can create the physical remains elusive.

In chapter 6 we observed that in traditional stories having God as a participant, both pagan and biblical, the deity communicates with people in ways that seem not to violate the natural order by influencing those natural occurrences that are not predictable or explainable by everyday humans (see pp. 128–29). For example, it is in the natural order of things that birds will often fly either to the right or to the left, but the direction is not normally within a human's power to determine. Ancient augurs claimed that the gods expressed their will through the direction of the flight and that through augury they could understand that will. For example, Livy reports that the decision of whether Romulus or Remus would be king of Rome was to have been decided by augury.[42] Or, as in the case of Jonah in the storm at sea, a drawing of lots enabled God to designate the person responsible for some malady. In the same way, the deity traditionally has caused diseases, earthquakes, and other natural events, operating invisibly through what seem to be events outside of human control.[43]

The idea that God works through what appear chance events is of fundamental importance for Ward and shows a continuity with ancient thinking. His exposition of the principle incorporates contemporary physics, just as we have observed scientists throughout the ages incorporating the physics of their day. Ward notes that according to quantum cosmology, in the 10^{-41} second after the Big Bang (the Planck time), the universe would have been only 10^{-33} cm across and so subject to quantum effects.[44] Quantum effects by their very nature cannot be predicted, but they are nevertheless subject to *probabilistic laws.* Our universe, he says, would have come into being only if the *probabilistic laws* at this crucial moment came out just so. That they were just so is highly indicative of the work of God, who, in his omnipotence, can use even probabilistic laws.

The genius of modern physics has been to conceive of probabilistic laws. Neither ancient natural philosophers nor those of the Enlightenment could conceive of such laws. The most that the ancient Epicureans could do to introduce unpredictability into their system was to assert a swerve, some unexplainable, purely indeterministic alteration in the downward fall of the atoms through the void. The swerve was a critical component of Epicurean physics, for without the swerve, there was no possibility of the atoms' combining or of free will. (In just the same way, some modern writers attribute free will to random quantum fluctuations!)[45] The swerve "just happened." Even the deities in the Epicurean system, like everything else, were made out of atoms and so were subject to deterministic laws, except, of course, for the occasional swerve. The swerve was a contrivance appropriately subjected to ridicule, and it rendered the whole system doubtful.

Also attempting to detect God's handiwork in the basic laws and structure of the universe are those who maintain what has come to be called the "anthropic principle." Although Ward does not use this term (and it does not appear in his book's index), he very much subscribes to ideas surrounding it.[46] The principle incorporates the true observation that even very small changes in some of the basic physical features of the universe just after the Big Bang, slight changes in the strengths of fundamental forces, infinitesimal changes in the masses or charges of subatomic particles—any one of these would have rendered the universe unsuitable for human life.[47] Although we have already discussed the anthropic principle in detail in our criticism of arguments for intelligent design (see pp. 263ff.), we might note here that a cockroach might make the same claim, if it could speak, for if any of the physical laws were ever so slightly different, there would be no cockroaches. And, no doubt, a bacterium born three billion years ago could have made the same claim (if it could have spoken). That the principle is in fact true would not be changed if we changed its name to the "roach principle" or the "bacterium principle" or the "rock principle" (for such and such a rock would surely not exist if the laws of the universe or the fundamental constants of nature were different). Indeed, the principle might refer even to an individual and not a species, for if the rules of the universe were different, a particular man, say, John Jacob Jingleheimer Schmidt, would not be here, and so it might just as well be the "John Jacob Jingleheimer Schmidt Principle." We might also note Ward's readiness to claim knowledge of the various possibilities and probabilities associated with the most basic features of the universe. Like other defenders of the anthropic principle, he claims to know, for example, that "many other arrays [of fundamental forces] and sets of laws [of the universe] are possible"[48] and, in another context, that the mathematical intelligibility of these laws is "immensely improbable."[49] As David Hume noted in the eighteenth century, however, claims about possibilities and probabilities are intrinsically speculative when applied to the universe as a whole (see p. 232).

If we leave aside the issue of probability as applied to the basic structure of the universe, we can consider the even more pressing issue of probability as applied to various explanations of the universe. As we have often observed, the issue of the prior probability of a hypothesis is as important as the issue of the explanatory power of that hypothesis when evaluating the hypothesis's plausibility. To assert the merits of a hypothesis on the basis of its explanatory power alone is insufficient, for such a strategy opens the door to wildly implausible—albeit powerfully explanatory—hypotheses. For example, if one postulates the existence of an extremely intelligent and powerful alien whose life's mission is to arrange the dust particles on one's office shelves, one has indeed come up with a hypothesis that would explain the dusty shelves. Such a hypothesis, however, is so implausible that its implausibility more than compensates for its (admittedly great) explanatory power. If the logic of explanation did not constrain explanations in this manner, there would be no limit on the sorts of imaginative yet bogus explanations one could advance.

Because Ward's overall position is that theism provides a better explanation than naturalistic alternatives, he must accept the task not only of showing that theism explains the phenomena but of arguing that the prior probability of theism is high. Ward fully accepts this responsibility. Although he issues the warning that it is "very doubtful whether the idea of probability applies to God at all" because "God is either necessary or God is impossible," he concludes that the existence of God, like all other (in his mind) necessary truths, has a probability of 1.[50]

On the surface, Ward's claim appears compelling, especially if one sympathizes with Anselm's ontological argument, which asserts that God cannot possibly fail to exist, i.e., that the probability of God's existence is as high as possible. If Anselm and Ward are correct, then the prior probability of God's existence, unlike that of the intelligent alien, cannot compromise the high explanatory power Ward has been intent on establishing. Unfortunately, there is a serious flaw in Ward's reasoning. Even if the *existence* of God has a probability of 1, the intention of God *to create* just the sort of world we observe may have a much lower probability. The probability of God's existence, considered abstractly, as in the ontological argument and in considerations of the necessity of God's existence, carries no guarantee that the probability of God's creating what he has allegedly created will be similarly high. A necessary being and a creator are distinct concepts.

It is important to note that all of Ward's arguments for the explanatory power of theism concern God in his creative capacity, not in his capacity as necessary being. Thus, for example, Ward argues that a benevolent God's desire to create valuable and beautiful things explains value and beauty in the world. A necessary being, insofar as it is a necessary being, would remain inscrutable as to creative desires and would thus be useless in establishing explanatory power. But just such a necessary being, considered precisely insofar as it is a necessary being, is what drives the argument for the high prior probability of theism. What is missing is a link between these two conceptions of God. Without such a link, an equivocation infects Ward's whole argument for the explanatory power of theism, namely, an equivocation between the necessary God whose prior probability is high and the creative God whose explanatory power is high.

Concluding his discussion of cosmogony, Ward embraces Anselm explicitly,[51] echoes Aristotle and Leibniz, and embraces the ancient and medieval doctrine of the inexpressibility of God's nature. He says that God is a cosmic mind that contemplates all the possibilities that could ever exist in any universe.[52] "Out of all the possibilities that exist, there is one possible being that actualises supreme perfection, the highest set of compossible values."[53] This, he says, is God. God is a cosmic mind who not only contemplates all possible values, but also chooses the best ones for himself, and he does this as pure actuality. For Ward, all this makes sense and "explains the existence of any universe that is elegantly formed to realise states of distinctive value, states that could not exist in any other universe." Finally, he writes, "The cosmic mind is beyond speech and utterance, beyond duality and description, beyond being as we can understand it, without beginning or end, without limitation or boundary."[54] Here is the doctrine of the *via negativa,* that is, that God can be spoken about only in terms of what he is not, since his nature is too mysterious to be described, too unlimited to be confined by any human words. What is striking, we think, is that Ward's system is a mélange of the various attempts of his predecessors, going back to antiquity, to save the marriage of God and science. Like those predecessors, he adheres both to traditional views of God and to the laws of physics as currently understood.

Ward next takes up the other major subject that challenges God and science—evolution. Just as in the Middle Ages one had to be an Aristotelian to be taken seriously as a scientist, so today anyone who denies or doubts evolution is relegated to an intellectual life on the margin. The challenge for those who would reconcile God and biology is somehow to reject the implications of Darwinism (a term that will be used here synonymously with "evolution theory") that would seem to render superfluous the guiding hand of a purposeful deity while at the same time adhering to enough of the theory so as not to be laughed out of academic circles. Ward accepts the basic view of Arthur Peacocke that God uses natural selection—the core of Darwinism—for his own purposes.[55] God is the true author of Darwinism, as he was of classical and relativistic mechanics.[56]

The genius of Darwin's theory of natural selection is that it offers a purely mechanical algorithm for evolutionary change. An organism with a characteristic that gives it even a minor advantage in passing on its genetic code succeeds in the evolutionary contest.[57] As the environment changes or as a species migrates to a different environment, those individuals with a greater ability to survive and reproduce in the new environment will pass along their genes with greater success, and so the species as a whole will gradually come to possess those advantages, provided, of course, that there is adequate selection pressure. We are all descended from some primordial living form whose DNA has developed by accretion and substitution through several billion years, with many creatures becoming extinct and new ones appearing. For individual creatures, the main occupations were eating, avoiding being eaten, and surviving long enough to reproduce. Species evolved over long stretches of time the various behaviors or attributes that helped them reproduce in the various environments in which they found themselves. Darwin's theory, described here in a very bald form with only a nod to its monumental synthesis with modern genetics, not only makes no mention of God and purpose—as one would expect from a methodologically naturalistic theory—but also, with its strikingly powerful explanatory mechanisms, seems to render explanation in terms of divine purpose superfluous.[58]

Of the several phenomena that Ward thinks theism explains better than does evolutionary theory or any other brand of naturalism, we shall focus on consciousness as representative of his views. As a dualist and antireductionist, Ward sees consciousness as qualitatively distinct from physical or biological processes.

> Conscious experiences are radically new elements of reality, which seem to come into existence when a certain stage of physically complex structure exists. We do not know why the firing of neurones in the brain should give rise to particular sensations or thoughts, though we assume that they do.[59]

It is important to realize that two sorts of questions can be asked about consciousness: (1) what it is and (2) whether evolution or theism better explains its presence in human beings. Although much of Ward's discussion involves saddling evolution theory with the first question, a notoriously difficult one for both the philosopher and the theist, Ward's answer to the second question is unequivocal: "The existence of consciousness is the refutation of materialism. It presents one with facts no materialist account could ever explain, in principle."[60] Ward's view, then, is that theism is the better explanation of consciousness, because it is the *only* explanation of that qualitatively unique phenomenon.

There are several ways in which Ward fails to give due credit to the opposing view, namely, to evolutionary accounts of consciousness. Instead of addressing the key issue of gradations in consciousness from humans to other primates and other mammals, and instead of dealing with the well-known proposals of how various degrees of consciousness serve various adaptive functions, Ward concerns himself entirely with claims about the impossibility of consciousness arising from physical entities or processes and about the plausibility of teleological explanations of consciousness.

Aside from assuming that dualism is true, Ward's arguments show no appreciation for the concept of emergent properties. For example, to say that a calculator is a physical object reducible to material entities that obey electromagnetic laws is not to deny that it performs calculations in a way that a bundle of wire or pile of copper cannot. Complex and intricate objects often exhibit emergent capabilities that in an important sense transcend the laws governing their individual parts. An example might be drawn from economics, where the competitive pressures arising from independently operating manufacturers lead to improved products for consumers. In his failure to acknowledge that complex organisms, especially those with brains, exhibit a host of properties that go beyond the individual cells and proteins that constitute them, Ward is not giving evolution its due. The reality of emergent properties reveals that he is attacking a straw man when he assumes that all reductionism is what Daniel Dennett calls "greedy reductionism,"[61] as, for example, Ward's claims that "materialist theories end up by denying the very realities of conscious experience they set out to explain"[62] or that "the materialist . . . simply eliminates the experienced world, or at best describes it as a causal by-product of the physical world."[63] Dennett's "good reductionism," which Ward does not acknowledge, recognizes emergent properties.

Ward also underestimates the efficacy of by-products in the evolutionist's arsenal of arguments. He wrongly assumes, for example, that "mere" by-products of physical processes can play no causal role in modifying those processes.[64] First of all, *every* product of evolution is a by-product, because none of the products are intentionally designed. Concerning consciousness itself, it is obvious that states of consciousness (e.g., embarrassment) affect physical states (e.g., by causing one to blush).[65] Regardless of how consciousness arose and regardless of whether consciousness involves an immaterial mind or just amounts to the workings of the brain, it is a fact that consciousness affects our bodily states. To criticize consciousness for being a by-product is therefore fallacious from the beginning.[66]

Failing to give evolution theory full credit, Ward says, "It is incredible to suppose that the brain originates by chance, and then translates its electrochemical states quite unpredictably into thoughts, feelings, and sensations."[67] This too is a straw man argument, for no evolutionist believes that chance alone—without selection operating over eons—gave rise to the human brain or that the translation of brain states into perceptions is unpredictable. In a similar vein, Ward avers,

> For an extreme Darwinian, it must always be an odd mischance, the incredible result of a million small errors in replication, that the universe, in human beings, has begun to understand its own structure and adapt it purposively to create a more stable and unequivocally desirable environment. How incredible it is that out of so many mistakes has emerged an outcome of such value![68]

Again, Ward speaks of Darwinism as if devoid of any mechanism of selection. Furthermore, genetic transcription errors are nothing like "mistakes" in the ordinary, negative sense of the term. Hence, the last sentence quoted above is no more than rhetoric. (We leave it for the reader to evaluate whether the environment we humans are creating is "unequivocally desirable.")

Besides failing to give evolution theory its due explanatory credit, Ward introduces a red herring by conflating metaphysical and methodological materialism. Scientific explanations in general, not just evolutionary ones, are methodologically materialist—and with good reason. The intelligibility of the universe in terms of natural laws (to which, incidentally, Ward is fond of appealing as evidence for purposeful creation) grounds explanation in the sciences. The world is predictable in scientific terms precisely because science systematically disallows appeal to the supernatural. The reason for this methodological restriction to natural, material laws and causes is a sound one. If one natural phenomenon, such as the fact that snakes have no legs, can be properly explained by appeal to the supernatural (e.g., because God condemned them to crawl on their bellies), then *any* natural phenomenon can be explained in this way. The case is the same for immaterial entities as it is for supernatural causes: if epilepsy can be explained in terms of possession by a demon, then *any* phenomenon can be explained by appeal to the spirit world. Neither supernatural nor immaterial forces can be controlled for in the way that natural influences can be measured and contained. Science does not deny the existence of such entities and forces; it simply makes no appeal to them, as a matter of methodological necessity.

But methodological materialism is not equivalent to metaphysical materialism, the claim that only material entities exist. Although one might be led to sympathize with metaphysical materialism by the power of naturalistic explanations— e.g., divine purposes are superfluous once an evolutionary explanation is in hand—naturalistic explanations by no means entail metaphysical materialism. As we have shown above, the materialism of scientific explanations is a matter of methodological necessity, not metaphysical commitment. To confuse methodology with metaphysics, as Ward does, is to set up yet another straw man: Ward's attacks on metaphysical materialism cannot possibly count as attacks on the adequacy of naturalistic explanations.

The thrust of Ward's position is that teleological explanations alone eliminate the contingencies inherent in evolutionary explanations. He does not seem to realize, however, that teleological explanations have their own particular problems. In many cases, a perfectly good non-teleological explanation reduces or eliminates the need for a teleological one, even though a teleological explanation is available. For example, a purely physical explanation can be given for the formation of the sun and moon. Given such an explanation, it is natural to think that the relationship between the apparent sizes of these two bodies is purely coincidental. In this case, a teleological explanation to the effect that God sized them to make solar eclipses more beautiful would strike most people as foolish, though, like other teleological explanations, the explanation is unfalsifiable.

A related sort of ad hocness affects Ward's teleology and leads to an interesting inconsistency. For example, Ward concludes that God's goal is not the end product, consciousness, but the evolutionary *process* that leads to consciousness. He needs to make this distinction because he realizes that embodied consciousness might not survive into the far future of the universe and hence cannot be the type of goal we would call an "end product." But the claim that the evolutionary process itself is God's goal accomplishes no explanatory work. The purported teleology becomes merely an ad hoc addendum to an otherwise self-contained evolutionary system. What is worse, locating the teleology in the process itself gives too much credit (for Ward) to evolution, for Ward has just argued that evolution alone cannot produce consciousness. It would make no sense for God to work through a process that is, by Ward's argument, in principle incapable of producing what God wants to produce.

Although Ward is more specific in answering *why* rather than *how* God creates by means of the evolutionary process, his central idea of creation through evolution amounts to mere handwaving. Consider the following typical passage.

> Why would God desire such an evolutionary system? . . . God creates . . . to actualise a distinctive sort of goodness . . . which lies in a process of creative learning, self-shaping and self-expression by conscious agents in community. . . . If such beings are to possess creative freedom, the basic processes of nature must be nondeterministic.[69]

As comforting as such words may sound, they tell us next to nothing about what "self-shaping" and "self-expression," which are perhaps relevant to individual psychology and to cultural evolution, have to do with mutation, selection, heritability, or shifts in gene frequencies. Moreover, even if we grant Ward the incompatibility between freedom and determinism, he gives us no clue as to *how* free creatures utilize indeterminism in nature or how creativity at the conscious level bears on indeterminism at the quantum level. Finally, although Ward suggests that God controls the indeterministic aspects of nature (including genetic mutations) probabilistically,[70] he provides no evidence for this suggestion, other than his purported insights into divine motives. One thing he has definitely not established is that the prior probability of there being a God with overriding reasons to create in this manner is high. A reconciliation of theistic and evolutionary explanations would require far more compelling argumentation than Ward is able to provide.

Ward finds other features of Darwinism objectionable. Drawing an analogy between the Marxist reduction of all historical causes to economic ones and the Darwinian reduction of all evolution to natural selection, he generously grants them both a nice "adolescent shock value."[71] He rejects Darwinian simplicity for being "exclusive,"[72] that is, for ignoring the real complexities in mind, purpose, and so on. Perhaps he finds the "inclusive" simplicity of his own theory, which he says "embraces and includes complexity and value in one integral unity of primordial fullness"[73] to possess the calming value of wise old age. As we have shown in the preceding pages, he thus overlooks what Darwinism *is* capable of explaining. Beauty and value are human artifacts, like radios and pajamas, and, like radios and pajamas, can be fitted into a general biological theory of natural selection as secondary or tertiary consequences of the intelligence that natural selection accounts for very well.

Mocking the ability to predict that is often said to be science's glory, he faults Darwin's theory for its lack of this ability.[74] As Ward realizes, the theory of evolution is more akin to archaeology in its deduction of what has happened in the past and in its fitting of vast amounts of evidence into a coherent explanatory scheme than it is to astronomy in its calculation of the next passing of a comet. In any case, in a broad sense, the theory of evolution *does* make predictions. It correctly predicts that species will adapt to environmental change and respond to selection pressures, whether natural or artificial. And in fact the theory has been borne out. The resistance of certain bacteria to antibiotics and of some insects to insecticides are clear examples of evolution at work. The theory of evolution makes strikingly specific predictions as well. For example, if a given segment of noncoding DNA[75] in humans and chimpanzees differs by, say 1 percent, the theory of evolution predicts that any other such segment will differ by a similar amount because every noncoding segment has had the same amount of time for genetic drift to occur, namely the time since humans and chimpanzees diverged from a common ancestor. Not only have such precise predictions proved true, but there are millions of independent segments of DNA that can be used for millions of predictions of this sort. Furthermore, there is an essentially inexhaustible supply of pairs of related species from which similar predictions can be generated. Similar predictions involving the structures of proteins coded for by the genes of related species yield similarly striking results. When, therefore, Ward faults evolution theory for its inability to predict the emergence of intelligent species, he both ignores the robust predictions of the theory and makes an entirely inappropriate demand for a prediction. Although not a theory that is "complete" in Ward's ultimate senses of making all events in its domain highly probable or of answering teleological "why questions," evolution theory certainly passes the threshold of adequate predictive and explanatory completeness, if any scientific theory does. We need not even mention the consilience of confirming evidence from fields as diverse as comparative anatomy, embryology, biogeography, molecular biology, genetics, and paleontology.

Would it be fair to evaluate the predictive power of *theism* according to Ward's standards?[76] Could anyone have predicted that a perfectly omnipotent, omniscient, and perfectly good deity would have created *this* world? Would it be fair, in the light of Ward's criticism, to evaluate the predictive power of Christianity, a religion that claims actual communication with God, the designer of everything that happens? Not only were early Christians repeatedly wrong about the end of the world that they foresaw as coming in their own lifetimes, or surely during the fall of Rome or surely in the year 1000, or surely any number of other times, but they were lamentably mistaken about what would happen if only the Emperor Constantine converted to Christianity and converted the empire with him. For they fully expected the messianic glories hinted in Virgil's "Fourth Eclogue," whereby a peaceful world would be governed by a benevolent father, a heavenly race would populate the globe, and a golden age of innocence and happiness would be restored. But we shall refrain from such evaluation.

The evidence of physics is revisited and elaborated to show how God "exerts the maximum influence for good compatible with the relative autonomy of nature and its probabilistic laws, and with the freedom of finite agents."[77] There is plenty of room in the universe as understood by modern science for God to influence nature in a noninterfering and undetectable manner. Ward sees two reasons for thinking (at least some of) God's actions undetectable: they are not quantifiable, and the inability of physicists to prove determinism leaves room for undetectable action.[78] Determinism cannot be proved, he shows, because deterministic prediction fails at small scales (on account of the Heisenberg Uncertainty Principle) and at large scales because of the extensions of those small-scale uncertainties, at least for chaotic systems. Chaos is often exemplified in the butterfly effect, whereby the actions of a butterfly in China may drastically alter the outcome of events in the United States years later. It is exemplified, in a simple manner, in the children's poem "For want of a nail, the shoe was lost," in which the downfall of a kingdom results from the loss of a nail in the shoe of a horse. It is a principle also exhibited very often in Herodotus, whereby small things, say, a boil on the breast of Queen Atossa, lead, by a curious chain of causes, to huge geo-political reversals. Thus, Ward concludes, God may intervene in human affairs in ways undetectable by us humans.[79] If Ward is right, of course, we would never be able to know it, for an omnipotent God should be able to ensure the undetectability of his actions by restricting his influence to the indeterministic realm.

That God intervenes in secret and subtle ways to affect the course of evolution, choosing which line of mutations will emerge triumphant, Ward finds a "simpler hypothesis" than natural selection alone.[80] This theory, one supposes, he finds "simple" in a good sense, not like the naïve simplicity he disparaged earlier. Simplicity disappears rapidly, however, once one considers the details. Let us say that a certain fish has a mutation that God favors, because three quarters of a billion years later one of the fish's descendants will be a professor of theology. God sees to it that the mutation occurs, because God foresees that this particular fish will swim fast enough to avoid being eaten by a certain predator only if it has the relevant mutation. (God would presumably also foresee that there is no other, simpler way to get the eventual theology professor than to tamper with the genetic material of that ancestral fish.) Such scenarios are baroque in their complexity. But there are billions of possible genetic loci for mutations. Furthermore, the effect of a given mutation is almost always interrelated to the effects of a host of other unmutated genes. At the phenotypic level, moreover, mutations lead to exceedingly complex interconnections with environmental factors. And there are billions of members of perhaps a billion historical species for God to keep track of! Described one way—as conscious intervention to bring about the desired outcome—the process appears simple; but described in all its necessary detail—detail that God must of necessity be conscious of—the process is anything but simple. Evolution, on the other hand, being mindless and undirected, cannot be accused of the same sort of complexity. The explanatory categories of selection, drift, and the like are intrinsically much simpler than multiple conscious interventions that require unimaginably complex planning to achieve their end.

Concluding his discussion of evolution, Ward confronts the fact that evolution, whether by random chance or by God's scripted plan, involves a great deal of pain and suffering for hundreds and hundreds of millions of years. Painful, violent deaths are the fate of millions of species and billions of individuals. To show how evolution *can* be a part of God's plan he Christianizes some of its features. First he converts the metaphor he uses for evolution. Where others speak about the "war of nature," he substitutes a "metaphor" of a "developing emergent whole."[81] (We put "metaphor" in quotation marks because we forebear to use the same term that we use for the implied comparisons of Shakespeare and Keats.) He also rightly points out that in addition to death and pitiless struggle, evolution involves cooperation.

Consistent with the long tradition of those who would reconcile God and science is Ward's rejection of the literal meaning of Scripture. In what is perhaps for him a difficult concession, he says that when explaining the presence of evil in the world and the fact that animals do not display antelapsarian courtesy to one another, one must reject a literal reading of Adam's fall. We now know, he admits, that carnivores and bacteria preceded Adam. What Adam's sin brought was *spiritual* death. He explains that spiritual death involves a fear of death, "because death is now seen not as a natural process but as a possibly final separation from God."[82] This is quite a galactic reversal in the traditional views of science and religion. The ancient poet of materialism, Lucretius, attempting in *On the Nature of Things* to free men from the fear of death, argued that death should not be feared *because* it is a natural process, one in which the atoms reorganized themselves into something else. It was *religion* that prevented people from seeing it as a natural process but instead made them see it as a punishment with terrors in an imaginary world to come. According to Ward, Adam had the Lucretian view *before* he sinned. The punishment of disobedience was the loss of science and the adoption of religion! Ward's entire analysis is marked by a curious desire to take biblical stories as both historical truth and as suggestive symbols at the same time. His method will not, we think, satisfy the orthodox believer, who accepts the magical story as reality, or the rationalist, who sees the tale as nothing other than poetic fiction.

Ward defends theism against the problem of evil by appealing both to the classical "greater good" argument, that a current evil leads to a greater good later (e.g., the pain of an inoculation leads to the greater good of freedom from disease) and to its variant in the standard free-will defense, that the good of human free will outweighs the evil humans do because they have free will. First, Ward sees much of the world's suffering as necessary for accomplishing God's goals, such as the creation of conscious, free, and morally sensitive beings. He also believes that the realization of these goals outweighs the associated costs. Although one might argue that creating conscious beings is not always worth the risk, given the extraordinary amount of suffering they can and do cause, we shall not take issue here with the part of Ward's "greater good" argument that concerns the justification of the means by the end. Instead, we wish to respond to the other major claim of his "greater good" argument, namely, that the actual quantity of suffering in the world was *necessary* to achieve these goals. The problem with such a claim of necessity is that it limits God, especially the sort of omnipotent God Ward affirms, the sort of God who is responsible for the very structure of the cosmos down to its smallest subatomic features. Surely *this* sort of God would not be bound, for example, by the biological limitations that cause so much human suffering. We doubt that Ward asserts that if even a single iota of all the suffering ever caused by the disease, injury, and decrepitude that have plagued humans (not to mention other animals) for tens of thousands of years had been removed, then humans would not have attained consciousness (or one of the other features Ward values). Yet, if the suffering were strictly necessary, he would have to make just such an assertion.

His analysis of the necessity of human suffering completely sidesteps this quantitative problem. Ward's key point is that without the sort of environment and nature we actually have we would not be humans. "Either we would not exist at all, or we have to exist in this very universe, with its general structural pattern of interaction, conflict, decay and renewal. . . . It is this pattern alone that makes *our* lives possible."[83] Ward's point is not the anthropocentric one that consciousness (i.e., rationality, freedom, morality, etc.) requires conscious beings to be embodied in a universe like the actual one. He is well aware that angels and God are conscious beings who do not require a physical universe. His point is rather that the *embodied* consciousness of human beings requires a physical universe roughly like the actual one in structure and (we are assuming for the sake of argument) that the benefits of embodied consciousness outweigh the costs. Even granting Ward's claim that embodied consciousness necessarily involves moral development and its attendant suffering, the question of the *quantity* of that suffering remains unanswered. For a God in the business of balancing means and ends, of weighing costs and benefits, this quantitative issue must be dealt with. We should have no more sympathy for a God who caused tens of thousands of years of suffering on the grounds that embodied consciousness involves suffering than we would for a parent who routinely tortures her child on the grounds that proper child-rearing involves torture.

In addition to this "greater good" argument, made, perhaps naïvely, in all innocence of the quantitative problem of evil, Ward offers a traditional free-will defense, that truly free creatures can cause their fellows to suffer in ways God neither intends nor desires. This argument has a powerful element of truth to it, for freedom is both of enormous value and incompatible with divine determination. If God is serious about making us free, he cannot *in principle* intervene in our free actions, even for what seems to be a greater good. Of the numerous available responses to the free-will defense, we wish to focus only on its inability to answer the quantitative problem posed above. For more than 99.9 percent of the time that living things have existed on earth—living things fully capable of intense suffering from disease, predation, starvation, and natural disasters—there were no humans whose free choices could possibly have caused any of that suffering. In Ward's view, furthermore, those nonhuman creatures, since they were not free (for only human beings have free will), could not have freely caused the suffering of their fellows. Unless warring angels (which Ward does not invoke) or some such thing were responsible for the animal suffering, the suffering remains untouched by the free-will defense. Similarly unexplained is the suffering—both of humans and of other animals—caused by natural forces clearly beyond the control of free human creatures. Even if the existence of free will accounts for the torture of children, it cannot account for the damage done by predators, bacteria, droughts, floods, earthquakes, and the myriad nonhuman causes of suffering. In light of these considerations, Ward's optimism rings hollow: "God constantly exercises a guiding influence, seeking to maximise good and eliminate evil, to the greatest extent compatible with preserving the autonomy of cosmic laws and the freedom of rational creatures."[84]

Finally, Ward develops a psychological theory of Darwinism. Temporarily losing sight of the many cooperative strategies employed by evolved species, Ward says Darwinism is motivated by a "gloomy and pessimistic view of nature as a battleground of irreconcilable forces,"[85] rather like Heraclitus's underlying war-metaphor for the dynamic interplay of opposing forces (see p. 82). Much better, he suggests, is James Lovelock's "Gaia-hypothesis," in which the world is an organic unit, all the various elements working together in symbiotic harmony. Ward also faults Darwin for an inability to find purpose in the evolutionary process, an inability "largely due to the fact that he [Darwin] saw purpose very much in terms of particular design." Darwin mistakenly thought, Ward continues, that the extinctions of millions of species and all the suffering entailed in those deaths are inconsistent with good design. Ward avoids Darwin's gloomy assessment of life by cheerfully redefining God. It is naïve, he says, to think of God as a parent who would try to eliminate waste and suffering. The laws of the evolutionary process, the laws of genetics are "supremely elegant." God's "apparently wasteful" extermination of individuals and species, he concludes, allows for the existence of the appreciation of beauty, moral action, and rational understanding. In other words, Ward's God is perfectly willing for billions of creatures to suffer miserably so that, after fourteen billion years of suffering, a few individuals can enjoy beauty, moral action, and rational understanding. This, he suggests is the cheerful, optimistic view. We, however, would suggest that Darwinism, when it leaves God out altogether, is far more charitable to God than Ward is.

To sum up, Ward has made the same use of the science of our day that the long line of theologians made of the science of their day. The variations and twists in his arguments are rather insignificant compared to the constancy of the themes. Many who believe in God will no doubt find Ward's arguments persuasive. We wonder, however, whether the arguments will be found comforting, or whether they will seem to have produced a deity not much different from Aristotle's remote Prime Mover. If on a ski outing someone is about to be buried by an avalanche, he wants his prayer to be answered by a God who will perform an immediate and breathtaking miracle, not one who will work through subtle changes in subatomic particles at the level of undetectable quantum physics. He wants the hundred thousand tons of ice and snow to stop in its tracks and roll back up the mountainside. The question of course is how Ward's views can help one find the God of the traditional religions that many humans appear to need.

ARTHUR PEACOCKE

An Anglican priest, biochemist, and winner of the Templeton Prize for Progress in Religion, Arthur Peacocke earnestly desires both his Christian faith and science to be true, not in the sense that one is true for religion and the other is true for science, but that both are true for the same single reality. In addition, he seeks consonance between the two fields: he strives for "a theology that has been refined . . . in the fires of the new perceptions of the world that the natural sciences have irreversibly established. Such a theology needs to be consonant and coherent with, though far from being derived from, scientific perspectives on the world."[86] In order to grasp Peacocke's brand of consonance, we shall focus on how Peacocke deals "scientifically" with a few traditional doctrines about Jesus Christ and the Creator.

After conceding that very little can be known with certainty about Jesus' nature, Peacocke investigates the plausible claim that Jesus was a complete human being who enjoyed a special relationship with God. What made the relationship special was a unity of purpose between them, a purpose embodied in the openness and harmony of an absence of sin.[87] If Jesus is merely human—and, to quote Ivy Compton Burnett, that's not very much to be—how, asks Peacocke, can we account for his miracles? After all, only supernatural beings can perform miracles. Peacocke's views about God's creation of an autonomous natural world lead him to the conclusion that there are "strong *theological* objections to the idea of a God who intervenes in and manipulates the world in ways that would disrupt the very fabric of relationships through which God is sustaining the world in being and continuing to create in and through it in its processes of becoming."[88] Indeed, he goes on to say,

> The whole edifice of theism in the Judeo-Christian tradition is constructed . . . on the foundation of the experienced intelligibility and rationality of the world as indicative of the existence and nature of its Creator and that God the Creator has limited God's own self by giving the creation its autonomous, orderly existence.[89]

There is, thus, on Peacocke's view, a theological presumption *against* the occurrence of miracles.

For Peacocke, Jesus' miracles of healing and exorcism can be easily explained as the sort of psychosomatic events and spontaneous cures that occur even today. Stories of Jesus' miracles involving nature, walking on water, changing water into wine, creating sufficient bread to feed a multitude, are "not convincing as accounts of 'what actually happened.' . . . The probabilities are stacked against their historicity."[90] Accounts of such miracles cannot be taken literally. Nor are miracles associated with Jesus' person, such as the virgin birth, to be taken literally. Jesus' full humanity demands that he inherited his DNA, as the rest of us have, from a human mother and a human father. Otherwise, Peacocke invites us to ask, would God have handpicked the genes associated with Jesus' hair and eye color, or would God have blessed Jesus with copies of the genes that Jesus *would* have inherited from Joseph, had it not been for the virgin birth? Peacocke again opts for an allegorical interpretation of accounts of miracles of this sort.

A traditional Christian might be hopeful when he begins reading Peacocke's account of the resurrection of Jesus. Peacocke emphasizes the difference between the virgin birth and the resurrection: "It is not at all clear that the narratives of the 'resurrection' are sensitive to scientific considerations in the way that beliefs concerning Jesus' birth are."[91] Peacocke's attempt to reconcile the Christian doctrine of the resurrection with a scientific worldview will thus put to the extreme test his desire to achieve consonance between the two.[92] But because he refuses to deny either the obvious irreversibility of death as a biological event or the accounts of a risen Jesus given by disciples who were willing to die for their beliefs, Peacocke is forced to settle for mystery rather than consonance.[93] Unlike the virgin birth, the resurrection constituted *some* sort of inscrutable, non-naturalistic event — one that would require exactly the sort of direct intervention in the autonomous natural world that Peacocke finds theologically and scientifically implausible. Peacocke's promise of consonance between science and religion, one that he makes good on in other cases by bringing his theology into line with science, here fades into "a realm of conjecture."[94] Instead of a miracle, the resurrection is renamed an "eschatological event,"[95] for which the reader is left looking in vain for a scientifically intelligible account. On this crucial point of Christian doctrine, science and religion part ways dramatically.

In an essay entitled "Science and God the Creator,"[96] Peacocke returns to his central project of refining theology with the help of scientific insights and of thereby achieving harmony between the two disciplines. Although he is primarily concerned in the essay with *describing* the basic features of a scientifically informed conception of God and of God's creative activity, he often slips into argument rather than description, claiming that God is the "best explanation" of various natural features of the universe. His venture beyond mere consonance into the realm of scientifically supported theology is what concerns us here, for the scientific support he offers is in every case extremely tenuous.

Because even a physical "theory of everything" would *not* explain *why* the (contingent) laws of physics are the way they are, Peacocke sees the need for a (necessary) "Ground of Being."[97] This is very similar to the cosmological argument for God's existence applied to modern physics. There is no need to rehearse the reasons that Hume, Kant, and others rejected this sort of argument. It is sufficient to point out that the modernness of the physics involved has nothing to do with the theistic argument, which turns on contingency alone. In other words, Peacocke's argument relies on the claim that the laws of physics that govern the universe might have been different; this contingency of the laws is what drives the argument and makes it a cosmological argument. It is, perhaps, hard to deny that science claims no resources for accounting for the sort of metaphysical contingency Peacocke has in mind; nevertheless, it is equally hard to see how the assertion of a tailor-made "Ground of Being" does any better.

Peacocke's case for the unity of God based on scientific evidence is quite weak. "From a scientific perspective," he argues, "the world exhibits an underlying unity beneath its remarkable diversity, fecundity, and complexity."[98] So far, so good. But he continues: "The 'best explanation' of such a world's existence and character . . . cannot but be grounded in *one* unifying source of creativity."[99] Following Hume, one might as well argue that the unity of a house or a ship or a space shuttle must have come from a single architect rather than the collaborative effort of several.

Peacocke derives another argument from the "intelligibility and putative comprehensibility of the world's entities, structures, and processes."[100] Instead of considering the vast amount we do not—and perhaps can not—know about the world or the fact that we would not have made much evolutionary headway if the world were not at least basically intelligible to us, Peacocke concludes that "this cannot but render more probable than ever before inference to the existence of a suprarational Being as Creator as the 'best explanation' of such a world's existence and character."[101] How he derives the supreme rationality of a creator from the partial intelligibility of the world, we will refrain from speculating.

Peacocke's least convincing arguments of all concern what he perceives to be the "anthropic universe," a concept that we have already discussed at length (see p. 263). Suffice it to say that, in inferring that the world is "finely tuned with respect to many physical features in a way conducive to the emergence of living organisms and so of human beings,"[102] Peacocke overlooks two crucial facts: the fine tuning in no way guarantees that life will arise in the universe, nor does it in any way privilege human life over, say, bacterial life. To say that "self-conscious life was bound to eventually appear"[103] flies in the face of the biological and astronomical evidence about the multiple contingencies of evolutionary pathways and environments. This point aside, the "scientific" evidence simply does not privilege persons over microbes. Peacocke's real motivation for attributing personhood to God is not scientific at all, but rests on the conviction that "the personal is the highest category of entity we can name."[104] Philosophy and theology, not science, are where he should be looking for his anthropomorphism.

Although Peacocke's theology—i.e., his interpretation of God's nature and creative activity in light of modern science—is fascinating, his attempts to use modern science as evidentiary support for that theology fail. Peacocke seems to be struggling not only to find evidence for his religious worldview in the discoveries of science, but to hold on to a core of (suitably reinterpreted) religious beliefs in the face of the scientific worldview he wholeheartedly endorses. He realizes that he cannot call himself a Christian if he converts every belief central to Christianity into legend or allegory.[105]

Paul made *belief* in the supernatural qualities of Jesus the core requirement for Christians, and *belief* in these unscientific qualities was reaffirmed in the Protestant Reformation, when it was faith that made one a Christian, not works—a faith that was not to be translated into mere allegorical encouragement to good works. Peacocke is too much a man of science to embrace a simple faith that ignores modern science; he is too much a man of faith, however, to give up on all his religious views. As a result, he is representative of the pattern we have observed through western history of reaching some sort of accommodation. Unfortunately, as in the other cases, the accommodation is not intellectually satisfactory.

JOHN POLKINGHORNE

John Polkinghorne, another scientist-minister and winner of the Templeton Prize, has given considerable creative thought to the reconciliation of science and religion. In an article entitled "The Metaphysics of Divine Action,"[106] he addresses the questions of ontological gaps and of how God might be able to bridge them, i.e., how a purely spiritual being might exert creative influence over a world governed by natural laws. It is important to note that "belief in divine providence," which "is founded in the religious experiences of prayer and of trust in a God who guides,"[107] causes this question to arise in the first place. It is thus a question uniquely faced by the religious believer who, like Polkinghorne, wishes to make philosophical and scientific sense of his beliefs. Polkinghorne's answer involves both a "contextual" theory of causality and a "dual-aspect" ontology.

His theory of causality capitalizes on the intrinsic unpredictability of chaotic systems and the impossibility of isolating (what Polkinghorne calls the "unisolability" of) such systems from their environments. These properties supposedly make such systems indeterministic enough for God to operate through them without violating any physical laws. Leaving aside the philosophical problems—similar to those Peacocke worried over—of an interventionist God, we find Polkinghorne's move from chaos to indeterminism unconvincing. First, unpredictability does not entail indeterminism, as Polkinghorne well realizes. Indeed, the whole interest of chaotic systems lies in their being both unpredictable and deterministic. (Collisions among billiard balls serve as a classic example of determinism in action. Yet, after fifteen successive collisions following the "break" of a rack of balls, the margin of error in predicting where the balls will lie exceeds the size of the table. It is therefore impossible even in principle—i.e., even if one knows the details of the initial collision within the limits of the Heisenberg Uncertainty Principle—to predict the final positions of the balls. The behavior of the balls is chaotic precisely because it is both deterministic and intrinsically unpredictable.) Second, the impossibility of isolating such systems from their environments, of which Polkinghorne speaks, concerns complexity but not indeterminism. Here is Polkinghorne's argument:

> The deterministic equations from which classical chaos theory developed are then to be interpreted as downward emergent approximations to a more subtle and supple physical reality. They are valid only in the limiting and special cases where bits and pieces are effectively insulated from the effects of their environment. In the general case, the effect of total context on the behavior of parts cannot be neglected.[108]

The "total context" might well be inscrutably complicated, but it is not therefore indeterministic. Without indeterminism, Polkinghorne's strategy for leaving God room to act in the world cannot succeed.

Polkinghorne is quick to point out that he does not think God acts by fiddling with the exceedingly sensitive initial conditions of chaotic systems. That sort of God would indeed be objectionably interventionist. But Polkinghorne's proposal, that "the behavior of parts" is "influenced by their overall context,"[109] is equally bizarre, if not unintelligible. Exactly how this is supposed to work is as unclear as the original question of how God influences physical processes without altering physical laws.

Polkinghorne's "dual-aspect monism" sheds roughly the same amount of light on the perennial issue of how physical and nonphysical entities can coexist. The key to Polkinghorne's proposal is that mind and matter constitute two aspects of one reality, in the same way that wavelikeness and particlelikeness constitute two aspects of the single entity of light. But light's behaving in different ways under different experimental conditions is far different from there existing two radically different kinds of entity in the world. The mode of interaction between mind and matter that dualists since Descartes have sought in vain cannot be found by simply proclaiming a metaphorically similar duality in physics. Besides, the dual nature of light is not exactly the sort of clear, common-sense analogy that would be helpful in clarifying the relationship between mind and matter. Polkinghorne admits that his theory is "largely conjectural and heuristic."[110]

Perhaps he should say that it is *entirely* conjectural.[111] Despite Polkinghorne's admittedly clever proposals, any person simultaneously serious about his religious and scientific commitments is left with the original puzzle of how a supernatural being can interact with an autonomous physical world.

In his essay, "A Potent Universe,"[112] Polkinghorne argues that the "anthropic fine-tuning" of the universe, which science by its nature stops short of trying to explain, can be accounted for by appeal to a divine designer, especially when the appeal is reinforced by independent lines of argument for a designer. After surveying some of the ways in which the universe seems "finely tuned" for intelligent life—it has the requisite kinds of laws, constituents, forces, and cosmic circumstances—Polkinghorne considers the possible explanations for such an unlikely yet "potent" universe. He quickly eliminates mere indifference to the radical contingency of the delicately balanced features of the universe that make our existence possible. He also eliminates the inadequate, though (in his view) slightly better, claim of the "weak anthropic principle" that the universe must of necessity exhibit the necessary conditions for everything, including humans. Instead of opting for a "strong anthropic principle," to the effect that the universe *must* for some reason be amenable to the existence of observers, Polkinghorne prefers what he calls the "moderate anthropic principle," according to which "the fine-tuning of a potent universe [is] an insight of significance that calls for some form of explanation."[113] Because the laws of physics themselves are what is being explained, Polkinghorne rightly points out that the explanation will be metaphysical rather than scientific (i.e., one that appeals to laws of physics). The two candidate explanations, in his mind, are many universes and creation. The former explains the "fine tuning" in terms of a selection effect, the latter in terms of the conscious purposes of a creator. Significantly, Polkinghorne thinks that the anthropic evidence needs to be supplemented before the creation hypothesis becomes preferable:

> In relation to the anthropic principle alone, there might seem to be equal coherence in [the many universes and creation explanations]. The latter gains much greater economy and persuasiveness when one takes into account that there are many other lines of argument that converge on the insight that behind the world of our experience there lies the fundamental Reality of God.[114]

For Polkinghorne, therefore, science and religion converge in an important way. Science reveals a universe that is, in its most fundamental constitution, remarkably fit for human habitation. To explain so basic a fitness, one must appeal either to a naturalistic principle such as the many-universes hypothesis or to the theistic alternative, creation. Although the scientific picture of a barely habitable universe does not by itself favor theism, this picture is a significant component in a cumulative-case argument for that position.

Although Polkinghorne asks exactly the right questions about how God fits in to the world of science and about whether scientific evidence might point to a creator, his answers prove, in the end, to be far from satisfying. Concerning the metaphysics of a spiritual God acting in the material world, Polkinghorne's theory of contextual causality fails because neither chaos nor interconnectedness achieves the required indeterminism and because the causal influence that context is supposed to exert remains inscrutable. Moreover, the metaphor that drives his dual-aspect ontology is incapable of solving the deep metaphysical problems of dualism. Finally, the fine-tuning arguments to which he appeals as one element of his cumulative-case argument for God's existence, although appealing at first glance, are as irremediably flawed as are the same fine-tuning arguments when employed in design inferences.

GOULD VERSUS DAWKINS: NON-OVERLAPPING MAGISTERIA?

Let us turn now to the question of whether science and religion deal with overlapping subject matters. The two most prominent recent popularizers of evolution, Stephen Jay Gould and Richard Dawkins, have squared off on the issue of whether science and religion share any common ground and can be reconciled. Gould's stance is a textbook case of a claim to independence for both science and religion; Dawkins's stance is that the two fields conflict.

Gould argues that, because science and religion investigate distinct subject matters and claim distinct realms of professional expertise, they cannot in principle conflict—although the two spheres abut each other closely and in complex ways.

> No such conflict [between science and religion] should exist because each subject has a legitimate magisterium, or domain of teaching authority—and these magisteria do not overlap (the principle that I would like to designate as NOMA, or "nonoverlapping magisteria"). The net of science covers the empirical realm: what is the universe made of (fact) and why does it work this way (theory). The net of religion extends over questions of moral meaning and value.[115]

Nevertheless,

> the two magisteria bump right up against each other, interdigitating in wondrously complex ways along their joint border. Many of our deepest questions call upon aspects of both magisteria for different parts of a full answer—and the sorting of legitimate domains can become quite complex and difficult.[116]

Although Gould speaks of the independence of religion in general and science in general, he focuses on Catholicism and evolution, citing official statements by Popes Pius XII and John Paul II as evidence that "the Catholic Church values scientific study, views science as no threat to religion in general or Catholic doctrine in particular, and has long accepted both the legitimacy of evolution as a field of study and the potential harmony of evolutionary conclusions with Catholic faith."[117] Pius XII, near the end of his 1950 *Humani Generis,* accepts in principle the scientific conclusions concerning evolution of the human body but reserves for God the role of infusing it with an individual soul. John Paul II, in his recent message on evolution to the Pontifical Academy of Sciences, concurs and even strengthens the concordance between science and religion by emphasizing that in the half century since Pius scientific evidence favoring evolution has mounted to the point that the theory is not just acceptable in principle but should be considered more than just a hypothesis. In addition (of course) to seconding John Paul's support of evolution, Gould agrees with both popes' assessment of the soul: "science cannot touch such a subject and therefore cannot be threatened by any theological position on such a legitimately and intrinsically religious issue."[118] Indeed, this principle of independence "cuts both ways. If religion can no longer dictate the nature of the factual conclusions residing properly within the magisterium of science, then scientists cannot claim higher insight into moral truth from any superior knowledge of the world's empirical constitution."[119] While prudently not delving into the controversial borderline cases, Gould claims there is virtually a consensus among scientists in favor of his NOMA principle and that the greatest strength of the principle lies in the fact that it encourages respectful discourse between scientists and religious believers.

Dawkins, by contrast, has no patience for such "respectful discourse." Although he would no doubt agree with the uncontroversial half of Gould's thesis, that much of science and much of religion have little to do with one another, he homes in on cases where the two domains, in his view, directly overlap and directly conflict. Despite the conciliatory statements of two popes, with which Gould agrees, Dawkins points out what he takes to be a direct contradiction between evolution and Catholicism: evolutionists view humans as continuous with their ancestral lineages, whereas Catholics think that God directly implanted a human soul into a previously nonhuman lineage. Dawkins is unsurprised by the contradiction, for he deems Catholic morality "speciesist to the core,"[120] based as it is on a sharp discontinuity between humans and other species. Hence, Catholic morality has scientific import in its reliance on a "fundamentally anti-evolutionary" gap between a single species and all others.[121]

What is worse (for Gould's view of independence), religions by no means restrict themselves to moral pronouncements.

A universe with a supernatural presence would be a fundamentally and qualitatively different kind of universe from one without. The difference is, inescapably, a scientific difference. Religions make existence claims, and this means scientific claims. . . . The Virgin Birth, the bodily Assumption of the Blessed Virgin Mary, the Resurrection of Jesus, the survival of our own souls after death: these are all claims of a clearly scientific nature. . . .

Either Mary's body decayed when she died, or it was physically removed from this planet to Heaven [e.g.]. . . . The Assumption of the Virgin is transparently a scientific theory. So is the theory that our souls survive bodily death and so are all stories of angelic visitations, Marian manifestations, and miracles of all types.[122]

Dawkins is particularly critical of the attempts by religious leaders—specifically Roman Catholic ones, to judge from the previous passage—to employ to their advantage miracle claims, which are appealing precisely because of their scientific import, and at the same time to reserve for miracles a religious status immune to scientific scrutiny.

Dawkins even doubts the commonly—and in his view uncritically—accepted authority of religions in moral matters. "The hope that religion might provide a bedrock, from which our otherwise sand-based morals can be derived, is a forlorn one,"[123] in part because we need some prior principle on which to judge which of the contradictory exhortations from Scripture, religious leaders, and religious traditions to adopt as moral guidelines. (Here we see hints of Euthyphro's dilemma over whether the gods obey a prior standard of goodness [see p. 96].)

Dawkins may have exaggerated his view that all existence claims are scientific, for religions typically invoke immaterial entities that are not subject to the laws of nature and that therefore lie beyond the domain of scientific investigation. (Such entities are of course beyond the realm of scientific confirmation as well.) But his central point about the untenability of Gould's independence thesis is valid: religions make numerous claims that are in principle subject to scientific investigation. This point seems to trump Gould's (correct) claim that many religious beliefs fall outside the scope of science.

If reconciliation between scientific and religious claims cannot be achieved via independence, the question is whether science and religion are hopelessly at odds in the cases in which their claims overlap. The answer, we suspect, is both yes and no. Yes, insofar as scientific explanations, such as the evolutionary explanation of human origins, undercut religious ones by providing a compelling alternative. Once one has in hand a plausible and well-confirmed scientific theory, one need not appeal to religious explanations. The answer is no, however, insofar as science is not in the business of disproving the existence of anything, including deities and immaterial souls. The science of meteorology serves as a clear illustration: it has rendered belief in Zeus's thunderbolts obsolete by providing a plausible alternative account of thunder and lightning; but this science does not aim at disproving the existence of Zeus or his wrath.

CONCLUSION

At the beginning of a new millennium we observe that fine minds are still engaged in the search to find room for both God and science. Our very human search for comfort in what might appear, without God, to be a meaningless universe and our very human hope for a benevolent deity who can help us in this vale-of-tears world continues to present the very same dilemma for us as it did for our predecessors in antiquity and the Middle Ages, and indeed for all who wish to explain the world by means of our most valuable human attribute—our reason—and by means of science—reason's most successful application. Where we have come and what conclusions we may draw from two and a half thousand years of inquiry into these difficult matters will form the subject of our concluding chapter.

DISCUSSION QUESTIONS

1. Is the sort of design argument proposed by "intelligent design" theory different in any fundamental way from the sort of design argument popular in the eighteenth century and earlier? Does the mathematical language in which the more recent argument is expressed make the argument more convincing to you?

2. Are all design arguments subject to the god-of-the-gaps fallacy? That is, are they vulnerable to being supplanted by future scientific explanations that would belie their claim that God alone can explain certain phenomena?

3. It is clear that modern science is naturalistic in its explanations: they make no reference to supernatural beings or divine intervention. Does science go further, *denying* the existence of the supernatural, i.e., is science *ontologically* naturalistic? Or is the supernatural simply beyond the scope of scientific investigation?

4. Can you think of a phenomenon having to do with living things that cannot in principle be accounted for by natural selection? If you can, are you sure that you have considered all possible selection hypotheses or all possible shifts in functionality? If you cannot, is natural selection in some objectionable sense tautologous or self-confirming (e.g., does it involve the circular claim that "survival of the fittest" means nothing other than "survival of those who survive" since the fittest are defined as "those who survive")?

5. Are you comfortable assigning probabilities to natural phenomena such as the occurrence of a certain structure in a living cell or the arrangement of the initial conditions in the Big Bang? On what grounds might such probabilities be assigned? Can the probability of a unique occurrence ever be known? Are examples drawn from dice and games of chance applicable to the natural world?

6. Do we know enough about the universe to set a universal bound on the probability that a given event will ever occur? What, if anything, can be concluded from the occurrence of an extremely improbable event, such as the drawing of a particular sequence of cards?

7. Are you convinced by Dembski's definition of "specification"? Can the specification of a given sort of event change through time? Might different persons disagree over whether or not a given event is specified? If so, how might such disagreements be adjudicated?

8. Is there a difference in principle between micro- and macroevolution? If so, what exactly is it? If the difference is merely quantitative, are there grounds on which a person can accept the former but reject the latter? Are the examples of hybridized plants and new strains of bacteria adequate evidence of the reality of macroevolution?

9. Do you find explanations in terms of design—where the designer remains unidentified or lacking any kind of description—intellectually satisfying? What positive explanatory power do such design inferences have? Why do you think proponents of intelligent design theory are so reluctant to identify the designer whose existence and activity they seek to establish? Are they like those affirming the doctrine of negative attributes (the *via negativa*) in the Middle Ages? What connection, if any, is there between the designer of intelligent design arguments and the God of traditional theism?

10. Does intelligent design theory have the marks of a *scientific* theory, such as falsifiability and predictive success? Does it have proper scientific credentials, such as publication in peer-reviewed journals and acceptance by the scientific community?

11. Have recent design arguments escaped the criticisms leveled at such arguments in earlier centuries? In particular, has the problem of suboptimal design been adequately answered, in your opinion? Are the relevant inductive and analogical arguments used in design inferences sound ones?

12. Do Ward, Peacocke, and Polkinghorne succeed in integrating the sciences of cosmology and evolutionary biology with Christian theology? Can science lead one to modify one's theology in legitimate ways, or do such modifications represent an unacceptable retreat of theology in the face of the scientific juggernaut?

13. What sense can you make of the idea that God works *through* evolution? How would you respond to someone who suggests that such thinking is a variation of a god-of-the-gaps strategy?

14. Should claims about Jesus Christ be subjected to scientific scrutiny? What advantage would there be in finding scientific confirmation for, say, some of Jesus' miracles? If, instead, science disconfirms Christian teaching, how is one to resolve the resulting dilemma?

15. Do the authors treated in this chapter suggest modifications in Christian doctrines beyond what you find acceptable? Would you prefer to consider science and religion as two separate and independent realms rather than to acquiesce to such modifications?

16. In your view, do chaos and indeterminism provide room for God to work in the world? Can *you* explain how a spiritual being operates in a material world, or would you prefer to classify such matters as mysteries?

17. Do you side with Gould or Dawkins in the debate over whether science and religion occupy totally separate realms? Does Gould underestimate

the "scientific" implications of religious doctrines? Does Dawkins focus too narrowly on Roman Catholic miracles?

NOTES

1. William A. Dembski, *The Design Inference* (Cambridge: Cambridge University Press, 1998).

2. William A. Dembski, *Intelligent Design: The Bridge between Science and Theology* (Downers Grove, Ill.: InterVarsity, 1999), 14. Subsequent references to Dembski are to this book.

3. Dembski, 46.

4. Fitelson et al. note, however, that Dembski equivocates on the notion of high probability, taking it to refer, variously, to noncontingency, lawlikeness, and determinism, in addition to probability. See Branden Fitelson, Christopher Stephens, and Elliott Sober, "How Not to Detect Design—Critical Notice: William A. Dembski, *The Design Inference,*" *Philosophy of Science* 66 (1999): 475.

5. Dembski, 148.

6. Dembski, 152.

7. A single coin toss represents one bit of information, for example, and a random sequence of five hundred tosses is complex enough to contain five hundred bits of information. The probability of getting such a long sequence by chance alone is roughly 10^{-150}.

8. Dembski, 238.

9. Dembski, 141.

10. Dembski, 174.

11. Dembski, 245.

12. Dembski, 245.

13. Dembski, 247.

14. Dembski, 17.

15. Dembski, 107.

16. Dembski, 111.

17. Dembski, 142.

18. Dembski, 223.

19. Young-earth creationists hold, on literalist biblical grounds, that God created the earth only a few thousand years ago.

20. Dembski, 258.

21. Dembski, 258.

22. Dembski, 264.

23. We note that the term *anthropic* is unjustifiably anthropocentric. As far as the universe is concerned, cockroaches, hummingbirds, and humans share exactly the same physical prerequisites.

24. Dembski, 268.

25. See Fitelson, Stephens, and Sober, "Critical Notice," 486.

26. Dembski, 271.

27. Here Dembski follows the same Elliott Sober who co-authored the recent devastating attack on Dembski's work.

28. Dembski, 274.

29. Dembski, 276.

30. Three serious technical problems not discussed in Dembski's appendix to *Intelligent Design* are worth noting. The first, which concerns the tractability and delimitation conditions on specification and is discussed by Fitelson, Stephens, and Sober ("Critical Notice," 481–82), is straightforward. The tractability and delimitation conditions may trivially be met simply by writing down a tautology, for coming up with a tautology such as "*p* entails *p*" from one's background knowledge is clearly a tractable problem, and any event whatsoever entails (or "delimits") a tautology. Hence the tractability and delimitation conditions bear no informational relevance to the event. The probability that an event will occur is an entirely different matter from whether one can generate a description of it. Yet Dembski needs something like these conditions in order to rule out ad hoc specifications.

The other technical problems pertain to Dembski's probability bounds. As Fitelson, Stephens, and Sober point out ("Critical Notice," 484–85), Dembski's provision that the probability of an event of type E occurring in the duration of the universe, given the hypothesis of chance, be less than one half in order to rule out chance as an explanation is absurd: improbable events sometimes occur, and the theories that predict that they probably will not occur may be perfectly good theories. (So they would modify the ancient poet Agathon's statement that "it is likely for unlikely things to happen" to "it is *unlikely* for unlikely things to happen.") Because there is no such thing as the probabilistic falsifiability of a theory, Dembski's concept of "probabilistic inconsistency" is indefensible.

Dembski's calculation of the universal upper bound on low probabilities is also problematic. The number of actual specifications possible in the lifetime of the universe, on which the calculation relies, is relevant to the probability of arriving at a given specification only if the list of specifications is generated without the benefit of selection. By capitalizing on selection, it is quite easy to meet Dembski's challenge of coming up with complex specified information below the 10^{-150} threshold that is not designed. (Thanks to Francisco Ayala for the following example.) Suppose a colony of 10^{12} bacteria are exposed to pathogen P1, to which only 10^{-10} of that species of bacteria are immune. Roughly one hundred survive and in a short time reconstitute a population of 10^{12}, all of which are immune to P1. This colony then encounters pathogen P2, to which only 10^{-10} are immune . . . and so on through P15. The final colony contains billions of bacteria immune to all fifteen pathogens, yet the probability of even one bacterium being immune to these fifteen pathogens is $(10^{-10})^{15} = 10^{-150}$. The example is realistic because the pathogens can be any chemical, biological, or environmental factor to which only a small fraction of a population is genetically immune. In rapidly reproducing species under heavy selection pressure, even remarkably improbable—and independently useful— adaptations will occur in astonishingly short periods of time. In short, Dembski's low probabilities are easy to come by. Putting aside for the moment what we take to be intractable problems with his concept of specification, this example clearly counts as a *specified* biological phenomenon as well: indeed, the final batch of bacteria exhibits a sort of irreducible complexity: if even one of the fifteen immunities were absent, the organisms could not survive. Dembski's claims about the holistic nature of complexity will not save his design inference: the holism of a complex structure means that it will not work if one of its parts is misplaced. We have been working on the even stronger assumption that one of the parts is removed entirely. If evolution can explain the *addition* of a supposedly indispensable part, it can certainly explain the *re-arrangement* of one. The power of natural selection to generate complex specified information, which Dembski system-

atically ignores, is obvious in this example. Equally obvious is the irrelevance of the total number of randomly generated specifications possible in the duration of the universe.

31. Keith Ward, *God, Chance, and Necessity* (Oxford: One World Publications, 1996).

32. Analogies are useful for where they show congruencies and for where they do not.
If the Western philosophical tradition is generally linear, with, say, the pre-Socratics followed by the classical Greek philosophers, followed by the medieval philosophers,
followed by the moderns, the family line of humans and chimpanzees branches from the
common ancestor several million years ago, with humans and chimpanzees then following separate evolutionary paths. A branching "family tree" might be drawn for philosophy
or religious sects, however, when one looks rather more deeply into the matter. For example, Socrates may be the common ancestor of the Academy, the Cynics, the Skeptics, and
the Stoics. Yet each of these schools developed in its own way with a line of teachers who
influenced the work of their successors.

33. Ward, *God*, 11.

34. Ward, *God*, 15.

35. Ward, *God*, 23.

36. Ward, *God*, 19.

37. See Aquinas, *Summa Theologica*, 1.2.3.2.

38. Ward, *God*, 25–26. While this faith is not faith in God, it is, according to Ward, akin
to it. In a discussion of Peter Atkins's idea that the human mind can understand all the secrets of the universe, Ward writes,

> It is clear that Dr Atkins begins with a faith of just the same nature as religious faith, a funda-
> mental postulate of the intelligibility, beauty and (mathematical) harmony of the universe, and of
> the possibility of human fulfillment in understanding its own ultimate environment. Monotheists
> will immediately recognize this faith as their own, and may even claim without self-deception
> that faith in science, in the rational structure of nature, has historically been strongly motivated
> by faith in a wise God who would be expected to provide such a structure.

Ward is suggesting a very strong kinship indeed!

39. Ward, *God*, 25.

40. The contradiction in these views is the subject of Kierkegaard's masterpiece *Fear
and Trembling*.

41. Ward, *God*, 38.

42. Livy, *Ab Urbe Condita*, 1.6. Another famous example reported by the ancient historians occurs before the Battle of Plataea, where, Herodotus reports (9.36–37), both the
Greeks and the Persians were waiting for the proper auguries. In the end, the Greeks began the battle.

43. Events that appear to some to result from chance appear to others as "acts of God," a
term that is used in legal contexts in the United States. When, for example, lightning strikes
one's house, it may be referred to as an "act of God." To some religious people, who believe
that God is responsible for everything, there is no such thing as chance, and this view is consistent with one of Aristotle's definitions of chance, as the intersection of independent orders
(*Physics*, 196b10–197a8). Boethius illustrates the Aristotelian definition with a wonderful example of a man who digs in his garden and "by chance" finds buried treasure (*Consolation of
Philosophy*, 5.1). But, as Boethius points out, the person who had buried the treasure had a
purpose in choosing the spot, and the farmer had a purpose in plowing his field. The event appears as chance because of each person's ignorance of the purpose and action of the other.

44. Ward, *God,* 39.

45. J. Gribbin, *A Brief History of Science* (New York: Barnes and Noble, 1998), 77, puts it thus:

> You may not like this, but you should. If the world ran in strict accordance with Newton's laws, like clockwork, then everything, down to the tiniest particle interaction, would be determined in advance. There would be no scope for free will. It is the quantum uncertainty that gives us the chance to run our own lives and make our own decisions rather than follow a preordained plan.

One might object (rightly, we think) that the will is no more free if it is the apparent result of a spontaneous "swerve" or quantum fluctuation than if it obeys deterministic laws. The same error is made by some who would say that modern chaos theory, where tiny fluctuations have unpredictable results, helps to make sense of free will. For example, J. P. Crutchfield, in his article on "Chaos" in *Chaos and Complexity: Scientific Perspectives on Divine Action,* ed. Robert J. Russell, Nancey Murphy, and Arthur R. Peacocke (Vatican City State: Vatican Observatory, 1995), 48, claims that "chaos provides a mechanism that allows for free will within a world governed by deterministic laws." Ward himself expresses sympathy with the view that quantum indeterminacy allows room for free will (*God,* 93). It is no surprise that he stops short of showing exactly how free creatures are supposed to capitalize on properties of the quantum domain when making free decisions. Ward and others are giving, in effect, a "freedom-of-the-gaps" argument by locating freedom in a convenient indeterministic gap.

46. Ward subscribes to the view: "The balance and precise strength of the fundamental gravitational, electro-magnetic and nuclear forces needs to be exactly what it is if conscious life is to exist" (Ward, *God,* 51).

47. For an account of the Anthropic Principle and its philosophical implications, see Patrick A. Wilson, "The Anthropic Principle," in *Cosmology: Historical, Literary, Philosophical, Religious, and Scientific Perspectives,* ed. Norriss S. Hetherington (New York: Garland, 1993), 505–14.

48. Ward, *God,* 40.

49. Ward, *God,* 56.

50. Ward, *God,* 112, 115.

51. Ward, *God,* 58.

52. Ward, *God,* 58.

53. Ward, *God,* 59.

54. Ward, *God,* 60. Though Ward seems to contradict himself since he has just called God "pure actuality," he can perhaps be forgiven inasmuch as "pure actuality" is not within human experience.

55. In *Theology for a Scientific Age,* Peacocke tells us what the purpose is (2d ed., London: SCM, 1993, 221):

> There can, it seems to me (*pace* Stephen Gould), be overall direction and implementation of purpose through the interplay of chance and law, without a deterministic plan fixing all the details of the structure(s) of that which emerges possessing personal qualities. Hence the emergence of self-conscious persons capable of relating personally to God can still be regarded as an intention of God continually creating through the processes of that to which he has given an existence of this kind and no other. (It certainly must have been "on the cards" since it actually happened—with us!)

56. Ward, *God,* 64.

57. The very terms we are using, *succeeds* and *contest,* are, however, value-laden terms that are not, of course, part of the Darwinian scheme. There is a difficulty in finding a vocabulary to express Darwin's views with complete objectivity. Perhaps it is enough to call attention to the difficulty of finding the appropriate words. A colleague of ours who teaches chemistry, Professor Herbert Sipe, lamented the same difficulty in describing to students—without anthropomophizing electrons—the "desire" of electrons to complete an orbital shell.

58. For an exceptionally lucid account of evolution, see Daniel Dennett, *Darwin's Dangerous Idea: Evolution and the Meaning of Life* (New York: Simon & Schuster, 1995).

59. Ward, *God,* 147.

60. Ward, *God,* 148.

61. Dennett, *Dangerous Idea,* 82.

62. Ward, *God,* 153.

63. Ward, *God,* 155.

64. Ward, *God,* 159.

65. Blushing and the mental processes that cause it are readily explained in terms of adaptive function, for example, the function of making it hard to fake cheating in a cooperative environment.

66. Indeed, Ward's earlier claim (*God,* 70) that consciousness, for the materialist, has no causal role in the world and hence no survival value presupposes an immaterialist definition of consciousness. For a materialist, the problem of how an immaterial consciousness interacts with material objects simply does not arise.

67. Ward, *God,* 158.

68. Ward, *God,* 160.

69. Ward, *God,* 131.

70. Ward, *God,* 134. Here, as elsewhere, Ward focuses on variation resulting from mutation, despite the fact that, in sexually reproducing species (which include all the conscious species on earth), the bulk of variation is due to sexual recombination, which is not related to indeterministic processes in the way some mutations are.

71. Ward, *God,* 71.

72. Ward, *God,* 84.

73. Ward, *God,* 85.

74. Ward, *God,* 72.

75. "Noncoding DNA" is DNA that does not lead to the production of a protein. Some noncoding DNA may serve to regulate various biological functions; some may be what is sometimes called "junk DNA"—DNA currently believed to serve no purpose whatsoever.

76. The predictive ability of theism, criticized here, is closely related to the explanatory power of theism, which in turn is related to the probability of various events occurring given the hypothesis of theism. The weaker theism is at predicting these events, the weaker it is at explaining them, and the lower the probability of theism. Even if Ward is correct in levying a similar criticism against the evolutionist, it is well to point out that the sword cuts both ways.

77. Ward, *God,* 80.

78. Ward, *God,* 80.

79. This view is expressed by many others, including W. J. Wildman and R. J. Russell in "Chaos: A Mathematical Introduction with Philosophical Reflections," in *Chaos and Complexity,* ed. Robert J. Russell, Nancey Murphy, and Arthur R. Peacocke (Vatican City State: Vatican Observatory, 1995), 83–86. As one might imagine, there are disagreements

even among the supporters of this general view. For example, John Polkinghorne believes that God intervenes in the world and that he does so through a "holistic," "top-down" manipulation of particles. But, Polkinghorne adds, "I do not suppose that either we or God interact with the world by carefully calculated adjustment of the infinitesimal details of initial conditions so as to bring about a desired result." And he objects to Peacocke for having claimed that God manipulates individual atoms and molecules. See "The Metaphysics of Divine Action," in *Chaos and Complexity,* 154.

80. Ward, *God,* 85.

81. Ward, *God,* 87.

82. Ward, *God,* 89.

83. Ward, *God,* 193.

84. Ward, *God,* 202.

85. Ward, *God,* 92.

86. Peacocke, *Theology,* ix.

87. Peacocke, *Theology,* 266.

88. Peacocke, *Theology,* 269.

89. Peacocke, *Theology,* 269–70.

90. Peacocke, *Theology,* 273.

91. Peacocke, *Theology,* 280.

92. Woody Allen is recorded to have said, "I don't want to achieve immortality through my work. . . . I want to achieve it by not dying." Perhaps Peacocke's Jesus may be thinking the same.

93. Peacocke could perhaps stand a dose of Hume's skepticism about the testimony concerning miracles and ask himself whether it is more likely that such a wholly inscrutable event occurred or that somewhere along the line the testimony got garbled. It is also important to point out that willingness to die for a belief, while certainly evidence for the firmness of that belief, does not necessarily have anything to do with the *truth* of that belief.

94. Peacocke, *Theology,* 286.

95. Peacocke, *Theology,* 287.

96. Arthur Peacocke, "Science and God the Creator," in *Evidence of Purpose: Scientists Discover the Creator,* ed. John Marks Templeton (New York: Continuum, 1994), 91–104.

97. Peacocke, "Science," 95.

98. Peacocke, "Science," 95.

99. Peacocke, "Science," 95.

100. Peacocke, "Science," 96.

101. Peacocke, "Science," 96.

102. Peacocke, "Science," 97.

103. Peacocke, "Science," 97.

104. Peacocke, "Science," 98.

105. We are reminded of G. Santayana, who said (*Reason in Religion* [New York: Dover, 1982], 137–38, 170) that Christianity would be beautiful if it were not taken literally. When it is taken literally, he adds, its dogmas, like the damnation of innocents, are absurd.

106. John Polkinghorne, "The Metaphysics of Divine Action," in *Chaos and Complexity,* ed. Robert J. Russell, Nancey Murphy, and Arthur R. Peacocke (Vatican City State: Vatican Observatory, 1995).

107. Polkinghorne, "Divine Action," 155.

108. Polkinghorne, "Divine Action," 153.

109. Polkinghorne, "Divine Action," 154.

110. Polkinghorne, "Divine Action," 155.

111. There is an abundance of earnest attempts to find a scientific basis for religious beliefs at which the skeptic can only marvel. Denis Edwards, invoking the inspiration of Peacocke and Polkinghorne, finds in chaos theory support for the trinity ("The Discovery of Chaos and the Retrieval of the Trinity," in *Chaos and Complexity*, ed. Robert J. Russell, Nancey Murphy, and Arthur R. Peacocke [Vatican City State: Vatican Observatory, 1995], 157–75); Stephen Happel finds in the scientific concept of self-ordering systems the conditions for cooperation with divine action without conflict ("Divine Providence and Instrumentality: Metaphors for Time in Self-Organizing Systems and Divine Action," in *Chaos and Complexity*, 177–203). After struggling mightily with showing how God might work in the world, William Stoeger finally admits that he is not able to solve the problem because of his ignorance of the nature of the key term *God* ("Describing God's Action in the World in the Light of Scientific Knowledge of Reality," in *Chaos and Complexity*, 239–61).

112. John Polkinghorne, "A Potent Universe," in *Evidence of Purpose: Scientists Discover the Creator*, ed. John Marks Templeton (New York: Continuum, 1994), 104–15.

113. Polkinghorne, "Universe," 114.

114. Polkinghorne, "Universe," 115.

115. Stephen Jay Gould, "Non-Overlapping Magisteria," *Skeptical Inquirer* 23, no. 4 (1999; reprinted from Gould's *Leonardo's Mountain of Clams and the Diet of Worms*): 58.

116. Gould, "Magisteria," 58.

117. Gould, "Magisteria," 57.

118. Gould, "Magisteria," 58.

119. Gould, "Magisteria," 60.

120. Richard Dawkins, "You Can't Have It Both Ways: Irreconcilable Differences?" *Skeptical Inquirer* 23, no. 4 (1999): 64.

121. Dawkins, "Differences," 64. Note that Ernan McMullin, a Catholic philosopher, sees spiritual meaning in the ideas of a common ancestry and of a continuity between humans and other species.

122. Dawkins, "Differences," 64.

123. Dawkins, "Differences," 63.

15

Conclusion

Blind is he who thinks he sees everything.

—Sholom Aleichem

UNSUCCESSFUL ATTEMPTS AT
RECONCILING SCIENCE AND RELIGION

We have frequently stated in these pages that the challenge to dualistic systems comes at the point where they interact. How does what is not corporeal actually affect what is corporeal? The answer of Aristotle and the Neoplatonists—that it stirred movement as object of desire—provided a recognizable experience for living things but lacked explanatory power at the level of the mind, for the theory could not show the mechanism by which the desired object actually produced the physical movement. And, of course, for inanimate entities, since they have no capacity to desire, the theory did not even evoke a recognizable experience. Other hypotheses that were offered, such as an action in the pineal gland, were insufficient to satisfy scientific rigor. Either they were not subject to experimentation or were not falsifiable.

Most disappointing of all have been attempts to assert the truth of specific religious doctrines and their compatibility with current science. Al Ghazali masterfully showed that his contemporaries failed—that twisting the meaning of Scripture by converting it to metaphor or allegory or simplistic, insipid tales for the stupid masses is intellectually dishonest. Al Ghazali concluded, for example, that science (which for him was identical to philosophy) could not prove the doctrine of resurrection or any other doctrine, and, given science's failure, a pious life required a pure, unquestioning faith. Among our contemporaries, Arthur Peacocke

302

asserts the compatibility of resurrection or other specific religious views with science, but he does so on no philosophical or scientific foundation whatsoever and hence fails to divert al Ghazali's criticism.

The theologians of the past were, we believe, at their noblest and most glorious when they humbly faced their intellectual limits. Augustine affirmed the superiority of Catholicism over Manichaeism because it did not claim to *know* what could be affirmed only by *faith*. Thus Catholicism was more intellectually honest than Manichaeism. Maimonides acknowledged philosophical *perplexity* as a reality he had to live with, and he did not assert as *science* propositions about which he was perplexed. Aquinas acknowledged that his philosophy could not conclusively answer the question of whether the world was created in time or was eternal and declared it would be wrong for philosophy to affirm as known what remained unknown. These, we maintain, were all honest acknowledgments of a failure to reconcile specific religious views with science.

Perhaps the most promising avenue for reconciling religion and science lay in the "argument from design." As we have seen, human thought, perhaps by nature, tends to be teleological, that is, to see purposes. To observe an intricate, regularly ordered thing, whether it be a clock or tidal patterns or the movement of the stars, and *not* to assume some purpose, whether consciously designed or not, requires an almost unnatural effort. Ancient science, with the remarkable exception of the Epicureans (whose explanation, because it required unaccountable, mysterious "swerves," was ultimately defective), could not conceive of design without conscious purpose. Contemporary reconcilers have hoped to find evidence of divine purpose in the modern variations of the argument from design, such as the "anthropic principle" or "intelligent design theory." We hope to have shown in the previous chapter that these modern design arguments are just as flawed as their ancient counterparts. Moreover, insights of modern science, especially contemporary Darwinism and inflation theory, offer scientific explanations of apparent design without appeal to purposes. These latter theories truly are "something new under the sun." Thus the quest for conclusive evidence of God through the argument from design remains at best elusive.

GENERAL COMMENTS

The desire to know, a desire nearly as strong in humans as the impulses towards food and sex, perhaps developed as a concomitant of the ability to learn and of the ability to use what was learned to control the environment. Practical knowledge made habitation outside the African savanna possible. People were able to exploit whatever opportunities were presented by the most inhospitable climates and terrains into which they migrated. Observation of regular effects resulting from the same causes is a process that occurs in many animals and allows them to be trained. A dog will eventually learn that sitting is followed by a biscuit after the same sound

"Sit!" Presumably the dog does not have an abstract idea of obedience or of sitting. Humans, whose brains are capable of abstracting general principles from the regularity of observations, are able to collect the "knowledge" that makes control of the environment possible.

When a few adventurous Greeks invented science, it became immediately clear that *scientific* knowledge might have practical advantages. An anecdote is recorded about Thales, the person credited as the inventor of science. Thales was famous for looking at the stars and for losing himself in abstruse thoughts. One day, the story goes, he fell into a well while looking skywards—an event that became emblematic of his inability to cope with this world. Thales decided that he would prove to the world that his ineptitude did not spring from stupidity but from a disinclination to devote himself to mundane matters. Having studied the climate, he predicted that there would be an unusually excellent crop of olives in a certain season. He raised the funds to acquire all the olive presses, so that anyone who wanted to make olive oil would be obliged to rent one of his machines. His monopoly enabled him to acquire fabulous wealth in a short period of time. He then returned to science, having proved that he could make money if he wanted to. (Many an impecunious professor has comforted himself with this tale!)

Aristotle divided the sciences into three kinds—those done for the sake of a product, such as the science of making olive presses; those done for the sake of an activity, such as ethics and politics; and those done for the sake of knowledge itself, such as geometry and metaphysics. As it was his practice to assign a rank to everything, Aristotle gave the crown to the sciences done for their own sake, that is, when the knowledge sought is for the sake of knowledge alone, not for any practical or productive good. This ranking still lingers, as some see engineering as a lower order of activity than physics, or pure research (note the normative term *pure*) as superior to applied research. Ancient science did not as a rule seek practical applications. Perhaps because of this gulf between theory and practice, theories could be maintained even if practice showed that they were mistaken.

In any case, it is obvious that knowledge of the world was slowly acquired, and this knowledge brought control over the environment. The ability of people to build shelters, to irrigate crops, to import products by sea-going vessels, and to formulate complex social laws so that large numbers of individuals could live together and engage in specialized labors all made life pleasant.

Control over nature was expected by supernatural means where it was not easily obtained by natural means. Since spirits seemed responsible for everything that happened, it was important to communicate with them, to appease them, and to coerce or persuade them to provide whatever was needed—good weather, good health, victory over enemies, and so forth. That a divine presence in the world interacts with human life is a belief doubted by very few in the history of the world; nevertheless, there has been little in common either in the conception of the spirits or in the rituals required to communicate. Moreover, refinements upon religious views have been continually made. Even in religions that look to their longevity as evidence of their validity, there have generally been innovations.

Even the most conservatively orthodox religious people think, and their thinking leads to modifications in ritual or belief. The great strength of Egypt was to stand still, though Kitchener scoffed at a country that (according to him) painted cats the same way for thousands of years. But even Egypt changed in its religious views in different periods and places.[1]

Once science arose, what constituted certainty became clear. The conclusions of geometry and logic—the models of what we have called strong or Aristotelian science—result from rigorous, systematic argument and exemplify a very high level of certainty. This strong science shows that reason alone is incapable of fully explaining, and of producing the same high level of certainty for, the characteristics of the divine—even whether the divine exists. Some thinkers felt either that it would be enough to show that science does not *contradict* received doctrines about divinity or that it would be enough to leave some room for God to operate.

As we have frequently observed, for the most part human minds rebel at the prospect of uncertainty. The uncertainty in the claim that there can be both natural and divine causes for things evidently disturbs many human souls. The deist notion that God's activity consists only of the initial creation of the universe and its physical laws was not found satisfying because of its limitation of God's power. As a consequence, there arose various theories to work out an intellectually satisfying co-existence of natural law and active, continuing divine action. We have suggested that those producing the theories are trying to maintain intellectual homeostasis: they want the world and human life with its spiritual inclinations to fit harmoniously and meaningfully together. They somehow feel that their reason is well satisfied by the laws of science that describe the physical universe but fear that their lives will be lost in a meaningless, empty, hopeless void without a superintending divinity. These efforts represent our human tendency to seek an order that puts everything in its place and in a hierarchical position vis-à-vis everything else.

The problem of this reconciliation may be illustrated by an analogy. Let us say that those seeking to understand the world scientifically are like children playing with Lego blocks and that those seeking to understand it by religion are like children playing with Lincoln Logs. Those seeking a reconciliation may be likened to children trying to make the two different types of toys fit together harmoniously without building a gangly monstrosity that instantly falls apart. Now children who have only one of the toys and never find out about the other suffer no intellectual crisis—they know of only one system of building forts or houses. The only children who experience the maddening frustration of combining the two toys will be those familiar with both. In the same way, those societies that never had contact with Greek thought and had only religion have not experienced— how could they?—the will to reconcile the two ways of understanding reality. The analogy might be examined further. Those who build with the toy blocks are not of course constructing reality; they are making imitations of it. Those who live a religious life and those who pursue scientific knowledge are dealing with reality. They would say that unlike children, who don't worry about the blocks themselves but accept them as a given, they *do* worry about the blocks—who made them, why they are here, and so on—for these questions are the subject matter of science and religion.

Most people, even in the West, have never questioned their faith. They accept it as they received it from their parents and their religion's authorities. This book has not been about them. If these people became aware of the other group—those who worry about science and religion—they probably would gaze on them with pity, as suffering from an illness, an illness of insufficient faith. For the faithful, that is, for those whose homeostasis consists of holding to their faith, this book has been a case study of those afflicted with the illness.

Despite all the problems we have outlined in this book, we can say that many of the various attempts to reconcile science and religion *have* indeed been successful, at least in part, and *have* managed to achieve a consistent worldview. These sorts of reconciliations, however, especially the first two discussed in the next section, are not likely to be very appealing, for they make profound compromises somewhere—either in the science or in the religion—and thus will not appease those who have strong convictions in either area.

TYPES OF "RECONCILIATION" THAT ARE POSSIBLE

Denial of God

One way to solve a problem is to eliminate it altogether. For example, when Rome found a certain city objectionable, an entirely efficacious option was to destroy it completely, root and branch. Total elimination of a social problem means reducing one of the parties to zero. For those who earnestly and sincerely believe that all religion is bunk and that no bunk should be tolerated, this is the best form of making peace between science and religion. Of the thinkers we have examined in this book, Richard Dawkins perhaps best exemplifies this view, although the ancient Epicureans and other atomists come close to a wholesale rejection of religion.

There are others who assume that where discrepant views are at odds, the truth *must* lie somewhere in the middle. But of course where the terms are exclusive, this "compromising" attitude is mistaken. For example, if a man must choose to be in Chicago for his sister's wedding on a certain date or in San Francisco for his friend's wedding on the same date, clearly he cannot compromise by going to Denver. If the position of religion is indeed wholly erroneous, rejection is the right choice. Better that one should acknowledge the unreality and absurdity of religion than live in delusion. Even if the delusion is comfortable and pleasing, would a rational, intelligent human being wish to live deceived in his one fleeting moment in this universe?

Those who consciously reject God believe either that everything can be explained by the laws of nature or that no explanation is possible at all or even needed. Biological entities can be explained as having arisen from simple organic molecules synthesized in earth's primordial soup two billion years ago. Physical phenomena can be traced to a few moments after the Big Bang, and these few moments, they believe, will become understood eventually, as our knowledge of science increases. As for what happened before the initial moment, either the word *before* is meaningless, since time is a function of the motion that came into being, or only highly speculative theories are possible.

The ancient Epicureans had essentially this latter view, though of course they did not put it in terms of the Big Bang. They believed that everything could be explained in terms of atoms and vacuity and the various laws that govern them. Even their gods are made of atoms and vacuity and obey the physical laws. They explained free will and chance by random "swerves." That the swerves exist was a postulate. How atoms came into being and why they fell were not questions that Epicureans addressed.

A number of modern physicists hold the same Epicurean views. Steven Weinberg, a Nobel laureate physicist, is representative of many modern scientists who hold them. At a recent conference sponsored by the Templeton Foundation, he called religion "an insult to human dignity" and a destructive force in society. In a statement that might have come from the pen of Lucretius, he added, "One of science's principal accomplishments had been in releasing intellectuals from the need to have religious faith."[2]

Those who believe in the deity of traditional religions will note that science cannot explain many of the profound circumstances of our life. It can offer few if any deep insights into love, loneliness, despair. It cannot explain beauty or laughter or the internal experience, with all its connotative associations, of the color red.[3] And, if they believe that faith in their religion is a requirement for salvation, well, clearly they will assign those who deny God to an eternal doom in hell. This worst of all possible outcomes does not, at least in this life, bother those who reject God, for they consider flimflam about an afterlife part of the bunk they reject.

Denial of Science

A rejection of science is also an intellectually satisfactory way of reconciling science and religion — insofar as it is intellectually satisfying to avoid the self-contradictions fatal to reason. If one adopts the appropriate first principles, the rejection of science will provide at least a consistent picture of the universe. If God is omnipotent, he may do anything that he wishes. If he chooses to act through the laws of nature, he may; if he chooses to violate the laws of nature, he may. If he chooses to deceive mankind with signs that the world is billions of years old, he may; and if he wishes to test people's faith by this misleading evidence, he may. The view that God is the cause of everything that happens, with the corollary that things apparently evil occur for some purpose in God's mind, is not subject to refutation. It may be that the claim is "uninteresting" in the sense that if it is true it is not debatable, but that something is "uninteresting" does not invalidate its truth.

This view, as we have seen, was held by Tertullian and, perhaps with more powerful acumen, by al Ghazali, who brilliantly exposed the inconsistencies of the science of his day. He showed that none of the arguments advanced by the philosophers held up to rigorous investigation and destroyed their arguments using their own logic. Because modern science is based on much stronger evidence and boasts a formidable track record, to refute it completely will be a very difficult task.

But modern religionists who understand science, people like Ward, Peacocke, and Polkinghorne, for example, do not use the arguments of science to undercut the science. Instead, they claim that science can lead us to God. Those who wish to reject modern science have yet to find their al Ghazali.

Redefining the Key Term—God

One of the most attractive ways of reconciling science and God is to define God in such a way as to eliminate any possible contradiction. The fact that there are so many different conceptions of God within and among various religions encourages latitude in choosing a definition that accommodates the needs of science.

Some of the pre-Socratics first attempted to identify God with the laws of nature or with the cosmic process. Spinoza did the same, declaring that the world *is* God under his attributes of thought and extension. Alternatively, God might be defined *as* the initiating or first cause, whether that cause is a Prime Mover (as Aristotle called him) or a cosmic clockmaker (as Paley called him) or the Big Bang itself. If God is defined as any of these things, or even as the principle of causality or as everything, there are no problems that contradict science. Nor are there problems if God's operations are similarly defined, as, say, the *process* of evolution, or as the law of gravity, or as quantum mechanics, and so forth. In other words, if we declare God to be the way things are, the problem of God and the reality uncovered by science evaporates.

With God so defined, "religion" and "religious experience" may be defined as that sense of awe and wonder that one has when marveling at the greatness and beauty of the world or the laws that describe it. Science may very well lead to "religious experience," when "religious experience" is defined in this way. When scientists talk about God and their deep religious feeling, they often have in mind rapturous ecstasy at the glories of their discoveries. They have seen the "mind of God" or the "wisdom of God," or some other poetic formulation.

Of course, the problem with this view is that the God of science does not listen to prayers, invites no ritual, has no dogma, requires no priests, does not intervene in human affairs, does not serve as a moral guide, and is generally silent. He has none of the pleasing qualities of personality that religious people traditionally desire. He would demand no churches, no monasteries, no mosques, no synagogues, no cemeteries, no symbols—nothing. If God is denuded of all human features, he cannot be much of a friend or comforter. Cosmic causality does not have ears to hear our cries for comfort or eyes to see our misery. Nevertheless, if the goal is *philosophical* consistency, then one can define oneself out of problems of self-contradiction by adopting one of these definitions of God.

Separating the Spheres of Religion and Science

It is possible to circumscribe science by confining it to what is observable by the senses and subject to testing in this life. One can then circumscribe religion by confining it to those matters that pertain to the mysterious—life after death, the communion of living and dead, communication with the divine, salvation and the judgment of the dead, the mysteries of the Trinity, the transformation of substances by miraculous intervention—in short, to those areas that conflict with reason and that most twentieth-century scientists would deny have anything to do with their work.

There will then be no conflict between science and religion because they will never intersect. Scientists will never bring their work home, so to speak, but leave it in the laboratory. When they leave work, they will become subject to a different set of laws. The spheres will never meet, like children who play with Lego blocks in one romper room and then move to another to play with Lincoln Logs.

This is the view often attributed to Averroës and recently put forth by Stephen Jay Gould, as discussed in the preceding chapter. The attractiveness of this view is that it allows each realm to have its own unchallenged jurisdiction. Even if we leave aside Dawkins' legitimate point that miracles involve scientific claims, the problem is that our lives do not compartmentalize so very neatly. It is not easy for a scientist to leave his rational mind at work, and even if it were easy, why should he? Is not the same exercise of thought likely to solve problems at home? And why should religion be narrowed to cultural and social activities? Those who take their religion seriously, who find real meaning in it, are not likely to admit of this dichotomous living. Indeed, the tradition of the West maintains the unitary nature of truth—one truth for all races, one truth for men and women, one truth for both religion and science.

Declaring God and His Operations Unknowable

Last, it is possible to attempt to reconcile science and religion with the assertion that God is unknowable and works through what is unknown. This solution has its roots in the earliest days of Greek philosophy, when Xenophanes and Heraclitus reasoned that the divine is so different from anything that we experience as to be ineffable and incomprehensible. Later on, the "doctrine of negative attributes" maintained that any actual terms used to describe God or his attributes are incapable of actually describing him, that since all words have definitions that limit their meaning, it is mistaken to use limited terms for a boundless God. God can be known only negatively, by what he is not—but to know God by what he is not is not really to know him at all. By this view, God and his operations are mysterious. What appears evil is, in his big scheme of things, actually good. Modern physics, with its theories of uncertainty in quantum fluctuations and of unpredictability from "chaos," has given God a place to work that is *demonstrably* unknowable. What is new is the apparent scientific validation and theoretical framework for unknowability. Now the claim that God's work is inherently unknowable appears to have a seal of approval from modern science. This solution has the enormous advantage of confirming the traditional view of God's participation in our world through ways mostly invisible to us. There is no conflict with science if we attribute to God something that science declares *inherently* unknowable. The cost is free. If the phenomenon is inherently unknowable, science loses nothing by granting God a role.

One critical problem with this line of thinking is that *how* exactly God works through the scientifically unknowable parts of nature must remain entirely mysterious. Another problem, of course, is the same found in other scientific or philosophical accounts of the divine. It ignores the God of our religions. As Augustine observes in the opening of his *Confessions,* if he does not know God, he might pray to something else by mistake. Augustine's solution was faith, but faith is not a scientific solution. Moreover, this solution involves really nothing but a substitution for the word *God.* Instead of saying "I don't know why such and such happened," one says "*God* is why such and such happened." In a fundamental way, this is but a return to the religious experience of primitive humans.

PROBLEMS

All of the proposed solutions are in some way irreligious by the standards of traditional religions. There is no way to derive the Ten Commandments or the Incarnation of Christ out of any of them. Arthur Peacocke, as we have observed, examined the various doctrines of Christianity and rejected them *seriatim,* except for the resurrection, which he accepted on faith for no coherent reason.

For a nonbeliever there is no problem, for there is nothing to reconcile. There is no need to reconcile the Easter Bunny with the spring equinox or Santa Claus with the winter solstice because, for the nonbeliever, Santa Claus and the Easter Bunny are, like the other supernatural characters in religion, phantoms of the imagination. For a devout believer, however, religion comes first, and nothing that science addresses can demonstrate its falsity. If science says one thing and religion another, science must yield. The masterstroke is the principle that God can do whatever he pleases because he is God and that the chief virtue of a believer is submission to this truth.

Reconciliation of science and religion is a problem only for believers who also want to accept science. For the most part these are people who were brought up in religious families, who drank religion with their infant formula, whose early religious associations are intermingled with family warmth, with the security of a kindly priest, with the comfort that religion evidently brought to their families in times of distress. The truth of particular religious doctrines, or at least of many of them, seems to these people self-evident. Yet they have attended universities. They have been persuaded of the laws of chemistry and physics. The evidence of evolution seems irrefutable. Here and there during their theological studies they have discovered statements that seem to anticipate scientific theories while somehow fitting in with God's plans. Though they accept the scientific explanations of causality, they cannot let go of the argument from design, for it convincingly confirms the image of God as a conscious mind somewhat like ours, the God that they have grown up with. So they have manipulated their science into an "anthropic principle" or some other catchy phrase that suggests a way for God to operate.

Yet the deity that they rescue proves not much different from Aristotle's Prime Mover, a God very different from the God of the Pentateuch and the prophets and the Gospels and the Qur'an. And when they try desperately to find some link between the dogmas of their traditional religion and their scientifically acceptable notion of God, they descend into nonsensical gibberish.

The gibberish reflects an effort to maintain the homeostasis that we have spoken of here. The human mind can live with gibberish; it cannot live with contradiction. So long as the gibberish is not self-contradictory, it can be called "plausible" or a "best guess" and can give some comfort to its advocate in virtue of its intellectual respectability.

A PROPOSAL

In his *Confessions,* Augustine says that he preferred the Catholic religion to Manichaeism because when Catholicism held a proposition for which it did not have *knowledge,* it called the proposition an article of *faith.* The Manichaeans, however, claimed to know what they did not know. Hence it was intellectually honest to be a Catholic and not to affirm knowledge where there was no knowledge.

What happened to this respectable view? Well, faith was metamorphosed into a virtue and declared to grasp truth. For Aristotle, truth was the object of *knowledge;* for Christianity, truth was the object also of *faith.* Christianity then required Christians to believe the "truths" of faith, and dictated that belief in these truths was required for salvation. This was a philosophical mistake. In requiring faith, Christianity, along with the other religions of faith, was demeaning knowledge, especially knowledge in the strong Aristotelian sense of understanding through causes. Since human beings by nature desire to *know,* the Church was demanding that they violate their nature. Now faith and knowledge both deal with causes and both result in a similar psychological state of intellectual calm (or "intellectual homeostasis"). Just as a safe medicine—methadone—might mimic the effect of an unsafe one—heroin—and fool the body into accepting it, so faith, with its explanations of cause, mimics the effect of knowledge and fools the mind. The Church, moreover, teaches that human beings are made in God's image and that the image is *logos* or reason itself, a prime quality of which is the search for understanding through causes. The Church asks that human beings violate the very nature it acknowledges. This contradictory stance is perhaps responsible for the civil war in the souls of those who seek to reconcile their religion with their science.

Those who seek evidence of God's purpose will find some appealing hints in the character of the universe. Their reason will lead them to a first cause, which they will call God. But they will not be able to *prove* demonstrably that God designed the system, or either consciously or unconsciously set the initial conditions, or sketched out either generally or in detail the laws of physics, or plotted the path of natural selection, or keeps the whole universe going by sustaining it as efficient cause, or intervenes with little adjustments now and again. Science cannot prove, either a priori or a posteriori, either from causes or from effects, anything about God's activities. Religion cannot offer any "demonstrative proofs" about God either. Therefore, all these features of God, if they are to be held, must be held by faith, for they are not subject to knowledge.

Human beings are fortunate in that they *can* know what they do not know. This bit of Socratic wisdom is something to which we can aspire. This wisdom can direct our investigations to our areas of ignorance, and it can lead us to the closure of *knowing* that certain things cannot be known. Rather than lament this information, we should rejoice in it and celebrate its advantages. One advantage—albeit a minor one—is that it allows us to play games of chance, games we could not play if there were no such thing as chance. A second advantage—a major one—is that it makes possible the range of moral actions that depend on a degree of ignorance. For example, courage requires knowledge of risk, and risk includes knowing that what will happen is not known. (A person who *knows* that he will be successful does not need courage; a person who *knows* he will fail will not make the attempt. The courageous person is the one who makes the attempt hoping for, but not certain of, success.) All humans know that they are going to die and they also know that they do *not* know when or how. Perhaps we are actually better off not knowing, and knowing that we do not know. So our proposal is that we gladly, even cheerfully, acknowledge what we do not know and not substitute tales or hopes or fears about it. This acknowledgment of our limits will enable us to know who we really are as human beings.

CONCLUSIONS ABOUT GOD AND HUMANKIND

We can attempt several conclusions. First, if there is no God, we do not have to draw any conclusions about him. But we can still draw conclusions about how we ought to live our lives. If we find ourselves alone in our corner of the universe, occupants of a little planet in the middle of the Milky Way, itself a galaxy in the middle of nowhere special, we should make the best of our situation. Making the best of it means living lives that are as good as they can be by seeking the greatest possible happiness. Fortunately, Aristotle's *Ethics* provides us with one possible formula: we ought to seek lives of rational activity in accordance with virtue. Such lives will fulfill our *biological* nature as rational bipeds, will make possible the fulfillment of our *social* natures in communities, and will give us the individual satisfaction of the most *human* of pleasures, intellectual pleasure. This intellectual pleasure will of course include acquiring as much knowledge of the universe as possible. Our lives will be meaningful in the limited way that they can be when they are not part of some greater scheme. This is not inconsequential. It is no insult to Lear that he is a character only in Shakespeare's *King Lear* and that he does not appear in *Ivanhoe*. It is no diminution of human existence that it is played out only on earth and not in the whole cosmos.

If there is a God and if he is the laws of nature, or if his mind is the laws and his body is the universe itself, we need do nothing at all, for the universe and God will continue to operate in accordance with the laws that are God. If God is the initial cause, the setter of initial conditions, the original clockmaker and so on, again we need do nothing, and for the same reason, since the laws will continue to operate as they have been set.

If there is a benevolent God who, like an artist, has particularly designed our natures in his image, we can conclude that it is incompatible with his goodness to demand that we hold to certain faiths, for to do so is to violate our nature as rational animals. He must want us to pursue knowledge; not to have this wish would be malevolent on his part. It would be like creating an eagle with wings but demanding that it always walk on the ground, or, even worse, creating it with wings and giving it only the *illusion* of flight. So if there is such a God, he should be pleased with human scientific inquiry.

Would such a God want us to embrace *revelation?* We think not, certainly not as we find revelation on our planet, for such a wish would be inconsistent with his goodness. It would be as though a parent told each of his many children that he has a different, special, exclusive truth for each of them, a "truth" inconsistent and contradictory to what he has told the other children. Such a parent would be malevolent. He would have given each child a sense of his own rightness, his own probity, and he would have stirred each child to depreciate the opinions of his siblings. Such a view is inconsistent with the view of a benevolent deity.

Without revelation can there be the rituals and communication of a personal deity? We do not see how there can be. Without a personal deity, without a creator-God we find ourselves without a divine comforter. This is indeed a great loss. It is far greater than the loss of both parents. Yet finding oneself alone is part of the excitement of life, part of the adventure of growing up—a sad adventure, to be sure, full of uncertainty and challenge.

NOTES

1. C. Hobson, *The World of the Pharaohs* (New York: Thames and Hudson, 1987), 132ff.

2. The information about the April 1999 conference, which was held in conjunction with the American Association for the Advancement of Science, is from the *Chronicle of Higher Education,* 30 April 1999, A17–18.

3. Such is the claim of Irwin Cohen, "The Paradox That Stumped Science," *Reform Judaism* 27, no. 4 (1999): 39–40. Cohen, an emeritus professor of chemistry, also gives an interesting version of Leibniz's view that ours is the best of all possible worlds. He argues that the world's imperfections are perfect for us, for they allow free will, inspire virtue, promote reflection. "This suggested—but didn't prove—that the world is no accident but was created; and quite possibly it was created for our benefit." Here is yet another version of the argument from design!

Works Cited

Afnan, M. *Avicenna: His Life and Works.* Westport, Conn.: Greenwood, 1958.

Al Farabi. *Mabadi' Ara Ahl Al-Madinah al-Fadilah.* Translated by Richard Walzer. Chicago: Great Books of the Islamic World; Distributed by KAZI Publications, 1998.

Al Ghazali. "Vivification of Theology." In *Averroës' Tahafut Al-Tahafut,* translated by S. Van Den Bergh. London: Gibb Memorial Trust, 1978.

Altmann, A. *Studies in Religious Philosophy and Mysticism.* Ithaca, N.Y.: Cornell University Press, 1969.

Arieti, James A. *Interpreting Plato: The Dialogues As Drama.* Savage, Md.: Rowman and Littlefield, 1991.

———. "Nudity in Greek Athletics." *The Classical World* 68 (1975): 431–36.

Arieti, Silvano. *Interpretation of Schizophrenia.* 2d ed. New York: Basic Books, 1974.

Aristotle. *Aristotle's Metaphysics.* Translated with commentaries by H. G. Apostle. Grinnell, Iowa: Peripatetic Press, 1979.

———. *Aristotle's Posterior Analytics.* Translated by H. G. Apostle. Grinnell, Iowa: Peripatetic Press, 1981.

———. *Problems.* Translated by E. S. Forster. In *The Complete Works of Aristotle: The Revised Oxford Translation,* edited by J. Barnes. Princeton, N.J.: Princeton University Press, 1984.

Armstrong, A. H., ed. *The Cambridge History of Later Greek and Early Medieval Philosophy.* Cambridge: Cambridge University Press, 1967.

Augustine. *The City of God.* Translated by M. Dods. Chicago: Encyclopaedia Britannica, 1952.

———. *Confessions.* Translated by Rex Warner. New York: New American Library, 1963.

Averroës. *Averroës' Tahafut al-tahafut (The Incoherence of the Incoherence).* Translated by S. Van den Bergh. London: Trustees of the "E. J. W. Gibb Memorial," 1978.

Bacon, Francis. *The Essays.* Mount Vernon, N.Y.: Peter Pauper, n.d.

Bahya ben Joseph ibn Pakuda. *The Duties of the Heart* [*Hovot ha-levavot*]. Translated by Yaakov Feldman. Northvale, N.J.: J. Aronson, 1996.

Beckmann, Petr. *A History of π.* New York: St. Martin's, 1971.

Bollack, Jean. *Empedocle.* Paris: Éditions de Minuit, 1965.

Bonaventure. *Opera Omnia.* Quaracchi: Ex Typographia Collegii S. Bonaventurae, 1882–1902.

Boswell, James. *Boswell's Life of Johnson.* Edited by G. B. Hill. New York: Harper and Brothers, n.d.

Brown, Peter. *The Body and Society: Men, Women, and Sexual Renunciation in Early Christianity.* New York: Columbia University Press, 1988.

Burghardt, W. J. *The Image of God in Man According to Cyril of Alexandria.* Woodstock, Md.: Woodstock College Press, 1957.

Casridini, M. T. "Il cosmo di Filolao." *Rivista Critica di Storia della Filosofia* 3 (1946): 322–33.

Chadwick, H. "Origen." In *The Cambridge History of Later Greek and Early Medieval Philosophy,* edited by A. H. Armstrong. Cambridge: Cambridge University Press, 1967.

——. "Philo." In *The Cambridge History of Later Greek and Early Medieval Philosophy,* edited by A. H. Armstrong. Cambridge: Cambridge University Press, 1967.

Cicero. *The Nature of the Gods.* Translated by H. C. McGregor. New York: Viking Penguin, 1985.

Cochrane, C. N. *Christianity and Classical Culture.* New York: Oxford University Press, 1940.

Cohen, Irwin. "The Paradox That Stumped Science." *Reform Judaism* 27, no. 4 (1999): 39.

Cooper, Lane. *Aristotle, Galileo, and the Tower of Pisa.* Ithaca, N.Y.: Cornell University Press, 1935.

Crutchfield, J. P. "Chaos." In *Chaos and Complexity: Scientific Perspectives on Divine Action,* edited by Robert J. Russell, Nancey Murphy, and Arthur R. Peacocke. Vatican City State: Vatican Observatory, 1995.

Dangelmayr, S. *Gotteserkenntnis und Gottesbegriff in den philosophischen Schriften des Nikolaus von Kues.* Meisenheim am Glan: Anton Hain, 1969.

Darwin, Charles. *On the Origin of Species by Means of Natural Selection; or, The Preservation of Favored Races in the Struggle for Life.* New York: New American Library, 1958.

David, Peter. "Moral Majority Intervenes." *Nature* 304 (1983): 201.

Davies, N. *Human Sacrifice in History and Today.* New York: Morrow, 1981.

Davis, B. *The Thought of Thomas Aquinas.* Oxford: Clarendon, 1992.

Dawkins, Richard. "You Can't Have It Both Ways: Irreconcilable Differences?" *Skeptical Inquirer* 23, no. 4 (1999): 62–64.

Dembski, William A. *The Design Inference.* Cambridge: Cambridge University Press, 1998.

——. *Intelligent Design: The Bridge between Science and Theology.* Downers Grove, Ill.: InterVarsity, 1999.

Dennett, Daniel. *Darwin's Dangerous Idea: Evolution and the Meaning of Life.* New York: Simon & Schuster, 1995.

Desmond, Adrian, and James Moore. *Darwin: The Life of a Tormented Evolutionist.* New York: Warner, 1991.

Dodds, E. R. *The Greeks and the Irrational.* Berkeley: University of California Press, 1964.

——. *Pagan and Christian in an Age of Anxiety: Some Aspects of Religious Experience from Marcus Aurelius to Constantine.* New York: Norton, 1965.

——. *Select Passages Illustrating Neoplatonism.* Chicago: Ares, 1979.

Dreyer, J. L. E. *A History of Astronomy from Thales to Kepler.* Revised by W. H. Stahl. New York: Dover, 1953.

Durant, W. *Rousseau and Revolution.* New York: Simon & Schuster, 1967.

——. *The Story of Philosophy.* New York: Simon & Schuster, 1926.

Edwards, Denis. "The Discovery of Chaos and the Retrieval of the Trinity." In *Chaos and Complexity: Scientific Perspectives on Divine Action,* edited by Robert J. Russell, Nancey Murphy, and Arthur R. Peacocke. Vatican City State: Vatican Observatory, 1995.

Einstein, Albert. "Autobiographical Notes." In *Albert Einstein: Philosopher-Scientist,* edited by P. A. Schilpp. New York: Tudor, 1951.

——. *The World As I See It.* Translated by Alan Harris. New York: Covici Friede, 1934.

Erasmus. *Erasmus-Luther: Discourse on Free Will.* Translated by E. F. Winter. New York: Frederick Ungar, 1961.

Fakhry, M. *A History of Islamic Philosophy.* New York: Columbia University Press, 1970.

——. *Islamic Occasionalism and Its Critique by Averroës and Aquinas.* London: Allen and Unwin, 1958.

Feynman, Richard. *What Do You Care What Other People Think? Further Adventures of a Curious Character.* New York: Bantam, 1989.

Fitelson, Branden, Christopher Stephens, and Elliott Sober. "How Not to Detect Design—Critical Notice: William A. Dembski, The Design Inference." *Philosophy of Science* 66 (1999): 472–88.

Fox, M. *Interpreting Maimonides: Studies in Methodology, Metaphysics, and Moral Philosophy.* Chicago: University of Chicago Press, 1990.

Frank, D. H. *New Introduction to Maimonides: The Guide of the Perplexed,* edited by J. Guttmann and translated by C. Rabin. Indianapolis: Hackett, 1995.

Frankel, E. *The Classic Tales: 4,000 Years of Jewish Lore.* Northvale, N.J.: Jason Aronson, 1993.

Frankel, H. *Early Greek Poetry and Philosophy.* Translated by M. Hadas and J. Willis. Oxford: Blackwell, 1975.

French, A. P., ed. *Einstein: A Centenary Volume.* Cambridge, Mass.: Harvard University Press, 1979.

Freud, S. "A Neurosis of Demoniacal Possession in the Seventeenth Century." In *Collected Papers,* translated by J. Riviere. New York: Basic Books, 1959.

——. "A Philosophy of Life, Lecture XXXV." In *New Introductory Lectures on Psycho-Analysis,* translated by W. J. H. Sprott. New York: Norton, 1933.

——. "The Question of Weltanschauung?" In *The Complete Introductory Lectures on Psychoanalysis,* translated by J. Strachley. New York: Norton, 1966.

Furley, D. "Self-Movers." In *Self-Motion: From Aristotle to Newton,* edited by M. L. Gill and J. G. Lennox. Princeton, N.J.: Princeton University Press, 1994.

Galileo. "Letter to the Grand Duchess Christina." In *Discoveries and Opinions of Galileo,* translated by S. Drake. New York: Doubleday, 1957.

——. "Il Saggiatore." In *Discoveries and Opinions of Galileo,* translated by S. Drake. New York: Doubleday, 1957.

Gibbon, E. *The Decline and Fall of the Roman Empire.* Great Books of the Western World Edition. Chicago: Encyclopedia Britannica, 1952.

Gill, M. L. "Aristotle on Self-Motion." In *Self-Motion: From Aristotle to Newton,* edited by M. L. Gill and J. G. Lennox. Princeton, N.J.: Princeton University Press, 1994.

Gomez-Lobo, A. "Definitions in Aristotle's Posterior Analytics." In *Studies in Aristotle,* edited by D. J. O'Meara. Washington: Catholic University Press, 1981.

Goodenough, E. *The Politics of Philo Judaeus with a General Bibliography of Philo.* New Haven, Conn.: Yale University Press, 1938.

Gould, Stephen Jay. "Non-Overlapping Magisteria." *Skeptical Inquirer* 23, no. 4 (1999; reprinted from Gould's *Leonardo's Mountain of Clams and the Diet of Worms*): 55–61.

Gribbin, J. *A Brief History of Science.* New York: Barnes and Noble, 1998.

Guttmann, J. Introduction to *Maimonides: The Guide of the Perplexed,* edited by J. Guttmann and translated by C. Rabin. Indianapolis: Hackett, 1995.

Happel, Stephen. "Divine Providence and Instrumentality: Metaphors for Time in Self-Organizing Systems and Divine Action." In *Chaos and Complexity: Scientific Perspectives on Divine Action,* edited by Robert J. Russell, Nancey Murphy, and Arthur R. Peacocke. Vatican City State: Vatican Observatory, 1995.

Heisenberg, Werner. *Across the Frontier.* New York: Harper & Row, 1974.

Hobson, C. *The World of the Pharaohs.* New York: Thames and Hudson, 1987.

Hume, David. *The History of England: From the Invasion of Julius Caesar to the Abdication of James the Second, 1688.* Philadelphia: J. B. Lippincott, 1865.

Husik, I. *A History of Mediaeval Jewish Philosophy.* Philadelphia: The Jewish Publication Society of America, 1916.

Ibn Daud. *The Exalted Faith.* Translated by N. Samuelson. Rutherford, N.J.: Fairleigh Dickinson, 1986.

Ibn Gabirol, Solomon. *"Keter Malkhuth" ("The Royal Crown").* In Selected Religious Poems of Solomon ibn Gabirol, translated by Israel Zangwill and edited by Israel Davidson. Philadelphia: Jewish Publication Society of America, 1952.

Inati, S. "Ibn Sina." In *History of Islamic Philosophy Part I,* edited by S. H. Nasr and O. Leaman. London: Routledge, 1996.

Jacobs, L. *Principles of the Jewish Faith.* Commentary Classics. New York: Basic Books, 1964.

Jaeger, Werner. *The Theology of the Early Greek Philosophers.* New York: Oxford University Press, 1967.

Joyce, G. H. *Principles of Natural Theology.* 3d ed. London: Longmans, 1934.

Kant, Immanuel. *The Critique of Judgment.* Translated by J. C. Meredith. Oxford: Clarendon, 1952.

——. *Religion within the Limits of Reason Alone.* Translated with an introduction and notes by Theodore M. Greene and Hoyt H. Hudson. Chicago: Open Court, 1934.

Keyt, D. "The Mad Craftsman of the Timaeus." *The Philosophical Review* 80 (1971): 230–35.

Kirk, G. S., and J. E. Raven. *The Presocratic Philosophers.* Cambridge: Cambridge University Press, 1966.

Klee, Robert. Introduction to the *Philosophy of Science: Cutting Nature at Its Seams.* New York: Oxford University Press, 1997.

Koestler, A. *The Watershed: A Biography of Johannes Kepler.* Garden City, N.Y.: Anchor, 1960.

Kretzmann, N., and E. Stump, eds. *The Cambridge Companion to Aquinas.* Cambridge: Cambridge University Press, 1993.

Kuhn, Thomas S. *The Structure of Scientific Revolutions.* Chicago: University of Chicago Press, 1970.

Leaman, O. *An Introduction to Medieval Islamic Philosophy.* Cambridge: Cambridge University Press, 1985.

——. *Moses Maimonides.* London: Routledge, 1990.

Liebeschütz, L. "Boethius and the Legacy of Antiquity." In *The Cambridge History of Later Greek and Early Medieval Philosophy,* edited by A. H. Armstrong. Cambridge: Cambridge University Press, 1967.

Livy. *Ab Urbe Condita.* Translated by A. de Sélincourt. New York: Penguin, 1971.

Lohr, C. H. "The Medieval Interpretation of Aristotle." In *The Cambridge Companion to Aquinas,* edited by N. Kretzmann and E. Stump. Cambridge: Cambridge University Press, 1993.

Longinus. *On the Sublime.* Translated and edited by James A. Arieti and John M. Crossett. New York: Edwin Mellen, 1985.

Lucretius. *On the Nature of the Universe.* Translated by R. E. Latham. New York: Penguin, 1994.

Maimonides. *The Guide of the Perplexed.* Translated by S. Pines. Chicago: University of Chicago Press, 1963.

McGuire, J. E. "Natural Motion and Its Causes: Newton on the 'Vis Insita' of Bodies." In *Self-Motion from Aristotle to Newton,* edited by M. L. Gill and J. G. Lennox. Princeton, N.J.: Princeton University Press, 1994.

Merlan, P. "Atticus and Other Platonists of the Second Century a.d." In *The Cambridge History of Later Greek and Early Medieval Philosophy,* edited by A. H. Armstrong. Cambridge: Cambridge University Press, 1967.

——. "Greek Philosophy from Plato to Plotinus." In *The Cambridge History of Later Greek and Early Medieval Philosophy,* edited by A. H. Armstrong. Cambridge: Cambridge University Press, 1967.

Miller, Hugh. *Testimony of the Rocks; or, Geology in Its Bearings on the Two Theologies, Natural and Revealed.* Edinburgh: Constable, 1856.

Mortley, R. J. "The Bond of the Cosmos: A Significant Metaphor (Tim. 31c ff.)." *Hermes* 97 (1969): 372–73.

Nehemiah. *The Mishnat ha Middot: The First Hebrew Geometry of about 150 C.E.; and The Geometry of Muhammad ibn Musa al-Khowarizmi: The First Arabic Geometry (c. 820) Representing the Arabic Version of the Mishnat ha Middot.* Translated by S. Gandz. Würzburg: jal-reprint, 1973.

Newton, Isaac. *Isaaci Newtoni opera quae exstant omnia.* London: Joannes Nichols, 1779–1785.

Nock, A. D. "The Loeb Philo." *The Classical Review* 75 (1943): 77–81.

Palmer, M. *Freud and Jung on Religion.* New York: Routledge, 1997.

Peacocke, Arthur. "Science and God the Creator." In *Evidence of Purpose: Scientists Discover the Creator,* edited by John Marks Templeton. New York: Continuum, 1994.

——. *Theology for a Scientific Age.* 2d ed. London: SCM, 1993.

Pegis, A. *Introduction to St. Thomas Aquinas.* New York: Modern Library, 1948.

Pike, N. *God and Timelessness.* London: Routledge and Kegan Paul, 1970.

Pines, S. "The Limitations of Human Knowledge According to Al-Farabi, Ibn Bajja and Maimonides." In *Studies in Medieval Jewish History and Literature,* edited by I. Twersky. Cambridge, Mass.: Harvard University Press, 1979.

Pinker, S. *How the Mind Works.* New York: Norton, 1997.

——. *The Language Instinct.* New York: HarperPerennial, 1995.

Planck, Max. *Where Is Science Going?* Translated by J. Murphy. New York: Norton, 1932.

Polkinghorne, John. "The Metaphysics of Divine Action." In *Chaos and Complexity: Scientific Perspectives on Divine Action,* edited by Robert J. Russell, Nancey Murphy, and Arthur R. Peacocke. Vatican City State: Vatican Observatory, 1995.

——. "A Potent Universe." In *Evidence of Purpose: Scientists Discover the Creator,* edited by John Marks Templeton. New York: Continuum, 1994.

Prager, D., and J. Telushkin. *The Nine Questions People Ask about Judaism.* New York: Simon and Schuster, 1981.

Raven, J. E. *Pythagoreans and Eleatics.* Cambridge: Cambridge University Press, 1948.

Ruse, M. *The Darwinian Revolution.* Chicago: University of Chicago Press, 1979.

Saadia ben Joseph. *Al-Amanat Wa-l-I 'tiqadat (The Book of Beliefs and Opinions).* Translated by S. Rosenblatt. New Haven, Conn.: Yale University Press, 1948.

Sagan, Carl. *The Demon-Haunted World: Science As a Candle in the Dark.* New York: Random House, 1995.

Saliba, D. *Étude sur la métaphysique d'Avicenne.* Paris: Les presses universitaires de France, 1926.

Samuelson, N. *The Exalted Faith.* Rutherford, N.J.: Fairleigh Dickinson, 1986.

Santayana, G. *Reason in Religion.* New York: Dover, 1982.

Sarton, G. *A History of Science.* Cambridge, Mass.: Harvard University Press, 1952.

Schilpp, P. A., ed. *Albert Einstein: Philosopher-Scientist.* New York: Tudor, 1951.

Sirat, C. *A History of Jewish Philosophy in the Middle Ages.* Cambridge: Cambridge University Press, 1985.

Smith, D. E. *History of Mathematics.* Boston: Ginn, 1923.

Smith, P. *History of Modern Culture.* New York: Holt, 1930.

Sophocles. *Oedipus Rex.* Translated by R. C. Jebb. Cambridge: Cambridge University Press, 1914.

Stoeger, William. "Describing God's Action in the World in the Light of Scientific Knowledge of Reality." In *Chaos and Complexity: Scientific Perspectives on Divine Action,* edited by Robert J. Russell, Nancey Murphy, and Arthur R. Peacocke. Vatican City State: Vatican Observatory, 1995.

Strauss, L. Introduction to *The Guide of the Perplexed,* by Maimonides. Translated by S. Pines. Chicago: University of Chicago Press, 1963.

Stump, E., and N. Kretzmann. "Eternity." *The Journal of Philosophy* 78 (1981): 429–58.

Tropfke, J. *Geschichte der Elementarmathematik. Vierter Band: Ebene Geometrie.* Berlin-Leipzig: Vereinigung wissenschaftlicher Verleger, 1923.

van Steenberghen, F. *Le problème de l'existence de Dieu dans les écrits de S. Thomas d'Aquin.* Louvain-La-Neuve: Editions de l'Institut supérieur de philosophie, 1980.

Vollert, C. *St. Thomas Aquinas: On the Eternity of the World and Selected Miscellaneous Texts.* Milwaukee: Marquette University Press, 1964.

Vollert, C., L. H. Kendzierski, and P. M. Byrne. *St. Thomas Aquinas, Siger of Brabant, St. Bonaventure: On the Eternity of the World.* Milwaukee: Marquette University Press, 1964.

Walzer, R. "The World, Man, and Society." In *The Cambridge History of Later Greek and Early Medieval Philosophy,* edited by A. H. Armstrong. Cambridge: Cambridge University Press, 1967.

Ward, Keith. *God, Chance, and Necessity.* Oxford: One World Publications, 1996.

Watt, W. M. *Muslim Intellectual: A Study of Al-Ghazali.* Edinburgh: Edinburgh University Press, 1963.

Whewell, William. *Philosophy of the Inductive Sciences.* London: Parker, 1840.

Wilber, K., ed. *Quantum Questions: Mystical Writings of the World's Great Physicists.* Boston: New Science Library, 1984.

Wildman, W. J., and R. J. Russell. "Chaos: A Mathematical Introduction with Philosophical Reflections." In *Chaos and Complexity: Scientific Perspectives on Divine Action,* edited by Robert J. Russell, Nancey Murphy, and Arthur R. Peacocke. Vatican City State: Vatican Observatory, 1995.

Wilson, E. O. *Consilience: The Unity of Knowledge.* New York: Knopf, 1998.

Wilson, Patrick A. "The Anthropic Principle." In *Cosmology: Historical, Literary, Philosophical, Religious, and Scientific Perspectives,* edited by Norriss S. Hetherington. New York: Garland, 1993.

Wippel, J. F. "Metaphysics." In *The Cambridge Companion to Aquinas,* edited by N. Kretzmann and E. Stump. Cambridge: Cambridge University Press, 1993.

Wolfson, H. A. *Philo: Foundations of Religious Philosophy in Judaism, Christianity, and Islam.* Cambridge, Mass.: Harvard University Press, 1947.

Index

paradox, 90, 132
and contradiction, 61–62
Parmenides, xiv, 45, 47, 79–82, 158
Aristotle's response to, 98–99
Democritus's response to, 84–85
Neoplatonic response to, 111
Way of Truth, 46
Pascal, 34
Peacocke, Arthur, 284–87, 303, 310
on the anthropic principle, 286–87
arguments for God's existence, 285–87
on the nature of Jesus, 284–85
on miracles, 284–85
on the resurrection, 285
Peter of Albano, 202
Philo of Alexandria, 144–51
On the Creation, 145–51
on the creation of man, 149–50
criticism of Epicureanism, 147
and *Logos,* 148–49
and Plato's *Timaeus,* 147–48, 150
similarity to Bonaventure, 203
Pico della Mirandola, 117, 138
Planck, Max, 244–45
Plato, 26, 46
Apology, 38
Aquinas's criticism of, 207
on change and identity, 46–47, 49
dialogues as drama, 49, 135
Euthyphro, 63, 96
definition of God, 96–97
Phaedo, 113, 163
Phaedrus, 149
versus the presocratics, 136–37
recalcitrant nature of matter, 138
Republic, 163
Symposium, 95, 150
Theaetetus, 191
Timaeus, 96, 135–41, 269
and Philo of Alexandria, 147–48, 150
Plato and Aristotle, reconciliation of, 110, 202
in Boethius, 114
in Islam, 154
in the Mutazilites, 155
in Neoplatonism, 110, 155
plausibility, 58–59, 132, 273

pleasure and pain, as standards, 87
Plotinus:
theory of emanation, 111–12
as criticized by Saadia Gaon, 180
Enneads, 110–13
definition of God, 110–13
Poincaré, Henri, 67
Polkinghorne, John, 287–90
on the anthropic principle, 289
contextual theory of causality, 287–88
on the design argument, 289
"dual-aspect monism," 288–89
Pope John Paul II, 290
Pope Pius XII, 290
Popper, Karl, 68
Porphyry, 110, 115
positivism, 67–68
potentiality and actuality, 98–100, 168
in Aquinas, 207
prayer, 30, 56, 78, 284
precision in science, 37
predictions:
of evolution theory for Ward, 279–80
quantitative, 77
premises, 52–53. *See also* first principles
presocratics, xiv, 168, 231
flaws of, 88
Plato's criticism of, 137
similarity to Leibniz, 228
similarity to Spinoza, 226
Prime Mover, 98, 102–3, 111, 271, 311
probabilistic laws, 272
Protestant Reformation, 219
pseudoscience, 67
Ptolemy, 186
purpose, 25
purposelessness, 25, 38–39, 70
Pythagoras, 23
Pythagoreans:
Plato's criticism of, 135
Xenophanes' mockery of, 95

Qur'an on God's knowledge, 169

Reason:
defective, 15–16
as generalization, 13–15, 24

About the Authors

James A. Arieti (B.A., Grinnell College, 1969; Ph.D., Stanford University, 1972) is Graves H. Thompson Professor of Classics at Hampden-Sydney College, where he has taught since 1978. Previously he taught at Stanford University, The Pennsylvania State University, and Cornell College. He is the author of five other books, *The Dating of Longinus* (1975), *Love Can Be Found* (1975), Longinus' *On the Sublime: Translated with Commentary* (1985), *Interpreting Plato: The Dialogues as Drama* (1991), and *Discourses on the First Book of Herodotus* (1995). He has edited four other books. He has delivered over sixty papers at professional conferences, colleges, and universities in North America and Europe and has published forty articles on subjects that include ancient medicine, Empedocles, Greek athletics, Greek and Roman rhetoric, Herodotus, Homer, Horace, Livy, Machiavelli, Philo, Plato, and the Septuagint. In 1997 he won a John M. Templeton Award for his course "Miletus to Los Alamos: Science and Religion, A Challenge Ancient and Modern." His doctoral dissertation dealt with the Septuagint, the translation of the Hebrew Bible into Greek, a translation from the language of revealed religion into the language of ancient science; in this sense, the subject matter of this book has been a vital interest to him for over three decades.

Patrick A. Wilson (B.A., University of Dallas, 1984; M.A. University of Notre Dame, 1987; Ph.D., University of Notre Dame, 1989) is an associate professor of philosophy at Hampden-Sydney College, where he has taught since 1990. He has published articles on design theory, evolutionary ethics, and the anthropic principle and has delivered seventeen papers on subjects such as the overlap between science and religion, the nature of morality, deistic evolution, teleology, and design. In 1997 he won a John M. Templeton

Award for his course "Science and Religion: Theistic and Naturalistic Perspectives on Cosmology and Evolution." His doctoral dissertation took a critical look at the anthropic principle, especially in its explanatory pretensions and its religious implications. He has cultivated an avid interest in the sciences and has been an observer of religion since his days as an undergraduate.